AMERICAN POLITICS IN THE MEDIA AGE

AMERICAN POLITICS IN THE MEDIA AGE

Thomas R. Dye
Florida State University

L. Harmon Zeigler
University of Oregon

Brooks/Cole Publishing Company
Monterey, California

Brooks/Cole Publishing Company
A Division of Wadsworth, Inc.

Printed in the United States of America
10 9 8 7 6 5 4 3 2 1

Library of Congress Cataloging in Publication Data

Dye, Thomas R.
   American politics in the media age.

   Includes bibliographical references and index.
   1. United States—Politics and government. 2. Mass
media—Political aspects—United States. I. Zeigler, L.
Harmon (Luther Harmon),   date. II. Title.
JK274.D97   1983   320.973   82-17710

Subject Editors: *Henry Staat and Marquita Flemming*
Production Editors: *John Bergez and Suzanne Ewing*
Production Assistant: *Louise Rixey*
Manuscript Editor: *William Waller*
Editorial Consultant: *David T. Yamada*
Permissions Editor: *Carline Haga*
Design Coordinators: *Jamie Sue Brooks and Vernon Boes*
Interior Design: © *Jurek Wajdowich*
Cover Design: *Jamie Sue Brooks*
Cover Photos: © *Jan Lukas*
Photoresearch: *Turner & Winston*
Art Coordinator: *Rebecca Tait*
Line Illustrations: *Florence Fujimoto*
Typesetting: *Allservice Phototypesetting Co., Phoenix, Arizona*

(Credits continue on page 475)

PREFACE

INTRODUCTION

Politics is the struggle over the allocation of values in society. It is lobbying, pressure, threat, bargaining, and compromise; it is serious and significant.

Politics is talk, expression, picture, and image; it is drama and entertainment.

Both aspects of politics—serious decision-making and drama and entertainment deserve our attention.

What political leaders *say* is as important as what leaders *do*. All government leaders—democratic and authoritarian, capitalist and socialist—use mass communication to legitimize their rule. The average person learns about political values and about political events and personalities from the mass media. The media help to set the "agenda" for national decision-making. The media determine what people will think about and talk about in public affairs.

American Politics in the Media Age is a basic introduction to American government with a special focus on the political role of the mass media. The book describes the basic elements of the American political system—beliefs and ideologies, constitutional arrangements, federalism, interest groups, parties and elections, Congress, the presidency, the bureaucracy, the courts, civil liberties, and civil rights. More importantly, it describes how these elements are symbolized and communicated to mass audiences and how these audiences respond to these symbols.

The functions of the mass media in politics are discussed—newsmaking, interpretation, socialization, persuasion, and agenda setting. The book describes the political parties, the volatility of the electorate, the recruitment of political leaders, the rise of single-interest groups, the changing nature of political campaigns, the representative role of the Congress, the symbolic role of the President, the functioning of the Washington bureaucracy. *American Politics in the Media Age* is written to help the reader understand both the symbols and realities of American politics. As political scientist Murray Edelman once wrote:

> Political analysis must, then, proceed at two levels
> simultaneously. It must examine how political actions get some

v

groups the tangible things they want from government, and at
the same time it must explore what these same actions mean to
the mass public and how it is placated or aroused by them.*

FEATURES OF THE BOOK

This book has helpful features to make the study of American politics
clear and interesting.

- Essentials boxes outline the basic structures and processes of
  American government.
- Interest boxes are included throughout the text highlighting
  topics of current interest.
- Important concepts are introduced in second color.
- Terms are defined in a running glossary throughout the book.
- End-of-chapter summaries review the main points and concepts
  presented in each chapter.
- Numerous illustrations—contemporary and historical photo-
  graphs, cartoons, charts, and graphs—give added meaning to the
  text discussion.

ACKNOWLEDGMENTS

We would like to thank the following people for the helpful comments in the early stages of the manuscript. Alan L. Clem, University
of South Dakota; Kenneth Dolbeare, Evergreen State College;
Charles Funderburk, Wright State University; Doris A. Graber, Uni-
versity of Illinois, Chicago Circle; Justin Green, Virginia Polytechnic
Institute and State University; Bernard Hennessy, Northern Ken-
tucky University; Larry Hough, East Carolina University; Robert
Huckshorn, Florida Atlantic University; Michael Johnston, Univer-
sity of Pittsburgh; Donald Matthews, University of Washington;
David Neubauer, University of New Orleans; Leroy N. Rieselbach,
Indiana University; Steven Robins; David T. Yamada, Monterey
Peninsula College; and Richard P. Young, University of Texas at
San Antonio.

We also appreciate the assistance of the staff at Brooks/Cole, especially Sue Ewing and Marquita Flemming.

Thomas R. Dye

L. Harmon Zeigler

*Murray Edelman, *The Symbolic Uses of Politics,* (Urbana: University of Illinois
Press, 1964), p. 12.

CONTENTS

7. INTEREST-GROUP POLITICS   224

8. CONGRESSIONAL POLITICS   258

9. PRESIDENTIAL POLITICS   298

10. BUREAUCRACY AND POLITICS   338

11. THE COURTS AND CIVIL LIBERTIES   368

12. THE POLITICS OF CIVIL RIGHTS

AMERICAN POLITICS
IN THE MEDIA AGE

CHAPTER 1

THE TWO FACES OF POLITICS

Politics is:

- Who?
- Gets what?
- When?
- How?

But politics is also:

- Who?
- Says what?
- In which channel?
- To whom?
- With what effect?*

Politics can be serious decision making about who gets what—the distribution of values in society. At the same time, politics can be about who says what—the communication of symbols to mass audiences. We can think of politics as a smoke-filled room where jobs, contracts, and money are dispensed; we can also think of politics as a room filled with cameras and lights where themes, messages, and images are dispensed.

*Both definitions were provided by the most distinguished American political scientist, the late Harold Lasswell. The first definition of politics is derived from an early book, *Politics: Who Gets What When and How* (New York: Free Press, 1936). The second definition is really Lasswell's description of mass communication, which is found in "The Structure and Function of Communication in Society," in Wilbur Schramm (Ed.), *Mass Communication* (Urbana: University of Illinois Press, 1960), p. 117.

Readying cameras
before the start of a
press conference.

Political science must be concerned with both aspects of politics—who *gets* what, and who *says* what. As one political scientist, Murray Edelman, wrote:

> Political analysis must, then, proceed at two levels simultaneously. It must examine how political actions get some groups the tangible things they want from government and at the same time it must explore what these same actions mean to the mass public and how it is placated or aroused by them.[1]

POLITICS AS WHO GETS WHAT

Politics: An activity by which people try to get more of whatever there is to get; specifically, the process by which society's values are allocated by authority to competing groups and individuals ("who gets what, when, and how").

If we define **politics** as who gets what when and how, then we are really saying that politics is an activity by which people try to get more of whatever there is to get—money, prestige, jobs, well-being, respect, sex, and power itself. "The study of politics," said Harold Lasswell, "is the study of influence and the influential. The influential are those who get the most of what there is to get."[2] Politics, then, is the struggle over the allocation of values in society. Politics, by this definition, could apply to all kinds of settings—office politics, student politics, sorority politics, corporate politics, union politics, church politics, and so forth. But (unfortunately, perhaps) political science has decided to limit its scope to government—to who gets what when and how in *government*.

Politics is the struggle over the allocation of values in society.

What distinguishes governmental politics from politics in other organizations and institutions? Government has the primary responsibility for resolving differences over the allocation of values *between* the different segments of society. Therefore, (1) government deci-

Politics defined—who *says* what, as well as who *gets* what.

sions extend to the whole of society, and (2) only government can legitimately use force.

Government, then, must *regulate conflict in society,* and the means it uses is politics. First of all, government establishes and enforces general rules by which conflict is to be carried on. It must ensure that group conflicts are settled in elections, legislatures, or courts, rather than in street fighting, terrorism, or civil war. Secondly, government must arrange settlements in the form of public policy— settlements that allocate values in a way that is accepted by both "winners" and "losers," at least temporarily. Public policy, then, is the outcome of the struggle in government over who gets what. Thirdly, government must impose these settlements on the parties to the disputes. In other words, government must enforce public policy by promising rewards or threatening punishments.

> Public policy is the outcome of the struggle in government over who gets what.

Why do we expect conflict in society over who gets what? Why can't we have a harmonious, loving, caring, sharing society of equals? Philosophers have pondered this question for centuries. James Madison (1751–1836), perhaps the first American to write systematically about politics and government, believed that the causes of "faction" (conflict) are found in human diversity,[3] which he defined as

a zeal for different opinions concerning religion, concerning government, and many other points, as well of speculation as of practice; an attachment to different leaders ambitiously contending for preeminence and power; or to persons of other descriptions whose fortunes have been interesting to human passions . . . .

So conflict arises from religion, ideology ("speculation"), and personal ambition. We could also add race, ethnicity, and region to Madison's list. But at the heart of the problem of conflict in society is inequality in the sources and distribution of wealth. According to Madison:

The most common and durable source of factions has been the various and unequal distribution of property. Those who hold, and those who are without property, have ever formed distinct interests in society. Those who are creditors, and those who are debtors, fall under like discrimination. A landed interest, a manufacturing interest, a mercantile interest, a monied interest, with many lesser interests, grow up of necessity in civilized nations, and divide them into different classes, actuated by different sentiments and views.

Politics as the activities (including voting) by which conflict is carried on.

In short, differences among people, particularly in the sources and amounts of their wealth, stimulate conflicts. And "politics arises out of conflicts and . . . consists of the activities—reasonable discussion, empassioned oratory, balloting, and street fighting—by which conflict is carried on."[4] It is the task of government to regulate these conflicts.

POLITICS AS WHO SAYS WHAT
Politics and communication are closely linked. When people engage in conflict, they derive the meaning of the conflict from communication. Communication not only provides meanings for abstract ideas and ideologies (democracy, liberalism, conservatism, radicalism, communism); it also defines for us key institutions (the presidency, Congress, the courts, the Republican party, the Democratic party). And it provides our images of key political figures (Ronald Reagan, Edward Kennedy, Jimmy Carter, George Bush).

What people think, feel, and do in politics arises out of the meanings they give to events, the perceptions they have of organizations and institutions, and the attitudes they have toward personalities. These events, organizations, institutions, and personalities are presented to them through the media of mass communication—newspapers, magazines, movies, books, radio, and, most of all, television.

Meanings, perceptions, and attitudes do not arise in advance of events and personalities but rather in the process of communication itself. Communication is not a mere transmission link; communication itself creates meanings, perceptions, and attitudes. It is true, of course, that people frequently screen out, or reinterpret for themselves, communications that differ from their own preconceived ideas. But these preconceived ideas themselves were formed with the help of thousands of previous communications. Communication is not neutral.

Communication is not a mere transmission link; communication itself creates meanings, perceptions, and attitudes.

Political communication is important in a mass society. What leaders *say* is as important as what leaders *do*. The importance of the communication of political symbols to mass audiences derives from (1) the *reassurance* these symbols provide the people that government is trying to do something to protect them from war or invasion, economic dislocation, crime and injustice, and other threats; (2) the *participation* of mass audiences in campaigns and elections by simply absorbing the media accounts of these events; and (3) the *legitimizing* of the political system through media presentations of the presidency, Congress, the courts, and elections.

The communication of words, pictures, symbols, and emotions *reassures* people that leaders in and out of government care about them. Even if government policies do not succeed in eliminating poverty, reforming welfare programs, preventing crime, halting inflation, reducing racial conflict, or protecting Americans abroad, it is still important that government *says* it wants to do these things. The statements of a government may tell us more about the aspirations of a society and its leadership than about actual conditions. Moreover, political campaigning, television debates, nightly newscasts, polls and predictions, speeches and press conferences, and election-night coverage of voting results all combine to reassure the people about the democratic character of the U. S. political system.

We can *participate* in politics by passively watching our television sets, responding with pride, patriotism, anger, or cynicism as the drama of politics is played for us between commercials. Even people who do not vote (about half the population), are nonetheless treated to year-long media coverage of presidential elections, from the early party caucuses and the New Hampshire primary to the November general election itself. It is difficult to avoid knowing that a presidential election is being held and who the Democratic and Republican candidates are. Elections for U. S. House and Senate seats and for governorships also receive considerable media coverage.

Legitimize: To convey governmental authority and its policies in such a way that they are accepted as "legal and proper" and deserving of the citizen's obedience and support.

Finally, all of this televised drama helps to **legitimize** both the government itself and public policies. We mean that the mass public comes to accept as "law" the actions of government. Television presents various dramatized versions of presidential initiatives, congressional actions, court decisions, and public issues and events. Government is portrayed as acting on national problems, and mass audiences are instructed that these governmental actions are the law of the land and ought to be obeyed. (This may seem simple in the United States today, but there are some societies where *no* institution is recognized as having a legitimate lawmaking power.) Democratic institutions—parties, elections, campaigns, and so on—provide additional legitimacy to government acts. People are instructed that they must obey the law because they had an opportunity (however indirect) to participate in the making of the law themselves. Therefore, citizens of a democratic nation have a greater obligation to obey the law than people living under authoritarian governments. But *all* governments—democratic and authoritarian, capitalist and socialist— use mass-communication channels to legitimize their rule.

> *All* governments—democratic and authoritarian, capitalist and socialist—use mass-communication channels to legitimize their rule.

Edelman summarized the use of political communication this way:

> To quiet resentments and doubts about particular political acts, reaffirm belief in the fundamental rationality and democratic character of the system, and thus fix conforming habits of future behavior, is demonstrably a key function of our persisting political institutions: elections, political discussions, legislatures, courts and administrations.[5]

POLITICAL FUNCTIONS OF THE MASS MEDIA

As children, Americans spend more time in front of television sets than in school. As adults, Americans spend nearly half of their leisure time watching television. On a typical evening, half of the nation's population will watch some television. In all, the average family spends more than six hours a day with television. Over two-thirds of Americans report that they receive all or most of their "news" from television. Perhaps more importantly, television is the "most trusted" media of communication. The political power of television is awesome.[6]

The political importance of television has emerged relatively recently. In 1952 only 19.8 percent of all U. S. homes had TV sets, compared with 99.8 percent in 1972. In other words, the United States acquired this form of mass communication in just twenty years. And not many scholars or textbooks have yet recognized the tremendous impact of television on U. S. society in general and on political life in particular.

Television—the "most trusted" medium of communications.

Realities and Symbols: Calling Balls and Strikes

Communication gives meaning to reality. Consider how the psychologist Hadley Cantril illustrated the distinction between "reality" and symbols:*

> Three umpires describe their job of calling balls and strikes in a baseball game.
> First Umpire: Some's balls and some's strikes and I calls 'em as they is.
> Second Umpire: Some's balls and some's strikes and I calls 'em as I sees 'em.
> Third Umpire: Some's balls and some's strikes but they ain't nothin' till I calls 'em.

The first umpire believes that there are balls and strikes in the "real world," and he merely observes and counts them. (There are very few people working in television or journalism who believe that they are only recording what goes on in the real world, although many will *say* that this is all they do.) The second umpire believes that there are "real" balls and strikes too, but he admits that he uses his own *judgment* in determining which are which. (Most television and newspaper reporters will admit to using some judgment about their descriptions of the "real world," if they are pressed to do so.) The third umpire understands that his own attachment of a symbol, "ball" or "strike," gives meaning to the pitch. His communication—calling out "ball" or "strike"—is a *creative* act. (Very few media people will admit that they themselves determine what is "news" or that "newsmaking" is a creative activity.) It is true that there are some commonly shared expectations about what a "ball" and a "strike" should look like; for example, a strike should not kick up dirt in front of the batter. The third umpire shares these expectations in labeling a pitch a "ball" or a "strike." But it is the communicator (the umpire) who gives meaning to otherwise meaningless acts.**

*Hadley Cantril, "Perception in Interpersonal Relations," *American Journal of Psychiatry,* 1957; also cited in Dan Nimmo, *Political Communication and Public Opinion in America* (Santa Monica, Calif.: Goodyear, 1978), p. 77.

**A leading commentator on mass communication, Marshall McLuhan, coined the phrase "The medium *is* the message." What he meant was that the communication itself, apart from the "real" information on which it is based, is the most important influence on mass audiences. Essentially, McLuhan was agreeing with our third umpire. See McLuhan, *Understanding Media: The Extensions of Man* (New York: McGraw-Hill, 1964).

Television is really the first form of *mass* communication—that is, communication that reaches nearly everyone: the poor, the illiterate, the aged, the sick, children. Newspapers always reported wars, riots, scandals, and disasters, just as they do today. But the masses of Americans did not always read the news sections of their daily paper, and fewer still chose to read the editorials on these topics. The television viewer today *must* see the news or else turn off the set; the newspaper reader can turn quickly to the sports and comics without confronting the political news.

Television is really the first form of *mass* communication— that is, communication that reaches nearly everyone.

Television also presents *visual* images, not merely printed words. The emotional impact that is conveyed by pictures enables television to communicate feelings as well as information in an especially powerful way.

What are the political functions of the mass media? We can establish five:

- *Newsmaking*: surveying of the world and deciding what people and events should be reported on
- *Interpretation*: analysis of the meaning of events and personalities
- *Socialization*: indoctrination of mass audiences into the prevailing political culture
- *Persuasion*: direct efforts to affect the behavior of mass audiences, as in political campaigns
- *Agenda setting*: deciding what will be decided; defining the problems of society and suggesting solutions

Newsmaking

Newsmaking involves all-important decisions about what is "news" and who is "newsworthy." Television executives and producers and newspaper and magazine editors must decide what people, organizations, and events will be given attention. This attention makes these topics matters of general public concern and political action. Without media coverage the general public would not "know" about these personalities, organizations, or events. They would not become objects of political discussion, nor would they be likely to be considered important by those government officials who did know about them.

Media coverage is especially important in describing conditions and defining conflicts with which mass audiences have little direct experience. For example, the activities of presidents, members of Congress, criminals, corporation presidents, bankers, astronauts, and foreign dictators are not generally experienced first hand by most

Newsmaking: The power of the mass media to decide what political issues, events, personalities, and conflicts will be brought to the public's attention.

people. Viewers are more likely to believe what they are told about these distant figures. But viewer opinions on race, ethnicity, or religion are not so likely to be shaped by media coverage. This is because many people have personal experiences on which to base their own views.

Media attention can create issues and personalities. Media *inat*tention can doom issues and personalities to obscurity. The television camera cannot be "a picture on the world," because the whole world cannot squeeze into the picture. Newsmakers must sort through a tremendous oversupply of information and decide what is "news."

> Newsmakers must sort through a tremendous oversupply of information and decide what is "news."

In addition to deciding what is, and what is not, news, the newsmakers provide cues to mass audiences about the degree of importance of an issue, personality, or event. Some matters are covered prominently by the media, with early placement on a newscast and several minutes of time or front-page coverage with big headlines and pictures. Prominent coverage tells us what is important and what is not.

Of course, politicians, professional public relations people, interest group "spokespersons," and various aspiring "celebrities" all *know* that the decisions of the newsmakers are vital to the success of their issue, their organization, and themselves. So they try to attract the attention of the media by deliberately engaging in behavior or manufacturing situations that are likely to win media coverage. The result

Attracting the attention of the news media.

is the **"media event"**—an activity arranged primarily to stimulate media coverage and thereby attract public attention to an issue or individual. Generally, the more bizarre, dramatic, and sensational it is, the more likely the media event is to attract coverage. A media event may be a press conference, to which reporters from the television stations and newspapers are invited by public figures, even when there is really no news to announce. Or it may be a staged debate, confrontation, or illustration of injustice. Political candidates may visit coal mines, ghetto neighborhoods, fires, or other disasters. Some protests and demonstrations, and even violence, have been staged primarily as media events in order to dramatize and communicate grievances.

Media event: An activity arranged primarily to stimulate media coverage and thereby attract public attention to an issue or individual.

How to Make "News"

Attracting media attention is vital to shaping politics. If you are a political candidate, party leader, interest-group spokesperson, or someone else who wishes to draw attention to yourself or your cause, here are a few guidelines for making *The Evening News*.

1. Schedule your "news" event so that it is convenient for television to cover it. The best time is between 10:00 A.M. and 2:30 P.M. on weekdays. After 2:30 your news cannot be edited in time for the 5:00 or 6:00 evening news. (The late news at 10:00 or 11:00 is only a rehash of the earlier program; seldom is any new news presented then.) If your news must wait twenty-four hours, it may no longer be newsworthy, or it may be pushed off the tube by newer news. Weekends are poor times for news. Very few network and station crews are working.

2. Make sure you have good "visuals." Television news directors want to avoid "talking heads"—the verbal communication of news without accompanying visual material. Make sure your visuals are attractive to the audience and that they make your point. Poor visuals can distract your audience or even contradict your message.

3. The more original, spectacular, or dramatic the event, the more likely you are to attract media coverage. Ordinary press conferences are dull. Walk the streets of a ghetto, appear at an unemployment line, visit a home for the elderly, swim in a polluted river, walk the entire length of the state, ride a bicycle backwards down a city street, or work one day as a stable boy or shrimp fisherman. (All of these "gimmicks" have been used by successful candidates for governor or U. S. senator.)

(continued)

The newsmakers who decide what news and entertainment will be seen by the masses of Americans are the top network executives—presidents, vice-presidents, directors, and producers—not Dan Rather, John Chancellor, nor Barbara Walters. The television network executives, however, exchange views with the editors of the *New York Times,* the *Washington Post, Newsweek, Time,* and a few of the larger newspaper chains. These television executives and producers and print editors and publishers can be considered collectively as the newsmakers.

Interpretation

The newsmakers not only decide what will be news; they also give an **interpretation,** put an event in context, and speculate about its consequences. Events, people, and organizations invariably lend

Interpretation: The "meaning" given by the media to a news story—a "meaning" that is not usually immune from political bias.

(*continued*)

4. Make sure that television and newspaper editors are informed well in advance of your event about where and when it will happen. Reschedule it if it is not convenient for television—for example, if they have other "news" planned for that day. Never begin your event until the television crew arrives. Even if newspaper reporters and onlookers become restless, remember that most people depend on television for the news. (Television crews usually run late.)

5. Keep your statement to ninety seconds or less. This is the longest television time you can reasonably expect to get. Pause every twenty seconds to allow for easy editing and cutting of comments. Do not introduce confusing facts or figures. Pass out copies of a typed press release of your statement. Make it easy on television and newspaper reporters. Remember that they usually do not know much about the stories they cover.

6. If anyone asks a tough or embarrassing question, do not change your facial expression, and respond with vague, rambling, long-winded talk. This will make the television film or tape unusable.

7. End the event quickly. Say what you want to say and then terminate the proceedings. This guards against mistakes. It helps ensure that television will show only what you planned.

8. Cultivate the friendship of editors, even more than that of reporters. Editors decide what will be news—what stories or personalities will be covered. The television assignment editor is particularly important, because he or she determines the schedule of the camera crews.

themselves to a variety of interpretations. Newsmakers try to find an "angle" on the story—an interpretation that affects the political consequences of the story. The decision to play up a particular angle is usually made before camera crews are sent out for filming or videotaping. By suggesting the causes and consequences of events, the media shape popular opinion.

Increasingly, television is turning to "news specials" or "special segments" of the nightly news to concentrate interpretation on a topic—the MX missile, migrant workers, Indian rights, gun control, Middle Eastern wars, and so on. But interpretation takes place in *every* news story. Film or videotape must be edited; this means that specific segments of it must be selected and mounted for showing. A script must be prepared with a "lead-in" (telling them what you are going to tell them).

In general, news interpretations have a "liberal" bias. Media executives and producers, as well as reporters, writers, and anchorpersons, are more liberal in their views than other segments of the nation's leadership. So interpretations are likely to cite as causes of unrest or disaster one of the following: disregard for the environment, corporate profit motives, racial antagonisms, support of right-wing regimes abroad, excessive military spending, and the like. The suggested remedies to the nation's ills are usually more governmental regulations, increased governmental spending, and new governmental programs and reforms.

The liberal bias is more comprehensive in television than it is in the press. Both conventionally "liberal" and "conservative" newspapers and magazines are prominent—for example, the *New York Times* (liberal) versus the *Wall Street Journal* (conservative), *Newsweek* (liberal) versus *U. S. News and World Report* (conservative), and *Harper's* (liberal) versus the *National Review* (conservative). But a liberal position is presented on all three major television networks, ABC, NBC, and CBS.

The newsmakers themselves, of course, generally deny any bias in the news. They may be sincere when they insist that they are impartial and objective, because in their world—the New York and Washington world of reporters, writers, producers, and intellectuals—liberal views are so widely held. Network entertainment programming, as well as newscasts and news specials, reflect liberal concerns for social reform, an interest in the problems of the poor and the minorities, a concern for ecology and the quality of life, and a willingness to use governmental power to "do good."

Socialization

A third function of the mass media is **political socialization**—the process of learning basic values and views of the world that prepares individuals for their place in the dominant culture. Governments cannot rely on force alone. They must have the acquiescence, if not the

Political socialization: The teaching of basic political values and attitudes to individuals by several agents, including the family, school, peers, workplace, and, increasingly, the mass media.

support, of most of their citizens. This means that most citizens must abide by the laws, pay their taxes, and view their government as legitimate. Until recently most scholars believed that parents and schools were the sources of political socialization. But recent studies have shown that the mass media are the primary factor in the political socialization of children.[7] The bulk of information that young people learn about the political world comes to them through television. This information includes specific facts as well as general values. Grade-school children spend an average of twenty-seven hours a week watching television, more time than they spend in school. The television set is the "new parent"; it puts even the youngest children in touch with mass-media images. This pattern of heavy media exposure continues throughout life. The average American spends nearly three hours a day watching television.

Political socialization is a lifelong process and so, as we have seen, is heavy media exposure. Political scientist Doris Graber commented:

> Much of what the average person learns about political norms, rules, and values, about events in the political universe, and about the way people cope with these happenings comes, of necessity, from the mass media. Those with the widest exposure to political news in the mass media generally are most aware of political issues and have more political opinions about these issues. Personal experiences are severely limited compared to the range of experiences that come to us directly or indirectly through the media.[8]

People do not necessarily remember all of the political facts reported by the media, nor do they necessarily adopt the specific attitudes and opinions delivered by the media. Nor do the media always directly determine political views and behavior. Lifelong political attitudes are difficult to change. People tend to pay more attention to information and opinions with which they agree. People tend to screen out, ignore, or overlook information and opinions with which they disagree. Nonetheless, information and opinions supplied by the mass media provide the ingredients that people use to adjust their existing attitudes and opinions to keep pace with a changing world.

Political socialization is brought about by entertainment shows as well as by news broadcasts.

Political socialization is brought about by entertainment shows as well as by news broadcasts. Entertainment shows have succeeded in "resocializing" Americans (changing their basic values and outlooks on life) in many areas—notably, tolerance with regard to sexual relations (sex outside of marriage, unmarried couples living together), divorce and feminism (divorced mothers raising children and living happily outside of marriage), interracial love affairs, and homosexuality. These themes appear regularly in the most popular shows. The producers and writers tend to be socially progressive. They may not make their decisions on entertainment based on any well-developed ideology, but they tend to introduce their own values in their "gate-keeping" function—determining what shows will be produced and shown to mass audiences.

Persuasion and Propaganda

Another function of the mass media is **political persuasion**— direct efforts to change people's attitudes and behavior through communication. Governments, corporations, unions, parties, and political candidates all make direct attempts to persuade mass audiences to accept political beliefs and engage in political activity. Persuasion is purposeful communication; it is intentionally designed to change people's beliefs, perceptions, values, and behavior. **Propaganda,** a form of persuasion, is the communication of facts, ideas, or opinions not for the audience's sake but for the benefit of the communicator. We have a negative reaction to the term *propaganda,* because it implies psychological manipulation of a mass audience for the benefit of one or a few.

Governments use direct advertising to urge people to pay their taxes by April 15, to join the armed forces, to obey speed limits, to fill out census forms, and, in general, to support current programs and

Political persuasion: Direct efforts to change people's attitudes and behavior through communication.

Propaganda: A highly selective form of persuasive communication intended to benefit the cause of the communicator through the transmission of information, facts, opinions, and allegations.

Persuasion and propaganda—governments using direct advertising.

policies. (Interestingly, Congress does not permit federal agencies to use the term *public relations,* because congressmen feel that the government should not be engaged in "propaganda." So advertising and public relations by the federal bureaucracy are called "public information." It is estimated that over 10,000 federal employees are directly engaged in public information. Congress acknowledges the need to engage in direct political persuasion only *outside* of the United States, through the U. S. International Communication Agency and its *Voice of America* broadcasts.) Corporations use direct political persuasion in commercials designed to make us believe that their profits are small and should not be heavily taxed, that they use their profits to drill more oil wells or seek new sources of energy, that their business is growing trees rather than selling lumber, that they are committed to a clean environment, that buying foreign cars is "un-American," and so on. A few unions (the International Ladies Garment Workers Union, for example) directly urge mass audiences to support unions and buy only union-made products ("Look for the union label").

Political leaders use persuasion and propaganda as the most important tools of their profession. Increasingly, presidents have tried to "go over the heads" of news directors, editors, and reporters to present direct appeals to mass audiences through televised speeches or news conferences. Presidents, by custom rather than by law, can command time from the television networks for speeches and announcements.

Increasingly, presidents have tried to "go over the heads" of news directors, editors, and reporters to present direct appeals to mass audiences through televised speeches or news conferences.

President Franklin D. Roosevelt set the tone of the modern presidential address to the nation with his "fireside chats" on the radio. Hitler's propaganda film *Triumph of the Will* (1936) is still considered a masterpiece of the political motion picture; it centers on a giant Nazi rally in Nuremberg where Hitler addresses tens of thousands of uniformed followers. Richard M. Nixon's televised "Checkers" speech in 1952 was the first highly effective use of television in a presidential campaign. (Nixon, the vice-presidential candidate running with Dwight D. Eisenhower, was accused of accepting money from California interests. Eisenhower was considering dropping him from the Republican ticket. Nixon made an emotional televised denial that he had received any gifts except a puppy named "Checkers," which his family loved and he would never give up. Hundreds of thousands of telegrams flooded Eisenhower headquarters urging that Nixon be kept on the ticket. He was.)

The first televised presidential debate was between John F. Kennedy and Richard M. Nixon in 1960. Nixon appeared to score debator's points in their exchanges, citing facts and figures in support of his positions. But the boyishly handsome, smiling, cool, confident image projected by Kennedy may have won the close election for him. In 1976, Gerald R. Ford was the first president in office to agree to a debate (probably because he was behind in the polls). Ford did well against Carter in the first of their debates, but he later stumbled badly in asserting that Eastern European nations were *not* under Soviet domination. Ford lost a very close election. In the 1980 presidential campaign, Reagan was supposed to be slightly ahead of Carter in the polls when Carter agreed to a nationally televised debate. Carter spoke rapidly and seriously, detailing programs and budgets, but he did not smile or warm to his audience. Reagan was relaxed, smiling, even joking. He spoke in commonplace generalities. He asked his audience simply: "Are you better off now than you were four years ago? Is it easier for you to go and buy things in the stores?" Reagan won in a landslide.

First televised presidential debate between Nixon and Kennedy.

Mass-media campaigns, directed by public relations specialists, have replaced the traditional campaigns run by Democratic or Republican party organizations. Candidates for president and vice-president, governor, and U. S. senator and representative generally create their own campaign organizations, separate from the party. These campaign organizations rely increasingly on professional public relations and advertising firms to manage media-oriented campaigns. As the image makers have taken over political campaigns, the importance of political parties has declined.

Mass-media campaigns, directed by public relations specialists, have replaced the traditional campaigns run by party organizations.

When voters can see and hear candidates in their own living room, they can make choices that differ from those of their party. Candidate image becomes a more important factor in determining voter choice. Candidates themselves can defy party organizations because television gives them direct access to voters. New faces, with the aid of the media, can gain a wide following very rapidly.

In short, persuasion is central to politics, and the mass media, particularly television, are the key to mass persuasion.

Live by the Tube, Die by the Tube*

Jimmy Carter was a media president. There is little likelihood that a one-term governor of Georgia would have been elected president without the instant celebrity that television brought him in 1976. Carter was known to corporate and political leaders as an original member of the Trilateral Commission (a prestigious group of officers of multinational corporations and government officials from the United States, Western Europe, and Japan). He had excellent financial connections through the Coca-Cola Company and Lockheed Aircraft Corporation. But he was unknown to the vast majority of Americans.

As early as 1974 Carter began his campaign to capture "name recognition" in the first two presidential primary elections, in New Hampshire and Florida. The first is a small state where he had two years to engage in face-to-face campaigning, and the second borders on Georgia. Although only a tiny fraction of the nation's electorate lives in New Hampshire, the state carries great political influence because it traditionally holds the first presidential primary. Every four years the state is overrun with presidential candidates, campaign aides, reporters, commentators, and camera crews. Carter understood that, if he won a "media victory" in New Hampshire, he would become the "front-runner," and the media would devote more time and space to him than to his Democratic rivals—Representative Morris K. Udall, Governor Edmund G. (Jerry) Brown, Jr., Senator Henry M. Jackson, Senator Frank Church, and former Senator Frank Harris. (The Democratic heavyweights—Senators Hubert H. Humphrey and Edward Kennedy—never got into the 1976 race. Although he was the choice of most Democrats in the polls, Humphrey was fighting a losing battle with cancer. Kennedy did not believe enough time had elapsed since the Chappaquidick incident to allow him to run.) Carter won in New Hampshire, captured the media spotlight, and never let it turn away from him.

After the pains of the Vietnam War and the Watergate scandal, the nation sought a new face, an original style, a high moral tone, a man of trust. Carter was "packaged" by Gerald Rafshoon, the head of an Atlanta advertising agency, as a "farmer, an engineer, a businessman, a former navy officer, a scientist, a governor, and a Christian." To blacks he was a friend of the family of the late Dr. Martin Luther King, Jr.; to Southern whites, he was a "good ole boy." He projected an image of a Washington "outsider," a down-home, God-fearing, trustworthy peanut farmer. He defeated the incumbent, Gerald Ford, in a close election.

To the extent that Carter governed at all, he governed through the media. Did the people want a more open government? He walked down Pennsylvania Avenue in his own inauguration parade. Did the people want to be heard in Washington? He held town meetings in small communities and stayed overnight with working-class families. Was there an energy crisis? He appeared on national television beside a fireplace in a sweater. Is nuclear power a danger? He strolled around the Three Mile Island nuclear power plant after an accident there.

In the fall of 1979, when Carter was at the lowest point any president had ever reached in the polls and Kennedy announced his candidacy for president, Carter was rescued temporarily by the taking of hostages at the U. S. Embassy in Tehran, Iran. It was a story the networks loved. It was exciting drama, with a hated foreign leader, students who demonstrated on cue for the cameras, emotional interviews with families of the hostages, and a president who changed from a lackluster politician to commander in chief of all of the people. The nation rallied to Carter. He defeated Kennedy from the White House Rose Garden without even campaigning. The media focus was on the president, and Kennedy was simply obliterated by the news from Iran. If the daring and dramatic military rescue attempt in April 1980 had been successful, Carter might still be president.

But what television gives, television can take away. Reagan has lived his life in front of a camera. The camera is the tool of both his trades, actor and politician. Newspaper

(*continued*)

(*continued*)

journalists could never understand Reagan's success. Reporters wrote down his commonplace observations and time-worn
slogans. The printed messages were uninspiring. But the reporters missed his true appeal as a comfortable, pleasant,
reassuring man of traditional American values. In 1980 the
past looked better than the present; the "good old days" had
never seemed better. Reagan turned his advancing age from a
liability into an asset—he knew that America could be great
again. Carter mistakenly tried to portray Reagan as an unstable warmonger, based on Reagan's opposition to a pending
strategic arms limitation treaty. But Reagan's polished style
and charm as a kindly, older, soft-spoken, western rancher
deflected the Carter thrust. Indeed, Carter's attacks appeared
personal and harsh; he was labeled "Jimmy the Mean."

Reagan even managed to turn some of his apparent blunders (or were they deliberate?) to his advantage. When he
used the word *depression* instead of *recession* in a campaign
speech, hordes of Carter economists explained that technically the nation was not in a depression and that Reagan had
misused the word. But instead of retracting it, Reagan made
it a standard campaign quip: "If he [Carter] wants a definition, I'll give him one. [pause for audience attention] Recession [split-second pause for emphasis] is when your neighbor

Reagan—comfortable and assured—campaigning for the presidential nomination in 1980.

loses his job. Depression [same short pause] is when you lose yours. [pause for audience laughter] And recovery [pause for audience attention] is when Jimmy Carter loses his." [pause for prolonged laughter and applause]

Although attacked by Carter as a threat to peace, Reagan in their televised debate seemed by contrast a pleasant, smiling, reassuring figure. Carter was clearly the master of substance: he talked about programs, figures, budgets. He talked rapidly and seriously. But during the ninety minutes of debate, Reagan was the master of the stage: he was relaxed, smiling, even joking. He never raised his voice or the tempo, and he managed in the process to treat the president of the United States as an overly aggressive younger man, regrettably given to exaggeration.

Reagan never said anything of great importance. He merely asked: "Are you better off now than you were four years ago?" Simple, yet highly effective. When it was over, it was plain that Carter had been bested by a true professional in the media skills in which Carter himself had once claimed supremacy.

In the final few days before the election, the media decided to publicize the first anniversary of the Iranian hostage taking. This decision sealed Carter's fate. By reminding Americans of international humiliations, military weaknesses, and administration blunders during the Carter years, the media set the stage for the Reagan landslide. In the end, NBC announced the winner on national television before the polls had closed in the West. And Carter, who understands as well as anyone the power of the media, conceded defeat even before the voting booths were closed.

*Phraseology courtesy David Halberstam in *Parade* magazine, January 11, 1981. Halberstam won a Pulitzer Prize while writing for the *New York Times*.

Agenda Setting: Deciding What Will Be Decided

Defining the problems of society, and suggesting alternative solutions, is the most important process in the determination of public policy. We can refer to the process as **agenda setting.** Conditions in society that are not defined as problems and for which solutions are never proposed never become political issues. They never get on the "agenda" of government decision makers. On the other hand, if certain conditions in society are defined as problems, then they become policy issues. Governments are forced to decide what to do.

Clearly then, the power to decide what will be decided—agenda setting—is crucial in politics. Deciding what the problems will be is

Agenda setting: Defining the problems of society and suggesting alternative solutions; the most important process in the determination of public policy.

even more important than deciding what the solutions will be. The political scientist E. E. Schattschneider once wrote: "As a matter of fact, the definition of the alternative is the supreme instrument of power; the antagonists can rarely agree on what the issues are because power is involved in the definition. He who determines what politics is about runs the country."[9]

Many civics textbooks imply that agenda setting just "happens." It is sometimes implied that in an open democracy such as the United States any problem can be discussed and placed on the agenda of government decision makers. Persons or groups, it is said, can easily assume the tasks of defining problems and suggesting solutions. It is true, of course, that people can *say* whatever they want about the society and call for "redress of grievances." These are rights guaranteed by the First Amendment of the U. S. Constitution. But will anyone *listen* to these complaints? Not if the complainers do not have access to the mass media.

In reality, political issues do not just "happen." Creating an issue, dramatizing it, calling attention to it, and pressuring government to do something about it are important political tactics. These are the tactics of agenda setting. They are employed by influential persons, organized interest groups, political candidates, government leaders, and, most importantly, the mass media themselves.

Media stories determine what mass audiences will think about and talk about. The power of television is not really in persuading viewers to take one side of an issue or another or to vote for one candidate or another. Instead, the power of television is in setting the agenda for decision making—deciding what issues will be given attention and what will be ignored.

The power of television is in setting the agenda for decision making.

The mass media also directly influence decision makers. Perhaps this influence is even more important than the media's influence on mass audiences. We know that government officials and other influential leaders follow the mass media more closely than the general public; leaders frequently look at the major newspapers (the *Washington Post*, the *New York Times*, the *Wall Street Journal*), the news magazines (*Time, Newsweek*) and all three television networks (ABC, NBC, CBS). When the media feature particular issues or events, politicians are likely to be asked to comment on them in interviews. This tends to force leaders to take positions on issues, and it certainly directs their personal attention to the issues. Their comments, in turn, further increase the importance of the selected issues or events and assure them of even more public attention.

Media role in special events—*The Washington Post* and Watergate.

The newsmakers themselves frequently deny their agenda-setting role. They sometimes contend that television is no more than a "mirror of society." Of course, the mirror analogy is nonsense: mirrors do not select what they present, edit film or write scripts, allot time or determine the order of presentation, or analyze or interpret what is presented. The mirror analogy even contradicts some of the claims that the media themselves have made about righting many of the country's wrongs—segregation, Vietnam, Watergate.

The media generally, and television particularly, credit themselves with the success of the civil rights movement of the 1960s. The dramatic televised images of nonviolent demonstrators being attacked by police officers with nightsticks, cattle prods, and vicious dogs helped to waken the nation and its political leadership to the injustices of segregation. The media also credit themselves with decisively changing Americans' opinion of the Vietnam War and forcing Lyndon Johnson out of the presidency. "Television for the first time brought an ongoing war into American living rooms. In vivid colors, it showed dead and wounded people, blazing villages, and the faces of horrified children."[10] Finally, television, together with the Washington press corps, also lays claim to the expulsion of Nixon from the presidency. The *Washington Post* conducted the investigative reporting that produced a continuous flow of embarrassing information about the president and his chief advisors. (Later, two *Post* reporters, Bob Woodward and Carl Bernstein, would be memorialized in a movie, *All the President's Men,* starring Robert Redford and Dustin

25

Hoffman.) But it was the television networks that maintained the continuous nightly attack on the Nixon White House for nearly two years and kept Watergate in the public eye. Nixon's approval rating in public-opinion polls dropped from a high of 68 percent in January, 1973, following the Vietnam peace agreement to a low of 24 percent less than a year later.[11] It is noteworthy that Nixon's approval rating went up and he was reelected *after* the Watergate break-in in June, 1972. His resignation came in August, 1974, after two years of aggressive and hostile media coverage.

It is difficult to *prove* that these major political events—the civil rights movement, the ending of the Vietnam War, Watergate, and the resignation of Nixon—would not have occurred without television. But certainly television does more than "mirror" reality. Television itself is a political reality.

HARD FLUFF AND SERIOUS DECISIONS

Television is entertainment, and television news must entertain its mass audience. The major source of distortion in the news is not the liberal bias of the newsmakers but the need for drama, action, and confrontation to hold audience attention. An NBC news executive, Reuven Frank, advised his producers in a memorandum: "The highest priority of television journalism is not in the transmission of information but in the transmission of experience—joy, sorrow, shock, fear—these are the stuff of the news."[12] Information must be visual to get on television. Interviews should contain emotionally charged rhetoric, and film or tape should show shocking incidents or dramatic confrontation. Race, sex, violence, and government corruption are favorite topics because of their popular interest. More complex and abstract problems (for example, inflation) must be either simplified or dramatized (a woman buying family groceries and showing shock and despair at the checkout counter), or else these topics must be ignored.

Hard fluff: A term used in television broadcasting to refer to dramatic or sensational presentations of news stories.

"**Hard fluff**" is a term used in television broadcasting to refer to dramatic or sensational presentations of news stories. The popular *60 Minutes* on CBS is the leading illustration of hard fluff—entertainment masquerading as news. Nearly 100 people are directly involved in the production of *60 Minutes* (including the four correspondents, Dan Rather, Morley Safer, Harry Reasoner, and Mike Wallace). But the key decisions about what will be said, when, and how are made by the executive producer, Don Hewitt. When asked for an explanation of his choices for stories, he responded:

> It's all instinctive. . . . I'm the least intellectual person I know. A
> lot of times I say to a producer, 'I see it and I hear it but I
> don't feel it in the pit of my stomach.' I don't make decisions

intellectually, I make them viscerally. When I get bored, I figure other people will get bored. I have the ability to put myself in the place of the viewer because I have the same short attention span he has.[13]

Few newsmakers are as candid as Hewitt. He acknowledges that his criteria for selecting "news" are emotional and not intellectual; that, above all, stories must not be boring; and that stories must satisfy people with a short attention span.

Politics is both "hard fluff" and serious decision making.

Politics is both "hard fluff" and serious decision making. Politics is talk, expression, picture, and image; and it is dramatic and emotional. Politics is also the struggle over allocating those things valued by society. It is lobbying, pressure, threat, bargaining, and compromising; it is serious and significant. Politics involves vital decisions that affect the lives of all of us—for example, whether to spend billions of dollars for a new mobile missile system to deter the Soviet Union from any attempt to launch a first-strike nuclear attack against the United States. Politics also involves the creation of images—for example, the image of Reagan as the defender of traditional American values of individualism, self-reliance, and common sense.

Both aspects of politics—hard fluff and serious decision making—deserve our attention.

CHAPTER SUMMARY

1. Politics involves both a struggle over the distribution of values and the communication of political symbols. In shorthand terms, the two key phrases become *who gets what* and *who says what.*

2. There is a close connection between politics and communication. Communication (a) provides meaning for political ideas, (b) defines key institutions of government, and (c) promotes leadership images. Communication of political symbols to mass audiences provides reassurance, encourages participation in political activities, and serves to legitimize the political system.

3. The major political functions of the mass media include newsmaking, interpretation, socialization, persuasion, and agenda setting. Through these functions the mass media create the important political issues for the public, define their meaning and consequences, and help to cause shifts in public opinions and attitudes.

4. The media do not necessarily monopolize the performance of these functions. All politics is not media politics; some areas of politics are more media-dominated than others. For example, the media

give more coverage to elections, presidents, and international relations than to the bureaucracy and the Supreme Court.

5. Agenda setting is vital to the public-policy process. If an issue is not defined as a problem by the mass media, then political leaders may not feel compelled to address the issue. Those issues that *are* emphasized by the mass media do command attention. Three examples of the agenda-setting function of the media are the civil rights movement, the Vietnam War, and the Watergate scandal.

6. In large measure, television news is "hard fluff"; that is, it is motivated by the need to convey information about political events in an antiintellectual, visceral manner. In-depth analysis of complex political and social problems is rarely a feature of network news programs.

7. Politics involves both hard-fluff images and major decisions affecting the distribution of values in society.

Notes

1. Murray Edelman, *The Symbolic Uses of Politics* (Urbana: University of Illinois Press, 1964), p. 12.
2. Harold Lasswell, *Politics: Who Gets What When and How* (New York: Free Press, 1936), p. 3.
3. Quotations from *The Federalist*, no. 10 [New York: Random House (Modern Library), 1937].
4. Edward C. Banfield and James Q. Wilson, *City Politics* (Cambridge, Mass.: Harvard University Press, 1963), p. 7.
5. Edelman, *Symbolic Uses of Politics*, p. 11.
6. *Public Opinion*, August/September 1979, p. 28.
7. The older studies include David Easton and Jack Dennis, *Children in the Political System* (New York: McGraw-Hill, 1969); and Fred I. Greenstein, *Children and Politics* (New Haven, Conn.: Yale University Press, 1965). Newer studies include Sidney Kraus and Dennis Davis, *The Effects of Mass Communication on Political Behavior* (University Park: Pennsylvania State University Press, 1976); and John M. Phelan, *Mediaworld: Programming the Public* (New York: Seaburg Press, 1977). See also Roberta S. Sigel (Ed.), *Learning about Politics: A Reader in Political Socialization* (New York: Random House, 1970); and Stanley A. Renshon (Ed.), *Handbook of Political Socialization: Theory and Research* (New York: The Free Press, 1977).
8. Doris A. Graber, *Mass Media and American Politics* (Washington: Congressional Quarterly Press, 1980), p. 127.
9. E. E. Schattschneider, *The Semisovereign People* (New York: Holt, Rinehart & Winston, 1961), p. 68.
10. Graber, *Mass Media and American Politics*, p. 12.
11. "Presidential Popularity: A 43-Year Review," *Gallup Opinion Index*, October/November 1980.
12. Edward J. Epstein, *News from Nowhere* (New York: Random House, 1973), p. 39.
13. Stephen Vito, "Inside 60 Minutes," *American Film*, December/January 1972, pp. 31–36, 55–57.

Close-Up and In-Depth Analyses

Ben H. Bagdikian. *The Information Machines.* New York: Harper & Row, 1971.

James David Barber. *Race for the Presidency: The Media and the Nominating Process.* Englewood Cliffs, N.J.: Prentice-Hall, 1978.

Dennis K. Davis and Stanley J. Baran. *Mass Communication and Everyday Life.* Belmont, Calif.: Wadsworth, 1981.

Murray Edelman. *The Symbolic Uses of Politics.* Chicago: University of Illinois Press, 1967.

Doris A. Graber. *Mass Media and American Politics.* Washington: Congressional Quarterly Press, 1980.

Mark W. Hopkins. *Mass Media in the Soviet Union.* Indianapolis: Pegasus, 1970.

Ray Eldon Huebert, Donald F. Ungurait, and Thomas W. Bohn. *Mass Media.* New York: Longman, 1979.

Sidney Kraus and Dennis Davis. *The Effects of Mass Communication on Political Behavior.* University Park: Pennsylvania State University Press, 1976.

Marshall McLuhan and Quentin Fiore. *The Medium Is the Message.* New York: Penguin, 1967.

David L. Paletz and Robert M. Entman. *Media Power Politics.* New York: Free Press, 1981.

Kevin P. Phillips. *Mediacracy.* Garden City, N. Y.: Doubleday, 1975.

Ann Rawley Saldich. *Electronic Democracy.* New York: Praeger, 1979.

IDEOLOGY AND GOVERNMENT

WHY DO WE NEED IDEOLOGY?
Ideas have power. People are influenced
by ideas—beliefs, symbols, doctrines—
more than they realize. Indeed, ideas
help to decide who gets what in society,
and then they help to justify the
outcome.

An ideology is an integrated system
of ideas that provides people with
rationalizations for a way of life, guides
for evaluating "right" and "wrong" in
public affairs, and emotional impulses
to action. Ideologies justify the
distribution of values in society.
Ideologies also justify the political
system itself. By providing a
justification for wealth and power, an
ideology itself becomes a source of
wealth and power. Without the added
legitimacy provided by an ideology,
people without power or wealth may
easily become resentful of the
distribution of values. This resentment
can lead to strikes, demonstrations,
terrorism, or revolution. Thus, it is
important to the leadership to gain
acceptance for the prevailing ideology—
whether it be capitalism, communism,
liberalism, conservatism, socialism, or
any other popular "ism."

Ideologies not only help regulate the
masses but also restrain leaders. Once
an ideology becomes deeply rooted in
society, leaders as well as nonleaders
become bound by it. An ideology that
justifies the distribution of power also
governs the behavior of power holders.
Leaders of democratic nations must

On the program
"Firing Line" William
F. Buckley, Jr. (left)
and John Kenneth
Galbraith discuss
political ideology.

abide by the outcome of elections and referenda; leaders of Communist-bloc nations must adhere to the principles of Marxism/Leninism.

DEMOCRACY: "WE HOLD THESE TRUTHS TO BE SELF-EVIDENT"

Democracy means individual participation in the decisions that affect one's life. The philosopher John Dewey wrote: "The keynote of democracy as a way of life may be expressed as the necessity for the participation of every mature human being in the formation of values that regulate the living of men together."[1]

Popular participation in decision making is valued in a democracy as fostering self-development. Responsibility for governing one's own conduct is viewed as promoting the development of character, self-reliance, intelligence, and moral judgment—in short, dignity. Even if a benevolent dictator could govern in the public interest, he or she would be rejected by the true democrat. The value of citizen participation in public affairs is *not* based on the policy outcomes it would produce but instead on the belief that individual involvement is essential to the full development of human character.

In a democracy, popular participation is to be achieved through majority rule and respect for the rights of minorities. Self-government can only be achieved by encouraging each individual to contribute to the development of public policy and by resolving conflicts over public policy through majority rule. Minorities that have had the opportunity to influence public policy but have not succeeded in winning majority support must accept the decisions of majorities. In return, majorities permit minorities to openly attempt to win majority support for their views. Minorities are guaranteed freedom of speech and press, freedom of dissent, freedom to form opposition political parties and organizations, and freedom to complain—"to petition the government for a redress of grievances." This freedom of expression is also necessary for learning what the majority views really are.

The underlying value of democracy is individual dignity. Human beings, by virtue of their existence, are entitled to life, liberty, property, and due process of law. A higher "natural law" guarantees to every person both liberty and property, and this natural law is morally superior to human law. John Locke (1632–1704), an English political philosopher whose writings most influenced the Founding Fathers of the United States, argued that even in a state of nature—that is, a world without governments—an individual possesses "certain inalienable Rights [and] that among these are Life, Liberty, and Property."[2] Locke meant that these rights are independent of government—that they are not given to us by government and cannot be taken away by government.

The underlying value of democracy is individual dignity.

Another vital aspect of democracy is a belief in equality. "All men are created equal," according to the Declaration of Independence. Early democrats in America believed in *equality before the law*—a person must not be judged by social position, economic class, religion, sex, or race. Many early democrats also believed in *political equality*—equal access of individuals to political influence. Political equality is frequently expressed today in the notion of "one person, one vote." Over time the notion of equality has been extended beyond legal and political affairs to include equality of opportunity in education, employment, housing, and public accommodations. Each person has an equal opportunity to develop his or her capacities to their fullest potential.

Remember, however, that the traditional idea of democracy always stressed *equality of opportunity* in education, wealth, and status, not *absolute equality*. Thomas Jefferson recognized a "natural aristocracy" of people having talent, ambition, and a willingness to work, and democrats since Jefferson have accepted inequalities that are a product of individual merit and hard work. Absolute equality, or "leveling" (as the Founding Fathers called it), is not a part of American democratic ideology.

Democracy is not a tightly organized system of thought, such as communism. Throughout history, many thinkers have contributed to our understanding of democracy. (Early Greek philosophers contributed the word *democracy* itself, which literally means "people power.") It is better, perhaps, to speak of democratic traditions rather than a single democratic ideology.

There is hardly a nation in the world that does not *claim* to be "democratic."

Unfortunately the looseness of the term *democracy* allows it to be perverted by very antidemocratic regimes. There is hardly a nation in the world that does not *claim* to be "democratic." Communist countries outlaw political opposition, suppress dissent, and deny fundamental freedoms of speech and press. Yet they frequently call themselves "democratic republics" (for example, the German Democratic Republic—Communist East Germany) or "people's republics" (for example, the Democratic People's Republic of Korea—Communist North Korea). Many nations use the term *democracy* to mean only that they believe that their policies conform to the wishes of their citizens. But these nations do not allow political freedoms or hold elections in order to find out whether their policies actually do conform to their citizens' wishes. Thus, they use the term *democracy* as a political slogan rather than a true description of their governmental process.

Democracy: Rhetoric or Reality?

Modern political scientists are in general agreement that "in all large-scale societies the decisions at any given time are typically in the hands of a small number of people." Direct popular participation in all of the decisions that shape our lives is not a real possibility. All societies—democratic and authoritarian, socialist and capitalist, traditional and advanced—are governed by a few. The political scientist Harold Lasswell wrote, "Government is always government by the few, whether in the name of the few, the one, or the many."[3]

"Government is always government by the few, whether in the name of the few, the one, or the many."

In a large society, direct democracy poses insurmountable problems. We may talk of "government by the people," but consider what that would mean if it were literally true: There are 226 million Americans spread over 4 million square miles. If we brought them all together, standing shoulder to shoulder in military formation, they would occupy sixty-six square miles. Just to shake the hands of 226 million people would take a century. One round of five-minute speeches by everyone would take 5,000 years. Generations of people would be born, grow old, and die while such an assembly tried to make one decision. Direct participatory democracy, then, is no more than an ideal.

No one seriously contends that American citizens participate directly in *all* of the decisions that shape their lives; that majority preferences always *prevail*; that the values of life, liberty, and property are *never* sacrificed; or that *every* American enjoys equality of oppor-

The town meeting is one of the few remaining forums for direct government in the U. S.

tunity. Indeed, most government and civics textbooks today acknowledge that direct participatory democracy is impossible, and they describe instead a limited form of self-government—pluralism—as the best possible approximation of democracy in a large society.

Pluralism: Government by Competing Interests

Pluralism is the belief that democratic values can be preserved by a system in which (a) there are many competing interest groups, (b) public policy is determined through bargaining and compromise, and (c) voters can influence policy by choosing among parties and candidates. Of course, pluralism is not the same as the democratic ideal of direct individual participation in decision making. Pluralists contend that individuals in the political system are *represented* by the leaders of large interest groups, parties, unions, corporations, and governments. The real decisions are made by these leaders.

Pluralism relies on the notion of *competition* among leaders to protect the interest of individuals. It is hoped that the existence of countervailing centers of power—for example, big business, big labor, and big government—will keep any single group of leaders from abusing their power or oppressing the individual. Citizens enjoy *indirect participation in policymaking* by helping to chose between competing groups of leaders in elections. According to the pluralists, the Democratic and Republican parties are really coalitions of interest groups: the Democratic party represents union members, big-city residents, blacks, Catholics, Jews, and, until recently, Southerners; the Republican party represents business and the professions, suburbanites, farmers, and White Anglo-Saxon Protestants. Citizens can indirectly affect policy by supporting candidates and parties—voting, contributing money, displaying bumper stickers, and so on. They can also indirectly affect policy by joining and supporting interest groups—for example, the Sierra Club for environmentalists, the American Civil Liberties Union for civil rights advocates, the National Association for the Advancement of Colored People or the Urban League for blacks, the American Legion for military advocates, the National Rifle Association for opponents of gun control, and so on.

Pluralism: The belief that democratic values can be preserved by a system in which (a) there are many competing interest groups, (b) public policy is determined through bargaining and compromise, and (c) voters can influence policy by choosing among parties and candidates.

Pluralists argue that groups that are influential in one kind of decision are not necessarily influential in another kind.

Pluralists believe that there are *multiple leadership groups* in society. (Sometimes this situation is referred to awkwardly as "polyarchy.") They contend that power is widely dispersed among these groups. More importantly, it is argued that groups that are influential in one kind of decision are not necessarily influential in another kind. For example, leadership groups that are influential in determining the military budget or deciding whether to build a new bomber are

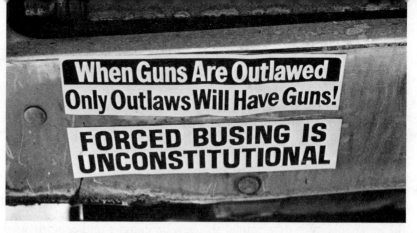

When Guns Are Outlawed
Only Outlaws Will Have Guns!

FORCED BUSING IS
UNCONSTITUTIONAL

Participation through
popular expression—
bumper stickers.

not the same groups that influence decisions about tax cuts or about interest rates on home mortgages. Different groups of leaders make decisions in different issue areas.

Public policy, according to the pluralists, is not necessarily majority preference. Instead it is the "equilibrium" achieved through interest-group interaction—competition, bargaining, and compromise. Public policy represents the balance of competing interest groups, and therefore, say the pluralists, it is a reasonable approximation of society's preferences.[4]

Elitism: Government by the Few

Not all scholars agree that pluralism accurately describes American democracy. Two hundred years ago, Alexander Hamilton, a delegate to the American Constitutional Convention and later secretary of the treasury under President George Washington, wrote:

> All governments divide themselves into the few and the many.
> The first are the rich and wellborn and the other, the masses of
> people. The voice of the people has been said to be the voice
> of god, and however generally this maxim has been quoted and
> believed it is not true in fact. The people are turbulent and
> changing. They seldom judge right.[5]

Elitism: The belief that all societies are governed by a small minority—drawn disproportionately from the wealthy, educated, socially prominent groups in society—who share a consensus about society's values and who are responsible for general policy direction in all issue areas.

Elitism is the belief that all societies are governed by a small minority—drawn disproportionately from the wealthy, educated, socially prominent groups—who share a consensus about society's values. This minority is viewed as responsible for general policy direction in all issue areas. Elitists believe that most people are uninterested in politics. They believe, therefore, that the survival of democratic values—individual dignity, freedom of speech and press, due process of law, personal liberty, and equality of opportunity—rests on the shoulders of the elite, not the masses.

Elitists believe that the survival of democratic values—individual dignity, freedom of speech and press, due process of law, personal liberty, and equality of opportunity—rests on the shoulders of the elite, not the masses.

Elitism contends that "the few" who govern are not typical of "the many" who are governed. The elite possesses greater wealth, education, status, information, ability to communicate, and skills of leadership than the masses. But elitism does *not* mean that individuals from the masses can never rise to positions of leadership. On the contrary, elitists argue, a certain amount of "circulation of elites" (upward mobility) is essential to the stability of the political system. This process skims off the cream of the lower classes and avoids potentially revolutionary oppositions from forming. And it strengthens the elite by bringing in new members who are talented and ambitious.

Elitism contends that leaders share a *consensus* about basic "rules of the game" and the fundamental values of society. It may support social welfare programs, minimum wages, civil rights legislation, environmental protection, and so on. But it is the elite that decides these matters, not the masses. Competition and disagreement take place within a very narrow range of issues. Members of the elite agree on

---

Essentials: Democracy, Pluralism, Elitism

Democracy's Central Ideas

1. People should participate in the decisions that shape their lives.

2. Government is by majority rule, with recognition of the rights of minorities to try to become majorities. These rights are freedom of speech, press, assembly, and petition, including the freedom to dissent, to form opposition parties, and to run for public office.

3. Key values are individual dignity and the preservation of life, liberty, property, and due process of law.

4. All individuals should have equal opportunity to develop their own capabilities to the fullest extent possible.

Pluralism's Central Ideas

1. Direct participatory democracy is impossible, but citizens can be represented by the leaders of large organizations.

2. Competition between organizations protects the individual.

3. Individuals can participate indirectly in policymaking by helping to choose between competing organizations and interest groups, by participating in elections, and by joining the supporting interest groups.

4. The existence of multiple leadership groups in society ensures wide dispersal of power. Leadership groups that are

(continued)

more matters than they disagree over, and disagreement usually occurs over *means* rather than *ends*.

According to the elitists, power is organized in a single pyramid with interlocking corporate, banking, civic, and governmental leaders at the top of this power structure. These leaders come together to set the general direction of both domestic and foreign policy for the nation.

Elitists generally believe that the masses are apathetic, uninterested, and ill-informed about policy questions. The masses are really not prepared to participate in public policymaking. Not only do they lack knowledge about public affairs; their values are also less "democratic" than those of the leaders. That is to say, the leaders give more consistent support to freedom of speech and press, freedom of dissent, due process of law, and equal opportunity than the masses. Parties and elections help to decide personnel but not policy. Parties and elections have very little issue content, and the masses have little influence over policy directions. Public policy reflects the values and

---

(continued)

influential in some decisions are not the same groups that are influential in other decisions.

5. Public policy is not necessarily majority preference but instead is the equilibrium, or balance, between competing interest groups.

Elitism's Central Ideas

1. In all societies, only a few can govern. These few—the elite—possess greater wealth, education, status, and other values than the many who are governed by them—the masses.

2. There is a consensus among the elite on the fundamental values of society. Competition centers on the best means of achieving these values.

3. Individuals in the mass have little influence over the elite. Parties and elections may help choose personnel but not policy. The masses are uninterested and ill-informed about public affairs and are probably less "democratic" in their values than the elite.

4. Power is organized in a single pyramid. At the top of the power structure business, financial, and governmental leaders come together to set general policy directions for all sections of society.

5. Public policy reflects the values and preferences of the elite, not the demands of the people. Mass attitudes toward public policy are shaped by the elite through the mass media.

preferences of the elite, not the demands of "the people." Mass opinion is shaped by elites (through the mass media). Elite opinion is seldom shaped by mass demands. This does *not* necessarily mean that the masses are exploited or oppressed by the elite. On the contrary, the elite may be very liberal and "public minded"—it may support social welfare programs, minimum wages, civil rights legislation, environmental protection, and so on. But it is the *elite* that decides these matters, not the masses.[6]

Conservatism:
"The Government Which Governs Best Governs Least"

"Conservatism" in the United States today traces its roots to the classical liberalism of an earlier era. Classical liberalism grew out of the eighteenth century Age of Reason, in which great philosophers such as Locke, Adam Smith, and Jefferson affirmed their faith in the rational abilities of human beings to determine their own destinies. Classical liberalism asserted *the dignity and worth of the individual.* It originated as an attack on feudal society, with its monarchy, privileged aristocracy, and state-established church. It asserted that "all men are created equal, that they are endowed by their Creator with certain inalienable Rights, [and] that among these are Life, Liberty, and the pursuit of Happiness." (Jefferson borrowed this phrase for use in the Declaration of Independence from Locke. However, Locke used the word *property* instead of *pursuit of happiness.* Jefferson thought that the two wordings were equivalent, because he believed that no one could pursue happiness without property.)

Classical liberalism asserted the dignity and worth of the individual.

This belief in the natural rights of individuals was coupled with a belief in *limited government*. Government is formed with the consent of the governed to protect individual liberty. It follows that government must never become so strong that it threatens liberty itself. Human beings form a "social contract" with one another to establish a government to protect their rights; they agree to accept some governmental activity in order to better protect life, liberty, and property. But this governmental authority should be kept to a minimum. The only restrictions on individuals should be those required to guarantee the freedom of other individuals.

Classical liberalism as a political ideology is closely related to *capitalism* as an economic ideology. Individual freedom includes being free to make contracts, to trade, to bargain for one's services, to move from one job to another, and to start one's own business. Laissez-faire economics stresses individual rationality in economic matters; freedom of choice in producing, buying, and selling; and limited government interference in the marketplace. Just as in politics people should be free to speak out, to form political parties, to vote as they please, and to pursue their political interest as they think best, in economics people should be free to find work, to start businesses, to spend their money as they please, and to pursue their economic interests as they think best. The role of government should be restricted to protecting private property, enforcing contracts, and performing only those functions that cannot be performed by the private market.

The "Neoconservatives"

Many traditional liberals have become disillusioned with costly large-scale, bureaucratic, governmental programs. The war in Vietnam, the vast expansion in social programs during the 1960s and '70s, urban rioting and campus unrest, the Watergate scandal, and the nation's spiraling inflation have combined over the past twenty years to raise doubt about the size and power of government. Enthusiasm has been dampened by the many failures and high costs of well-meaning yet ineffective government social programs. The result has been that many traditional liberals have become critical of such programs and suspicious of new government plans to solve society's problems. These are the "neo" (or new) conservatives.

The neoconservatives believe that society's problems cannot be solved simply by passing a law, creating a new bureaucracy, and throwing several billion dollars in the general direction of the problem. They argue that poverty, ill health, discrimination, crime, ignorance, pollution, joblessness, and inflation have afflicted societies for a long time. Neoconservatives would like to solve these problems, but they no longer assume that the problems can be solved by massive government intervention. Instead, they have greater respect for the free-market system; they generally support fewer regulations on business; they believe that many government social programs only make things worse; they are respectful toward traditional values and institutions, including religion, family, and community; and they believe that the United States must maintain a strong national defense and protect itself and its allies from Communist aggression.

The neoconservatives disapprove of unequal treatment suffered by racial minorities. But they generally oppose affirmative-action or busing programs that involve racial quotas. They believe in *equality of opportunity,* with all people free to strive for whatever they wish; but they do not

Conservatives today retain their faith in the early classical "liberal" values of Locke and Jefferson. Conservatives claim to be the true "liberals," because they stress individual freedom from government controls, maximum personal liberty, reliance on individual initiative and effort, support for a free-enterprise economy with a minimum of governmental intervention, and rewards for initiative, skill, risk, and hard work—in contrast to government-imposed "leveling" of income. The result, of course, is often a confusion in ideologi-

Conservatives (contemporary): Today's political conservatives believe in individualism, fiscal responsibility, an economy free from excessive government controls, and state initiatives over federal actions.

believe in *absolute equality*, with the government trying to give everyone equal shares of everything. Neoconservatives believe that government is "overloaded" with tasks that should be left to the individual, the family, the church, or the free-market system. Government has tried to do too much for its citizens, and by failure to meet its promises it has lost respect.

The neoconservative movement began as a reaction by a few intellectuals to the social unrest of the 1960s and the massive new government programs of President Lyndon Johnson's Great Society. The early movement included the sociologists Nathan Glazer, Irving Kristol, and Daniel Bell; the political scientists James Q. Wilson, Aaron Wildavsky, and Daniel Patrick Moynihan (now a U. S. senator from New York); and the political sociologist Seymour Martin Lipset. They captured control of an established liberal journal, *Commentary*, and they established a new journal of their own, *The Public Interest*. A neoconservative base has emerged in the American Enterprise Institute, a Washington "think tank" that has grown in recent years to challenge the liberalism of the more prestigious Brookings Institution.

The neoconservatives are not always warmly welcomed by the established conservatives. Conservatives such as William F. Buckley, Jr., editor of the *National Review*, know that the neoconservatives are recent converts and that many of them were liberals (and even socialists) in years past. Moreover, the neoconservatives, while critical of big government and supportive of the free market, are not always "conservative" on controversial social issues such as abortion, prayer in public schools, and the Equal Rights Amendment. In short, some traditional conservatives do not always trust the loyalty of the "neoconservatives."

See Peter Steinfels, *The New Conservatives* (New York: Simon & Schuster, 1979).

cal labels. Many conservatives today charge that modern liberals have abandoned the principles of individualism, limited government, and free enterprise.

Conservatives generally have an *evolutionary* view of social progress. Revolutionary change is believed to create more problems than it solves. It is better to rely on the cumulative experience of society to produce workable arrangements to ease social problems than it is to engage in radical experimentation. Gradual progress is possible, but only if people do not destroy the acquired wisdom of the past in favor of untried, utopian solutions that jeopardize the well-being of society. Certainly no government possesses the wisdom to resolve all social problems. Governments are likely to make things worse rather than better.

Liberalism: The Power of Positive Government

Modern liberalism rationalizes and justifies the growth of government in the United States in the twentieth century. Contemporary **liberals** retain their faith in individual dignity, civil rights, due process of law, and equality of opportunity. But they emphasize the importance of social and economic security for the whole population as a prerequisite to individual self-realization and self-development. Whereas classical liberalism looked with suspicion on government as a potential threat to individual freedom, modern liberals look on government as a positive force to be used to combat social and economic barriers to freedom, equality, and self-development.

Liberals (contemporary): Today's political liberals believe in the positive power of government to reduce inequalities, correct serious societal abuses, and expand the scope of human freedoms.

Modern liberals believe that they can change people's lives through the use of governmental power—ending racial and sexual discrimination, abolishing poverty, eliminating slums, creating jobs, providing medical care for all, educating young and old, and instilling humanitarian values in everyone. The prevailing impulse in modern liberalism is to use the government to *do good*—to perform public services, to end injustice, and to assist the least fortunate in society. Today's liberals are impatient with what they see as slow progress through individual initiative and private enterprise toward the solution of social and economic problems. So they seek to use the power of the national government to find immediate and comprehensive solutions to society's troubles.

> The prevailing impulse in modern liberalism is to use government to *do good*—to perform public services, to end injustice, and to assist the least fortunate in society.

Modern liberalism is critical of some aspects of capitalism—"excess" profits, low wages, environmental damage, unsafe consumer products, and lack of health and safety in the work place. Both liberals and socialists are critical of capitalism, but liberals propose to

Americans: Left, Right, or Center?

The terms *liberal* and *conservative* have been used with different meanings over the years. So it is difficult to know whether Americans are really liberal or conservative on the issues. We can ask them, "How would you describe your own political philosophy—conservative, middle-of-the-road, or liberal?" The results over recent years are shown below. More of those polled described themselves as *middle-of-the-road* than either conservative or liberal. However, self-described conservatives outnumbered liberals by a large margin: about 40 percent of the general population described itself as conservative, compared with a little over 20 percent that described itself as liberal.

What do Americans mean when they label themselves as liberal, middle-of-the-road, or conservative? There is no clear answer to this question. People who labeled themselves conservative did not *consistently* oppose social welfare programs, government regulation of the economy, or change in society. People who labeled themselves liberals did not *consistently* support social welfare programs or government regulation of the economy.

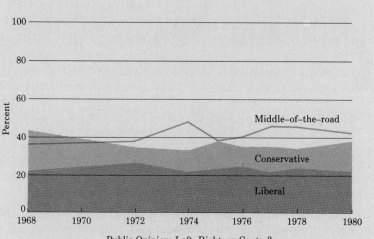

Public Opinion: Left, Right, or Center?

Question: How would you describe your own personal political philosophy—conservative, middle-of-the-road, liberal, or radical? (Source: Surveys by American Institute of Public Opinion—Gallup, latest that of August 11–14, 1978; Louis Harris and Associates, latest that of December 27–January 10, 1978. From *Public Opinion*, Sept./Oct. 1978, Feb./March 1981.)

Students and Professors: Liberal or Conservative?
College students are more liberal than the general population, although conservatism among students has been growing in recent years. Most of the students polled, however,
described themselves as middle-of-the-road. College or university life did not necessarily make a student more liberal.
Indeed, liberals outnumbered conservatives among entering
freshmen classes; this indicates that college students are
more liberal than the general population even before they
begin their classes.

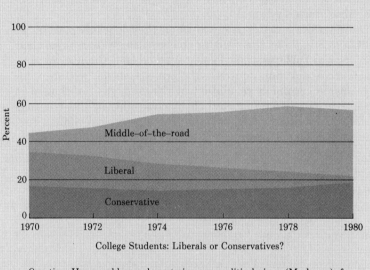

College Students: Liberals or Conservatives?

Question: How would you characterize your political views (Mark one): far
left, liberal, middle-of-the-road, conservative, far right? (Source: Surveys of
the Cooperative Institutional Research Program of the Laboratory for Research on Higher Education, UCLA, and the American Council on Education;
latest that of 1978—Austin Study. From *Public Opinion*, June/July 1979.)

reform capitalism rather than replace it with socialism. Liberals generally support government bureaucracies and regulations designed to
oversee business and financial practices, guarantee minimum wages,
protect unions, ensure environmental protection, guarantee consumer
safety, and protect occupational health.

Modern liberalism stresses the ability of government fiscal policies—taxing and spending—to maintain full employment. Liberals
are generally committed to an enlargement of the governmental sector in society—in education, welfare, medicine, civil rights, housing,

The stereotype of the liberal college professor is widely accepted both on and off of the campus. And it is true that the college professors polled were more liberal than either students or the general population. About 45 percent of all college faculty members described themselves as liberal as opposed to 35 percent who described themselves as conservative. This was a reversal of the situation in the general population.

However, students should note what field their professors are in before estimating the likelihood that they are liberal or conservative. There was a great deal of difference between professors in the social sciences and humanities (59 percent of whom described themselves as liberal) and professors in business and engineering (28 percent of whom described themselves as liberal) and agriculture (22 percent of whom described themselves as liberal). Other fields included the natural sciences (40 percent liberal) and law and medicine (31 percent liberal).

employment, job training, child care, transportation, and so on. Modern liberalism envisions a larger role for government in the future—setting new goals, managing the economy, protecting individual health and safety, meeting popular demands, and redirecting national resources away from private wants toward public needs.

Modern liberals call for the reduction of extreme inequalities in society. Classical liberals and conservatives place great value on *equality of opportunity,* but they accept differences in wealth and income that are a product of differences in talent, initiative, risk taking, skill, education, and the like. In contrast, modern liberals contend that individual dignity depends on the elimination of extreme inequalities in society. They contend that true equality of opportunity and individual dignity cannot be achieved if there are significant numbers of people suffering from hunger, remediable illness, or extreme hardship in life. Thus, modern liberals generally support governmental efforts to reduce inequalities in society by transferring income, goods, and services from the affluent to the poor.[7]

Democratic Socialism: "Economic Democracy"

Socialism means collective ownership of the means of production, distribution, and service. There are a number of forms of socialism and a bewildering array of socialist parties and groups. But socialists agree on one point: private property in land, buildings, factories, and stores must be transformed into social, collective property.

Socialism: An ideology that emphasizes collective ownership of the means of production, the equitable distribution of wealth to all members of society, and cooperation in place of competition for private profit.

Socialism shares with communism (see the section following) a condemnation of capitalist profit making as exploitive of the working classes. Communists and socialists agree on the "evils" of industrial capitalism—the concentration of wealth, the insensitivity of the profit motive to human needs, the insecurities and sufferings brought on by the business cycle, the conflict of class interests, and the tendency of capitalist nations to involve themselves in imperialist wars. However, socialists are committed to the *democratic process* as a means to replacing capitalism with collective ownership of economic enterprise.

Modern socialists frequently contend that socialism in the economic sector is essential in achieving democracy and equality in the political sector. In other words, they believe that true democracy cannot be achieved until wealth is equally distributed among the people and business and industry are collectively owned by the people. To socialists, "economic democracy" is essential to political democracy.

> To socialists, "economic democracy" is essential to political democracy.

Socialists generally reject the notion of violent revolution as a way to replace capitalism and instead advocate peaceful, constitutional roads to socialism. Moreover, many socialists are prepared to govern in a free society under democratic principles, including freedom of speech and press and the right to organize political parties and oppose government policy.

Socialists are generally committed to an evolutionary approach to the achievement of collective ownership of the economy. They are prepared for a gradual restructuring of society, a restructuring that can take place within the framework of liberal democratic traditions. Socialists are willing to cooperate with liberals to achieve improvements in the conditions of the working class—to alleviate poverty, to maintain full employment, to provide national health care, to expand educational opportunities, and so on. Socialists can also be found allied with liberal reformers at the forefront of attacks on American business, in environmental movements, in antinuclear organizations, and in consumer-interest groups. Unlike the liberals, however, the socialists hope to discredit the private enterprise system sufficiently to see it replaced with government ownership, not merely reformed or regulated. Socialists generally propose to begin by "nationalizing" the railroads, the steel industry, the automobile industry, privately owned public utilities, or other specific segments of the economy.

Socialism is equalitarian, seeking to reduce or eliminate inequalities in the distribution of wealth. It would attempt to achieve absolute equality, rather than mere equality of opportunity.[8]

COMMUNISM: "WORKERS OF THE WORLD, UNITE"

The first stirrings of socialism date back to the days of the French Revolution beginning in 1789. A number of "utopian socialists" tried over the years to develop schemes to replace the free-market system with cooperative, equalitarian communities. This socialism was neither political nor violent. Utopian socialism and communal living never amounted to a strong political movement. The man who finally made socialism into an effective ideology and a successful political movement was Karl Marx (1818–1883).

Marxism arose out of the Industrial Revolution and the social evils and economic inequalities it generated. Classical liberalism began as an eighteenth century revolt against the hereditary aristocracy of a feudal system; Marxism began as a nineteenth century revolt against the privileged wealth of a capitalist system. Even though the Industrial Revolution eventually led to great increases in the standards of living of Western democracies, throughout much of the nineteenth century the only beneficiaries seemed to be the successful

After the Russian revolution in 1917, Lenin sent propaganda trains equipped with movies and recordings around the country to teach peasants contemporary communist theory.

manufacturers, bankers, merchants, and speculators. The masses of industrial workers seemed hopelessly impoverished. It appeared as if liberalism and capitalism had simply substituted an aristocracy of wealth for an aristocracy of birth.

Like many other socialists, Marx was not an impoverished worker but rather an upper-middle-class intellectual. He began his academic career as a student of law, then changed to philosophy. Later he was supported by Friedrich Engels (1820–1895), a wealthy young intellectual who not only assisted Marx financially but also collaborated with him on many of his writings. Marx wrote many books and essays, but his pamphlet the *Communist Manifesto* (1848) was politically more important. It was concise and full of dramatic phrases: "Workers of the world, unite. You have nothing to lose but your chains." It provided a political ideology to what had previously been only scattered protests against injustices. Later Marx would elaborate on his ideas in great detail in *Das Kapital*.

Let us summarize some of the basic ideas of Marxism.

Economic determinism: Marx's assertion that economic structure determines all other aspects of a society, including politics, culture, art, and religion.

Economic determinism. Marxism teaches that the economic system, "the mode of production," is basic to all of the rest of society. The mode of production determines the class structure, the political system, religion, education, family life, law, and even art and literature. The economic system of capitalism creates a class structure composed of a wealthy *bourgeoisie* (the property-owning class of capitalists) and an oppressed proletariat (the property-less worker class).

The class struggle: The Marxist theory that historical change has been caused by the inevitable conflict between the exploiting "haves" and the exploited "have-nots" in every society.

The class struggle. The first sentence in the *Communist Manifesto* proclaims, "The history of all hitherto existing societies is the history of the class struggle." The class that controls the mode of production (the economic system) is the dominant class, and it always exploits the other classes. This exploitation creates antagonisms, which eventually produce revolution. Just as the landed aristocracy was supplanted by the industrial capitalists, eventually the capitalists will be supplanted by the working proletariat.

The theory of surplus value. According to Marx, *labor* is the only real source of value. Laborers deserve the full value of any product they make, but under capitalism laborers only receive a small part of it—just enough for their subsistence. The rest, which Marx called **"surplus value,"** is taken by the capitalists as profit for their own enrichment. According to Marx, the capitalist profit system is a gigantic scheme for exploiting the workers by taking much of the value they have created.

Surplus value: The profit "squeezed" out of the worker's labor that allows the exploiting class to become wealthier.

The inevitability of revolution. As capitalists continuously try to maximize their profits, the rich become richer and the poor become poorer. Competition squeezes out the smaller capitalists, and ownership is gradually concentrated in the hands of a few giant corporations. As exploitation increases, the ranks of the proletariat grow and class hostilities rise. As capitalists drive down wages, capitalism becomes plagued by its own "internal contradictions"—depression, unemployment, and human misery. These generate class consciousness among the workers—a realization that they are being exploited by the capitalists—which eventually leads to strikes, unrest, and revolution itself.

The dictatorship of the proletariat.   The capitalists will never peacefully give up their ruling position. Only a violent revolution will place the proletariat in power. When the proletariat finally revolts, it, like the ruling capitalist class before it, will establish a government of its own—a dictatorship of the proletariat—to protect its class interest. It will seize the property of the capitalists and establish "collective ownership" (state control) of the entire economy—manufacturing plants, banks, utilities, stores, schools, newspapers, television, and so on. The bourgeoisie will be eliminated as a class.

Withering away of the state.   As a result of collective ownership of everything, Marx predicted, a "classless" society will emerge from the revolution. Since the purpose of government is to assist the ruling class in exploiting and oppressing the other classes, once a classless society is established, the government will have no real purpose. It will simply "wither away." After the establishment of the communist state, the rule of distribution will be "from each according to his ability, to each according to his needs."[9]

The task fell to V. I. Lenin (1870–1924) to reinterpret Marxism as a revolutionary ideology and to apply it to the Russian Revolution in 1917. In revising Marxism, Lenin contributed so many new ideas that contemporary communist ideology is frequently referred to as Marxism/Leninism. Two of Lenin's ideas deserve special mention, the totalitarian party and the theory of imperialism.[10]

The totalitarian party.   According to Lenin, the key to a successful revolution is the organizing of a small, disciplined, hard-core group of professional revolutionaries into a centralized, totalitarian party. The Communist party will be organized according to the principle of "democratic centralism." Discussion of alternative actions is permitted before the leadership makes a decision, but once a decision has been made, the party will obey commands like a well-trained army. The Communist party will be the "vanguard of the proletariat"—the most advanced and class-conscious sector of the proletariat, which has the right to act as its voice and to exercise its dictatorial powers over the rest of society.

The Mass Media in a Communist Regime

In the Union of Soviet Socialist Republics the Communist party is the only legal political party. It enrolls about 16 million members out of a national population of 280 million. Since the end of the Stalinist era, the regime has tolerated a few individual dissenters. But this tiny minority, which faces daily threats of imprisonment or deportation, is not permitted access to the mass media. Dissidents must, at great risk to themselves, family, and friends, secretly circulate their own illegal writings.

The only recognized function of the mass media in the U. S. S. R. is political persuasion. It was Lenin himself who lectured on the power of the media and set forth their political uses: (1) agitation and propaganda to serve the purposes of the state—strengthening loyalty, improving worker output, and encouraging obedience to the regime; (2) education in Marxism—increasing mass solidarity, improving support for the party, and encouraging hostility toward bourgeois (Western democratic) ideas; and (3) spread of proletarian (communist) cultural values—through art, music, theater,

Another communist country, the People's Republic of China, has begun to enter the TV age. About 400 million of China's 1 billion people have access to TVs.

ballet, sports, and so on—in order to extol the virtues of communism. *All* media communication must serve the state.

There are no privately owned media in the U. S. S. R. All newspapers are published by either the Communist party or the government itself. The national news agency, Telegrafnoye Agentsvo Sovretskovo Soyuza (TASS), collects and disseminates all of the "news." Its headquarters is in Moscow, and it maintains reporters in cities throughout the Soviet Union and around the world. All stories are checked for political "errors" before being released to newspapers and radio and television stations. There are perhaps 750 daily newspapers in the Soviet Union, including regional papers and a number published in languages other than Russian for the many nationalities within the country. But the national Communist party newspaper, *Pravda* ("Truth"), has the largest circulation. The government has its own newspaper, *Izvestia* ("News"), which tends to concentrate on foreign affairs. Regional and local papers do not deviate from the official "news" sent to them by TASS or published by *Pravda* or *Izvestia*. These papers also cover regional or local news. A major section of these newspapers is devoted to letters from the general public; no political criticisms are permitted, but writers may criticize slow progress on projects, sloppy workmanship, long food lines, poorly made goods, and the like.

Television is even more tightly controlled by the state. The chairman of state television and radio is a member of the Council of Ministers (the cabinet) and a high-ranking Communist party official. Television has rapidly expanded in the Soviet Union over the last decade. Today about two-thirds of all homes have television sets. Soviet television now broadcasts in color, but most sets are black and white. National broadcasts originate from the State Television Ministry in Moscow and are transmitted over thousands of miles and many time zones to distant parts of the country. Moscow usually broadcasts evening television with a choice of news and political commentary and educational, cultural, and sports programs. There is no advertising, although news items may appear about new products or ones that are overstocked at government stores. By U. S. standards, there is little program "entertainment"; Soviet television resembles educational programming in the United States—heavy on classical music, ballet, theater, and education. Entertainment for its own sake is not considered a legitimate objective in broadcasting. The purpose of all broadcasting is to advance Communist policies and improve the "socialist state."

The theory of imperialism.   Lenin also tried to come to grips with some obvious problems in Marx's theories: capitalist societies were still flourishing in the twentieth century contrary to Marx's predictions about revolution; and the condition of the working classes was improving rather than deteriorating. So Lenin devised the theory of **imperialism,** which holds that advanced capitalist countries turn to war and colonialism to obtain cheap raw materials and create new markets for their goods. By "exporting poverty abroad" the capitalists manage to keep their own workers relatively prosperous, at the expense of exploiting workers in the Third World through giant multinational corporations. This delays the development of true proletarian class consciousness in the advanced capitalist countries.

> **Imperialism:** Lenin's theory that advanced capitalist societies turn to war and colonialism, exploiting under-developed nations and delaying the development of a proletarian class consciousness among their own workers.

The theory of imperialism helped to explain why no revolution had occurred. Lenin believed that the whole world was being divided into exploiters and exploited, with underdeveloped nations providing the surplus labor for advanced capitalist nations. Of course, as rival capitalist nations tried to expand their markets and sources of raw materials, they came into conflict with one another and continually fought imperialist wars. The idea of worldwide imperialism and exploitation helps revolutionary leaders in Third World countries to arouse the masses, and it assists the Soviet Union in directing hatred toward the United States.

THE AMERICAN LEFT: BEYOND SOCIALISM

The Left in the United States covers a wide spectrum of reformers, Marxists, "progressives," and even violent revolutionaries. It is linked to a subculture, or "counterculture," that deliberately rejects the familiar middle-class way of life—in clothes, hairstyles, living arrangements, drug use, language, and behavior. Much of the American Left is devoid of a coherent ideology; it is not specifically socialist or communist. However, certain targets for opposition recur in the movement—poverty in the midst of affluence, racism, imperialist wars, unresponsive bureaucracy, materialism, and production for profit rather than for use. Two American scholars who have had a strong influence on the thinking of the Left are the philosopher Herbert Marcuse (1898–1979) and the sociologist C. Wright Mills (1916–1962).[11]

Herbert Marcuse

The radicalism of Marcuse begins with a sweeping condemnation of contemporary society as a highly industrialized, "bureaucratized" machine, in which human nature is twisted and destroyed.[12] (Marcuse viewed American society with its capitalist ethos as the most materialistic of all societies, but he considered his critique to be almost equally applicable to communist nations such as the Soviet Union.) Marcuse was primarily concerned with the quality of human life and spirit, and he saw advanced technological society as destructive of human characteristics. He believed that the present ruinous use of technology is ironic, because for the first time in history people possess the opportunity to satisfy all their material needs with relatively little work, leaving them free to live a full, creative life. When life's sustaining resources were scarce, human beings were violent and competitive, lacking attitudes of human solidarity and cooperativeness, but now they can really become more humane.

Marcuse believed that only a *radical restructuring* of social and economic institutions will succeed in liberating people for humanistic, cooperative life-styles. The existing institutions have conditioned them to be materialistic, competitive, and violent. The individual has been transformed into a "one-dimensional" person in whom genuine humanistic values are repressed. In other words, *institutions* have thoroughly distorted human nature. The implication is that without these institutions life would be loving, cooperative, and compassionate. The problem of social change is truly monumental, because the values and institutions of American society are deeply rooted. Since most people are not aware that they are one-dimensional, the first step in social change is "consciousness raising"—that is, making people aware of their misery.

Bureaucracy, rationality, efficiency, and productivity are "dehumanizing" ideas that grow out of technology and materialism. Bureaucracies, both in socialist governments and in capitalist corporations, are insensitive to human needs. But the American capitalist system is the worst of all. Profitability, rather than humanistic values, remains the criterion of decision making in the economy, and this is the reason for poverty and misery despite material abundance.

Marcuse gave no specific prescription for change; he was pessimistic about changing American society. Contemporary radicals are not necessarily committed to work for change within the existing framework of society; many endorse extralegal and sometimes violent alternatives as the only means of dealing with a system they regard as violent itself. The emphasis in contemporary radicalism is on destroying institutions—governments, corporations, universities, the military, and so on—that are bureaucratic and inattentive to human needs.

Many radicals are vague about the kind of society they want to replace the present one with after the revolution. But radical writings imply that the new society will be humanistic rather than materialistic, spontaneous rather than bureaucratic. Popular participation in the spirit of solidarity and brotherhood will replace the bargaining, compromising, and competition that are characteristic of contemporary society.

Radical writings imply that the new society will be humanistic rather than materialistic, spontaneous rather than bureaucratic. Popular participation in the spirit of solidarity and brotherhood will replace the bargaining, compromising, and competition that are characteristic of contemporary society.

In the new society, based on the principles of cooperation and brotherhood rather than competition, love will overcome materialism. This new society will be organized not to foster technological or material progress but to develop human qualities. The Left is not always socialist, because socialism implies large, unresponsive state bureaucracies. However, the Left emphasizes the need for *collectivist control* over the economic resources of society and popular participation in decisions about the use of these resources. **Participatory democracy** must replace bureaucratization and centralization in decision making. Participatory democracy does not involve elections, bargains, or compromises but has to do with group interaction in a spirit of solidarity with a view toward developing consensus. It is not merely a way of registering individual preferences and deciding issues by majority rule but also a group process in which individuals are transformed into a whole community with a shared purpose. Participatory democracy will bring people out of isolation and powerlessness into solidarity and control. Institutions should not be governed from the top down but by the individuals who compose them. Participatory democracy should extend to work, school, neighborhood, prison, and so forth. Thus, besides political institutions, all other major societal institutions must be restructured to meet the criteria for participatory democracy.

> **Participatory democracy:** The view that institutions should be governed, not from the top down, but by the people who compose them; a group process in which consensus and shared purpose are to replace majority rule and competing interests.

Other characteristics of contemporary radicalism include:

1. emphasis on the community rather than the individual
2. belief in the superiority of direct experience over rational knowledge
3. stress on cooperation rather than competition, and
4. emphasis on naturalness in appearance (rejection of makeup, suits, ties).

Contemporary radicalism has yet to find a mass base on which to found a revolution; most radicals are upper-middle-class intellectuals and students.

Radicalism does not have a clear, comprehensive theory of social change. Radicals do not accept the necessity of "working within the system," believing as they do that present institutions are inflexible and incapable of transformation. However, it is not clear how the revolution will come about. Contemporary radicalism has yet to find a mass base on which to found a revolution; most radicals are upper-middle-class intellectuals and students. They know they must form coalitions with broader-based groups in society. Yet the New Left is fragmented over such questions as the role of black people in the movement, the organizational potential of the working class, and the ethics of violence. Radical meetings are frequently endless debates over such questions as these: Is violence or nonviolence the better revolutionary tactic? With whom and under what conditions should coalitions be formed? How should current popular issues be exploited? Should radicals cooperate with liberals? Is the youth culture with its interest in drugs, pop music, and communal living a source of social change or a cop-out from the revolutionary struggle?

C. Wright Mills

The most popular and controversial analysis of power in the United States is Mills's *The Power Elite*.[13] Since its appearance in 1956, most American leftist writings have relied heavily on this important study.

According to Mills, power is concentrated at the top of American corporate, governmental, and military organizations, which closely interlock to form a single structure of power—a **power elite.** Power rests in these three domains—"the corporation chieftains, the political directorate, and the military warlords." Occasionally there is tension among them, but they share a broad consensus about the general direction of public policy and the main course of society. Other institutions (the family, churches, schools, and so forth) are subordinate to the three major institutions of power: "Families and churches and schools adapt to modern life. Governments and armies and corporations shape it, and, as they do, they turn these lesser institutions into means for their ends" (p. 6).

The power elite: An alliance of huge corporations, the military, and key government officials that, according to Mills, controls American society.

The emergence of the power elite is a product of *technology, bureaucracy,* and *centralization.* The economy—once a scattering of many small competing units—is now dominated by a few hundred giant corporate and financial institutions. The political system—once a decentralized structure of states and communities with a small central government—has become a giant centralized bureaucracy in Washington that has assumed power over nearly every aspect of American life. The military—once a slim establishment depending largely on citizen soldiers to meet specific crises—has become the largest and most expensive function of government and a sprawling bureaucratic domain.

As these sectors of society enlarged and centralized, they increasingly came together to coordinate decision making.

At the pinnacle of each of the three enlarged and centralized domains, there have arisen those higher circles which make up the economic, the political, and the military elites. At the top of the economy, among the corporate rich, there are the chief executives; at the top of the political order, the members of the political directorate; at the top of the military establishment, the elite of soldier-statesmen clustered in and around the Joint Chiefs of Staff and the upper echelon. As each of these domains has coincided with the others, as decisions tend to become total in their consequences, the leading men in each of the three domains of power—the warlords, the corporation chieftains, the political directorate—tend to come together, to form the power elite of America [pp. 8–9].

Mills is aware that his description of power conflicts with the pluralist interpretation. But he believes that notions of power holders who balance and compromise interests or who engage in competition

Americans Choose Free Enterprise

While public opinion in the United States is often critical of specific business practices, the free-enterprise system enjoys widespread support. (See figure below.) Most of those polled said they believed that the system provided them with the highest living standards in the world, and most "strongly believed" that Americans must make necessary sacrifices to preserve it.

Free Enterprise Worth Sacrifice

Question: Now here are some statements which represent some traditional American values. Will you tell me for each one whether you strongly believe in this statement, partially believe it or don't believe it.... We must be ready to make sacrifices if necessary to preserve the free enterprise system.

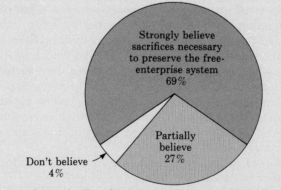

Source: Survey by Time/Yankelovich, Skelly, and White, January 1976.

between parties and groups apply to the middle level of power and not to the top power elite. Political journalists and scholars write about middle levels because that is all they know about or understand; these levels provide the noisy content of most "political" news and gossip. The major directions of national and international policy are determined by people beyond the "clang and clash of American politics." Political campaigns actually distract attention from the really important national and international decisions.

The *unity* of the top elite rests on several factors. First of all, these people are recruited from the same upper social classes; they have similar education, wealth, and upbringing. Moreover, they continue to associate with one another, which reinforces their common feelings. They belong to the same clubs, attend the same parties, meet at the same resorts, and serve on the same civic, cultural, and philanthropic committees. Factions exist, and individual ambitions

More importantly, most of the Americans polled believed that the free-market system (capitalism) is essential to the preservation of individual liberty.

Free Enterprise and Personal Liberty

Question: Some people say that a free market economy is necessary for personal liberty and democracy and that if you take away the free market we will lose liberty. Other people say that the two aren't really related and we can be free and democratic in any kind of economy. Is a free market economy essential to freedom or not?

Not essential
17%

Not sure
24%

Free market
essential to
freedom
59%

Source: Survey by *Cambridge Reports,* May 29–June 13, 1979.

Socialism as an ideological label has very little support. Most of those polled said they opposed the introduction of socialism in the United States; only about 10 percent said they favored it.

(continued)

(*continued*)

Opposition to Socialism

Question: Would you favor or oppose introducing socialism in the United States?

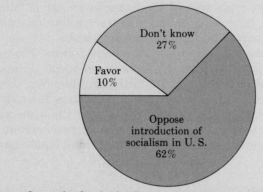

Source: Survey by *Cambridge Reports,* March 12–22, 1976.

More importantly, most of those polled opposed the principal program of democratic socialism—government ownership of major business enterprises. Seventy-four percent disagreed with the idea of a government takeover of big business "as in certain European countries"; only 9 percent strongly agreed, and 17 percent partially agreed.

Opposition to Government Takeover of Big Business

Question: A number of controversial proposals are being discussed these days. I'd like you to tell me for each one whether you strongly agree with it, partially agree with it, or disagree with it. . . .

The country would be better off if big business were taken over by the government, as in certain European countries.

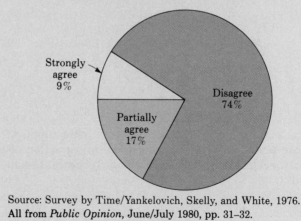

Source: Survey by Time/Yankelovich, Skelly, and White, 1976.
All from *Public Opinion,* June/July 1980, pp. 31–32.

clash, but their community of interest is far greater than any divisions that exist. Perhaps what accounts for their consensus more than anything else is their experience in command positions in giant institutions. "As the requirements of the top places in each of the major hierarchies become similar, the types of men occupying these roles at the top—by selection and by training in the jobs—become similar" (p. 19).

Mills finds American democracy severely deficient, and his work is frequently cited by radical critics of American society. According to Mills, the power elite is guilty of "a higher immorality," which is not necessarily personal corruption or even mistaken policies and deeds but rather the moral insensitivity of institutional bureaucracy. More importantly, it is the failure of the power elite to be responsive and responsible to "knowledgeable publics." Mills implies that true democracy is possible only where those in power are truly responsible to "men of Knowledge." He is not very specific about who the "men of Knowledge" are, but the reader is left with the impression that he means intellectuals like himself.

CHAPTER SUMMARY

1. All ideologies—democracy, communism, socialism, liberalism, conservatism—justify the distribution of values in society, the political system's legitimacy, and what is *acceptable* (or legal) political behavior on the part of both leaders and the electorate. In addition, ideologies influence *political* perceptions, morality, and actions.

2. Democracy places great stress on the individual's dignity and fundamental legal equality. People are free to participate in political life, guided by the principles of majority rule and minority rights. Theoretically, the state may not infringe on the individual's rights of life, liberty, and property without observing due process of law. This democratic view is frequently expropriated by authoritarian regimes that base their legitimacy on "the will of the people."

3. Direct participatory democracy is an ideal that presents insurmountable problems of application in a large, modern society. All societies are governed by a minority of citizens.

4. Pluralism can be viewed as a substitute for "direct democracy." The ideology assumes that interest-group competition will preserve democracy by fragmenting power and producing public policies that are the products of necessary bargaining and compromise. Pluralism encourages individuals to participate in political life through membership in interest groups and indirectly through the voting booth.

5. The "elitist" model of American democracy argues that: only a qualified few can rule in society; American elites differ over means, not ends, and are more committed to democratic values than the "masses"; political power is pyramidally structured, embracing top

policymakers from business and government; and public policy reflects elite preferences, not mass opinion.

6. Classical liberalism, the forerunner of contemporary conservative thinking, emphasized the importance of the individual's freedom from unnecessary governmental interference. Conservatives continue to believe in limited government. They also argue that social progress must be cognizant of and reconciled with the wisdom of past experience. Radical change is damaging to society.

7. Neoconservatives are liberals who have become disillusioned with costly, large-scale, bureaucratic governmental programs. They are concerned with social problems, but they no longer have great confidence that these problems can be solved with massive government programs.

8. Modern liberalism insists on the power of government "to do good"—that is, to increase individual freedom, reduce social and economic inequalities, and curb the excesses of capitalism. Modern liberals also believe that the scope of governmental power and regulation must increase as society becomes more complex.

9. Democratic socialism seeks to replace capitalism with collective ownership of economic enterprise and a redistribution of wealth. These goals are to be achieved peacefully through the democratic process.

10. Marxism concentrates on the importance of economic forces, particularly property ownership, in determining the shape of society. Marxism envisions the violent overthrow of the wealthy bourgeoisie by the exploited proletariat. Subsequently, economic classes and the structure of the state will "wither away" as a utopian, communist society emerges.

11. Lenin modified Marx's theories to include, among other ideas, the importance of a disciplined Communist party and the notion of global imperialism.

12. The American Left embraces a wide range of groups that have in common an opposition to poverty, racism, imperialist wars, bureaucracy, materialism, and production for profit rather than for use. It is not, however, a unified ideology, and contemporary radicals disagree about how their goals are to be realized.

Notes

1. John Dewey, "Democracy and Educational Administration," *School and Society,* April 1937.
2. See R. I. Aaron, *John Locke* (New York: Oxford University Press, 1956).
3. Harold Lasswell and Daniel Lerner, *The Comparative Study of Elites* (Stanford: Stanford University Press, 1952), p. 7.
4. See Robert A. Dahl, *A Preface to Democratic Theory* (Chicago: University of Chicago Press, 1956), for the classic statement of pluralism.
5. Alexander Hamilton, as reported in Max Farrand, *Records of the Federal Convention of 1787,* Vol. 1, pp. 299–300.

6. See C. Wright Mills, *The Power Elite* (New York: Oxford University Press, 1956), for the classic statement of elitism. See also Thomas R. Dye, *Who's Running America?* (Englewood Cliffs, N. J.: Prentice-Hall, 1976); G. William Domhoff, *Who Rules America?* (Englewood Cliffs, N. J.: Prentice-Hall, 1967).

7. See John Kenneth Galbraith, *Economics and the Public Purpose* (Boston: Houghton Mifflin Co., 1973); and Henry K. Girvetz, *The Evolution of Liberalism* (New York: Collier Books, 1963).

8. See Michael Harrington, *Socialism* (New York: Saturday Review Press, 1972).

9. V. I. Lenin, *State and Revolution* (New York: International Publishers Co., 1943).

10. See V. I. Lenin, *Imperialism: The Highest Stage of Capitalism* (New York: International Publishers Co., 1939); and C. Wright Mills, *The Marxists* (New York: Delta, 1962).

11. See Kenneth M. Dolbeare and Patricia Dolbeare, *American Ideologies* (Chicago: Markham, 1971).

12. Herbert Marcuse, *One-Dimensional Man* (Boston: Beacon Press, 1964).

13. C. Wright Mills, *The Power Elite* (New York: Oxford University Press, 1956).

Close-Up and In-Depth Analyses

Peter Bachrach. *The Theory of Democratic Elitism.* Boston: Little, Brown, 1967.

William F. Buckley, Jr. *Up from Liberalism.* New York: Honor Books, 1959.

Kenneth M. Dolbeare and Patricia Dolbeare. *American Ideologies.* Chicago: Markham, 1971.

Thomas R. Dye and Harmon Zeigler. *The Irony of Democracy,* 5th ed. Monterey, Calif.: Brooks/Cole, 1981.

William Ebenstein and Edwin Fogelman. *Today's Isms,* 8th ed. Englewood Cliffs, N. J.: Prentice-Hall, 1980.

Louis Hartz. *The Liberal Tradition in America.* New York: Harcourt, Brace & World, 1955.

Richard Hofstadter. *The American Political Tradition.* New York: Knopf, 1948.

Seymour Martin Lipset. *Political Man.* New York: Doubleday (Anchor Books), 1963.

Theodore Lowi. *The End of Liberalism.* Chicago: Norton, 1969.

Herbert Marcuse. *One-Dimensional Man.* Boston: Beacon Press, 1964.

C. Wright Mills. *The Power Elite.* New York: Oxford University Press, 1956.

Clinton Rossiter. *Conservatism in America.* New York: Knopf, 1965.

THE CONSTITUTION: RULES OF THE POLITICAL GAME

WHY DOES THE NATION NEED A CONSTITUTION?

Every new nation must create its own symbols and myths. They help to bind society together and provide a sense of nationhood. They give us unity and purpose and pride. The Declaration of Independence and the Constitution are the cornerstones of the American political culture. Their symbolic importance in the nation's political history cannot be underestimated.

Constitutionalism is the belief that governmental power should be limited and controlled. A fundamental ideal of constitutionalism—a government of laws, not of men—means that those who exercise authority are restricted in their use of it by a higher law.

A constitution governs a government. It establishes governmental bodies (the House of Representatives, the Senate, the presidency, the Supreme Court); it grants them powers; and at the same time it limits their exercise of authority over people. In other words, a constitution defines what governmental authorities can and cannot do. It should not be changed by the ordinary acts of governmental bodies; change should come only through a process of general popular consent. The U. S. Constitution, then, is superior to ordinary laws of Congress, orders of the president, decisions of the courts, acts of the state legislatures, or regulations of the bureaucracies. Indeed, the Constitution is "the supreme law of the land."

The Constitution
and a set of scales
symbolizing the checks
and balances of U. S.
government.

Constitutionalism:
The belief that
governmental power
should be limited
and controlled.

Above all, a constitution must truly limit and control the exercise of authority by government. It does so by setting forth individual liberties that the government—even with majority consent—cannot violate. In this way individual freedoms, such as freedom of speech and religion, are placed beyond the reach of government and beyond the reach of majorities. Of course, to be effective in protecting the individual from government, a constitution must be respected—by both the people and the government. Government officials must believe that they are in fact limited by the constitution, and private citizens must believe that they are in fact protected by it. The constitution is a national symbol that must be taken seriously if it is to be effective in limiting government and protecting liberty.

AGENDA SETTING IN 1787

Contrary to the public statements of the Founding Fathers, the Articles of Confederation had served the new American republic very well. The articles had been adopted by the Continental Congress in 1777, creating a "firm league of Friendship" among the states "for their common defense, the security of their liberties, and their mutual and general welfare." The national government was thought of as an alliance of states, not as a government "of the People." Congress was given the power to declare war, to make treaties, to manage Indian affairs, to establish post offices, and to build an army and a navy.

Under the articles the United States achieved independence from the world's most powerful colonial nation, defeated vastly superior forces in a prolonged war for independence, established a viable peace, won powerful allies (such as France) in the international community, created an effective army and navy, established a postal system, and laid the foundations for national unity. But despite the successes of the new government in war and diplomacy, the political arrangements under the articles were unsatisfactory to many influential groups—notably, bankers and investors who held U. S. government bonds, plantation owners, real estate developers, and merchants and shippers.

Under the Articles of Confederation, two important governmental powers were denied to Congress—the power to tax and the power to regulate interstate commerce. Without the power to tax, the federal government had to ask the states for money to pay its expenses, particularly the expenses of fighting the long and costly War of Independence with Great Britain. There was no way to force the states to make their payments to the federal government; it is estimated that 90 percent of the funds requisitioned by Congress from the states were never paid. So Congress borrowed money to fight the war from

A copy of the *Boston Newsletter*, an early colonial newspaper.

wealthy investors such as Robert Morris, the "patriot financier" and president of the Bank of Philadelphia, the largest in the nation at that time. But without the power to tax, Congress could not pay off these debts. Indeed, the value of U. S. government bonds fell to about ten cents for every dollar's worth, because few people believed the bonds would ever be paid off. Congress even stopped making interest payments on these bonds.

Under the Articles of Confederation, two important governmental powers were denied to Congress—the power to tax and the power to regulate interstate commerce.

Without the power to regulate interstate commerce, the federal government was unable to protect merchants from heavy tariffs imposed on shipments from state to state. Southern planters could not ship their cotton, tobacco, and other agricultural products to northern cities without paying state-imposed tariffs, and northern merchants could not ship manufactured products from state to state without interference. Merchants, manufacturers, shippers, and planters all wanted to develop national markets and to prevent the states from imposing tariffs or restrictions on interstate trade. States competed with one another by passing low tariffs on foreign goods (to encourage the shipment of goods through their own ports) and by passing high tariffs against one another's goods (to protect their own markets). The result was a great deal of confusion and bad feeling—as well as a great deal of smuggling.

Under the articles the states themselves had the power to issue their own money, regulate its value, and require that it be accepted in payment of debts. (States had their own "legal tender" laws, which required creditors to accept state money if "tendered" in payment of debt.) This meant that various forms of money were circulating: Virginia dollars, Rhode Island dollars, Pennsylvania dollars, and so on. Some states (Rhode Island, for example) printed a great deal of money, creating inflation in their currency and alienating banks and investors whose loans were being paid in this cheap currency. If creditors refused payment in a particular state's currency, the debt could be abolished in that state. So finances throughout the states were very unstable, and banks and creditors were threatened by cheap paper money.

The Constitutional Convention of 1787 did not just "happen." It was carefully planned by leading investors and bondholders, planters, merchants, and landowners. In the spring of 1785 some wealthy merchants from Virginia and Maryland met at Alexandria, Virginia, to try to resolve a conflict between the two states over commerce and navigation on the Potomac River and Chesapeake Bay. General George Washington, the new nation's most prominent citizen, took a personal interest in the meeting. As a wealthy plantation owner and a land speculator who owned over thirty thousand acres of land upstream on the Potomac, Washington was keenly interested in commercial problems under the articles. He lent his great prestige to the Alexandria meeting by inviting the participants to his house at Mount Vernon. Out of this conference came the idea for a general economic conference for all of the states to be held in Annapolis, Maryland, in September 1786.

The Constitutional Convention of 1787 did not just "happen." It was carefully planned by leading investors and bondholders, planters, merchants, and landowners.

The Annapolis convention turned out to be a key stepping stone to the Constitutional Convention of 1787. Instead of concentrating on commerce and navigation between the states, the delegates at Annapolis, including Alexander Hamilton and James Madison, called for a general constitutional convention to suggest remedies to what they saw as defects in the Articles of Confederation.

Shays' Rebellion provided the dramatic news that moved the proposed constitutional convention to the top of the nation's agenda. In several states debtors had already engaged in open revolt against tax collectors and sheriffs who were attempting to repossess farms on

Shays' Rebellion (1786): An armed uprising of farmers seeking to prevent the foreclosure of mortgages on their farms. Shays' Rebellion helped to convince property owners of the need for a strong central government.

behalf of creditors who held unpaid mortgages. The most serious rebellion broke out in the summer of 1786 in western Massachusetts when a band of 2,000 insurgent farmers captured the courthouses in several counties and briefly held the city of Springfield. Deeds, mortgages, and tax records were burned, so that farmers who worked the land would no longer be indebted to the owners. Led by Daniel Shays, a veteran of the Revolutionary War battle at Bunker Hill, the insurgent army posed a direct threat to investors, bankers, creditors, and tax collectors. Shays' Rebellion, as it was called, was finally put down by a small mercenary army, paid for by well-to-do citizens of Boston.

Reports of Shays' Rebellion filled the newspapers of the large eastern cities. Washington, Hamilton, Madison, and many other prominent Americans wrote their friends about it. The event galvanized men of property in support of the movement to create a strong central government capable of dealing with "radicalism." Only a strong central government could "insure domestic tranquility," guarantee "a republican form of government," and protect property "against domestic violence." It is no accident that all of these phrases appear in the Constitution of 1787.

On February 21, 1787, Congress confirmed the call for a convention to meet in Philadelphia

> for the sole and express purpose of revising the Articles of Confederation and reporting to the Congress and the several legislatures such alterations and provisions therein as shall, when agreed to in Congress and confirmed by the states, render the federal Constitution adequate to the exigencies of government and the preservation of the union.

Notice that Congress did *not* authorize the Convention to write a new constitution or to submit its work to any bodies except Congress and state legislatures. Later we will see that the Founding Fathers ignored this congressional mandate.

CONSENSUS BUILDING IN THE NEW NATION

The Founding Fathers—the fifty-five men who met in the summer of 1787 to establish a new government for the United States—quickly chose George Washington to preside over the assembly. By doing so they immediately gave the convention great prestige. Washington was at the height of his power. As Commander in Chief of the successful Revolutionary Army and defender of the new nation, he had overwhelming charismatic appeal among his countrymen. Not only was he a soldier, statesman, and founder of a nation; he was also one of the richest men in the country, with a large estate on the

Potomac, hundreds of slaves, and thousands of acres of undeveloped land in western Virginia. He owned major shares of the Potomac Company and the James River Company (what we would call today real estate development firms) and of the Bank of Columbia and the Bank of Alexandria. He also held large amounts of unpaid U. S. government bonds.

The Founding Fathers had impressive educational backgrounds and lengthy experience in government. At a period in history when few Americans attended any school at all, over half of the delegates at Philadelphia had been educated at Princeton, Yale, Harvard, Columbia, Pennsylvania, or William and Mary or in England. Most of the delegates had studied law. The debates made frequent references to the classics: Aristotle, Plutarch, Cicero, Locke, and Montesquieu. Eight of the delegates had signed the Declaration of Independence twelve years earlier. Eleven had served as officers in Washington's army. Forty-two of the fifty-five had held high state office. Even at the moment of the convention, over forty delegates held high state offices: Benjamin Franklin was governor of Pennsylvania; Robert Livingston was governor of New York; and Edmund Randolph was governor of Virginia. Only Thomas Jefferson and John Adams were missing: Jefferson was in Paris as U. S. ambassador to France, and Adams was in London as U. S. ambassador to Great Britain, both key posts at the time.

Scholars and textbooks frequently focus on the arguments that divided the delegates and the compromises that were worked out. But actually the delegates agreed on the essential questions of politics.

Protecting Property

To the Founding Fathers the protection of life, liberty, and property was the fundamental object of government. The phraseology was courtesy of John Locke. Jefferson borrowed it and substituted *the pursuit of happiness* for *property,* but he explained that the terms meant the same thing, because no one could pursue happiness without property. The delegates agreed that government had to ensure that property was not stolen or destroyed, that debts were paid, that deeds and contracts were enforced, that crippling taxes or tariffs were not imposed, and that slaves (who were considered "property") were returned to their owners.

> To the Founding Fathers the protection of life, liberty, and property was the fundamental object of government.

Natural rights: The belief that individuals are born with basic rights on which government must not infringe.

The Founding Fathers believed that life, liberty, and property were **natural rights** on which government could not infringe. Indeed, the early American leaders believed that "all men" were entitled to have their natural rights respected regardless of their class or social position. This differed a great deal from the prevailing aristocratic ideas in Europe, where "nobles" and "commoners" had very different rights under the law. Most of the Founding Fathers, even slave owners such as Jefferson, were aware of the inconsistency between their stated belief in equality and the practice of slavery.

The Social Contract

The Founding Fathers agreed with Locke's notion of a **social contract,** in which the people agreed to obey just laws in return for the protection of their life, liberty, and property. Government itself was viewed as a contract among people, not as a creation of the gods or of kings. Government was founded on the consent of the governed as a means of better protecting their rights and liberties.

Social contract: John Locke's view of government as an agreement among people to obey just laws in return for government's protection of their life, liberty, and property.

Controlling Faction

According to Madison, "the principal task" of government was to control **faction.** "Faction" meant social and political conflict in society, especially conflict between the wealthy and the poor. "The most common and durable source of faction has been the various and unequal distribution of property. Those who hold and those who are without property have ever formed distinct interests in society."

Faction: James Madison's term for societal conflict, especially between the wealthy and the poor; in its more familiar sense, "faction" refers to one of the competing interests.

Used in its other, more familiar, sense, the word *faction* referred to one of the competing interests. Thus, a faction might be composed of wealthy citizens who would use government for their own gain at the expense of the community as a whole. Or more likely, said Madison, a faction might be composed of a majority of poor and propertyless people who would use government to seize the property of the wealthy and redistribute it. Shays' Rebellion had reminded the Founding Fathers of the threat of radicalism in the new nation. According to Madison, a new national government must be established to suppress "factious" issues. And Madison did not hesitate to name these issues—"a rage for paper money, for an abolition of debts, for an equal division of property, or any other improper or wicked project."[1] Note that all of Madison's examples represented threats to private wealth.

Republicanism

The Founding Fathers believed in **republican government**—a representative, responsible, and nonhereditary government. This was a radical belief at a time when most European countries were governed by hereditary monarchies and aristocracies of birth. But the Founding Fathers distinguished between republicanism and mass democracy, with direct participation by the people in decision making. They believed that the masses should consent to be governed by men of "principle and property" out of a recognition of their abilities, education, and stake in preserving liberty and order. They also believed that the masses should select *some portion* of the nation's leaders,

Republican government: A form of government in which representatives of the people exercise power on their behalf according to law. To be distinguished from *mass democracy,* in which the people themselves are directly involved in government and policy making.

not all of them. (The Constitution of 1787 originally provided for four decision-making bodies—the House of Representatives, the Senate, the president, and the Supreme Court. Only the House of Representatives was to be directly elected by the people.)

Limited Government

The Founding Fathers believed that government should be limited in its powers by a written constitution. It is true that those men who attended the Philadelphia convention in 1787 generally wanted a stronger federal government. (Eventually most of them would be labeled "federalists" in later political battles.) But they all believed in the general notion of a government of limited power over its citizens. The Founding Fathers also accepted the idea of dividing powers in order to prevent any one government, or any one branch of government, from gaining so much power that it threatened liberty and property. Thus, the Constitution of 1787 recognized *federalism*—the division of responsibilities between independent states and the nation—and *separation of power*—the creation of separate legislative, executive, and judicial branches of the national government, each capable of checking the powers of the others.

Nationalism

Above all, the Founding Fathers were convinced that only a strong national government would be able to "establish justice, insure domestic tranquility, provide for the common defense, promote the general welfare and secure the blessings of liberty," as the Constitution was to put it. These leaders increasingly thought of themselves as "Americans" rather than only Virginians or Pennsylvanians. They wanted the United States to play a greater role in the international community of nations. They shared a common English heritage, they spoke the same language, and they had inherited the same political culture. The War of Independence had united them against a common opponent. Nationalism was on the rise.

CONVENTIONEERING IN PHILADELPHIA

If the Founding Fathers had not already developed a consensus on the fundamental need for a new national government, the Constitutional Convention of 1787 would have been a failure. But the agenda for decision making had been carefully set, and a consensus had been developed on the underlying issues—protecting property, suppressing radicalism, paying off the national debt, establishing a national monetary system, restricting state powers over commerce and finance, opening up western land, and attaining world recognition. The differences that needed to be resolved in Philadelphia were relatively minor compared with these major objectives. The famous "compromises" in the Constitution did not involve conflict over fundamental issues.

The Representation Compromise

On May 25, 1787, the Constitutional Convention opened and immediately adopted a resolution that all of the proceedings be kept secret. The Founding Fathers stuck to their resolution: the Constitution itself was not "leaked" until September 19, 1787, and most of what we know about the debates comes from secret notes made by Madison and published many years later.*

Governor Randolph of Virginia began debate with the presentation of a draft of a new constitution, quickly dubbed the **"Virginia Plan."** The Virginia Plan proposed a two-house Congress; the lower house would be elected by the people based on population, but the upper house would be elected by the lower house. Separate executive and judicial branches of government would be established, but their members would be selected by Congress. Congress would also have the power to nullify any state laws that differed from its own.

Virginia Plan: A proposal for a two-house Congress; the lower house would be elected by the people based on population and the upper house would be elected by the lower house.

This Virginia Plan appeared to overlook the concern of small states for representation in the government. Debate over the plan continued for several weeks. There were no great questions of economic interest or ideology to be resolved, since the delegates from large and small states did not divide along economic or ideological lines. But the Virginia Plan failed to ensure that the small states would obtain membership in the upper house of the legislature or in the executive or judicial branches.

William Paterson of New Jersey presented a counterproposal. In the **"New Jersey Plan"** each state was granted equal representation in Congress, regardless of its size. But the New Jersey Plan was *not* simply an attempt to retain the Articles of Confederation. On the contrary, this plan, too, recognized the supremacy of the constitution and laws of Congress over the states and proposed the creation of separate executive and judicial branches.

New Jersey Plan: A proposal that each state be granted equal representation in Congress, regardless of the size of the state.

On June 29 William Samuel Johnson of Connecticut proposed the obvious compromise—representation in a lower house of Congress based on population and representation in an upper house based on an equal number (two) from each state. The **"Connecticut Compromise"** even provided that equal representation of the states in the Senate could not be altered, even by constitutional amendment.

Connecticut Compromise: The compromise accepted by the Constitutional Convention. It called for a two-house legislature, with representation in the lower house to be based on a state's population and equal representation for each state in the upper house.

The Slavery Compromise

Another question to be compromised was that of slavery and the counting of slaves for representation and taxation. Seventy-five years

*See Max Farrand, ed., *The Records of the Federal Convention of 1787* (New Haven, Conn.: Yale University Press, 1911).

later, in the Civil War, the northern and southern states would go to war over the future of slavery and the plantation system. Slavery was indeed an important economic and ideological issue. But in 1787 the northern states were willing to guarantee the protection of slavery in slave states and even guarantee the return of escaped slaves in the interest of national unity. In return, the southern states agreed to end the importation of slaves after 1808. (This twenty-year delay would allow the undeveloped southern states to acquire as many slaves as they needed before the slave trade ended.)

Of course, the southern states would have preferred to count slaves as "persons" in apportioning representatives to the states; the northern states argued that "persons" should be "free inhabitants." When the issue was taxes, the positions of the northern and southern states were reversed: southern states did not wish to count slaves for purposes of direct taxation, but the northern states wished to do so. Debate on this issue of counting slaves produced the famous **"three-fifths compromise"**: three-fifths of the slaves of each state would be counted for the purposes of both representation and taxation. Thus, the Founding Fathers determined that a black slave was three-fifths of a person.

Three-fifths Compromise: The agreement reached at the Constitutional Convention to count a slave as three-fifths of a person in determining state representation and taxation formulas.

The Export Tax Compromise

Both agricultural interests and commercial interests wanted to halt state tariffs and trade restrictions. They wanted to give power over interstate commerce to the federal government. But the agricultural interests were fearful that the federal government itself might tax exports, particularly the cotton and tobacco trade of the large southern plantations. So the planters and merchants reached another compromise: neither the states nor the federal government could levy a tax or duty on articles exported from any state. All interstate commerce and foreign commerce would be regulated by the federal government. The federal government would tax only foreign imports. Indeed, import taxes were the major source of revenue for the federal government until the twentieth century.

The Voter Qualification Compromise

An important compromise, which receives very little attention in the Constitution itself but occupied a great deal of time in the convention, concerned property qualifications for voting and holding office in the new government. The Founding Fathers generally favored property qualifications, yet none appears in the Constitution itself. The problem was one of deciding what *kind* of property should be required as a condition of voting or holding office. Various propositions to establish property qualifications were defeated on the floor of the convention, not because the Founding Fathers opposed property qualifications but because of differences in the kinds of property

Democracy and the Founding Fathers

The Founding Fathers rejected the idea of an aristocracy by birth, with its lords and ladies and kings and queens. But they believed in a "natural aristocracy" (Thomas Jefferson's phrase). They believed in government by the talented, informed, educated, and courageous men of principle and property. Many of the comments the Founding Fathers made during the debates at the Constitutional Convention of 1787 reveal a skepticism about democracy:

"The evils that we experience flow from the excess of democracy."—Elbridge Gerry.

"The people immediately should have as little to do as may be about the government."—Roger Sherman.

"A representative of the people is appointed to think for, and not with, his constituents."—George Clymer.

Property qualifications for voting are "a necessary defense against the dangerous influence of those multitudes without property and without principle, with which our country like all others, will in time abound."—John Dickinson.

"Are you not ... abundantly depressed at the theoretical nonsense of an election of Congress by the people? In the first instance, it is clearly and practically wrong, and it will in the end be the means of bringing our councils into contempt."—Charles Pinckney.

represented at the convention. Requiring land ownership was supported by the plantation owners but opposed by the merchants, whose property was in goods, warehouses, and ships. Others had their money in bonds, stocks, bank deposits, and other forms of assets. Even Madison, a plantation owner, admitted that "landed possessions were no certain evidence of real wealth. Many enjoyed them to a great extent who were more in debt than they are worth."[2]

The Founding Fathers generally favored property qualifications for voting and holding office, yet none appears in the Constitution itself. The problem was one of deciding what *kind* of property should be required.

Since the convention could not agree on specific property qualifications, a compromise was approved to allow the states themselves to impose whatever property qualifications they wished. The Constitution provided that "the electors in each state should have the qualifications requisite for electors of the most numerous branch of the state legislature." This appeared to be a safe course of action in

1787. All of the states had property qualifications for voting. And only the House of Representatives was to be elected by popular vote anyhow. The other three governmental bodies—the Senate, the presidency, and the Supreme Court—were removed from direct popular selection.

THE CONSTITUTION OF 1787

The document that emerged from the Philadelphia convention on September 17, 1787, did not amend the Articles of Confederation. Instead, it founded a national government with a unique structure and enhanced powers.

National Supremacy

National-supremacy clause: The assertion in Article VI of the Constitution that the Constitution and federal laws take precedence over state laws.

At the heart of the new Constitution was the **national-supremacy clause** of Article VI:

> This Constitution, and the laws of the United States which shall be made in Pursuance thereof, and all treaties made, or which shall be made, under the authority of the United States, *shall be the supreme law of the land*; and the judges in every state shall be bound thereby, anything in the constitution or Laws of any state to the contrary notwithstanding [italics added].

This clause made it very clear that the laws of Congress would supersede the laws of the states.

Powers of Congress

The Founding Fathers tried to implement Locke's idea of limited government by granting to the national government only certain *enumerated* powers (sometimes called *delegated* powers), together with some powers that might be *implied* from the enumerated powers. The Constitution includes a fairly long list of specific powers expressly delegated to Congress (Article I, Section 8). These powers include:

1. the power to tax and spend to pay debts and to provide for "the common defense and the general welfare of the United States"
2. the power to regulate interstate and foreign commerce, including power over bankruptcy, money, patents and copyrights, and post offices and post roads
3. the power to declare war, "to raise and support" military forces, and to call out the militia to "suppress insurrections and repel invasions"
4. the power "to make all laws which shall be necessary and

proper" for carrying out all of the other powers vested in the national government by the Constitution

This **necessary-and-proper clause** would turn out to be a major source of growth in national power over the years. The original idea was to limit national government to *only* those powers expressly enumerated in the Constitution or reasonably implied from them. But as we will see later, this particular approach to limited government gradually disappeared over time. Today Congress can legislate on a wide range of topics never mentioned in the Constitution. The power of the national government has expanded with the expansion of federal taxing and spending powers; the expansion of the interstate commerce power; the growth of federal civil rights legislation enforcing the Fourteenth Amendment; and a very broad interpretation of the necessary-and-proper clause.

Necessary-and-proper clause: The Constitutional provision that allows Congress to make whatever laws are needed for the national government to perform its Constitutional functions.

Restrictions on the States

The powers granted to the national government are accompanied by certain restrictions on the powers of the states. Generally, these reinforce federal supremacy in various areas. States may *not*:

1. enter into treaties with foreign nations
2. maintain armies or engage in war without congressional consent
3. issue paper money or coins
4. impair contracts
5. tax imports or exports

Later, additional restrictions were placed on the states in the interest of guaranteeing civil rights. States may not:

6. permit slavery (Thirteenth Amendment, 1865)
7. deny the privileges and immunities of citizenship (Fourteenth Amendment, 1868)
8. deny the right to life, liberty, and property without due process of law (Fourteenth Amendment, 1868)
9. deny equal protection of the law (Fourteenth Amendment, 1868)
10. deny the right to vote because of race (Fifteenth Amendment, 1870)
11. deny the right to vote because of sex (Nineteenth Amendment, 1920)
12. deny the right to vote for failure to pay any tax (Twenty-fourth Amendment, 1964)
13. deny the right to vote because of age over 18 (Twenty-sixth Amendment, 1971)

The first black casting his vote after the passage of the Fifteenth Amendment.

Alice Paul, national director of Congressional Union for Woman Suffrage, toasting the passage of the Nineteenth Amendment.

Federalism: The division of power between the nation and the states. Both can pass and enforce laws, levy taxes, and maintain courts. Each is restricted in its power to infringe on the other.

Federalism

The Constitution *divides* power between the nation and the states. Both the nation and the states have legal authority over their citizens; they can pass their own laws, levy their own taxes, and maintain their own courts. This arrangement is known as **federalism.** The states cannot alter or abolish the national government without amending the Constitution, and the national government cannot alter or abolish the states.

The U. S. government is frequently called the federal government or the national government. As part of a federal system the U. S. government has no formal authority to change the boundaries of states or to dictate to state officials about state and local governmental affairs. Thus, a federal system differs from a **unitary system of government,** in which all formal authority is given in the constitution to the national government and subunits of government are merely administrative outposts of the national government. But a federal system also differs from a *confederation,* in which the national government must depend on the states to levy taxes and enforce laws.

Actually, most governments in the world today are unitary governments. This is true of Communist bloc nations as well as democracies such as Great Britain, France, and Japan. Even the American states themselves are unitary governments within their own borders. Local governments—cities, counties, towns, villages, school districts, special districts, and so on—are created by state laws and constitutions. Local governments in the United States are not mentioned in the Constitution; they are considered subdivisions of state government. States can (and do) alter their boundaries, determine their form of government, decide what taxes they can collect, and decide what powers they can exercise.

Unitary system of government: A form of government in which formal authority is given exclusively to the national government; subunits of government are merely administrative outposts of the national government.

Republicanism

To the Founding Fathers a *republican* government meant the delegation of powers by the people to a small number of gifted individuals "whose wisdom may discern the true interests of their country, and whose patriotism and love of justice will be least likely to be sacrificed to temporary or partial considerations."[3] The Founding Fathers believed that enlightened men of principle and property could govern the people better than the people could govern themselves. So they gave the voters only a limited voice in the selection of government leaders.

> The Founding Fathers believed that enlightened men of principle and property could govern the people better than the people could govern themselves.

In the Constitution of 1787, U. S. senators were to be elected by state legislatures, not by the people. The president was to be elected by "electors," who themselves would be chosen as the state legislatures saw fit. Finally, all federal judges, including Supreme Court justices, were to be appointed for life by the president and confirmed by the Senate.

The Founding Fathers cannot be labeled "reactionaries" because of these early undemocratic features of the Constitution of 1787. On the contrary, the idea of republicanism itself—the notion that citizens are entitled to any participation in the selection of their leaders—was an advanced idea at the time.

Later, of course, democratic impulses in the nation greatly altered the original Constitution. The national government became much more democratic as a result of:

1. the states' gradual dropping of property qualifications for voting in the early 1800s
2. the rise of political parties and the practice of voting for slates of presidential electors pledged to cast their vote for one party candidate or the other
3. the expansion of the right to vote to all races (Fifteenth Amendment, 1870)
4. the election of U. S. senators by popular vote instead of by state legislatures (Seventeenth Amendment, 1913)
5. the extension of the right to vote to women (Nineteenth Amendment, 1920)
6. the elimination of tax payments as a prerequisite to voting (Twenty-fourth Amendment, 1964)
7. the extension of the right to vote to everyone age eighteen or over (Twenty-sixth Amendment, 1971)
8. civil rights laws, particularly the Voting Rights Act of 1965, which provided additional protection for voting rights and increased the proportion of black voters, particularly in the southern states

Separation of Powers and Checks and Balances

Separation of powers: The Constitution's allocation of authority among three branches of the national government: a Congress, a president, and a Supreme Court.

The Founding Fathers' fear of popular majorities is also reflected in the **separation of powers** built into the structure of the new national government (see Figure 3-1). Three separate governing authorities are created in the first three articles of the Constitution—a Congress, a president, and a Supreme Court. Congress itself is divided into a popularly elected House of Representatives and a Senate elected by the state legislatures. According to Madison:

> Ambition must be made to counteract ambition. . . . If men were angels, no government would be necessary. If angels were to govern men, neither external nor internal controls on government would be necessary. In framing a government which is to be administered by men over men, the great difficulty lies in this: You must first enable the government to control the governed; and in the next place oblige it to control itself.[4]

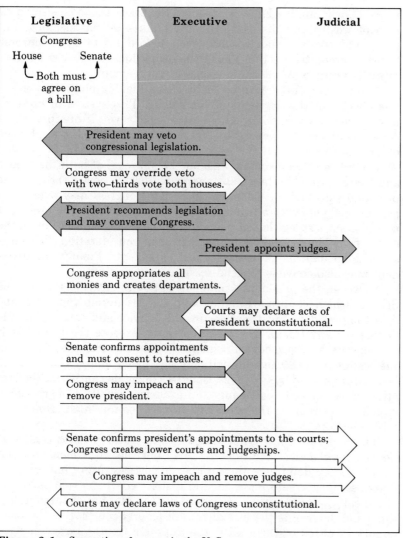

Legislative

Congress

House   Senate

⎩ Both must ⎭
agree on
a bill.

President may veto
congressional legislation.

Congress may override veto
with two–thirds vote both houses.

President recommends legislation
and may convene Congress.

President appoints judges.

Congress appropriates all
monies and creates departments.

Courts may declare acts of
president unconstitutional.

Senate confirms appointments
and must consent to treaties.

Congress may impeach and
remove president.

Senate confirms president's appointments to the courts;
Congress creates lower courts and judgeships.

Congress may impeach and remove judges.

Courts may declare laws of Congress unconstitutional.

Executive

Judicial

Figure 3-1.   Separation of powers in the U. S. government

If a popular movement sweeps the nation, several years may be
needed for its full effect on the composition of the government to be
felt. Each of the four decision-making bodies has a different tenure.
The House is elected every two years. (The Founding Fathers expected the House to be the voice of the people.) A senator is elected
every six years, with one-third of the Senate up for election every two
years. (The Founding Fathers expected senators to be elected by
state legislators, but, as we have seen, the Seventeenth Amendment
provided for their direct election.) The president is elected every four

years. (The Founding Fathers expected the president to be elected by men of wealth and distinction in the states—official electors—but party and custom changed that even before 1800.) The Supreme Court is appointed for life. Thus, "the people" must wait years before capturing control of all the branches of government.

More importantly, each of the decision-making bodies has effective checks on the decisions of the others. This system of **checks and balances** was designed to ensure that, even if one branch of government were influenced by "factions," it could be limited by the other branches.

Checks and balances: The Constitutional provisions whereby the three branches of the national government restrict one another's authority, thus preventing a concentration of political power in any one branch.

No bill can become a law without the approval of both the House and the Senate. The president shares legislative power through the power to veto laws of Congress, although Congress may override a presidential veto with a two-thirds vote in each house. The president may also suggest legislation, "give to the Congress information on the state of the Union, and recommend to their consideration such measures as he shall judge necessary and expedient." Finally, the president may also convene "special sessions" of Congress.

However, the president's power of appointment is shared by the Senate, which confirms Cabinet and ambassadorial appointments. And the president must also secure the "advice and consent" of the Senate for any treaty. The president must execute the laws, but it is Congress that provides the money to do so. The president and the rest of the executive branch may not spend money that has not been appropriated by Congress. Congress must also authorize the creation of executive departments and agencies. Finally, Congress may impeach and remove the president from office for "high crimes and misdemeanors."

The Supreme Court is appointed by the president, with confirmation by the Senate. Traditionally, this Court has nine members, but Congress may determine the number of justices. More importantly, Congress must create lower federal district courts as well as courts of appeal. Congress must also determine the number of these judgeships and determine the jurisdiction of federal courts. But the most important check of them all is the Supreme Court's power of judicial review.

Judicial Review

Judicial review: The power of the courts to invalidate acts of Congress and the president that the courts believe violate the Constitution.

Judicial review is not specifically described in the Constitution itself. It is the power to overturn laws of Congress and acts of the president that the courts believe violate the Constitution. Many Federalists, including Alexander Hamilton, believed that the Constitution of 1787 clearly implied that the Supreme Court could invalidate any laws of Congress or presidential actions that it believed to be unconstitutional. But it wasn't until *Marbury* v. *Madison* in 1803 that Chief Justice John Marshall asserted in a case that the Supreme Court possessed the power of judicial review over laws of Congress.

Essentials: *Marbury* v. *Madison*

In the election of 1800 electors pledged to the Democratic presidential candidate, Thomas Jefferson, won out over electors pledged to the Federalist president, John Adams. Like many defeated presidents to follow, Adams used his last few weeks in office to appoint as many of his own party workers to high office as possible. Indeed, Adams allegedly stayed up all night signing appointments on his last day as president.

One of these last-minute appointments was for William Marbury to serve as justice of the peace in the District of Columbia. When the Jeffersonians came into office, the new secretary of state, James Madison, found Marbury's appointment on his desk. Madison refused to deliver the appointment, and Marbury found himself out of a job.

Marbury sued Madison to get his appointment. Marbury asked for a writ of mandamus (a court order compelling a public official to act) against Madison. He cited the Judiciary Act of 1789, which gave original jurisdiction in such cases to the Supreme Court. Since Marbury knew that a fellow Federalist, John Marshall, was chief justice, he expected to win easily.

But Marshall realized that, if he ordered Madison to act, Madison would probably refuse, President Jefferson would support Madison, and the Supreme Court would be shown to be weak. So Marshall devised a shrewd strategy that sacrificed Marbury but asserted the power of the Supreme Court.

Marshall held that the Judiciary Act of 1789, which gave the Supreme Court original jurisdiction in such cases, was unconstitutional. According to Marshall, the Judiciary Act conflicted with the original jurisdiction clause in the Constitution itself. He threw out Marbury's case in order to make the point that the Supreme Court could invalidate an act of Congress.

In his opinion Marshall argued convincingly (1) that the "judicial power" was given in the Constitution to the Supreme Court, (2) that historically the judicial power had included the power to interpret the meaning of laws, (3) that the national supremacy clause made the Constitution the "supreme law of the land," (4) that laws of the United States must be made "in pursuance thereof," (5) that judges are sworn to uphold the Constitution, and (6) that judges must therefore declare void any act of Congress that conflicts with the Constitution.

THE SELLING OF THE CONSTITUTION

Although today we think of the Constitution as a work of genius, the Founding Fathers themselves had real doubts about whether they could get it accepted as the "Supreme Law of the Land." When their secret meetings in Philadelphia ended on September 17, copies of the new Constitution were distributed to the leading newspapers. Almost immediately "antifederalist" opposition began to surface.

The antifederalists charged, not without justification, that the new Constitution would create an "aristocratic tyranny." They attacked the motives of the Founding Fathers: "These federalists, men of learning and moneyed men . . . expect to get into Congress themselves . . . and get all of the power and money into their own hands."[5] Secondly, the antifederalists contended that the new Constitution created an overpowering central government, over which there were very few checks. In the original Constitution of 1787 there were no constitutional guarantees of freedom of speech or press or religion or of the right of people to assemble and petition their government for a redress of grievances. Finally, the antifederalists argued that the Constitution weakened the powers of the states—which it certainly did. The Virginia patriot Patrick Henry urged its defeat "to preserve the poor commonwealth of Virginia."[6]

But the Founding Fathers had expected this opposition even before ending their convention. Indeed, they knew that they would lose if they obeyed the procedures for amending the Articles of Confederation. These procedures called for the *state legislatures of all thirteen states* to approve any changes in the articles. But the state legislatures could not be relied on to vote for a new constitution that reduced their own power. So the Founding Fathers called for ratification by special state ratifying conventions instead of the legislatures. They also declared that the Constitution would be considered ratified if *three-fourths* of the states approved, rather than all of the states. In other words, they ignored the Articles of Confederation, which was then the law of the land, and rewrote the rules of ratification to favor their own side.

> The Founding Fathers ignored the Articles of Confederation, which was then the law of the land, and rewrote the rules of ratification to favor their own side.

The Founding Fathers also mounted a very professional (for 1787) campaign. They began by calling ratifying conventions as quickly as possible, so that the opposition could not get itself organized. They met in the winter, so that it was difficult for those living far from the cities of the East Coast to make the trip to the conventions. But, most importantly, the federalists maintained the support of the press.

Patrick Henry

Eighty-five press releases on behalf of the Constitution were written by Madison, Hamilton, and John Jay. Each signed their essays as "Publius," and the names of the authors were kept secret at the time. Major newspapers ran the essays, which later were collected and published as *The Federalist* papers.

Table 3-1. Ratification of the Constitution

State	Date	Vote in convention	Rank in population
1. Delaware	December 7, 1787	unanimous	13
2. Pennsylvania	December 12, 1787	46 to 23	3
3. New Jersey	December 18, 1787	unanimous	9
4. Georgia	January 2, 1788	unanimous	11
5. Connecticut	January 9, 1788	128 to 40	8
6. Massachusetts	February 6, 1788	187 to 168	2
7. Maryland	April 28, 1788	63 to 11	6
8. South Carolina	May 23, 1788	149 to 73	7
9. New Hampshire	June 21, 1788	57 to 46	10
10. Virginia	June 25, 1788	89 to 79	1
11. New York	July 26, 1788	30 to 27	5
12. North Carolina	November 21, 1789	195 to 77	4
13. Rhode Island	May 29, 1790	34 to 32	12

Although the federalists managed a series of quick victories, it was clear that they had to win in the big states of Virginia, Massachusetts, and New York to create a truly national government. But the antifederalists began to draw blood with their attacks on the failure of the Constitution to protect individual liberty. The omission of a bill of rights was particularly glaring since all of the state constitutions contained one. It is an interesting commentary on the psychology of the Founding Fathers that a bill of rights was never even mentioned in the Philadelphia convention until the last week of discussions; even then it was given little consideration. A few liberties were written into the body of the Constitution: protection against bills of attainder and ex post facto laws; a guarantee of the writ of habeas corpus; a limited definition of treason; and a guarantee of jury trial. But there was no explicit bill of rights in the original Constitution of 1787.

The federalists argued that there was really no need for a bill of rights, because (1) the national government was one of enumerated powers and could not exercise any powers not expressly delegated to it in the Constitution; (2) the power to interfere in free speech, press,

James Madison

Alexander Hamilton

John Jay

The Selling of the Constitution

An example of an early mass media campaign was a series of articles released to the press in 1787 and 1789 by James Madison, Alexander Hamilton, and John Jay—articles that urged support for the new Constitution. Altogether, eighty-five articles were published under the pen name "Publius." Later the essays were collected and published in book form as *The Federalist*. They have lasting value as an authoritative explanation of the Constitution by the men who helped write it.

52   THE FEDERALIST.

long as it exists by a conftitutional neceffity for local purpofes, though it fhould be in perfect fubordination to the general authority of the union, it would ftill be, in fact and in theory, an affociation of ftates, or a confederacy. The propofed conftitution, fo far from implying an abolition of the ftate governments, makes them conftituent parts of the national fovereignty by allowing them a direct reprefentation in the fenate, and leaves in their poffeffion certain exclufive and very important portions of fovereign power. This fully correfponds, in every rational import of the terms, with the idea of a federal government.

In the Lycian confederacy, which confifted of twenty-three CITIES, or republics, the largeft were intitled to *three* votes in the COMMON COUNCIL, thofe of the middle clafs to *two*, and the fmalleft to *one*. The COMMON COUNCIL had the appointment of all the judges and magiftrates of the refpective CITIES. This was certainly the moft delicate fpecies of interference in their internal adminiftration ; for if there be any thing that feems exclufively appropriated to the local jurifdictions, it is the appointment of their own officers. Yet Montefquieu, fpeaking of this affociation, fays, " Were I to give a model of an excellent " confederate republic, it would be that of Lycia." Thus we perceive that the diftinctions infifted upon were not within the contemplation of this enlightened Civilian, and we fhall be led to conclude, that they are the novel refinements of an erroneous theory.

PUBLIUS.

NUMBER X. *J. Madi*

The fame Subject continued.

AMONG the numerous advantages promifed by a well conftructed union, none deferves to be more accurately developed than its tendency to break and control the violence of faction. The friend of popular governments

THE FEDERALIST.   53

governments, never finds himfelf fo much alarmed for their character and fate, as when he contemplates their propenfity to this dangerous vice. He will not fail therefore to fet a due value on any plan which, without violating the principles to which he is attached, provides a proper cure for it. The inftability, injuftice and confufion introduced into the public councils, have in truth been the mortal difeafes under which popular governments have every where perifhed ; as they continue to be the favorite and fruitful topics from which the adverfaries to liberty derive their moft fpecious declamations. The valuable improvements made by the American conftitutions on the popular models, both antient and modern, cannot certainly be too much admired ; but it would be an unwarrantable partiality, to contend that they have as effectually obviated the danger on this fide as was wifhed and expected. Complaints are every where heard from our moft confiderate and virtuous citizens, equally the friends of public and private faith, and of public and perfonal liberty ; that our governments are too unftable ; that the public good is difregarded in the conflicts of rival parties ; and that meafures are too often decided, not according to the rules of juftice, and the rights of the minor party ; but by the fuperior force of an interefted and overbearing majority. However anxioufly we may wifh that thefe complaints had no foundation, the evidence of known facts will not permit us to deny that they are in fome degree true. It will be found indeed, on a candid review of our fituation, that fome of the diftreffes under which we labour, have been erroneoufly charged on the operation of our governments ; but it will be found at the fame time, that other caufes will not alone account for many of our heavieft misfortunes ; and particularly, for that prevailing and increafing diftruft of public engagements, and alarm for private rights, which are echoed from one end of the continent to the other. Thefe muft be chiefly, if not

E 3   wholly,

The absence of a bill of rights seemed to confirm the suspicion that the Founding Fathers were more interested in preserving property than in protecting individual freedom.[7]

or religion or otherwise restrain liberty was not among the enumerated powers; (3) therefore, it was not necessary to specifically deny these powers to the new federal government. But this logic was unconvincing. The absence of a bill of rights seemed to confirm the suspicion that the Founding Fathers were more interested in preserving property than in protecting individual freedom. So the federalists backed down and made a solemn promise to support a Bill of Rights as the first amendments to the Constitution.

AMENDING THE CONSTITUTION

On April 30, 1789, George Washington assumed the office of president as the unanimous choice of the new nation's presidential electors. The capital was then New York City; Washington, D. C., had not yet been built. In the spring of 1790 Madison fulfilled the federalist promise and introduced a bill of rights into the first Congress to meet under the new Constitution. This bill of rights closely followed the one in Virginia. Congress approved. Ten of these amendments were promptly ratified by the states and went into effect in 1791.

All of the first ten amendments were originally designed to limit the powers of the *national* government. The Bill of Rights begins with the command "Congress shall make no law . . ." It was not until after the Civil War that the Constitution also prohibited *states* from violating individual rights. The Fourteenth Amendment begins with the command "No state shall . . ." Today virtually all of the rights guaranteed in the Constitution protect the individual from the national government and its agencies, departments, and bureaus *and* the state governments and their cities, counties, school districts, and other subdivisions.

Both the national government and the states have an important role in amending the Constitution. A constitutional amendment must first be proposed, and then it must be ratified. The Constitution allows two methods of *proposing* a constitutional amendment: (1) by passage in the House and the Senate with a two-thirds vote or (2) by passage in a national convention called by Congress in response to petitions by two-thirds of the states. Congress then chooses the method of *ratification,* which can be either (1) by majority vote in the legislatures of three-fourths of the states or (2) by conventions called for the purpose in three-fourths of the states.

Of the four possible combinations of proposal and ratification, the method involving proposal by a two-thirds vote of Congress and ratification by three-quarters of the legislatures has been used for all the amendments except one. Only for the Twenty-first Amendment's repeal of Prohibition did Congress call for state ratifying conventions. (This was because Congress feared that Southern Bible Belt fundamentalist state legislatures would vote against repeal.) The method of proposal by national convention has never been used.

CHAPTER SUMMARY

1. The Constitution was written to correct what influential men of property saw as major political and economic weaknesses of the Articles of Confederation. Under the articles, the nation was an alliance of states that lacked a strong central government capable of resolving serious national problems.

2. The Founding Fathers (the fifty-five men who met in Philadelphia in 1787) were not a typical cross section of the American population. They were generally better educated and wealthier. Their major concern was to have an effective government that could protect property against radical political and social movements or dangerous "factions."

3. Although they were not advocates of mass democracy, the Founding Fathers did believe in a republican form of government that allowed a degree of popular participation while entrusting government to men of position and property.

4. Central to the Founding Fathers' political philosophy was the idea that the role of government is to protect the individual's rights of life, liberty, and property. A "social contract" establishes mutual obligations between the rulers and the ruled.

5. The Constitutional Convention of 1787 was marked by a series of compromises on such issues as representation in Congress, the counting of slaves, the question of export taxes, and qualifications for voting and holding office.

6. The Constitution created a federal form of government, dividing powers between the national government and the states.

7. The Constitution also divided power *within* the national government by establishing three major branches, together with a system of checks and balances designed to prevent the concentration of power in any one branch.

8. One key check in the American political system is the practice of *judicial review*—the power of the courts to declare acts of Congress or of the executive unconstitutional. The first notable enunciation of this principle was the 1803 case of *Marbury* v. *Madison*.

9. The Founding Fathers declared that the Constitution required ratification by at least nine states. The proponents of the Constitution, the federalists, cleverly used the press and political maneuvers to defeat the antifederalists. To assure ratification, however, it be-

came necessary to provide for a "bill of rights" limiting the power of the government with respect to individual freedoms.

10. Twenty-six amendments have been added to the Constitution since its adoption. Although various methods for proposal and ratification of amendments are possible, all but one of the twenty-six have been first proposed by a two-thirds vote in Congress and subsequently ratified by at least three-fourths of the state legislatures.

Notes

1. James Madison, Alexander Hamilton, and John Jay, *The Federalist,* Number 10 [New York: Random House (Modern Library), 1937], p. 55.
2. Richard Hofstadter, *The American Political Tradition* (New York: Knopf, 1948), p. 14.
3. *The Federalist,* Number 10, p. 59.
4. *The Federalist,* Number 51, p. 55.
5. See Cecelia M. Kenyon (Ed.), *The Antifederalists* (Indianapolis, Ind.: Bobbs-Merrill, 1966), p. 102.
6. Jackson T. Main, *The Antifederalists: Critics of the Constitution* (Chapel Hill, N. C.: University of North Carolina Press, 1961), p. 61.

Close-Up and In-Depth Analyses

Charles A. Beard. *An Economic Interpretation of the Constitution.* New York: Macmillan, 1935. (Originally published in 1913.)

Edward S. Corwin and Jack W. Peltason. *Understanding the Constitution.* New York: Holt, Rinehart & Winston, 1973.

Max Farrand. *The Framing of the Constitution of the United States.* New Haven, Conn.: Yale University Press, 1913.

Seymour Martin Lipset. *The First New Nation.* New York: Norton, 1979.

James Madison, Alexander Hamilton, and John Jay. *The Federalist.* New York: Random House (Modern Library), 1937.

Clinton Rossiter. *1787 The Grand Convention.* New York: Macmillan, 1966.

AMERICAN FEDERALISM: EIGHTY THOUSAND GOVERNMENTS

While the mass media are focusing on what happens in Washington, nearly eighty thousand other governments are taxing, spending, and regulating the lives of Americans. These eighty thousand governments—states, counties, municipalities, townships, school districts, and special districts—receive relatively sparse attention, even on the "local" news. The major television networks focus almost exclusively on the national government. But every day important issues are being dealt with in state capitols, county courthouses, and city halls.

"AN INDESTRUCTIBLE UNION OF INDESTRUCTIBLE STATES"

In 1861 eleven southern states attempted to secede from the Union. There was no provision for secession in the Constitution. President Abraham Lincoln declared these states to be in rebellion and sent federal troops to put down the rebellion. The result was the nation's bloodiest war: four years and over a quarter of a million lives lost out of a population of only 30 million. Following the war, the Chief Justice of the United States, Salmon P. Chase, described the legal character of American federalism: "The preservation of the states and the maintenance of their governments are as much within the design and care of the Constitution

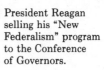

President Reagan selling his "New Federalism" program to the Conference of Governors.

as the preservation of the Union and the maintenance of the national government. The Constitution, in all of its provisions, looks to an indestructible union, composed of indestructible states."[1]

What is meant by "an indestructible union, composed of indestructible states"? The Constitution divides power between two separate authorities—the nation and the states. Each of these authorities may raise taxes, spend money, and directly enforce its laws on citizens through its own courts. The American federal union is an indissoluble partnership between the states and the national government. The Constitution itself is the only legal source of authority for the division of powers between these two authorities, and it may not be amended without the approval of both national and state bodies.

WHY FEDERALISM?

Why do we have state and local governments? Why not govern the entire nation from Washington? Why not have a unitary government—a centralized regime responsible to all of the people and capable of carrying out uniform policies throughout the country?

Advantages of Federalism

The argument for American federalism—for dividing powers between national and state governments (and for further dividing state powers among many types of local governments)—centers on the advantages of decentralization.

1. Federalism permits diversity. Local governments may deal directly with local problems. The entire nation is not "strait-jacketed" with a uniform policy that every state and community must conform to. State and local governments may be better suited to deal with specific state and local problems. Washington bureaucrats do not always know best about what to do in Commerce, Texas.

2. Federalism helps manage conflict. Permitting states and communities to pursue their own policies reduces the pressures that would build up in Washington if the national government had to decide everything. Federalism permits citizens to decide many things at the state and local levels of government and avoid battling over single national policies to be applied uniformly throughout the land.

3. Federalism disperses power. The widespread distribution of power is generally regarded as a protection against tyranny. To the extent that pluralism thrives in the United States, state and local governments have contributed to its success. State and local governments also provide a political base for the survival of the opposition party when it has lost national elections.

4. Federalism increases political participation. It allows more people to run for and hold political office. Nearly a million people hold some kind of political office in counties, cities, townships, school

As a local leader, Mayor Kevin White of Boston can better govern that city than an "unknown" from Washington—one advantage of federalism.

districts, and special districts. These local leaders are often regarded as "closer to the people" than Washington officials. Public-opinion polls show that Americans believe that their local governments are more manageable and responsive than the national government.

5. Federalism improves efficiency. Even though we may think of having 80,000 governments as inefficient, governing the entire nation from Washington would be even worse. Imagine the bureaucracy, red tape, delays, and confusion if every government activity in every community in the nation—police, schools, roads, fire fighting, garbage collection, sewage disposal, street lighting, and so on—were controlled by a central government in Washington. Even in the Soviet Union, where centralized discipline and party control are a matter of political ideology, leaders have been forced to resort to decentralization simply as a practical matter. Moreover, federalism encourages experimentation and innovation in public policy in the states.

Disadvantages of Federalism

However, federalism has its drawbacks.

1. Federalism allows special interests to protect their privileges. For many years segregationists used the argument of "states' rights" to avoid federal laws designed to guarantee equality and prevent discrimination. Indeed, the states' rights argument has been used so often in defense of racial discrimination that it has become a "code word" (innocent-looking symbol) for racism.

2. Federalism allows local leaders to frustrate national policy. They can obstruct not only civil-rights policies but also those in areas as diverse as energy, poverty, and pollution.

Women in Chicago, May 1978, show their support for ERA. (See "ERA in the Federal System" on p. 93.)

3. Federalism allows the benefits and costs of government to be spread unevenly. Some states spend more than twice as much per capita as other states on education. Even in the same state, some wealthy school districts spend two or three times as much as poorer districts. The taxes in some states are much higher than in other states; five states have no state income tax at all.

4. Federalism disadvantages poorer states and communities, which generally provide lower levels of education, health and welfare services, police protection, environmental protection, and so on than wealthier states and communities.

5. Federalism obstructs action on national issues. Although decentralization may reduce conflict at the national level, the result may be one of "sweeping under the rug" some very serious national issues. For many years, decentralizing the issue of civil rights allowed segregation to flourish. Only when the issue was nationalized in the 1960s by the civil rights movement was there any significant progress. Minorities can usually expect better treatment by national agencies than by state or local authorities.

Table 4-1. How Many American Governments Are There?

Federal government		1
State government		50
Local government		79,862
Counties	3,042	
Municipalities	18,862	
Townships	16,822	
School districts	15,174	
Special districts	25,962	
Total		79,913

ERA in the Federal System

The power of the states in the American federal system has been demonstrated in the struggle to add an Equal Rights Amendment (ERA) to the U. S. Constitution. According to Article V, *the Constitution cannot be amended without the approval of three-fourths of the states, either by the state legislatures or state ratifying conventions.* When Congress proposed ERA to the states in 1972, it did so by more than the necessary two-thirds vote of both the Senate and the House of Representatives. Indeed, Republicans and Democrats; Presidents Richard M. Nixon, Gerald R. Ford, and Jimmy Carter; and most other national political leaders endorsed the simple language of the amendment: "Equality of rights under law shall not be denied or abridged by the United States or by any state on account of sex." Congress followed constitutional tradition and allowed seven years for the states to ratify the amendment. ERA won quick ratification in about half of the states, but by 1975 a growing "Stop ERA" movement slowed progress in the states. In an effort to save ERA from defeat, Congress granted an unprecedented extension of time (from seven to ten years) to try to obtain the necessary two-thirds (38) of the states' ratifications.

Pros. Proponents of ERA argued in the state legislatures that most of the progress women have made toward equality in marriage, property, employment, credit, education, and so on, depends upon state and federal *law.* The guarantee of equality of the sexes would be much more secure if this guarantee were part of the U. S. Constitution. Moreover, ERA would eliminate the need to pass separate laws in a wide variety of fields to ensure sexual equality. ERA, as a permanent part of the U. S. Constitution, would provide a sweeping guarantee of equality, directly enforceable by court action. Finally, ERA took on a great deal of symbolic meaning: even if current federal and state laws prohibited sexual discrimination, it was still important for ERA to become part of the U. S. Constitution—"the Supreme Law of the Land."

Cons. Opponents of ERA suggested that it could eliminate many legal protections for women—financial support by husbands, an interest in the husband's property, exemption from military service, and so forth. In addition to these specific objections, the opposition to "women's liberation" in

(continued)

One of the many
political buttons made
that supported the
ratification of ERA.

(*continued*)

general charged that the movement weakened the family and
demoralized women who wished to devote their lives to their
families, husbands, and children. Finally, some state legislators objected that the vague wording of ERA would greatly
increase the power of the federal courts and Congress to intervene in the affairs of states, communities, and private
citizens.

The ratification battle. While writers have devoted a
great deal of attention to the leaders of the feminist movement in America,* less has been said about the large, active
group of women who successfully lobbied *against* ERA in
state legislatures. In spite of overwhelming support for ERA
by a majority of Americans surveyed by national polling organizations, the "ladies in pink" halted the ratification of ERA
in the states. (The phrase "ladies in pink" refers to a common
practice of anti-ERA women lobbyists wearing pink, dressing
well, baking apple pies for legislators, and otherwise adopting
the traditional symbols of femininity.) Most of the lobbying
against ERA in state legislatures was done by *women's*
groups. While not as well organized as the leading feminist
groups (N.O.W., the League of Women Voters, the Womens'
Political Caucus, and so on), the "ladies in pink" were very
much in evidence when a state legislature took up ratification
of ERA.

One interesting study comparing pro-ERA and anti-ERA
lobbyists revealed the following differences.**

- *Occupation*: Nearly three-quarters of the anti-ERA
  women were homemakers.
- *Education and income*: The pro-ERA women were
  drawn from higher socioeconomic class groups than
  the anti-ERA women.
- *Age*: A majority of pro-ERA women lobbyists were under 35, while a majority of the anti-ERA were over 35.
- *Religion*: Fully 98% of the "ladies in pink" were church
  members, compared to only 48% of the pro-ERA
  women.

In addition to being younger, better employed, more educated, more affluent, and less religious, the pro-ERA women
were decidedly more liberal in their political ideology than
were the anti-ERA women. The "ladies in pink" tended to

share moderate to conservative ideas on a variety of political issues. The pro-ERA women were more active in politics generally and displayed greater interest in, and information about, public affairs. The surprise is that the "ladies in pink"—mostly homemakers, middle-aged, religious, less educated, less affluent, politically conservative, and less active and knowledgeable about politics—were so effective in halting the Equal Rights Amendment.

    The future of ERA.   According to its supporters, "ERA won't go away." The failure of ERA to be ratified by the necessary 38 states by June 1982 ended immediate prospects for a constitutional amendment guaranteeing sexual equality. But support for ERA still runs high in national opinion polls and pro-ERA groups have not given up the fight.

    Three-quarters of the states must concur in any constitutional amendment. This is a powerful tool of the states in the federal system. The states can obstruct formal changes in the Constitution, even if a majority of Americans as well as national leaders support such a change.

    *See J. Freeman, *The Politics of Women's Liberation* (New York: David McKay, 1975); Amundsen, *The Selected Majority* (Englewood Cliffs, N. J.: Prentice-Hall, 1975); Karen DeCrow, "Who are We? Survey of N.O.W.'s Membership" (New York: National Organization for Women, 1974).
    **See Kent L. Tedin et al., "Social Background and Political Differences between Pro- and Anti-ERA Activists," *American Politics Quarterly,* July 1977, pp. 395–408.

THE DEVELOPMENT OF AMERICAN FEDERALISM

The importance of formal constitutional arrangements should not be underestimated. However, the American federal system is also shaped by the interpretations placed on constitutional principles. The real meaning of American federalism has emerged in the heat of political conflict between the states and the nation.

> The real meaning of American federalism has emerged in the heat of political conflict between the states and the nation.

Implied Federal Powers

In the early days of the new republic Chief Justice John Marshall, who presided over the Supreme Court from 1801 to 1835, became a major architect of American federalism. Marshall was responsible for making the necessary-and-proper clause the most significant grant of

Implied powers: Authority that is implicit in, or derived from, the powers expressly granted to the national government in the Constitution.

constitutional power to the national government.

Political conflict over the scope of national power is as old as the nation itself. In 1790 Alexander Hamilton, as Secretary of the Treasury, proposed the establishment of a national bank. Congress acted on Hamilton's suggestion in 1791, establishing a national bank to serve as a depository for federal money and to aid the federal government in borrowing funds. Jeffersonians believed that the national bank was a dangerous centralization in government. They objected that the power to establish it was nowhere to be found in the enumerated powers of Congress. Jefferson argued that Congress had no constitutional authority to establish a bank, because a bank was not "indispensably necessary" in carrying out its delegated functions. Hamilton replied that Congress could derive the power to establish a bank from grants of authority in the Constitution relating to money, in combination with the clause authorizing Congress "to make all laws which will be necessary and proper for carrying into execution the foregoing powers." Jefferson interpreted the word "necessary" to mean "indispensable," but Hamilton argued that the national government had the right to choose the manner and means of performing its delegated functions and was not restricted to employing only those means considered indispensable in the performance of its functions. The question eventually reached the Supreme Court in 1819 when Maryland levied a tax on the national bank and the bank refused to pay it. In the case of *McCulloch* v. *Maryland*, Chief Justice Marshall accepted the broader Hamiltonian version of the necessary-and-proper clause: "Let the end be legitimate, let it be within the scope of the Constitution, and all means which are appropriate, which are plainly adopted to that end, which are not prohibited but consistently with the letter and the spirit of the Constitution, are constitutional."[2]

Chief Justice
John Marshall

The *McCulloch* case firmly established the principle that the necessary-and-proper clause gives Congress the right to choose its means for carrying out the enumerated powers of the national government. Today Congress can devise programs, create agencies, and establish national laws on the basis of long chains of reasoning from the most meager phrases of the constitutional text because of the broad interpretation of the necessary-and-proper clause.

National Supremacy

The case of *McCulloch* v. *Maryland* also made a major contribution to the interpretation of the national-supremacy clause. Chief Justice Marshall held Maryland's tax on the national bank to be unconstitutional on the ground that it interfered with a national activity being carried out under the Constitution and laws "made in pursuance thereof." Thus, Maryland's state tax law was declared unconstitutional because it conflicted with the federal law establishing the national bank. From Marshall's time to the present, the national-supremacy clause has meant that states cannot refuse to obey federal laws.

Of course, it was one thing to announce that states had no constitutional right to resist federal authority and quite another thing to establish this principle as a political reality. In the famous Virginia and Kentucky Resolutions, the early Jeffersonians set forth a doctrine of state **"interposition."** This was the assertion that a state had a right to resist enforcement of a national law that the state believed to be unconstitutional. The Resolutions were passed by Kentucky and Virginia in response to the Alien and Sedition Acts of 1798, which had been fashioned by a Federalist Congress. The Jeffersonians argued—rightly, no doubt—that the Alien and Sedition Acts violated constitutional guarantees of free speech and freedom of the press. (The Acts included provisions for halting the publication of "seditious" newspapers.) The interposition argument asserted that a state could "interpose" itself between its people and the operation of what, in the eyes of the state, was an unconstitutional federal law. Because the Jeffersonians captured the presidency in 1800 and a Jeffersonian Congress repealed the Alien and Sedition Acts in 1801, the interposition argument in the Kentucky and Virginia Resolutions was never formally challenged in the courts.

Interposition: The doctrine that a state can "interpose" its authority between its people and a law of the national government that the state believes to be unconstitutional.

Secession and Civil War

The Civil War was the greatest crisis of the American federal system. Did a state have the right to oppose national law to the point of secession? In the years preceding the war, John C. Calhoun argued that the Constitution was a compact made by the *states* in their sovereign capacity rather than by the *people* in their national capacity. Calhoun contended that the federal government was an agent of the states, that the states retained their sovereignty in this compact, and that the federal government must not violate the compact, under the penalty of state nullification or even secession. Calhoun's doctrine was embodied in the constitution of the Confederacy, which began with the words "We, the people of the Confederate States, each state acting in its sovereign and independent character, in order to form a permanent federal government. . . ." This wording contrasts with the preamble of the U. S. Constitution: "We, the people of the United States, in order to form a more perfect union. . . ."

The states' rights doctrine and political disputes over the character of American federalism did not disappear with Lee's surrender at Appomattox.

What was decided on the battlefield between 1861 and 1865 was confirmed by the Supreme Court in 1869: "Ours is an indestructible union, composed of indestructible states."[3] Yet the states' rights doctrine and political disputes over the character of American federalism did not disappear with Lee's surrender at Appomattox. The Thirteenth, Fourteenth, and Fifteenth Amendments, passed by the Reconstruction Congress, were clearly aimed at limiting state power in the interests of individual freedom. The Thirteenth Amendment eliminated slavery in the states; the Fifteenth Amendment prevented states from denying the vote on the basis of race, color, or previous enslavement; and the Fourteenth Amendment declared: "No state shall make or enforce any law which shall abridge the privileges or immunities of citizens of the United States; nor shall any state deprive any person of life, liberty, or property, without due process of law; nor deny to any person within its jurisdiction the equal protection of the laws." These amendments delegated to Congress the power to secure their enforcement. Yet for several generations they were narrowly construed and added little, if anything, to national power. By tacit agreement, after Southern states demonstrated their continued political importance in the disputed presidential election of 1876, the federal government refrained from using its power to enforce these civil rights.

Civil Rights

After World War II, however, the Supreme Court began to build a national system of civil rights based on the Fourteenth Amendment. The Court had held that the Fourteenth Amendment prevented states from interfering with free speech, free press, or religious practices.[4] Not until 1954, however, in the desegregation decision in *Brown* v. *Board of Education of Topeka,* did the Court begin to call for the full assertion of national authority on behalf of civil rights.[5] When the Court decided that the Fourteenth Amendment prohibited the states from segregating the races in public schools, it was asserting national authority over deeply held beliefs and long-standing practices in many of the states.

The Supreme Court used the Fourteenth Amendment to ensure a national system of civil rights supported by the power of the federal government. This was an important step in the evolution of the American federal system. The controversy over federally imposed desegregation in the Southern states renewed the debate over states' rights versus national authority. The vigorous resistance to desegregation in the South following *Brown* testified to the continued strength of the states in the American federal system. Despite the clear mandate of the Supreme Court, the Southern states succeeded in avoiding all but token integration for more than ten years.[6] Yet only occasionally did resistance take the form of "interposition." Governor Orval Faubus called out the Arkansas National Guard to prevent a federal court from desegregating Little Rock Central High

In Little Rock, Arkansas, United States Army troops helped enforce a federal court order calling for desegregation.

School in 1957. But this "interposition" was ended quickly when President Eisenhower ordered the National Guard removed and sent units of the United States Army to enforce national authority. In 1962 President John F. Kennedy took a similar action when Governor Ross Barnett of Mississippi personally barred the entry of a black student to the University of Mississippi, despite a federal court order requiring his admission. Governor George Wallace literally stood in the doorway to prevent desegregation at the University of Alabama but moved aside several hours later when federal marshals arrived. These actions failed to alter the principle of national supremacy in the American political system.

Interstate Commerce

The growth of national power under the interstate commerce clause of the Constitution is also an important development in the evolution of American federalism. The Industrial Revolution in the United States created a national economy with a nationwide network of transportation and communications and the potential for national economic depressions. In response to this growth Congress progressively widened the definition of *interstate commerce* to include the regulation of interstate transportation (particularly the railroads) and of communications (particularly the telephone and telegraph). Industrialization created interstate businesses that could be regulated only by the national government; this reality was recognized in the passage of the Sherman Antitrust Act in 1890. Yet for a time the Supreme Court placed obstacles in the way of national authority over the economy and by so doing created a crisis in American federalism. For many years the Court narrowly construed "interstate commerce" to mean only the movement of goods and services across state lines, and until the late 1930s it insisted that agriculture, mining, manufacturing, and labor relations were outside the reach of the delegated powers of the national government. However, when confronted with the Great Depression of the 1930s and the threat of presidential attack on the membership of the Court itself, it yielded. The Court recognized the principle that production and distribution of goods and services for a national market could be regulated by Congress under the interstate commerce clause. The effect was to give the national government effective control over the national economy, and today few economic activities are not within the reach of congressional power.

Essentials: The Framework of American Federalism

The framework of American federalism is determined by (1) the powers delegated by the Constitution to the national government, (2) the constitutional guarantees reserved for the states, (3) the powers denied by the Constitution to both the national government and the states, (4) the constitutional provisions giving the states a role in the composition of the national government, and (5) the subsequent interpretation of these constitutional provisions by the courts.

1. *Delegated powers.* Article I, Section 8 of the Constitution lists eighteen grants of **delegated powers** to Congress. One set of powers includes authority over matters of war and foreign affairs—the power to declare war, raise armies, equip navies, and so on. Another series of delegated powers is related to control of the economy, including the power to coin money, to control its value, and to regulate foreign and interstate commerce. The national government has been given independent powers of taxation "to pay the debts and provide for the common defense and general welfare of the United States." It has the power to establish its own court system. The national government was given the authority to grant copyrights and patents, establish post offices, enact bankruptcy laws, punish counterfeiting, punish crimes committed on the high seas, and govern the District of Columbia. Finally, after seventeen specific grants of power comes the power "to make all laws which shall be necessary and proper for carrying into execution the foregoing powers, and all other powers vested by this Constitution in the government of the United States or in any department or officer thereof." This is generally referred to as the necessary-and-proper clause.

These delegated powers, when coupled with the national supremacy clause of Article VI, ensured a powerful national government. The national supremacy clause is quite specific regarding the relationship between the national government

Delegated powers: Powers of the national government specifically listed in the Constitution.

and the states. In questions involving conflict between state laws and the Constitution, laws, or treaties of the United States, "This Constitution, and the laws of the United States which shall be made in pursuance thereof . . . shall be the supreme law of the land . . . anything in the constitution or laws of any state to the contrary notwithstanding."

2. *Reserved powers.* Despite these broad grants of power to the national government, the states retained a great deal of authority over the lives of their citizens. The Tenth Amendment reaffirmed the idea that the national government had only certain delegated powers and that all powers not delegated to it were retained by the states: "The powers not delegated to the United States by the Constitution, nor prohibited by it to the states, are reserved to the states respectively, or to the people." The states retained control over the ownership and use of property; the regulation of offenses against persons and property (criminal law and civil law); the regulation of marriage and divorce; the control of business, labor, farming, trades, and professions; the provision of education, hospitals, and other aspects of social welfare; and the provision of highways, roads, canals, and other public works. The states also retained full authority over the organization and control of units of local government. Finally, the states, like the federal government, were given the power to tax and spend for the general welfare.

3. *Powers denied to the nation and states.* The Constitution denies some powers to both the national and the state governments; these denials generally safeguard individual rights. Both nation and states were forbidden to pass ex post facto laws or bills of attainder. The first eight amendments to the Constitution, the Bill of Rights, originally applied only to the federal government, but the Fourteenth Amendment, ratified in 1867, provided that the states must also adhere to fundamental guarantees of individual liberty.

> No state shall make or enforce any law which shall abridge the privileges or immunities of the citizens of the United States; nor shall any state deprive any person of life, liberty, or property, without due process of law; nor deny to any person within its jurisdiction equal protection of the laws.

Some powers were denied only to the states, generally as a safeguard to national unity, including the power to coin money, enter into treaties with foreign powers, interfere with

(continued)

Reserved powers: The authority of the states under the Constitution to exercise any powers not specifically delegated to the national government or prohibited by the Constitution.

(continued)

the obligations of contracts, levy duties on imports or exports without congressional consent, maintain military forces in peacetime, engage in war, or enter into compacts with foreign nations or other states.

4. *State role in national government.* The states also play an important role in the composition of the national government. U. S. representatives must be apportioned among the states according to their population every ten years. Governors have the authority to fill vacancies in Congress, and every state must have at least one representative regardless of population. The Senate of the United States is composed of two senators from each state regardless of the state's population. The times, places, and manner of holding elections for Congress are determined by the states. The president is chosen by electors, allotted to each state on the basis of its senators and representatives. Finally, amendments to the Constitution must be ratified by three-fourths of the states.

MONEY AND POWER IN WASHINGTON

Today the national government exercises much greater power in the federal system than the Founding Fathers originally envisioned. The growth of power in Washington has not necessarily meant a reduction in the powers of state and local governments; in fact, *all* governments have vastly increased their powers and responsibilities in the twentieth century. Nevertheless, the national government is no longer really a government with only "delegated," or "enumerated," powers. Its delegated powers are now so broadly defined—particularly the power to tax and spend for the general welfare and the authority over interstate commerce—that the government in Washington is involved in every aspect of American life. There are really no segments of public activity "reserved" to the states or the people.

> The growth of power in Washington has not necessarily meant a reduction in the power of state and local governments; in fact, *all* governments have vastly increased their powers and responsibilities in the twentieth century.

The Earliest Federal Aid

Even in the earliest days of the republic the national government was deeply involved in public activities that were not specifically delegated to it in the Constitution.[7] The first Congress of the United States passed the famous Northwest Ordinance, providing for the government of the territories to the west of the Appalachian Mountains. This statute authorized grants of federal land for the establishment of public schools and, by so doing, showed a concern for education, an area reserved to the states by the Constitution. Again, in 1863 in the Morrill Land Grant Act, Congress provided grants of land to the states to promote higher education.

The Income Tax

The Sixteenth Amendment (1913) gave the federal government the power to tax income directly. This was the beginning of a new era in American federalism. The Sixteenth Amendment helped to shift the balance of financial power from the states to Washington, giving Congress the power to tax the incomes of corporations and individuals on a progressive basis. The income tax gave the federal government the ability to raise large sums of money, which it proceeded to spend for the general welfare as well as for the military. It is no coincidence that the first major grant-in-aid programs (agricultural extension in 1914, highways in 1916, vocational education in 1917, and public health in 1918) all came shortly after the inauguration of the federal income tax.

Centralizing finances.   At the beginning of the twentieth century most government activity was carried on at the local level. Table 4-2 reveals that local governments once made 59 percent of all government expenditures in the United States, compared with 35 percent

Table 4-2. A Comparison of the Expenditures of Federal, State, and Local Governments

| | Percentages of total general expenditures of governments | | |
	Federal	*State*	*Local*
1902	35%	6%	59%
1927	31	13	56
1936	50	14	36
1944	90	3	7
1950	64	12	24
1960	62	13	25
1970	64	13	23
1975	61	18	21
1980	58	19	23

Note: Figures for federal government include Social Security and trust fund expenditures as well as grants to state and local governments. State payments to local governments are shown as local expenditures.

for the federal government and 6 percent for state governments. In 1970 centralization in the American federal system had proceeded to the point at which local governments were making only 23 percent of government expenditures, compared with 64 percent for the federal government and 13 percent for state governments. Over the past decade, however, state and local government spending increased *faster* than federal spending. Yet federal spending still accounts for well over half of all government spending in the nation.

Wars and Depressions

Wars and the Great Depression had a great deal to do with the shift away from reliance on local government. During national emergencies, both foreign and domestic, Americans have turned to the federal government for help. After the emergency, federal activity decreases somewhat in relation to state and local activity, but it never returns to the earlier level. Thus, during World War I, World War II, the Korean War, and the Vietnam War, the federal government's percentage of total government activity increased (see Table 4-2). Since the federal government has the primary responsibility for national defense, this is what we would expect to occur during wartime. Moreover, the federal government also expands its activities in response to domestic crisis; it was during the 1930s that federal expenditures surpassed those of states and communities combined.

Although foreign and domestic crises have brought about increasing centralization in American government, it should be repeated that expanded federal activity has not come at the expense of state and local activity. Federal power and state and local power are *not* at the opposite ends of the seesaw. National activity has expanded in the twentieth century, but so has the activity of state and local governments.

The extent of centralization of government activity in the American federal system varies widely according to policy area (see Table 4-3). In the fields of the armed forces, space research, and the postal service, the federal government assumes almost exclusive responsibility. In all other fields, state and local governments share responsibility and costs with the federal government. State and local governments assume the major share of the costs of education, highways, health and hospitals, sanitation, and fire and police protection. Welfare costs are gradually being shifted to the federal government, and it is also assuming the major share of the costs of natural-resource development and Social Security.

NATIONAL POWER AND FEDERAL GRANTS

The federal grant-in-aid has become a principal instrument in the expansion of national power. It should be noted that there is no general grant of power to the national government in the Constitution to

Table 4-3. Federal and State/Local Shares of Expenditures by Policy Areas, 1927–1980

	1927		1938		1970		1975		1980	
	Federal	State and local	Federal	State and local	Federal	State and local	Federal	State and local	Federal	State and local
National defense	100%	0%	100%	0%	100%	0%	100%	0%	100%	0%
Space research	100	0	100	0	100	0	100	0	100	0
Postal service	100	0	100	0	100	0	100	0	100	0
Education	1	99	6	94	10	90	18	82	16	84
Highways	1	99	23	77	29	71	28	72	21	79
Welfare	6	94	13	87	58	42	63	37	64	36
Health and hospitals	18	82	19	81	33	67	32	68	31	69
Natural resources	31	69	81	19	80	20	82	18	74	26
Housing and urban renewal	—	—	—	—	82	18	85	15	85	39

Note: Federal grants are shown as federal expenditures.

protect and advance the public health, safety, welfare, or morals. Theoretically, the national government may not enact laws dealing directly with housing, streets, zoning, schools, health, police protection, fire fighting, crime, and so on simply because such a law might contribute to the general welfare. However, it may *tax or borrow or spend money* for the general welfare, even though it has no power in the Constitution to regulate welfare activities directly.

> There is no general grant of power to the national government in the Constitution to protect and advance the public health, safety, welfare, or morals.

This is a subtle distinction, but it is an important one. For example, Congress may not outlaw billboards on highways, because billboard regulation is not among the enumerated powers of Congress in the Constitution. However, the federal government, through its power to tax and spend, can provide financial assistance to the states to build highways and then pass a law threatening to withdraw financial aid if the states do not regulate billboards themselves. Thus, the federal government can involve itself in billboard regulation through its taxing power and financial resources, even though this field is "reserved" to the states.

Growth of Federal Grants

The Great Depression of the 1930s brought pressure on the national government to use its tax and spending powers in a wide variety of areas formerly reserved to states and communities. The federal government initiated grant programs to states and communities for public assistance, unemployment compensation, employment services, child welfare, public housing, urban renewal, and so on; it also expanded federal grant programs for highways, vocational education, and rehabilitation. The inadequacy of state and local revenue systems to meet the financial crisis created by the depression contributed significantly to the expansion of federal power.

During World War II and the Cold War that followed, federal grant programs were expanded and given labels that made them appear to be part of the military effort. Aid to public schools came in a program to help school districts experiencing rapid population growth because of military bases, defense industries, or other federal installations. In 1956 the Interstate and Defense Highway Act greatly expanded aid for the construction of the interstate highway system. In the National Defense Education Act of 1957, federal grants and loans for higher education were authorized.

The Great Society programs of the 1960s brought a myriad of new federal grant programs in health, urban affairs, economic development, job training, and education. From 1965 to 1972 federal grants grew from $10 billion a year to $30 billion. The Carter administration added temporary public jobs and local public works to counteract a recession. *All* grant programs grew at an astonishing rate in the 1970s. Figure 4-1 shows the expansion of federal grant programs in a

Food stamps, one federally funded program administered through state and local governments.

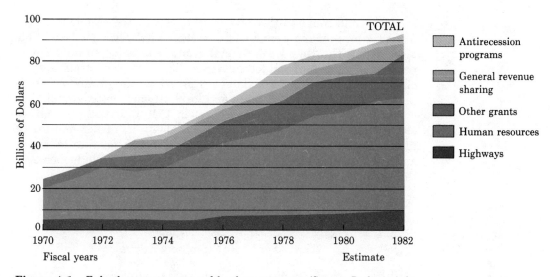

Figure 4-1. Federal grants to state and local governments. (Source: *Budget of the United States Government 1982*. Washington, D. C.: U. S. Government Printing Office, 1981.)

single decade. In 1972 Congress passed the State and Local Fiscal Assistance Act—general revenue sharing—which distributes federal money to state and local governments for general purposes. Federal grants to states and cities total more than $80 billion a year, or nearly 20 percent of all federal expenditures.

Federal Grant-in-Aid

Grant-in-aid programs are the single most important source of federal influence over state policy. Approximately one-fifth of all state and local government revenues are from federal grants. This money is paid out through perhaps 500 different programs. So numerous and diverse are they that there is a substantial lack of information about their availability, purpose, and requirements. Learning about the availability of federal grants and mastering the art of grant application place a heavy burden on state and local officials. Moreover, the problem of program coordination, not only between levels of government but also among federal agencies, is a difficult one.

Federal grants are available in nearly every major category of state and local government activity. These categorical grants are made for particular projects or activities in a city or state. Federal grants can be obtained for the preservation of historic buildings, the development of minority-owned businesses, aid to foreign refugees, the drainage of abandoned mines, riot control, and school milk. Welfare, Medicaid (for the poor), food stamps, and highways, however, account for over two-thirds of federal aid money.

States and communities have come to rely on the national government for an ever-increasing share of their total revenues (see Table
4-4). Before the New Deal, federal grants amounted to only 2 or 3
percent of total state and local revenue. The New Deal itself, in spite
of all of its innovations in federal aid programs, only raised this proportion to 7 or 8 percent. State and local reliance on federal aid has
continued to increase, from 8 percent in 1946 to over 23 percent in
1980. Thus, no matter how it is measured—in increased number of
programs, increased dollar amounts, or increased reliance by states
and communities—federal aid has grown into a major influence over
the activities of state and local governments.

**Table 4-4. Impact of Federal Grants on
State and Local Finances**

	Total federal grants (in millions)	Federal grants as a percentage of state and local revenue
1902	$ 7	*
1913	12	*
1922	118	2.1
1927	123	1.6
1932	232	2.9
1938	800	7.2
1940	945	8.1
1944	954	6.8
1948	1,861	8.6
1950	2,486	9.7
1955	3,131	8.3
1960	6,974	11.6
1962	7,871	11.3
1967	15,366	14.0
1970	25,029	14.8
1972	36,080	16.6
1976	55,632	22.2
1980	82,858	24.4
1982 (est.)	99,529	26.3

*Less than 1 percent

Arguments Supporting the Federal Aid Program

Several arguments are made in support of federal aid. First of all,
these grants allow the federal government to single out and support
those services of state and local government in which it has a particular interest. Grants allow the national government to set national
goals and priorities at lower levels of government without formally
altering the federal structure. Thus, as problems of public assistance,
urban renewal, highway construction, education, poverty, and so on
acquire national significance, they can be dealt with by the application of national resources.

Second, the grant-in-aid system helps to overcome the inadequacies of state and local sources of revenue. Contrary to the political rhetoric accusing the states of excessive fiscal conservatism, the states have actually demonstrated a great deal of fiscal courage, effort, and ingenuity in trying to cope with money problems. In the last two decades, as we have seen, state and local expenditures have risen at a faster *rate* than federal expenditures. These fiscal efforts have meant increased income taxes or sales taxes in nearly every state in the past ten years as well as increased liquor and gasoline taxes. Yet in spite of these efforts by the states, their fiscal problems continue to multiply.

States and communities must raise revenue and at the same time compete for industry and wealth. Although the influence of tax considerations on decisions about where to locate industries may be overstated by most lawmakers, this overstatement itself is part of the political lore at statehouses and courthouses and operates to impede revenue raising.

A third general argument on behalf of federal grants centers on the greater progressiveness of the federal tax structure. If a government program is funded through state and local taxes, it is funded on a tax structure that is regressive or only mildly progressive. In contrast, if a particular program is funded out of federal taxes, it is funded on a more progressive basis.

Fourth, grants-in-aid provide an opportunity for the national government to ensure a uniform, minimum level of public service throughout the nation. For example, federal grants can help achieve equality in educational opportunity in all parts of the nation or help ensure a minimum level of subsistence for the poverty-striken regardless of where they live. This aspect of federal policy assumes that some state and local governments are unable or perhaps unwilling to devote their resources to raising public-service levels to minimum national standards.

Finally, federal guidelines that accompany grants have often improved standards of administration, personnel policies, and fiscal practices in states and communities. More importantly, federal guidelines have helped to ensure that states and communities do not engage in racial discrimination in federally aided programs.

Arguments Opposing the Federal Aid Program

Equally persuasive arguments are made in opposition to the current federal grant system. First of all, whenever the national government contributes financially to state or local programs, officials at those levels are left with less freedom of choice than they would have had otherwise. Federal grants are invariably accompanied by federal standards, or guidelines, which must be adhered to if states and communities are to receive their money. The national government gives money to states and communities only if they are willing to meet conditions specified by Congress. Often Congress delegates to federal agencies the power to establish the conditions.

No state is required to accept a federal grant and its restrictions. However, it is very difficult for states and communities to resist the pressure to accept federal money. It is sometimes said that states are "bribed" by the temptation of much-needed federal money and "blackmailed" by the thought that other states will get the money, which was contributed in part by their own citizens through federal taxation.

The centralization of power in Washington has created some serious problems in the implementation of public policy. First, federal grants frequently work at cross purposes, reflecting fragmentation of federal programs. For example, urban renewal grants attempt to save central cities from deterioration and population loss, but federal highway grants go to build expressways that make possible the exodus to the suburbs. Federal public housing programs have tried to increase the supply of low-rent housing for the poor, but federally funded urban renewal programs have torn down low-rent housing.

Second, the federal government has never set any significant priorities among its hundreds of grant programs. The result is that too few dollars chase too many goals. Cities are pressured to apply for funds for projects they do not really need, simply because federal money is available, but they may receive little or no federal assistance for more vital programs. Federal grant money is frequently provided for "innovative" or "demonstration" programs, when the real crisis facing states and communities may be in traditional public services—police, sewage, street repair, and so forth.

Third, the administrative quagmire created by the maze of separate federal grant programs threatens to drown state and local officials in red tape. The 500 separate programs with separate purposes and guidelines are uncoordinated and bureaucratic. State and local officials spend a great deal of their time in "grantsmanship"—learning where to find federal funds, how to apply, and how to write applications in such a way as to appear to meet guidelines.

Categorical grant: A federal grant-in-aid to a state or local government that specifies the purpose for which the grant funds are to be employed.

Finally, the current **categorical grant** system assumes that federal officials are better judges of goals and priorities at all levels of government than state or local officials. State and local officials do not determine which activities will receive federal money. Moreover, federal officials must approve each federally funded project—a public housing project in Des Moines, an airport in Pittsburgh, a new set of welfare regulations in California, a sewage disposal system in Baton Rouge, an urban renewal project in Atlanta, a highway in North Dakota. Whether federal officials or state and local officials are better judges of public goals and priorities is, of course, a political question.

Sun Belt and Frost Belt

Americans are increasingly recognizing an important national division brought about by the rise of the Sun Belt and the decline of the Frost Belt. This new recognition of regionalism in American social, economic, and political life is *not* the equivalent of the traditional notion that the South (the eleven states of the old Confederacy) is "different." Instead, the distinction is based on real differences in *growth rates* in the West and South as opposed to the Northeast and Midwest. States and communities in the Sun Belt have shown more-rapid increases in recent years in population, income, employment, and productivity than states and communities of the Frost Belt.

Sun Belt and *Frost Belt* are terms used frequently by journalists and commentators, but there are no official definitions for them. For our purposes let us draw a line across the United States separating nineteen Sun Belt states—Hawaii, California, Nevada, Utah, Colorado, Arizona, New Mexico, Texas, Oklahoma, Arkansas, Louisiana, Tennessee, Mississippi, Alabama, Georgia, Florida, North Carolina, South Carolina, and Virginia—from the thirty-one Frost Belt states.

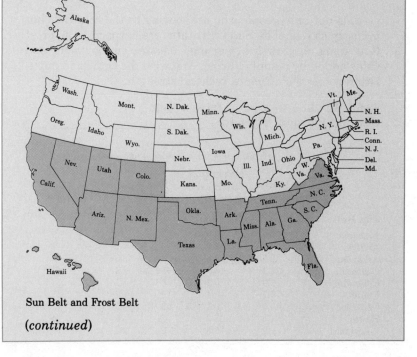

Sun Belt and Frost Belt

(continued)

(*continued*)

The Sun Belt states have an average annual population growth rate of 2.5 percent, compared with 0.4 percent for the Frost Belt states. This translates into a 22.8 percent increase in the 1970s for the Sun Belt, compared with 4.3 percent for the Frost Belt.

Table A. Sun Belt versus Frost Belt: Contrasts in Growth

	Sun Belt	Frost Belt
Population growth (average annual change)	2.5%	0.4%
Income growth (average annual change)	7.7	5.5
Employment growth (average annual change in nonagricultural jobs)	4.2	2.8
Productivity growth (average annual change in value added by manufacturing)	10.0	9.2

Note: Figures are means for nineteen Sun Belt and thirty-one Frost Belt states. Population growth figures are average annual rates, 1970–1980; income, employment, and productivity growth are 1970–1978.

It is not only people who are moving to the Sun Belt but industry as well. The Sun Belt states are outpacing the Frost Belt states in growth in personal income, employment, and value added by manufacturing. And with the change in population comes a shifting of political strength.

Table B. Sun Belt versus Frost Belt: Shifting Political Strength

	Population		U. S. Representatives		Electoral College votes
	1980 (millions)	Percentage increase from 1970	1980	Change from 1970	1980
Sun Belt					
Alabama	3.9	12.9	7	0	9
Arizona	2.7	53.1	5	+1	7
Arkansas	2.3	18.8	4	0	6
California	23.7	18.5	45	+2	47
Colorado	2.9	30.7	6	+1	8
Florida	9.7	43.4	19	+4	21
Georgia	5.5	19.1	10	0	12
Hawaii	1.0	25.3	2	0	4
Louisiana	4.2	15.3	8	0	10

Table B, continued

	1980 (millions)	Percentage increase from 1970	1980	Change from 1970	1980
Mississippi	2.5	13.7	5	0	7
Nevada	.8	63.5	2	+1	4
New Mexico	1.3	27.8	3	+1	5
North Carolina	5.9	15.5	11	0	13
Oklahoma	3.0	18.2	6	0	8
South Carolina	3.1	20.4	6	0	8
Tennessee	4.5	16.9	9	+1	11
Texas	14.2	27.1	27	+3	29
Utah	1.5	37.9	3	+1	5
Virginia	5.3	14.9	10	0	12
Total	**98.0**	**22.8**	**188**	**+15**	**226**
Frost Belt					
Alaska	.4	32.4	1	0	3
Connecticut	3.1	2.5	6	0	8
Delaware	.6	8.6	1	0	3
Dist. of Col.	.6	18.6	*	*	3
Idaho	.9	32.4	2	0	4
Illinois	11.4	2.8	22	−2	24
Indiana	5.5	5.7	10	−1	12
Iowa	2.9	3.1	6	0	8
Kansas	2.4	5.1	5	0	7
Kentucky	3.7	13.7	7	0	9
Maine	1.1	13.2	2	0	4
Maryland	4.2	7.5	8	0	10
Massachusetts	5.7	.8	11	−1	13
Michigan	9.3	4.2	18	−1	20
Minnesota	4.1	7.1	8	0	10
Missouri	4.9	5.1	9	−1	11
Montana	.8	13.3	2	0	4
Nebraska	1.6	5.7	3	0	5
New Hampshire	.9	24.8	2	0	4
New Jersey	7.5	2.7	14	−1	16
New York	17.6	−3.8	34	−5	36
North Dakota	.7	5.6	1	0	3
Ohio	10.8	1.3	21	−2	23
Oregon	2.6	25.9	5	+1	7
Pennsylvania	11.9	.6	23	−2	25
Rhode Island	.9	−.3	2	0	4
South Dakota	.7	3.6	1	−1	3
Vermont	.5	15.0	1	0	3
Washington	4.1	21.0	8	+1	10
West Virginia	1.9	11.8	4	0	6
Wisconsin	4.7	6.5	9	0	11
Wyoming	.5	41.6	1	0	3
Total	**128.5**	**4.3**	**247**	**−15**	**312**

*The District of Columbia does not elect U. S. senators or representatives, but the District was given three electoral votes by the Twenty-fourth Amendment in 1961.

(continued)

(*continued*)

One explanation for the growth of the Sun Belt is that lower costs in the region are attracting industries from the North. These lower costs include cheap land for expanded manufacturing activities, lower wage rates, and lower taxes. Although these factors may help to explain why some older, low-wage industries (such as textile manufacturing) have moved from the Northeast to the South, they do not explain the growth of new industries in the Sun Belt. Houston and Phoenix are not just relocated versions of Providence and Pittsburgh. The rapid rise of the Sun Belt can be attributed primarily to the growth in the region of dynamic new industries since World War II:

1. oil and natural gas
2. aerospace and defense
3. computers, cameras, and business machines
4. real estate development
5. drugs and fast foods
6. tourism*

No doubt the milder climate of the Sun Belt has attracted tourists, retirees, and light industries that are not tied to sources of heavy raw material (coal, iron ore, and so forth). The average mean temperature in the largest cities of the Sun Belt states is sixty-two degrees Fahrenheit, compared with fifty degrees for the Frost Belt states. But, more importantly, the Sun Belt states are not saddled with an obsolescent industrial foundation. The Sun Belt has been in a more flexible position to accommodate new enterprises and to shift with the changing needs of the national economy. It is not encrusted with the outmoded buildings, aging facilities, and characteristic habits of old economies. So it is capturing a disproportionate share of the new, growing industries.

The rapid rise of the Sun Belt is creating political rivalries as well as economic competition. New leaders who have acquired their wealth in the post–World War II era of dramatic growth in Sun Belt industries have been referred to as "cowboys." In contrast, the established "Yankees" represent established corporations, Washington law firms, Eastern banking and investment firms, well-known foundations, and Ivy League universities. According to one popular journalist:

There is a broadly metaphorical but rather apt way of describing these rival power bases, the one of the

Northeast and the other of the Southern Rim, as the *yankee* and the *cowboys*. Taken loosely, that is meant to suggest the traditional, staid, oldtime, button-down, Ivy League, tight-lipped, patrician, New England rooted WASP culture on the one hand, and the aggressive, flamboyant, restless, swaggering, newfangled, open-collar, can-do, Southern-rooted Baptist culture of the Southern Rim on the other . . . [Sale, *Power Shift*, pp. 5–6].*

The cowboys do not fully share in the liberal social welfarism of the still dominant Eastern Yankees. The leading cowboys are often self-made people who acquired wealth and power in a competitive struggle that continues to shape their outlook on life. They are individualistic, upwardly mobile, competitive, very patriotic—sometimes vocally "anti-Communist"—and moderate to conservative on many national policy issues. The leading Yankees have often inherited wealth or acquired it over a long climb up the corporate or legal ladder of large institutions or firms. They have been taught in prestigious private schools and universities that it is their responsibility to "do good"—to abolish poverty, end discrimination, eliminate slums, ensure employment, uplift the poor, end sickness, and educate the masses—and to use government power to achieve these high-minded goals.

Established Yankees are still dominant in national politics and economics, but the challenge from the Sun Belt is real. Reapportionment after the 1980 census switched 17 seats in the U. S. House of Representatives (and 17 electoral college votes in presidential elections) from the Frost Belt states to the Sun Belt states. In the 1980s the 18 Sun Belt states have 182 representatives (up from 165 in the 1970s), and the 32 Frost Belt states have 253 representatives (down from 270 in the 1970s).

*See Kirkpatrick Sale, *Power Shift* (New York: Vintage, 1976).

CUTTING FEDERAL STRINGS

Revenue Sharing

The many dissatisfactions with the conditional grant system led to new approaches to federal financial assistance to state and local governments. In 1972, at the urging of President Richard M. Nixon, Congress adopted the idea of **revenue sharing**—the turning over

Revenue sharing: A program whereby the federal government redistributes tax dollars among state and local governments.

of federal tax dollars to state and local governments for use as they saw fit. The idea of revenue sharing assumes that the federal government is better at collecting revenue than state or local governments but that state and local governments are better at spending it. Consequently, revenue sharing was said to combine the best features of each level of government. More importantly, revenue sharing promised to reverse the flow of money and power to Washington, to end excessive red tape, and to revitalize state and local governments.

The State and Local Fiscal Assistance Act of 1972 authorized general revenue sharing—the distribution of billions of dollars per year of federal money to states and communities with very few restrictions on its use. Revenue sharing under this act does not replace any existing grant programs but does provide states and communities with new unrestricted revenues. No applications are required; the U. S. Treasury Department sends revenue-sharing money to states and communities on a formula basis that considers population, income, and local tax effort. Restrictions are minor compared with the maze of guidelines surrounding categorical federal grants.

What happens to federal revenue-sharing funds? Generally cities spend them in the same way they spend tax funds that they raise themselves. Most revenue-sharing funds go to police and fire protection, education, streets and highways, health, recreation, and general government in roughly the same proportions as state and local governments spend for these same purposes.[8] Revenue sharing does *not* give any more help to fiscally troubled big cities than it does to smaller cities with less-pressing needs. In other words, it does not direct money to where it is needed most.[9] Corpus Christi, Texas, reported spending $100,000 of federal shared revenues on its municipal golf course.[10] Mayors are strong supporters of the program. Former New Orleans Mayor Moon Landrieu, later President Jimmy Carter's Secretary of Housing and Human Development, exclaimed: "General revenue sharing has been the best thing since ice cream!"[11]

Block Grants

Block grant: A federal grant that specifies a general category or purpose within which states and communities may decide on specific projects.

Another approach to cutting federal strings is the **block grant.** Block grants may be used by states and communities for specific projects decided on at the local level within a broad category—for example, community development or law enforcement. Block grants carry many of the requirements and restrictions of ordinary categorical federal grants. However, in the Housing and Community Development Act of 1974, for example, specific public housing projects, urban renewal projects, and community facilities projects were incorporated into a general block-grant program. The federal Department of Housing and Urban Development still supervises community development block grants, but specific projects are supposed to be decided at the local level. Obviously, block grants do *not* give states and communities the same freedom as revenue-sharing money. However, they provide greater flexibility than traditional categorical grants.

The Reagan administration persuaded Congress to consolidate hundreds of categorical-grant programs into nine large block-grant programs: social services; community development; elementary and secondary education; alcohol and drug abuse; mental health; maternal and child health; community services; primary health care; and preventive health care. However, the total amount of federal dollars provided under the block grants was smaller than the total of the categorical programs that were consolidated. Officials in the Reagan administration argued that cities and states could get along with less money, because block grants eliminate the costs of "people processing paper" and allow local officials to use the money for the most urgent needs of their area. Critics of Reagan's approach argued that it was just another way to cut federal spending. Reduced federal funding under block grants forces state and local governments to determine exactly what to cut and frees the Reagan people from this unhappy chore.

CHAPTER SUMMARY

1. The nearly 80,000 state and local governments play a vital role within the American federal union. It is true that the specific delegated powers given to the federal government in the Constitution along with the national supremacy clause ensure national dominance. However, the broad grant of powers *reserved* to the states constitutes substantial authority over the lives of the American citizenry. Finally, powers that would infringe on individual freedoms are *denied* to both the national government and state governments.

2. The states also affect or control congressional representation, elections, and the amendment process to the Constitution.

3. The 1819 case of *McCulloch* v. *Maryland* was important because it expanded the scope and jurisdiction of federal power. Chief Justice John Marshall ruled that Congress may choose the means required to implement its enumerated powers. Of equal importance, Marshall ruled that federal law supersedes state law.

4. The theory of states' rights has had a long history, extending from the Virginia and Kentucky Resolutions to Calhoun's nullification theory and the practice of secession. It was only after World War II that the Supreme Court began to actively limit states' rights through judicial interpretation of the Fourteenth Amendment.

5. Another expansion of federal power occurred under the interstate commerce clause of the Constitution. As the national economy grew, Congress passed legislation to regulate communications, trans-

portation, or commerce that collectively involved "the production and distribution of goods and services for a national market."

6. Federal aid to the states has existed virtually from the start of the republic, an example being the Northwest Ordinance. It was the Sixteenth Amendment that accelerated the shift of financial power to the federal government. Vast sums of tax money could now be spent on defense *and* the general welfare. Federal "financial centralization," at least in certain policy areas, became a reality.

7. The federal grant has become an important policy tool in influencing the actions of state governments. The use of federal taxing and spending powers first gained strength during the Great Depression as a means of aiding the states. Then the programs of the Great Society and subsequent revenue sharing expanded the federal role of support for the states. Today, there are over 500 different federal grant programs.

8. The increase in federal aid to the states allows the national government to (a) structure its goals and priorities within the states, (b) make up for the states' fiscal inadequacies, (c) fund on a progressive tax basis, and (d) provide a uniform public service (such as educational opportunity) throughout all of the states. Conversely, federal aid has (a) constricted state and local choices, (b) involved some cumbersome guidelines, and (c) forced the states into a "bribe and blackmail" syndrome. Further, federal grant programs have suffered from fragmentation and diffuseness and have assumed that state and local officials are less capable judges of priorities than their federal counterparts.

9. Revenue sharing allows federal tax dollars to be sent back to the states with few onerous guidelines. Block grants also provide greater flexibility than the traditional categorical type.

10. Regional rivalries have emerged between states in the Sun Belt and those in the Frost Belt. Sun Belt states have had higher growth rates, largely due to the attraction of new, high-technology industries. However, the Frost Belt's population still has higher levels of income and education. This regional rivalry can be personified in the contrast between the "Yankee" concerned with social welfare and the new "cowboy" class of self-made leaders.

Notes

1. *Texas* v. *White,* 7 Wallace 700 (1869).
2. *McCulloch* v. *Maryland,* 4 Wheaton 316 (1819).
3. *Texas* v. *White.*
4. E.g., *Gitlan* v. *New York,* 286 U. S. 652 (1925); *Near* v. *Minnesota,* 283 U. S. 697 (1931); *Minersville School District* v. *Gobitis,* 310 U. S. 586 (1940).
5. *Brown* v. *Board of Education of Topeka,* 347 U. S. 483 (1954).
6. See Chapter 12, "The Politics of Civil Rights."

7. See Daniel J. Elazer, *The American Partnership: Inter-Governmental Cooperation in Nineteenth Century United States* (Chicago: University of Chicago Press, 1962).
8. Richard P. Nathan et al., *Monitoring Revenue Sharing* (Washington: Brookings Institution, 1975).
9. Richard P. Nathan and Charles F. Adams, Jr., *Revenue Sharing: The Second Round* (Washington: Brookings Institution, 1977).
10. *Washington Post,* June 18, 1973, p. A20.
11. *National Journal,* August 9, 1975, p. 1142.

Close-Up and In-Depth Analyses

Daniel J. Elazar. *American Federalism: A View from the States.* New York: Harper & Row, 1972.

Parris N. Glendeming and Mavis Mann Reeves. *Pragmatic Federalism.* San Francisco: Palisades Publishers, 1971.

Morton Grodzins. *The American System.* Chicago: Rand McNally, 1966.

Michael D. Reagan. *The New Federalism.* New York: Oxford University Press, 1972.

William H. Riker. *Federalism: Origin, Operation, Significance.* Boston: Little, Brown, 1964.

Deil S. Wright. *Understanding Intergovernmental Relations,* 2nd ed. Monterey, Calif.: Brooks/Cole, 1982.

CHAPTER
5

MASS MEDIA: IMAGES
OF AMERICAN POLITICS

Communication is the manipulation of
symbols—words, pictures, expressions.
What people think, feel, and do in
American politics arises out of their
response to these symbols. What is
communicated to us through the mass
media are symbols, not realities. Unless
we ourselves are in the White House
Oval Office, on the floor of Congress, in
the chambers of the Supreme Court, or
on a foreign battlefield, we cannot really
"know" what is happening. We can only
know our political world through the
symbols communicated to us by the
media.

> We can only know our political
> world through the symbols
> communicated to us by
> the media.

Political scientist Murray Edelman
explains: "For most people most of the
time politics is a series of pictures in the
mind, placed there by television news,
newspapers, magazines, and discussions.
The pictures create a moving panorama
taking place in a world the mass public
never quite touches, yet one its
members come to fear and cheer, often
with passion and sometimes with
action.... Politics for most of us is a
passing parade of abstract symbols."[1]

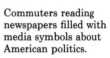

Commuters reading newspapers filled with media symbols about American politics.

THE STRUCTURE OF THE MASS MEDIA

Mass media: All the channels of communication—books, records, movies, newspapers, magazines, radio, and television—that carry messages to the general public.

The **"mass media"** are all the channels of communication that carry messages to the general public.[2] There are seven principal mass media:

- *Books*: About 40,000 books are published each year by 1,500 publishing companies, but only 300 companies publish a majority of these books; most publishers are in New York City.
- *Newspapers*: About 1,800 daily newspapers are published. The ten largest chains of newspapers own nearly 50 percent of these papers. About half of the nation's newspapers subscribe to the Associated Press (AP) to obtain the bulk of their nonlocal news, and about half subscribe to the competing United Press International (UPI).
- *Motion pictures*: Seven major studios dominate film distribution: Columbia, MGM, Warner Brothers, 20th Century Fox, Paramount, United Artists, and Universal. They finance most films and book them into 12,000 local theaters and 4,000 drive-ins throughout the nation.
- *Radio*: About 4,500 AM stations and 2,800 FM stations broadcast daily. There is a wide range of programming formats; the prevailing format is music, news, weather, and sports, with music selected for a specialized audience.
- *Magazines*: About 10,000 magazines are published each year. Most of these are highly specialized monthly publications; others are weekly publications, including the major news magazines—*Time, Newsweek,* and *U. S. News and World Report.* (See Table 5-1.)

Television, the most popular mass medium, can reach us even while waiting in a bus station.

- *Television*: About 700 local television stations are licensed to broadcast by the Federal Communications Commission (FCC). However, the three national television networks (ABC, CBS, and NBC) supply nearly 90 percent of the programming appearing on local stations.
- *Recordings*: About 1,500 companies produce records and tapes. But half a dozen companies—CBS, Capitol, RCA, Motown, ABC, and United Artists—control over half of the market.

Table 5-1. The Most Popular Magazines in the United States

Magazine	Circulation (millions)
1. *TV Guide*	19.9
2. *Reader's Digest*	18.3
3. *National Geographic*	10.0
4. *Family Circle*	8.3
5. *Better Homes and Gardens*	8.0
6. *Woman's Day*	8.0
7. *McCall's*	6.5
8. *Ladies Home Journal*	6.0
9. *National Enquirer*	5.7
10. *Good Housekeeping*	5.2
11. *Playboy*	4.8
12. *Penthouse*	4.5
13. *Redbook*	4.4
14. *Time*	4.3
15. *Star*	3.0
16. *Newsweek*	2.9
17. *Cosmopolitan*	2.7
18. *Sports Illustrated*	2.3
19. *People*	2.3
20. *U. S. News and World Report*	2.1

Source: *The World Almanac and Book of Facts, 1982* (New York: Newspaper Enterprises Association, Inc., 1981).

Of these media of communication, television is the most popular. Over 98 percent of all households own a television set; more than 50 percent own two sets. The average family uses its set more than 40 hours a week. Television is the dominant medium in the United States today (see Figure 5-1 on the next page).

Over 98 percent of all households have a radio, and most automobiles are equipped with one. The average American listens to the radio eighteen hours a week.

About 77 percent of the population reads newspapers. The average American spends about 3½ hours a week reading newspapers.

Motion picture attendance in the United States has declined more than 50 percent since 1960. About 23 million people (a little over 10 percent of the population) will attend a motion picture in a year. About 225 feature pictures are produced in the country each year;

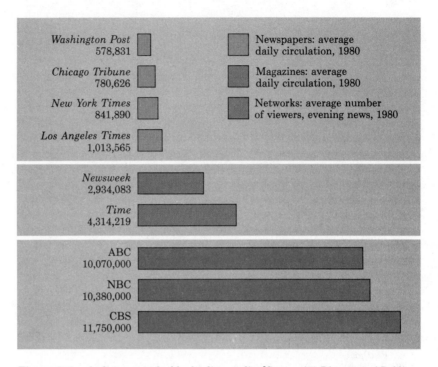

Figure 5-1. Audiences reached by leading media. [Source: *'80 Directory of Publications* (Bala Cynwyd, Pa.: Ayer Press, 1980), and ABC News.]

this is about half the number produced in the 1940s and 1950s.

The average American is exposed to at least two magazines a week and spends about an hour and a half reading them. The nation's most popular magazine is *TV Guide,* followed by *Reader's Digest.*

About half of all the books published in a year are textbooks for the elementary, secondary, and college levels. The growth of book clubs and the emergence of a large paperback market has meant an increase in the number of other books sold. However, the amount of time spent each week by the average American on book reading is infinitesimal compared with the time spent on television viewing.

American television is dominated by three private corporations—the American Broadcasting Company (ABC), CBS, Incorporated, and the National Broadcasting Company (NBC), which is a division of the RCA Corporation. Most of the 700 local television stations are forced to affiliate with one or another of these networks because of the high cost of producing news and entertainment programs. Local stations restrict themselves to local news coverage and then broadcast the network "feeds" of the "Evening News," rebroadcasting it in shorter form as part of their late news program. In addition, each network owns five stations itself, the maximum number under the rules of the Federal Communications Commission (FCC). These network-owned stations are found in the largest "market" cities, and they cover 38 percent of all "TV households" in the nation.[3]

Some media conglomerates own interests in many different channels of communication. Consider, for example, the extensive media holdings of:

- CBS, Incorporated: CBS television network; five television stations; fourteen radio stations; twenty-two magazines; Columbia Records; and publishers, including Holt, Rinehart & Winston and Praeger.
- American Broadcasting Company: ABC television network; five TV stations; six book publishing companies; and various recreational attractions, including Weeki Wachee, Silver Springs, and Wild Waters in Florida.
- National Broadcasting Company: NBC television is a subsidiary of RCA along with five television stations and four publishing companies.
- New York Times Company: *New York Times* plus fourteen other daily newspapers, as well as radio and television stations.
- Time, Incorporated: *Time, Sports Illustrated, Fortune,* and *People* magazines; five television stations; Home Box Office; the publisher Little, Brown & Company; and Book-of-the-Month Club, Incorporated.
- Washington Post Company: *Washington Post, Newsweek,* and five television stations.

Prime time (8:00 P.M. to 11:00 P.M.) is the most important time in television, and it is dominated by the three networks. Potentially, all 80 million homes in America with TV sets (98 percent of all homes) could tune in, and these homes house over 200 million people. The networks broadcast mostly action and adventure series (30 percent), situation comedies (25 percent) and movies (16 percent) on prime time. Specials and mini-series are becoming more popular. The only regular "live" programs on prime time are sports events, such as ABC's *NFL Monday Night Football.* Most other programs are filmed or videotaped.

Local stations do the actual broadcasting. Almost all stations are affiliated with one of the networks. The stations are paid by the networks to carry network prime-time shows. Networks do not make payments to stations to carry news, sports, or late-night programs. However, the networks allow a certain number of advertising slots in those programs to be filled by local stations.

Public Opinion about Television

Public reliance on television for both news and entertainment has remained very high over the past twenty years. Surveys disclose that on an average day, the average American watches television for about three hours.

Table A.   Average Time Spent Per Day Watching Television

1961	1963	1967	1971	1974	1976	1978	1980
2:17	2:34	2:41	2:50	3:02	2:53	3:08	2:55

Source: *Public Opinion,* October/November 1981.

Further, in a ranking of the "honesty and ethical standards" of various professions, TV reporters and commentators rank relatively high.

Table B.   Public Ranking of "Honesty and Ethical Standards" for Various Professions

Profession	Percent saying "very high" or "high"
Clergymen	63%
Druggists, pharmacists	59
Dentists	52
Medical doctors	50
Engineers	48
College teachers	45
Policemen	44
Bankers	39
TV reporters, commentators	**36**
Journalists	32
Newspaper reporters	30
Funeral directors	30
Lawyers	25
Stockbrokers	21
Senators	19
Business executives	19
Building contractors	19
Congressmen	20
Local political officeholders	14
Realtors	14
Labor union leaders	14
State political officeholders	12
Insurance salesmen	11
Advertising practitioners	9
Car salesmen	6

Source: *The Gallup Opinion Index,* September 1981.

Most people report getting most of their news from television. And television news is found more believable than that of any other medium. (See two accompanying figures.) But

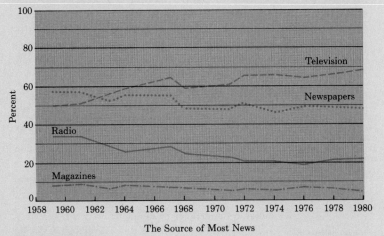

The Source of Most News

Question: I'd like to ask you where you usually get most of your news about what's going on in the world today—from the newspapers or radio or magazines or talking to people or where? (Note: Some respondents gave more than one answer.) Source: Surveys by the Roper Organization for the Television Information Office, latest that of November 1978. From *Public Opinion*, August/September, 1979.

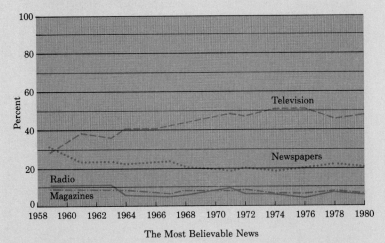

The Most Believable News

Question: If you got conflicting or different reports of the same news story from radio, television, the magazines, and the newspapers, which of the four versions would you be most inclined to believe—the one on radio or television or magazines, or newspapers? Source: Surveys by the Roper Organization for the Television Information Office, latest that of November 1978. From *Public Opinion*, August/September, 1979.

(continued)

(continued)

programming is not so favorably regarded. There has been an increase in the number of people saying that television presents "too much violence," "programs that insult your intelligence," and "too much sex." Most people agree with the statement that television and other media in the United States reflect permissive and immoral values that are bad for the country (see figure).

Question: A number of criticisms and suggestions are also being made these days. Will you tell me for each of the following whether you mostly agree or mostly disagree with each one? Let's start with (Read first statement on list). Do you mostly agree or mostly disagree with this? (Record one answer below and continue with list).... Television and other media in this country reflect a permissive and immoral set of values which are bad for the country.

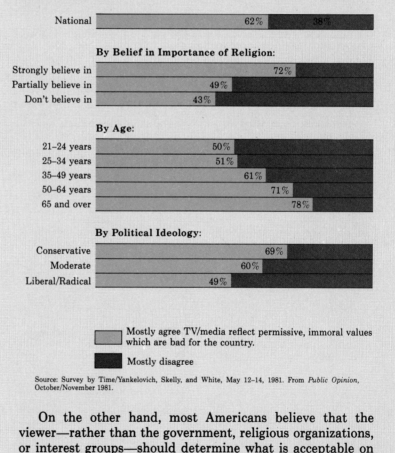

Source: Survey by Time/Yankelovich, Skelly, and White, May 12–14, 1981. From *Public Opinion*, October/November 1981.

On the other hand, most Americans believe that the viewer—rather than the government, religious organizations, or interest groups—should determine what is acceptable on television. Table C shows responses to the question "Television offers a wide variety of programming, not all of which is acceptable to everyone. Who do you think should have the primary responsibility to determine what is acceptable?"

Table C.   Public Identification of the Responsibility for Acceptable TV Programming

Viewer	67%
Network/station	24
Government	3
Religion	2
Advertisers	2
Interest groups	2

Source: *Public Opinion*, October/November 1981.

HARD FLUFF: NEWS AS ENTERTAINMENT

The producer of *60 Minutes,* Don Hewitt, once gave an excellent explanation of why the news must entertain its audience:

> When an idea [for news] comes in, my first reaction is always "Does anybody care? Is anyone gonna watch this?" It's not important in TV what you tell people. If you bombard them with a lot of facts in a dull fashion just to discharge your public duty, you perform no service at all. If you can entertain people, you can keep them close to the show and they'll come back next week. I don't want to broadcast in a vacuum.[4]

Dan Rather (right), Tom Brokaw (next), and others from news media assemble for a press conference to gather "entertaining" facts.

It is important to all three networks that their evening news program attract as large an audience as possible. It is important not only because a large audience means that they can sell higher-priced commercial time on the news itself but also because they know that many American families leave their TV dial untouched after the news. A popular news show will promote audiences for later entertainment shows.

The news must entertain. It must be "hyped" to capture and hold audience attention with drama, action, conflict, violence, or disaster.

Like any good entertainment show, a news show must have recognizable characters doing something interesting, who are involved in struggles and conflicts with important prizes at stake. There must be a dramatic story line, but one that can be introduced, developed, and concluded in less than two minutes. The news must be made to appear timely, and it must be shown to affect us directly.

"Hard fluff" is entertainment masquerading as news. The term refers to a broadcast news story that has all the drama, suspense, action, and sensationalism of a successful entertainment show. A story must have the necessary "fluff"—sex, corruption, violence, tragedy, and the like—to make it interesting. And yet it must be "hard"—it cannot be entirely fiction but must refer to something that occurred in the real world.

"Hard fluff" is entertainment masquerading as news.

The need to make the news entertaining results in some interesting criteria for the selection of "news."

1. Violence is more "newsworthy" than nonviolence. War, crime, conflict, and disasters excite audiences. Violent behavior is remembered better than nonviolent behavior. The murder and suicide of 900 Americans in Jonestown, Guyana, in 1978 was the most remembered story of that year, with 98 percent of the Gallup Poll respondents saying that they knew about the event—a figure matched only by the Japanese attack on Pearl Harbor in 1941 and the dropping of atomic bombs on Japan in 1945.[5]

2. The "news" should have a direct impact on the lives of viewers. Millions of starving people in central Africa will not get as much coverage as a hotel fire in Las Vegas. Dramatic film of starving African children may help get the story on the air; but film of fire victims leaping to their deaths from high buildings is better. After all, nearly everyone in the United States has stayed in a hotel at one time or another, but very few have gone to Africa.

3. Stories about celebrities are more "newsworthy" than stories about people unfamiliar to the audience. Scandal, sex, accidents, personal grief, and even the daily habits of prominent and famous people make "news." Newscasters themselves are hired primarily for person-

The Ayatollah Khomeini answers questions about his foreign policy.

ality, rather than journalistic skill. And the emphasis on personality extends to interpretation of the news. Personalities are substituted for explanation. For example, foreign policy is explained as a consequence of Alexander Haig, the Ayatollah Khomeini, or Anwar Sadat.

4. "News" should be timely and novel. This means only that the "news" should not have been reported in the previous 24 hours. Most of the evening news on all three networks is composed of "preplanned" stories—stories about events or situations that are not spontaneous. However, insofar as possible these preplanned stories must be made to appear novel and timely.

5. "News" must be an event, rather than a trend or an idea. It must be an event that can be filmed and seen and heard. Even if inflation is the single most important problem confronting Americans, according to national surveys, this topic will be pushed aside in favor of coverage of presidential visits, ceremonial bill signings, strikes, protests, accidents, or fires for which action film is available.

When inflation is covered at all, it will be through a brief announcement of newly released inflation figures or some interviews with shoppers complaining of high prices. The news chiefs are not trying to hide inflation; the problem is that inflation is not an event that produces good film.

6. Every "news" story should have a dramatic quality—a clear conflict with identifiable antagonists and a real prize at stake. The "news" cannot report ideas in the abstract. Stories work better on television when there are clear antagonists, especially when they are physically different. It is best when confrontation occurs between men and women, blacks and whites, young and old, rich and poor. Ideal antagonists will shout, cry, shake fists, or otherwise show intense emotions. There should be "good guys" and "bad guys," and either side can be shown as winning.

7. Finally, a "news" story must be short. The entire drama must be introduced, played out, and summarized in less than two minutes. Anything longer is a "documentary."[6]

WHAT'S IN TV NEWS?

The relationship between television news and government can be demonstrated by examining who and what is reported. As Table 5-2 indicates, the largest number of television news stories is about government, including conflicts, ceremonies, and personnel changes. The second most frequent news stories are those about crime, scandal, or corruption. Many of these stories are also about government officials. The third most frequent news stories are those about disasters, both actual and imagined. The fourth most frequent news stories involve protests, including strikes. Another fairly common type of news story involves some innovation or tradition—the first women at West Point, the last edition of a bankrupt newspaper, the first black four-star general, and the like.

Who are the "actors" in the news? Again, it turns out that most of the people portrayed as doing something in the news are government officials—the president, members of Congress, and other federal officials, including Supreme Court justices. Most of the news figures are national officials, but state and local officials—governors and mayors of large cities—get some exposure. The next largest category of person in the news is the accused criminal. Other frequent actors in the news are business leaders, labor union officials, and civil rights leaders.

The vast majority of those in the news (over 80 percent) are public officials and well-known celebrities. "Unknowns" receive far less attention. These include victims of crimes or disasters, individual strikers or protesters, "typical" voters, or respondents to surveys.

Table 5-2. Who and What Are in TV News

Type of item	Percentage of TV news stories
Activities	
Government	**35%**
Conflicts	17
Decisions, ceremonies	12
Personnel changes	6
Nongovernment	**65%**
Crimes, scandal, corruption	28
Disasters	14
Protests, strikes	10
Innovation and tradition	8
Other	5
Persons	
Government	**66%**
President	17
Members of Congress	16
All other federal officials (including cabinet and Supreme Court)	22
State and local officials	11
Nongovernment	**34%**
Accused criminals	10
Business, labor leaders	7
Civil rights leaders	4
Other known figures	13

Source: Derived from figures provided in Herbert J. Gans, *Deciding What's News* (New York: Random House, 1979), Chapter 1.

BIAS IN TV NEWS

Bias in the news originates from four major sources: (1) the need to "hype" the news to hold audience attention; (2) the production requirements that force executives and producers to choose "news" well in advance of broadcasting; (3) the geographic focus on the government in Washington; and (4) the liberal values of the newsmakers themselves.

There is very little diversity in television news. The three networks—ABC, CBS, and NBC—present nearly identical news "packages" each evening. They are "rivals in conformity."[7] In newspapers and magazines, by contrast, conventionally "liberal" and "conservative" views can be found—for example, in the liberal *New York Times* and the conservative *Wall Street Journal,* in *Newsweek* and *U. S. News and World Report,* and in *Harper's* and the *National Review.* But a conventional liberal position is presented on all three television networks. Moreover, the same stories, and even the same "angle" on each story, are usually found. **"Pack journalism"** refers to the tendency of reporters and news organizations to adopt the same ideas of what is news and how it should be presented.

Pack journalism: The tendency of reporters and news organizations to adopt the same approach to news presentations.

"Hype"

The principal source of bias in the news is not the liberal politics of the newsmakers but rather the need to "hype" the news—to capture and hold audience attention with drama, action, and confrontation. Because they are presented in the early evening, the news programs determine the evening-long network viewing patterns for some viewers. Topics are *not* selected for "news" because of their social or political significance. Instead, the need to attract large audiences biases the news toward violence, conflict, confrontation, scandal, sex, people the audience can identify with, and the personal problems of "celebrities."

> The principal source of bias in the news is not the liberal politics of the newsmakers but rather the need to "hype" the news.

Production Requirements

A second major source of bias in the news is the technological requirement that many decisions be made well in advance of broadcast time. It is impossible to put any half-hour television show together in twelve hours. News executives and producers must make some of their decisions weeks and months in advance of scheduled broadcasts. Network television crews must be sent on location to obtain videotapes, which later must be transported, processed, and edited. A script must be written, with a lead-in, a narration, and a recapitula-

"We're at the home of Jim and Mindy Marks, who are about to discover that their utility bill has gone sky-high. Let's watch."
(Drawing by Maslin. © 1980 *The New Yorker*, Inc.)

tion. The order of stories must be decided as well as the amount of time to be given to each of them. All of these tasks require advance decision making.

All news can be categorized as either "spontaneous" or "preplanned." Spontaneous news includes fires, floods, accidents, shootings, and the like. These events occur the day of the news broadcast and are not planned by the medium itself or by others for the medium. In contrast, preplanned events may occur days, weeks, or months before the broadcast. Or they may be planned to occur by the media or by others for media coverage on that day. The most common preplanned events are congressional hearings and investigations, meetings of government leaders, and staged press conferences. These are usually coordinated by government press agents and network producers. Ideally the press agents and producers try to predict "slow" news days to schedule their events. They are not always successful. If the Mount St. Helens volcano blows its top on the day the networks planned to cover a congressional hearing (and if film of the volcano is available), then the spontaneous event may push the preplanned event off the newscast.

In television news, almost 70 percent of all stories are preplanned. One careful study of stories presented on ABC, NBC, and CBS weekday evening newscasts in 1978 presented the following breakdown of stories:[8]

- commentary on preplanned events, 38.1 percent of news time
- preplanned events, 31.8 percent
- spontaneous events, 19.8 percent
- comment on spontaneous events, 10.3 percent

The planning requirement of television news helps create the "media event"—an activity arranged primarily for media coverage. It is not only the press agents, professional public-relations people, spokespersons, and politicians who benefit from media events. It is also the network executives and producers who are searching for dramatic, sensational, or bizarre activities to videotape and who appreciate notification well in advance of these activities so they can assign camera crews and plan broadcasting time.

Another production requirement that shapes television news is the short time that can be allocated to each story. The average television news story is sixty seconds. Ninety seconds or two minutes is considered "heavy" coverage. Therefore, nothing really complex can be broadcast on television news. Complex issues must either be simplified and dramatized or dropped. Even "in-depth" special segments of network news run only 2½ or 3 minutes, and they may cover public issues as broad as gun control, abortion, campaign financing, the Middle East, or the arms race.

Geographical Bias

A third major source of bias is the overrepresentation of Washington, New York, and California in the news. Half of the national network news focuses on Washington. Two-thirds of the news comes from three places—Washington, New York, and California.[9] Moreover, the Washington emphasis is even worse when we consider that many stories originating elsewhere are "reaction stories" that focus on how people or communities will adjust or react to programs or policies decided upon in Washington. News organizations have a bias toward government. Government leaders and government agencies, especially in Washington, are the prime "actors" in television news.[10] Private people and organizations—large corporations and interest groups, as well as individuals, families, and communities—are shown as the "acted upon" in news stories. Television news presents a narrative in which government is the dominant subject. Even foreign news generally relates to government activities, including other countries' reactions to what happens in Washington.

The major news organizations, including the television networks, establish "beats" at various centers of government in Washington—the White House, Congress, the State Department, the Supreme Court, and so on. But even the large networks cannot afford to place full teams of reporters and camera crews all over the country. The networks place permanent crews in Washington, New York, Chicago, and Los Angeles. They may send additional crews on special assignment to other locations if news is expected. Otherwise, the networks can only rely on local stations to forward videotape to them.

Liberal Values of Newsmakers

Finally, the liberal bias of the news originates in the values of the newsmakers themselves. Newsmakers may be sincere when they insist that they are impartial, objective, and unbiased, because, in their world of reporting and writing in Washington and New York, the liberal point of view is so widely held. However, network news and even network entertainment programs are designed to communicate liberal values: a concern for social reform, an interest in the problems of the poor and the minorities, a distrust of big business, a concern for the environment and the quality of life, and a willingness to use governmental power to "do good."

Newsmakers must rely on their own values in making decisions about what will be "news." They must choose, from among an almost infinite number of stories in the real world, what stories will be presented. Even as broadcast time approaches, hundreds of stories and hundreds of hours of film and videotape are available for selection as "news." Most of these stories must be rejected; there is simply not enough time to report all the news. It would be impossible for editors' own values *not* to affect these decisions.

> Newsmakers must rely on their own values in making decisions about what will be "news."

The owners (stockholders) of the major corporations that control the television networks, news services, and major newspaper chains usually share the moderate conservatism and Republicanism of the big business community; but the executives, producers, directors, reporters, and other media professionals are clearly "left-leaning" and Democratic in their political views. Generally, newsmakers in larger, more prestigious organizations, including the television networks, are more "liberal" in their social, cultural, and political values than those in smaller, regional organizations, including individual television stations.

One study of top news executives reported that over two-thirds came from upper-middle-class families with fathers in professional or managerial jobs.[11] Fewer than 10 percent of the top newsmakers surveyed were women. Over three-quarters were college graduates. These newsmakers were usually either Democrats or liberal independents. Very few were Republicans. (As Table 5-3 indicates, the survey found 44 percent to be Democrats, 45 percent to be independents, and 9 percent to be Republicans. At the time of the survey, 40 percent of the general population reported itself as Democratic, 34 percent as independent, and 23 percent as Republican. Moreover,

**Table 5-3. Prominent News Executives:
Social and Political Characteristics**

Characteristic	Percentage of news executives
Social class	
Father professional or managerial	66%
Sex	
Male	91
Education	
College graduate	75
Party	
Independent	45
Democratic	44
Republican	9
Other	3
Ideology	
Left-leaning	63
Middle-of-the-road	27
Right-leaning	10

Source: Derived from data in John Johnstone et al., *The Newspeople* (Urbana: University of Illinois Press, 1976), pp. 225–226.

63 percent of these executives classified themselves as "left-leaning," in contrast to 10 percent who were "right-leaning" and 27 percent who were "middle-of-the-road."

The political scientist Doris A. Graber writes: "The political orientations of the personnel frequently are reflected in the overall tone of the media. Economic and social liberalism prevails, as does a preference for an internationalist foreign policy, caution about military intervention, and some suspicion of the ethics of established large institutions, particularly the government." However, she adds that during general election campaigns the media try to treat major-party candidates evenly in "anticipation of scrutiny and criticism in this area."[12]

The Washington Press Corps

The media are as much a part of the government of the United States as the president, Congress, or the Supreme Court. They are a vital part of the governmental process that they are supposed to be reporting. Stories involving Washington directly or reporting reactions from across the country to something occurring in Washington make up 80 percent of the lead items on network television news and nearly half of the front-page lead items in newspapers.

Not only do the masses of people learn about Washington from the media, but most government officials also learn about Washington from reading the *Washington Post*, the *New York Times*, or the *Wall Street Journal*. Former Secretary Joseph A. Califano, Jr., of the Department of Health, Education, and Welfare, was quoted as saying: "Most Congressmen never read even a partial text of a presidential message. They read about it in the *Washington Post*."[13] The press cannot tell people what to think, but it certainly tells them what to think about.*

The Washington press corps is the working mechanism of media involvement in government. It is composed of over 3,000 officially accredited reporters from television, newspapers, wire services, and magazines. Overall media policies and major themes in the news are determined by network executives and producers and newspaper and magazine editors and executives. But day-to-day decisions must be made by reporters on the Washington scene.

Yet most reporters follow the lead of the *New York Times* and the *Washington Post*—even television reporters. Once either of these two newspapers gives front-page attention to a story, the instinct for "pack journalism" compels the television networks, other newspapers, and the news magazines to cover the same story, whether they agree that it is really newsworthy or not. As one Washington reporter explained: "You may spend half of your week saying that a story [played up by the *Times* or the *Post*] is bull, but still have to write about it." The power of the *New York Times* and the *Washington Post* is not that many people across the nation read these papers, but rather that the people who count in official Washington read them and react to them. In this way, news breeds news, and the Washington press corps plays follow the leader.

Washington reporters rate themselves highly satisfied in their work: 40 percent are "very satisfied," 44 percent are "satisfied," 14 percent are "somewhat dissatisfied," and 2 percent are "very dissatisfied." However, there are frequent complaints:

> I have a hell of a fight with [my editor] over the "trivialization" of news. Editors are getting fed up with serious institutional problems, with articles on what government should and shouldn't do. It took me a week to get an article in the paper on government reorganization, then [the editor] attacked it as "another story of government glop."

> Editors feel they aren't doing their thing if they don't screw around with your copy.

> We're being used by publicity seeking members of Congress.

> Reporters are suspicious of bureaucrats; we consider them always ready to hide behind regulations, unending paper-shufflers. [Quotations from Stephen Hess, *The Washington Reporters* (Washington, D. C.: Brookings Institution, 1981), p. 1. Reprinted by permission.]

There is a recognized pecking order among reporters. In recent years television reporters have captured the attention of politicians seeking to get their faces on the evening news. Therefore, network reporters and camera crews are given preference in "media events" and "photo opportunities." Only a few years ago, the senior writers for the *New York Times* or the *Washington Post* could complain loudly and effectively

(continued)

Copyright, 1978, G. B. Trudeau. Reprinted with permission of Universal Press Syndicate. All rights reserved.

(continued)

whenever a microphone or camera got in their way. But now the print reporters must step aside as the camera crews push by with a shouted "coming through." Some tension exists between print and electronic journalists; the senior print journalists believe their work is more insightful, intellectual, and important than "picture-taking." Most Washington reporters believe that, if a politician wants to be seen by a large number of people, then television is the way to do it. But if politicians are trying to influence other politicians—to win a hearing for their own program or create an obstacle for someone else's—then they should go to the journalists and columnists.

At the top of the pecking order are the network television reporters, the syndicated columnists, reporters for the three major weekly news magazines, and reporters for the *Washington Post,* the *New York Times,* and the *Wall Street Journal.* Their influence is primarily a product of the organizations they represent. But they can improve their influence by personally acquiring greater access to information. Simply "knowing people," preferably on a first-name basis, is the key to success in Washington for reporters as well as everyone else. Occasionally it is suggested that reporters should be transferred out of Washington for a while, back into the "real America," in order to improve their perspective. But there is always the same objection: Washington contacts are vital to the job, so it does not make sense to transfer experienced reporters.

Wire-service reporters for the Associated Press and United Press International and reporters for newspapers outside of Washington are lower in the press corps pecking order. They seldom get exclusive interviews with national figures. They are herded in large numbers to and from press conferences and media events. They are hopeful of a guest appearance on *Meet the Press* or *Washington Week in Review* in order to improve their visibility in Washington. They attend cocktail parties to try to ferret out pieces of information not already reported by others.

The Washington press corps pecking order is also determined by "beats." Beats are regular assignments given to reporters. Good assignments include the White House beat, the Congressional beat, the State Department beat, and the Pentagon beat. Lesser beats include economics, law and the Supreme Court, science, the regulatory agencies, and the domestic departments (agriculture, labor, energy, and so on).

The most envied reporters are those who are *not* given any beat—those who are free to cover any story anywhere in Washington.

The Washington press corps is composed mainly of liberal, well-educated, white males from Eastern elite colleges and universities. Only 20 percent of the Washington press corps is female, and women reporters tend to be assigned to less prestigious beats. Most Washington reporters are in their thirties or forties. Many move up later in their own news organization to editor or bureau chief. Others move into higher-paying jobs in advertising and public relations. Almost all are college graduates, and one-third have an advanced degree. When Washington reporters themselves were asked if there is political bias in the Washington press corps, 51 percent agreed and 49 percent disagreed. Of those who agreed that there is bias, 96 percent described the bias as "liberal." When reporters were asked to describe their own politics, 42 percent said "liberal," 39 percent said "middle-of-the-road," and 19 percent said "conservative."

*Both television and newspaper reporters like to be referred to as "the press" rather than "the media." Arthur Ochs Sulzberger, owner and publisher of the *New York Times,* was once quoted as having said: "Let me pass along a tip on how to detect bias in any speeches on this subject: If he talks about 'the press' he's for us." In this text, we have chosen to use the term *media* not out of bias, we hope, but instead because *the media* connotes television and radio, whereas *the press* connotes only print journalism. See Stephen Hess, *The Washington Reporters* (Washington, D. C.: Brookings Institution, 1981), p. 2.

SOFT FLUFF: ENTERTAINMENT AS SOCIALIZATION

Prime-time entertainment programming suggests to Americans how they ought to live and what values they ought to hold. **Socialization**—the learning, accepting, and approving of customs, values, and life-styles—is an important function of the mass media. Network television entertainment is the most widely shared experience in the country. America's favorite TV shows average over 25 million viewers (see Table 5-4 on the next page). This is two-and-one-half times the average audience for network news. The network executives who decide what will be shown as entertainment have a tremendous impact on the values, aspirations, and life-styles of Americans.

Socialization: The learning, accepting, and approving of customs, values, and life-styles.

Prime-time entertainment programming suggests to Americans how they ought to live and what values they ought to hold.

Table 5-4. America's Favorite Television Programs of 1981

Program	Average number of households viewing (millions)
1. *Dallas*	34.9
2. *60 Minutes*	28.3
3. *Dukes of Hazzard*	26.7
4. *Love Boat*	25.7
5. *Alice*	25.6
6. *One Day at a Time*	25.2
7. *The Jeffersons*	25.2
8. *Happy Days*	24.4
9. *Archie Bunker's Place*	24.2
10. *Three's Company*	23.3
11. *Laverne and Shirley*	23.0
12. *NBC Tuesday Night Movie*	22.6
13. *Too Close for Comfort*	22.1
14. *Little House on the Prairie*	22.1
15. *M*A*S*H*	22.0
16. *Fantasy Island*	21.8
17. *Diff'rent Strokes*	19.8
18. *NFL Monday Night Football*	19.7
Total TV households	77.8

Source: A. C. Nielsen, as reported in *The World Almanac 1982* (New York: Newspaper Enterprises Association, Inc., 1981), p. 429.

Throughout the 1970s no one had a more direct effect on the themes of television entertainment than Fred Silverman. Silverman was vice-president for programming at CBS-TV from 1970 to 1975, president of entertainment for ABC-TV from 1975 to 1978, and president of NBC-TV from 1978 to 1981. It was Silverman who championed liberal programming with *M*A*S*H* (antiwar), *All in the Family* (antiracist), and later *Roots* (black experience). He favored the producer Norman Lear, whose work—*All in the Family, Maude, The Jeffersons, One Day at a Time,* and *Mary Hartman, Mary Hartman*—emphasized different and often controversial life-styles. When Silverman moved to ABC, he boldly predicted that he would make a lackluster network into number one in viewing audience. He did just that. It was Silverman, more than anyone else, who introduced sex-oriented shows to prime-time television with *Charlie's Angels* and *Three's Company*. He also went after younger audiences—*Happy Days* and *Laverne and Shirley*—with the notion that children in the family really control the TV dial. Silverman was never accused of overestimating the intelligence of TV audiences.

When he moved to NBC, Silverman faced the problem of beating his own program lineups on CBS and ABC. By 1978, NBC had dropped to third in the audience ratings. Its biggest success was *The*

American children receive much of their socialization from television entertainment and advertising.

Tonight Show, and the star of that show, Johnny Carson, was demanding a reduction in his workload and threatening to move to another network. Silverman held on to Carson. He made numerous changes in program lineups to try to restore NBC audience ratings. But he failed. He spent millions on poor shows such as *Supertrain,* and in 1981 NBC was still in the network cellar. It lost a chance to televise the Moscow Olympics when the United States boycotted the games. Its only long-run, top-ten show, *Little House on the Prairie,* predated Silverman's tenure and emphasized traditional family values. When a new chairman, Thornton Bradshaw, took over the reins of NBC's parent company, RCA, Silverman was encouraged to resign. His replacement was Grant Tinker.

Tinker had founded MTM Enterprises with his former wife, Mary Tyler Moore. He had produced shows generally considered superior to those of Silverman: *The Mary Tyler Moore Show, Phyllis, Rhoda,* and *Lou Grant.* These shows emphasized feminism, liberalism, and crusading journalism.

Silverman, Tinker, and other top network executives and producers are generally "coast oriented" in their values and life-styles; that is, they reflect popular culture in New York and California. Typical themes include tolerance toward sexual relations, including interracial affairs and homosexuality, and toward divorce and feminism. Network executives and producers are genuinely perplexed when it is charged that their programming does not reflect the values of a majority of Americans. It is noteworthy that the few shows that reflect traditional American values (family, work, and community) are placed by these programmers in a historical setting (*Little House on the Prairie*—1890s; *The Waltons*—1930s; and even *Happy Days*— early 1960s). The implied message is that these values are quaint and interesting as history but not relevant today.

"We live in terms of the stories we tell—stories about what things exist, stories about how things work, and stories about what to do. . . . Increasingly, media-cultivated facts and values become standards by which we judge."[14] Much of our learning is subconscious. We learn how New York cab drivers live from *Taxi,* how Texas oil families live from *Dallas,* how waitresses live from *Alice,* and so on. If these televised images are inaccurate, we end up with wrong impressions of American life. If television shows emphasize sex and violence, we come to believe that there is more sex and violence in America than is actually the case.

"Increasingly, media-cultivated facts and values become standards by which we judge."

Occasionally, voices are raised against sex and violence on prime-time television. In 1981, fundamentalist religious groups threatened to boycott the products of companies that advertised on shows that included sex, violence, or profanity. The networks promptly labeled the proposed boycott an infringement of their freedom of the press. But the advertisers listened. Proctor and Gamble, the nation's largest single advertiser, announced that it would withdraw its ads from shows with "gratuitous sex, violence, and profanity." Religious groups claimed a temporary victory and dropped their proposed boycott. Network television may "clean up its act" for a season, but in the long run it can be expected to broadcast whatever it believes will attract viewing audiences.

For millions of Americans, television is a way of keeping in touch with their environment. Both entertainment and advertising provide model ways of life. People are shown products, services, and lifestyles that they are expected to desire and imitate. By creating these desires and expectations, the media help to define how Americans should live.

Selective perception: The "screening-out" of information with which one disagrees; specifically, the tendency of TV viewers to hear and see only those portions of news and entertainment programs that fit in with their own values and beliefs.

SELECTIVE PERCEPTION: DEFENDING AGAINST THE MEDIA

The viewer's psychological mechanism of **"selective perception"** helps to defend against bias in news and entertainment programming. Selective perception means mentally screening out information or images with which one disagrees. It causes people to tend to see and hear only what they want to see and hear. Selective perception reduces the impact of television bias on viewer attitudes and behavior.

Consider the example of the enormously popular television show *All in the Family*. Its producer, Norman Lear, and the leadership of CBS believed that the crude, bumbling, working-class, conservative, superpatriotic, racist Archie Bunker would be an effective tool against prejudice. Bigotry would be made to appear ridiculous; Archie would always end up suffering some defeat because of his bigotry; and the masses would be instructed in liberal, reformist values. But evidence soon developed that many viewers applauded Archie's bigotry, believing he was "telling it like it is."[15] They missed the satire altogether. Sixty percent of the viewers liked or admired the bigoted Archie more than his liberal son-in-law, Mike. Vidmar and Rokeach's study indicated that highly prejudiced people enjoyed and watched the show more than less-prejudiced people; and few people believed that Archie was being "made fun of." When these trends in public opinion became apparent, the show was sharply attacked by the *New York Times*.[16] But by that time *All in the Family* had the number-one rating on television. CBS optimistically predicted that the humor of the program would eventually help break down bigotry.[17] But it seems clear that the network vastly underestimated "selective perception."

The networks' concentration on scandal, abuse, and corruption in government has not always produced the desired liberal, reformist notions in the minds of the masses of viewers. Contrary to the expectations of network executives, their focus on governmental scandals—Watergate, illicit activities by the Central Intelligence Agency, abuses by the Federal Bureau of Investigation, congressional sex scandals, and power struggles between Congress and the executive branch—has produced feelings of general political distrust and cynicism toward government and "the system." These feelings have been labeled **"television malaise"**—a combination of social distrust, political cynicism, feelings of powerlessness, and disaffection from parties and politics that seems to stem from television's emphasis on the negative aspects of American life.[18]

Network executives do not *intend* to create "television malaise" among the masses. But scandal, sex, abuse of power, and corruption attract large audiences and increase ratings. "Bad" news is placed up front in the telecast, usually with some dramatic visual aids. Negative television journalism "is concerned with what is *wrong* with our governmental system, our leaders, our prisons, schools, roads, automobiles, race relations, traffic systems, pollution laws, every aspect of our society. In Europe, there is much less emphasis on exposing what is wrong, much more satisfaction with the status quo."[19]

Television malaise:
A combination of distrust, cynicism, feelings of powerlessness, and disaffection from parties and politics that seems to stem from television's emphasis on the negative aspects of American life.

THE ECONOMICS OF TELEVISION

To understand American television, we must remember that networks and stations "sell" audiences to advertisers, who recover their costs when they sell their products to the audiences. This means that networks and stations must attract audiences with news, sports, and entertainment. "Economic pressures are even more potent than political pressures in molding the news and entertainment which media produce."[20]

> "Economic pressures are even more potent than political pressures in molding the news and entertainment which media produce."

Independent rating services, such as the Nielsen ratings, provide the most accurate estimates of viewing audiences for each network show. A popular "sitcom" (situation comedy) may be estimated to average 16.5 million viewers; *NFL Monday Night Football* may be estimated to reach 14.5 million viewers; and *CBS Evening News with Dan Rather* may be estimated to average 10 million viewers. The television networks use figures such as these to sell commercial advertising time on each show. A thirty-second spot commercial on a popular sitcom may cost $100,000. This would be the cost of the time on the air only and would not include the cost of producing the commercial itself. If the sitcom regularly attracted 16.5 million viewers, the advertisers might be told that their cost of advertising one thirty-second spot would be $6 per thousand viewers, or $99,000. Thus, a show with only 14.5 million viewers at the same rate would bring the networks only about $88,000. So the networks' income and profits are directly tied to their ratings.

Network broadcasting is a very profitable business. The networks' return on invested capital is usually well above 20 percent per year, a figure matched by few other industries. Each half-hour of commercial broadcasting carries at least twelve thirty-second commercials—that is, a minimum of six minutes of commercials for twenty-four minutes of programming. A popular prime-time show, then, may bring the network over a million dollars in gross advertising revenue.

It is true, of course, that program production costs are high. Production costs fall into two basic categories: (1) "above-the-line" costs, covering writing, directing, acting, and producing; and (2) "below-the-line" costs, including the use of studio facilities, location, equipment, editing and processing tape, and administrative overhead. Because "below-the-line" costs are difficult to attribute to any one show, it is hard to estimate the total costs of a particular program. But costs of $300,000 to $500,000 for a popular, prime-time, half-hour show would not be unusual.

Reruns reduce costs and increase profits for the networks. Today, most prime-time series produce thirteen to twenty-four shows each season, which makes it possible for each episode to be run twice a year. In theory, this cuts production costs in half. Old prime-time shows can be shown again in the daytime. Time on daytime TV is sold for less than half of the cost of prime-time, but network programming costs are minimal.

Today, the networks themselves do not create or produce very many entertainment shows. They produce primarily news, sports, and documentaries while purchasing entertainment series from independent production companies. For example, MTM Productions (Mary Tyler Moore) has sold a number of prime-time shows to NBC (the original *Mary Tyler Moore Show, Rhoda, Phyllis, Lou Grant,* and others). These independent producers employ the writers, directors, actors, and technical personnel. They may produce a "pilot" program and attempt to sell a series to a network based on it. Or they may produce a special "television feature film" to be shown on the *Movie of the Week* or the *Tuesday Night Movie.* If the initial ratings are good, a series will be developed. Financial relations between independent producers and the networks are very complicated. The producers must use network studios and facilities to produce shows that the networks may or may not purchase. So it is difficult to view the producers as truly independent.

In contrast, there are a very few "syndicated" shows, which are sold by producers directly to stations across the country, bypassing the networks altogether. The most successful of these shows, over the years, have been *The Lawrence Welk Show* and *Hee Haw.*

The networks must also pay their affiliated stations across the country a fee to use their local broadcasting facilities, and the networks must pay the American Telephone and Telegraph Company (AT&T) a small fee to use its cable and satellite relay system.

The cost of making the commercial itself is borne by the advertiser. Well-produced commercials can cost several hundred thousand dollars or even more if stars appear in them. Commercials are usually made by advertising agencies, which develop a theme and produce a series of TV commercials and related print advertisements. The agencies also determine when to show the commercials (matching the type of audience likely to watch a particular program with the type of person likely to buy the product). Advertising agencies usually charge their clients a 15 percent commission, based on the cost of producing and broadcasting the commercials.

Edward Jay Epstein writes in his study of network television, *News from Nowhere*: "Before network news can be properly analyzed as a journalistic enterprise, it is necessary to understand the business enterprise that it is a part of, and the logic that proceeds from it."[21]

Television advertising requires insight into the visual images and nonverbal cues that motivate people to buy products. Written or spoken messages inform but seldom motivate, according to one author: "The visual symbols communicate much faster, much more directly, than any long involved argument in words. There is no work called for, no mental effort."[22]

Television advertising frequently seeks to create an association between people's fantasies and specific products. The most common source of human fantasies is sex. So the advertiser tries to associate the product with a sexual fantasy—a beautiful woman in a car, the stares of men at fashionable stockings, men and women succumbing to perfume and after-shave lotion. Buying the product then becomes a step toward acting out the fantasy.

> I don't wear dark glasses just to keep the sun out of my eyes. I'm much more interested in the overtones: being, for the moment, a racer, a movie star, a mountain climber, a skiing champion, an airline pilot. These are by far the most impelling product benefits to me, not some mumbo-jumbo about what the glasses are made of.[23]

Advertising aimed at personal fears is just as effective as advertising aimed at personal fantasies. Such fears can be exploited, and specific products can be associated with a reduction of fear. The fear of bad breath or underarm "wetness" has sold billions of dollars of products.

Motivational commercials now dominate television advertising. They have proven enormously successful in selling products. Fantasy advertising is more successful in motivating those who find life generally meaningless. Fear advertising is more successful in motivating those who are insecure in interpersonal relations. In short, the more psychologically defenseless the viewer, the greater the impact of advertising.

THE EFFECTS OF THE MEDIA ON POLITICS

The mass media—particularly television—have brought about major changes in the American political system. These changes involve (1) the decline of political parties; (2) the increased power of the media to decide who the candidates will be; (3) the portrayal of elections as popularity contests, with the focus on candidate style and image rather than policy issues; (4) the development of media campaigns with professional public-relations techniques.

The Decline of Political Parties

The media have become the focus of political campaigning. Instead of seeking meetings with party leaders, candidates now spend most of their time going from one media market to another, seeking coverage by local news organizations and by the national reporters accompanying them on the campaign trail. Campaigns are organized as media events; the networks' evening news programs are the major targets of campaign activities. Furthermore, television advertising has become the most costly activity of a political campaign. The voters have come to depend more heavily on television than on any other source of information.

The media have replaced the party as the principal link between the candidates and the voters. Party organizations can no longer "deliver the vote." Even in those few places where party organizations still exist, they can be bypassed by candidates who appeal directly to the voters through television. Party organizations have all but withered away at the local (ward and precinct) level. Party loyalty has declined; there are more "independents" in the electorate than ever before; and among party affiliates there are many who will switch votes for a popular candidate.

> The media have replaced the party as the principal link between the candidates and the voters.

Primary elections have largely replaced caucuses and conventions as means of selecting presidential delegates to the national party conventions. Party leaders can no longer "control" state delegations. The presidential primaries have become a series of media events conducted every fourth year. Elections are now more sensitive to short-term influences, such as candidate personality and style and current events. The weakening of party organizations and the decline of party voting have made elections less predictable and more volatile.

The Media as Kingmakers

The mass media play a central role in deciding who will be the candidates in an election. Because television will bring the image of the candidates directly into the homes of millions of voters, it is necessary to eliminate candidates who look unimpressive or fail to perform well in front of a camera. An ugly Abraham Lincoln or an overweight William Howard Taft might never have made it to the White House in the television era. The pool of available recruits for high public office has been altered by eliminating candidates who cannot project a good image on the tube.

Favorable media reporting over a period of time can create presidential candidates out of senators, governors, and other political figures. The media create "name recognition," an essential quality of a presidential candidate. Conversely, the media can condemn an aspiring candidate to obscurity by simply failing to report his or her activities.

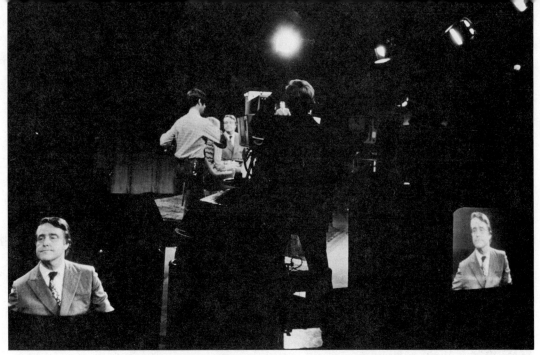

A TV camera crew prepares vice-presidential hopeful Sargent Shriver for one of his many appearances during the 1972 presidential campaign.

More importantly, the media sort out "serious" candidates at the beginning of a race. This is particularly true in primary elections. The media assign roles to candidates early in the campaign—"the front runner," "the candidate to beat," "the favorite," "the head of the pack," and so on. The media even set vote "quotas" that each candidate is expected to attain in a state primary. If the favorite does not win by as large a margin as the media have predicted, they may declare the runner-up to be the "real winner." In the Democratic primary in New Hampshire in 1968, President Lyndon B. Johnson, a write-in candidate, received more votes than his challenger, Eugene McCarthy, who was on the ballot. But the media declared McCarthy the "winner" because he had exceeded their expectations. Later, Johnson's abrupt withdrawal from the race made McCarthy a "loser" when he garnered "only" 58 percent of the vote in Wisconsin. Campaigning in Indiana, McCarthy observed wryly:

> I don't really know how to assess my position at this point. I got 42 percent in New Hampshire and they said I won. ... Then I got 58 percent in Wisconsin, and they said I lost. ... Chet Huntley [an anchorman for NBC] at 7:30 said, all of a sudden, he said, he's got to get 60 percent. He never explained. ... I mean, I thought it was a magic number or something out of the Bible, a multiple of seven, or something like that. But he never explained. ... Now in Indiana we haven't established yet what the standard is. I hope it will be all right.[24]

Media standards remained flexible, however. In New Hampshire in 1972, the "man to beat," Senator Edmund Muskie, outpolled

George McGovern, but the media declared McGovern the "real winner."

The New Hampshire primary, deliberately scheduled by that state's legislature to be the nation's earliest presidential primary, is an important media event. It is, according to the media, "the first important test of the candidates' grass-roots strength." But in reality fewer than 180,000 votes are cast, and New Hampshire accounts for only about 1 percent of the Democratic and Republican delegates to the national convention. Winning the New Hampshire primary means very little in terms of delegates. But it means a great deal in terms of media coverage.

The media search for a "winner." Each primary election in a presidential campaign is treated as a separate battle and not as a part of a larger nominating process. The naming of a winner makes good "hard" news. The polls are regarded as "soft" news, and even the delegate count is not given as much attention as the early primaries. When their predictions go wrong, the media respond with references to "shocking victories," "stunning turnabouts," and "surprising results."

Once the media have settled on a "winner" in a party, he receives the bulk of media coverage, and his opponents are condemned to obscurity. This increased coverage, then, gains additional recognition and support for the "winner." Financial contributions to opponents begin to dry up; no one wants to contribute to a losing cause. "Big Mo" (momentum) shifts to the media-designated "winner." Only a rare "stunning upset" will prevent the media's chosen candidate from winning the presidential nomination.

Media Elections: Covering the Game

In its election coverage, the media largely bypass questions of national policy and focus attention on the political "game"—the activities of the candidates in pursuit of electoral victory. The campaign is presented to the viewers (voters) not as a policy debate but rather as a struggle for power between the candidates. The media present the campaign as a series of speeches, rallies, press conferences, meetings, travels, and perhaps debates between the candidates. They also report on who is winning or losing, what their strategy is, how much money they are spending, how they look in public appearances, what the response of their audience was, and so on. The media give much less attention to issues or policies, the prior record of candidates, or endorsements by other political leaders. Consider Table 5-5 on the next page, showing the proportion of presidential election coverage devoted to the "game" and the proportion devoted to substantive issues and records. All of the media represented in the table—network news, the two magazines, and the newspaper—devoted a majority of their coverage to the game. Winning and losing, strategy, public appearances, and campaign hoopla received over half of the campaign coverage by all media forms. Issues, policies, traits, records, and endorsements received around one-third of the campaign coverage.

> The campaign is presented to the viewers (voters) not as a policy debate but rather as a struggle for power between the candidates.

It is not surprising that policy issues do not play a very large role in voters' decisions. The media do not pay much attention to policy issues. Elections are presented to voters as struggles between competing personalities. Media coverage emphasizes the popularity of candidates, their position in the race, and their personal characteristics—their style, charm, and vigor.

Table 5-5. Presidential Election Coverage

Subject of coverage	Network evening news	Los Angeles Times	Time and Newsweek
Games	**58%**	**51%**	**54%**
Winning and losing	24	20	23
Strategy, logistics	17	19	22
Appearances, hoopla	17	12	9
Substance	**29%**	**35%**	**32%**
Issues, policies	18	21	17
Traits, records	7	8	11
Endorsements	4	6	4
Other	**13%**	**14%**	**14%**

Source: Based on figures provided in Thomas E. Patterson, *The Mass Media Election* (New York: Praeger, 1980), p. 24. The election studied was the 1976 presidential election from January 1 to November 2.

The Media Campaign

If marketing, advertising, and public-relations firms can sell mouthwash, toothpaste, and deodorant, why not political candidates? Indeed, why not? Today, professional media campaign management includes planning the entire campaign; developing computerized mailing lists for fund raising; selecting a campaign theme and coming up with a desired candidate image; monitoring the progress of the campaign with continuous polling of the voters; producing television tapes for commercials, newspaper advertisements, signs, bumper stickers, and radio spots; selecting clothing and hair styles for the candidates; writing speeches and scheduling appearances; and even planning the victory party.

The first objective in a professional media campaign is to increase the candidate's name recognition among the voters. Years ago, name recognition was achieved only through years of service in minor public or party offices (or owning a well-known family name). Today, expert media advisors (and lots of money) can create "instant celebrity."

Frequently, polling is at the center of media campaign planning. At the beginning of the campaign, polls test name recognition and at the same time learn what concerns are uppermost in the minds of the voters. The results of these early polls will be used to determine a general strategy—developing a favorable image for the candidate and focusing on a popular campaign theme. Polls can detect weaknesses in the candidate, which can then be overcome by the right advertising. (Is there anything you do not like about Joe Jones? Too rich? Then show him in blue jeans digging ditches. Too intellectual? Then show him in a hog-calling contest.) During the campaign, polls can chart the progress of a candidate and even assess the effectiveness of specific themes. Finally, polls can identify the undecided vote toward the end of the campaign and help direct last-minute time and money.

The emphasis in professional media campaigns is on simplicity: a few themes, brief speeches, uncluttered ads, quick and catchy spot commercials. Finding the right theme or slogan is essential; this effort is not much different from that of launching an advertising campaign for a new detergent. A campaign theme may be as simple as "A leader you can trust." The candidate can then be "packaged" as honest and trustworthy (and his opponent as a shady wheeler-dealer).

A good media campaign manager knows that television producers do not like "talking heads"—that is, to show only the faces of speakers. So candidates must engage in activities that convey attractive pictures. The candidate visits an old people's home, a black ghetto, a coal mine, a pig farm, and so forth. These activities are more likely to achieve a spot on the evening news than a thoughtful speech on nuclear arms control. Moreover, these activities usually help to proclaim the candidate's friendliness toward particular groups.

Because reporters believe that conflict and confrontation are the real stuff of the news, they try to badger the candidates into strong attacks on each other or emotional displays of temperament. The prudent campaign manager tries to keep the candidate away from potentially explosive topics. (However, Ronald Reagan's display of temper in Manchester, New Hampshire, in early 1980 against an overbearing, impolite newspaper official may have helped him to win the primary and the Republican nomination.)

The movie *The Candidate,* starring Robert Redford, portrays an attractive, intelligent, young social activist who agrees to run for public office when approached by a professional campaign manager. The candidate is packaged and sold by a team of pollsters, filmmakers, advertising agents, speech writers, makeup artists, cameramen, and others. Gradually the candidate abandons his idealism as he is molded into a media image. After victory at the polls he begins to wonder whether he is really qualified to hold the office. His professional campaign manager, a hired gun already looking for new faces and more races, is leaving. "But what do I do now?" asks the victorious candidate. Without his image makers, he feels lost in the political world.

Battle of Political Commercials

In the 1982 congressional elections, the Republican and Democratic parties both claimed to be protectors of the nation's social security system. Although the Reagan administration had considered limiting the annual cost-of-living allowance for social security recipients, the president dropped this idea when the Democrats in Congress accused him of failing to live up to his campaign promise not to cut social security benefits. Later, in the congressional campaign, the Republicans took credit for continuing the cost-of-living increases in social security, much to the distress of the Democrats. In a controversial Republican television commercial, a kindly letter carrier is shown delivering a higher social security check to a grateful older woman and praising President Reagan for keeping his campaign promise.

I'm probably one of the most popular people in town.

In spite of those stick-in-the-muds who try to keep him from doing what we elected him to do.

He has kept his word and it is a beginning.

For gosh sake, let's give the guy a chance.

But the Democrats struck back with their own political commercial. A pair of scissors is shown clipping away at a social security card. The implication is that Republican budget-cutting will eventually destroy the benefits of social security. The simple theme, "It isn't fair, it's Republican," is given dramatic portrayal in the destruction of the social security card.

PUBLIC OPINION AND THE POLLSTERS

Politicians and the media both seek "feedback"—knowledge about the reactions of the public to presidents, candidates, parties, and issues. The pollsters play a major role in political campaigns, just as the ratings play a major role in television broadcasting. The major polls today—Gallup, Harris, and Roper—are supplemented by polls conducted by the media themselves—the *Washington Post*; CBS News/*New York Times*; ABC News/Harris; and NBC News/Associated Press. Moreover, there are about 200 private polling organizations that sell their services to political candidates and commercial advertisers.

Polls are an important part of the political landscape and a vital tool in the media age. No serious presidential candidate would be without a personal pollster. In 1980 Ronald Reagan relied on Richard Wirthlin, and Jimmy Carter relied on Patrick Caddell.

Most polling organizations measure national opinion on the basis of questions submitted to about 1,500 people selected at random throughout the country. How can the opinions of only 1,500 people represent the views of 226 million Americans? The answer lies in probability theory: if every person in the United States has an equal chance of being selected in the 1,500, then the *sample* should be representative of the 226 million *universe*. The real problem is to make sure that everyone in the population (or universe) has an equal chance of being selected for the sample. Many pollsters use random selection to determine cities, blocks, and bases for face-to-face interviews. Other pollsters select sample residential telephone numbers from the universe of all residential telephone numbers in the United States and conduct their interviews by phone. (This method excludes from the sample all of those people who have no telephone, but today there are not very many people in that category.)

Despite the media attention given to polls and the importance placed in them by candidates, the polls have a dismal record in predicting election outcomes. In a notorious instance, most polls reported Thomas E. Dewey as the winner over Harry Truman in 1948. But even when the polls correctly predicted the winner, the poll results still varied several percentage points from the actual vote. Table 5-6 shows the final poll results in the 1980 presidential elections: note the difference between the close election predicted by the polls and the actual Reagan victory.

Table 5-6. 1980 U. S. Presidential Election

	Reagan	*Carter*	*Anderson*	*Others/ undecided*
Result of the popular vote (November 4)	51%	41%	7%	1%
Final Poll Results				
Washington Post (Oct. 29–30)	39	42	7	12
CBS News/*New York Times* (Oct. 30–Nov. 1)	41	40	7	12
Gallup (Oct. 30–Nov. 1)	46	43	7	4
ABC News/Harris (Oct. 22–Nov. 3)	46	41	10	3
NBC News/Associated Press (Oct. 22–24)	42	36	9	13

Source: *Public Opinion*, October/November 1981.

Why are the polls often in error? First of all, public opinion is volatile. Opinions change from week to week. Voting preferences may change a day or two before the election. Secondly, the polls report many "undecideds"; these people may not eventually divide their votes in the same proportion as those who have already decided on a candidate. Thirdly, the opinions of the mass public may not be strongly held. Many people feel obliged to give a pollster an answer about a candidate or issue that they have never really thought about before the interview. This "doorstep" opinion is easily changed. Fourth, the opinions of the mass public are not very "constrained"— that is, not very organized and consistent. Opinions are shaped more by immediate events or popular images than by philosophy or ideology. Finally, the polls have difficulty in identifying those who are likely to go out and vote on election day for the candidate they say they prefer. Old style politicians knew the importance of "getting out the vote." Pollsters have difficulty knowing whether their sample accurately predicts the people who will vote.

AGENDA SETTING AND THE MASS MEDIA
The most important power of the mass media is agenda setting. Agenda setting is deciding what will be decided—what events, personalities, and conditions in society will be brought to the attention of mass audiences and placed on the agenda of decision makers. Events, personalities, and conditions that are ignored by the mass media are seldom talked about by the people or their leaders.

The mass media set the agenda for conversation among people and debate among their leaders. The media create some issues and obscure others. They spotlight some personalities and condemn others to anonymity. They define some conditions in society as problems, or even crises, and allow other conditions to go unnoticed. "TV is the Great Legitimator. TV confers reality. Nothing happens in America, practically everyone seems to agree, until it happens on television."[25]

The mass media set the agenda for conversation among people and debate among their leaders.

The power to set the national agenda is an awesome one. The popular political writer Theodore White put it this way:

The power of the press in America is a primordial one. It sets the agenda of public discussions; and this sweeping political power is unrestrained by any law. It determines what people will talk and think about—an authority that in other nations is reserved for tyrants, priests, parties, and potentates.[26]

Access to the mass media is a very valuable political asset. The president of the United States has easy access to the media; he can call a press conference or ask the networks for prime time for a presidential address. The president is rarely refused access. In contrast,

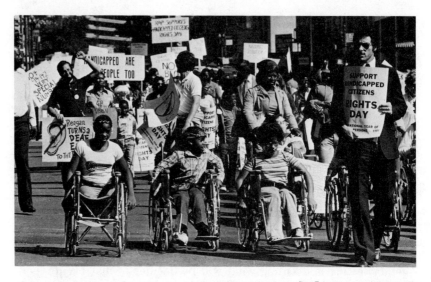

To gain media coverage, the powerless groups in our society resort to demonstrations and civil disturbances.

the powerless groups in our society must resort to civil disturbances to obtain access to the media. Indeed, the first problem confronting groups with little power, prestige, or celebrity is that of creating a *public issue*. Injustices affecting the powerless must be dramatized and sensationalized in order to gain access to the media. Demonstrations, civil disobedience, and violence help to attract media coverage. The media are essential in constructing an "issue" or "problem" or "crisis" for popular conversation and for action by decision makers.

Most Americans agree that the media have an important impact on politics and public opinion, and certainly politicians behave as if they believe the same thing. But many political scientists deny that the media are very influential. This discrepancy may be a product of voter studies showing that few people *change* their voting intentions based on media coverage of candidates or on newspaper endorsements. And it is true that the media can seldom change voter attitudes once they are formed. Party, region, and interest-group affiliation have been shown to be the long-term factors that affect voter behavior. The image of the candidates and specific political issues are only short-term factors. The media's more important influence is on short-term factors—determining the issues and building candidate images.

Systematic research has shown that the issues that receive greatest attention in the media are the issues that are viewed by the voters as most important.[27] Mass audiences generally adopt the media's agenda of issue importance. We look at the front page of a newspaper and expect to find the most important stories there. We also expect to find the most important items mentioned in the opening minutes of the evening news, and we expect to see more time devoted to these items. Media selection of the issues is most important in areas beyond the realm of the viewer's personal experience. If viewers have some personal experience with a topic, they may notice even a brief article on a back page or a short item at the tail end of a newscast. But audiences will generally identify as most important those issues that are given the greatest media coverage.

CHAPTER SUMMARY

1. The media, particularly television, communicate important political symbols to the public. Apparently, most Americans trust television news, despite their dislike of some of its entertainment "values." Along with the most popular media form, television, the less dominant media—radio, magazines, motion pictures, recordings, and newspapers—also reach millions of people.

2. "Hard fluff" television news stresses dramatic violence and conflict over in-depth analysis. In order to meet the criterion of "entertainment," television news must have a direct impact on viewers' lives, be oriented toward personalities and political celebrities, be novel and timely, consist of "events" capable of being captured on film or videotape, and be short (less than two minutes) in regard to air-time consumed.

3. Television news stories emphasize, first and foremost, governmental events, then accounts of crime or scandal, followed by disasters, and protests and strikes. "People in the news" are most often national public officials.

4. *Bias* in television news can result from four factors: (a) the *hype* factor (holding the audience's attention by overdramatizing conflict or violence); (b) production requirements and the preponderance of preplanned news events; (c) the geographical overrepresentation of news events from Washington, D. C., New York City, and California; and (d) the liberal values of the chief newsmakers in the media.

5. Television also "socializes" the American people, imparting social values and life-styles through its dramatic and comedy shows. Periodically, these values may come under attack as immoral or unAmerican by various concerned interest groups.

6. Television bias is countered to some degree by viewers' selective perception of TV images. Contrary to the expectations of TV executives, both news and entertainment have contributed to "television malaise"—viewer alienation resulting from TV's often negative portrayal of American life.

7. Because television is so highly dependent upon advertising revenues, it must create programming that will please both the audience and the sponsor. High ratings mean increased revenue for the networks *and* more people who may buy the advertised products. The

necessary "social symbols" of advertising can be readily transferred to the political imagery inherent in news reporting as well.

8. Political campaigns in America have become "media events." The media emphasis on candidate image has eroded the importance of political parties, largely determined who is perceived as the winners or losers in presidential primaries, led to extensive coverage of a campaign's "political games," and enhanced the role of professional media campaign managers.

9. Both the media and political candidates pay close attention to public opinion polls, although poll accuracy is not always assured. Voter volatility, independent voters, and weakly held opinions may all distort the final poll projection.

10. The mass media influence the national policy agenda by identifying the problems or crises that should be considered by leaders and the public. Although the power of the media to change already-formed attitudes may be limited, the media do play a powerful role in determining what the public thinks *about*.

Notes

1. Murray Edelman, *The Symbolic Uses of Politics* (Urbana: University of Illinois Press, 1967), p. 5.
2. *Media* is a plural term. Television is one *medium*.
3. CBS owns WCBS (New York), WBBM (Chicago), WCAU (Philadelphia), KMOX (St. Louis), and KNXT (Los Angeles). ABC owns WABC (New York), WCS (Chicago), KGO (San Francisco), KABC (Los Angeles), and WXYZ (Detroit). NBC owns WNBC (New York), WKYC (Cleveland), KNBC (Los Angeles), KMAG (Chicago), and WRC (Washington).
4. Quoted in Stephen Vito, "Inside 60 Minutes," *American Film*, December/January 1972, p. 55.
5. See Doris A. Graber, *Mass Media and American Politics* (Washington, D. C.: Congressional Quarterly Press, 1980), p. 65.
6. See William A. Henry, "News as Entertainment," in Elie Abel (Ed.), *What's News* (San Francisco: Institute for Contemporary Studies, 1981).
7. Graber, p. 68.
8. Robert Rutherford Smith, "Mythic Elements in Television News," *Journal of Communication*, Winter 1979, pp. 78–82.
9. Joseph R. Dominick, "Geographical Bias in National TV News," *Journal of Communication*, Autumn 1977, pp. 94–99.
10. Smith, "Mythic Elements."
11. John Johnstone, Edward Slawski, and William Bowman, *The Newspeople* (Urbana: University of Illinois Press, 1976).
12. Graber, p. 41.
13. *Newsweek*, May 25, 1981.
14. George Gerbner, "Cultural Indicators," *Journal of Communication*, Summer 1978, pp. 176–207. Also cited by Graber, p. 122.
15. See Neil Vidmar and Milton Rokeach, "Archie Bunker's Bigotry: A Study in Selective Perception and Exposure," *Journal of Communication*, Winter 1974, pp. 36–47.

16. L. Z. Hobson, "As I Listened to Archie Say 'Hebe,'" *New York Times,* September 12, 1972.
17. Norman Lear, "As I Read How Laura Saw Archie," *New York Times,* October 10, 1971.
18. Michael J. Robinson, "Public Affairs Television and the Growth of Political Malaise," *American Political Science Review,* June 1976, pp. 409–432; and "Television and American Politics," *The Public Interest,* Summer 1977, pp. 3–39.
19. Merritt Panitt, "America Out of Focus," *TV Guide,* January 15, 1972, p. 6.
20. Graber, p. 61.
21. Edward Jay Epstein, *News from Nowhere* (New York: Random House, 1973), p. 69.
22. Pierre Martineau, *Motivation in Advertising: Motives That Make People Buy* (New York: McGraw-Hill, 1957), p. 4.
23. Martineau, p. 50.
24. Speech to the Fort Wayne Gridiron Club, April 27, 1968.
25. Henry, "News as Entertainment," p. 134.
26. Theodore White, *The Making of the President 1972* (New York: Atheneum, 1973), p. 327.
27. J. M. McLeod, L. B. Becker, and J. E. Byrne, "Another Look at the Agenda-Setting Functions of the Press," *Communications Research,* April 1974, pp. 131–166; also "The Political Consequences of Agenda-Setting," *Mass Communications Review,* Spring 1976, pp. 8–15, and M. E. McCombs, "Agenda-Setting Research: A Bibliographic Essay," *Political Communication Review,* March 1976, pp. 1–7.

Close-Up and In-Depth Analyses

Elie Abel (Ed.). *What's News.* San Francisco: Institute for Contemporary Studies, 1981.
Erik Barnouw. *The Image Empire.* New York: Oxford University Press, 1970.
Edith Efron. *The News Twisters.* Los Angeles: Nash Publishing, 1971.
Herbert J. Gans. *Deciding What's News.* New York: Vintage, 1980.
David Halberstam. *The Powers That Be.* New York: Knopf, 1979.
Richard Hofstetter. *Bias in the News.* Columbus: Ohio State University Press, 1976.
Dan Nimmo. *The Political Persuaders.* Englewood Cliffs, N. J.: Prentice-Hall, 1970.
Thomas E. Patterson. *The Mass Media Election.* New York: Praeger, 1980.
Ron Powers. *The Newscasters.* New York: St. Martin's, 1977.

POLITICS, PARTIES, AND ELECTIONS

The media, especially television, have reshaped American politics. Televised debates, political advertising on television, and election-night coverage are among the more obvious effects of television on politics. But as we began to see in the last chapter, there are other less obvious but equally important effects: the decline of political parties, the eroding influence of party leaders, the growing number and importance of primary elections, the recruitment of new "instant" candidates, the increase in campaign costs, and the role of the media in selecting "winners."

In the 1980 presidential election, for the first time, two media candidates faced each other. Both major contestants—Republican Ronald Reagan and Democrat Jimmy Carter—owed their career to the media, not to political parties. In this chapter we will use the 1980 election and the examples of Reagan and Carter to illustrate fundamental changes in the electoral system, many of which can be attributed to the dominance of television. Our discussion will concentrate on the changing role of parties and interest groups, the changing nature of candidates and elections, and the growing relationships between the candidates and the media.

RONALD REAGAN: PRODUCT OF THE MEDIA

Reagan's career illustrates the influence of the mass media in recruiting national

The 1980 Republican convention.

leaders. Reagan is usually described as a political amateur; that is, he did not have much experience in government. He did not pretend to know much about the complexities of government. But he was a professional communicator. He was the ideal contemporary candidate, because he has had a lifetime of experience in using the media. As an actor, he was regarded as a "quick study" who could learn lines easily and deliver them well. He made fifty-four movies in twenty-seven years, most of them forgettable. He was never nominated for an Oscar, but he never blew up on the set. He showed up for work on time, never argued with directors, and was comfortable before the camera. He had a naturally relaxed manner that made him pleasing if not exciting.

Reagan grew up in the Midwest, in small towns far removed from the power of Washington or the glitter of Hollywood. He was a self-made success. His father was an economic failure and a personal tragedy—an alcoholic shoe salesman who could not contribute to his son's education. Reagan washed dishes at tiny Eureka College, hardly a training ground for national leadership. Later he won an athletic scholarship and played football. Graduating in 1932, he landed a job as a sports announcer in Des Moines, Iowa. When he was assigned to cover spring training for the Chicago Cubs in California, he managed a screen test with Warner Brothers and was given a standard studio contract.

Reagan was a hard-working professional. Many Hollywood stars in those days did not trouble themselves with the problems of supporting actors and "extras," but Reagan always identified with the rank and file. He was elected president of the Screen Actors Guild. During World War II he made training films for the Army Air Corps, a task surely beneath the dignity of Humphrey Bogart, who, at the same time, was filming *Casablanca*. After the war, acting jobs went to a new generation of stars. Always beneath the level of the Bogarts, Flynns, and Cagneys, he was now displaced by Brando, Newman, and Holden. Before the war he played opposite Pat O'Brien in *Knute Rockne, All American,* by any standards a good performance in a good film. But after the war he was reduced to playing opposite a chimpanzee in *Bedtime for Bonzo*.

His apparently doomed career was rescued from obscurity by Ralph J. Cordiner, president of the General Electric Company. The firm was planning a weekly television series, *G. E. Theatre*. At the time, television was just emerging as a serious competitor to the movies, and there was little crossover between the two media. Reagan switched to television simply because he needed a job, but it was a very fortunate choice. It was through television that he gained genuine mass exposure. *G. E. Theatre* ran for seven years on prime time before being supplanted by one of Reagan's personal favorites, *Bonanza*. Reagan's job as host involved no more than introducing each show. He did not have to act; he merely appeared in millions of homes every Sunday night, looking comfortable, relaxed, and friendly.

General Electric also used Reagan as a goodwill ambassador for free enterprise. During his Hollywood years he had been an active liberal Democrat. As General Electric's roving ambassador, he developed a standard speech about the ever-present danger of socialism and the threat that the federal bureaucracy would reduce business efficiency. He delivered his lines well; after all, he had been delivering them all his life. Whether he believed them or not is no longer important. Actors are paid to appear sincere, and he was a competent actor. It is possible that his staunch conservatism developed as a consequence of his delivery of conservative appeals with sincerity. In any case, his conservatism soon went beyond that of his sponsor. General Electric, after all, had huge defense contracts with the "evil bureaucracy."

The origins of "the speech" (Reagan's defense of free enterprise) can be traced directly to his first television job. Armed with the speech, which had been delivered, polished, and adjusted over the years, Reagan appeared to have a promising future as a representative of business interests. When *Bonanza* replaced *G. E. Theatre*, Reagan suffered another loss in prestige. He became the host of *Death Valley Days* at a lower salary, and was no longer doing public relations for General Electric. But he was marketable, especially with "the speech."

His marketability was fortunate, because he was in debt by 1964. He had made a lot of money but spent it quickly, and he was being hounded for back taxes. His inept personal financial behavior was hardly unique; many actors end up in similar circumstances. However, Reagan's new enthusiasm for conservatism and his skill at communicating served him well. A group headed by Justin Dart (Dart Industries, Rexall Drugs, Kraft Foods), Holmes Tuttle (a California Ford dealer), William French Smith (a wealthy Los Angeles attorney) and A. S. Rubel (chairman of Union Oil), formed a Reagan Trust Fund to manage his personal finances, leaving him free to pursue a new avocation: conservative politics.

At an age when most are looking forward to retirement, Reagan began his second career.

At an age when most are looking forward to retirement, Reagan began his second career on the foundations of his first. He produced a film to assist the Republican presidential nominee, Senator Barry Goldwater, in 1964. The film was enormously successful and generated substantial revenue. The money rolled in, even if the votes did not. Although Goldwater was trounced, Reagan had won the loyalty of the conservative wing of the Republican party. He was, by then, as conservative as Goldwater; but he was more charming. Indeed, he was *the* media politician.

In 1966, Reagan won his first election and became governor of California. He defeated Edmund G. ("Pat") Brown, the man who had crushed Richard Nixon for the job in 1962. The media politician was a new phenomenon. Brown, a politician of the old school, underestimated Reagan's mass appeal. According to Brown, Reagan sounded simplistic; his speech was silly; and he did not understand government. Brown would not be the last to underestimate Reagan's appeal. The very qualities that make him appear childish to sophisticated professors of government endear him to some voters.

As governor of California, Reagan did not succeed in creating a conservative government, as he had promised during the campaign. Although he had promised to halt the growth of government spending, to clean up the "welfare mess," and to crack down on campus rioting, California's spending doubled during his eight years as governor. Welfare administration was only slightly improved, and campus rioting remained routine.

Yet as governor he extracted grudging admiration from those with whom he came into personal contact. Despite his public image as a rigid conservative, he was quite willing to compromise. When he could not win, he would at least try to avoid losing badly. He did not halt the growth of government, so he satisfied himself with reducing its *rate* of growth. He was not an obsessive conservative; he was also charming and personable. He rarely displayed much of a temper and did not become bitter when he lost. Reagan knew about images. He also knew about administration. He was willing, indeed eager, to delegate responsibility to his staff. He arrived for work at a reasonable hour and left in plenty of time for a relaxing evening. He was so relaxed that he often ended work in the early afternoon, and he spent his weekends on his ranch.

He recruited a competent staff. Men who later became familiar as key White House aides were selected during his years as governor of California—Edwin Meese, Michael Deaver, William Clark. He also developed his support base among the business community, and Dart and Smith became trusted advisor and attorney general, respectively.

His political success (reelection in 1970 by another wide margin) was accompanied by financial success. His trust fund had converted him from a debtor into a millionaire. He was worth over $2 million in 1980. He could thank his wealthy friends for his financial success.

In 1976 Reagan decided to make a run at the presidency. It is generally considered foolish to challenge an incumbent president of one's party, but Gerald Ford was not a "real" (elected) incumbent, having replaced the disgraced Nixon. Still, it is unusual for a party to

Reagan campaigns in 1980 at the Chrysler assembly plant for the presidential nomination.

deny its nomination to its own incumbent president. However, this traditional wisdom is invalidated by the primary election process. There is no party to deny the nomination to an incumbent; the party's nominee is whoever wins the most primaries. Ford was not as invulnerable as traditional wisdom suggested, because primaries and their media focus reduce the advantage of incumbency. To go after Ford, Reagan hired a media consultant, John Sears. Sears was a mistake, since he had less instinct for the media than did Reagan. He counseled Reagan to mute his conservatism and broaden his appeal. Reagan did, and lost the nomination. But he almost defeated the incumbent president.

His narrow defeat, impressive though it was, convinced Reagan that his second career was over. He was old, financially secure, and planned to enjoy his newly acquired fortune. But Ford lost to Carter, Carter stumbled badly, and Reagan decided to give it another try in 1980.

> The camera is the tool of both of Reagan's trades, acting
> and politics.

This time Reagan did it *his* way. Sears was fired, and Reagan relied on his own professional skills. The camera is the tool of both of Reagan's trades, acting and politics. Newsmen covering Reagan's primary campaign agreed with Sears. They thought his hackneyed phrases and simplistic slogans were tiresome. They were bored by "the speech." Yet the professionals in the media misjudged the extent to which a comfortable, pleasant, reassuring man could use this image to win. (Carter allegedly hoped that Reagan would win the Republican nomination, believing that Reagan would be easy to beat.) Reagan was a communicator first and a politician second. True, he made laughable mistakes when, carried away by an enthusiastic crowd, he departed from the speech. But even these mistakes were almost endearing. Most of us have a poor command of details; so does Reagan. But all of this was of no matter. In a media age, a media expert became president.

JIMMY CARTER: THE FIRST MEDIA PRESIDENT

Reagan's opponent was the first media president. But Carter was an amateur in front of a camera, whereas Reagan was a professional. Carter learned the art of media manipulation on his own. Before winning the presidency in 1976 he had an obscure and mediocre career. As a state legislator and later governor in Georgia, he was hardly in the same position as Reagan. Reagan was known to millions even before he became governor of the nation's most populous state; Carter was unknown even after he had served as governor of a smaller state. One year before he was elected president, three-quarters of the American people had never even heard of him.

Carter did, however, have a personal fortune. He liked to emphasize his humble beginnings (all candidates like to emphasize their humble beginnings). He grew up in Sumter County, Georgia, and rebuilt the family peanut business from the brink of poverty to a net worth of over $4 million. He graduated from Annapolis, spent seven years in the Navy, made his fortune in the family business, served in the legislature, and served one term as governor. These are not impressive credentials for the presidency.

What reason did he have for thinking he could become president? In December, 1974, he announced his intention to seek the Democratic nomination. The country was struggling to forget Watergate, and Carter proved to be a shrewd judge of national mood. His candidacy was based on a single assumption: the public was sick of corruption, "politics as usual," defeat in Vietnam, scandal in the Nixon administration, and especially the perceived immorality of Washington.

Carter based his campaign not on ideology but on image. "My name is Jimmy Carter, and I won't lie to you" became "the speech." Thus, he turned what would normally be a crippling handicap—his total inexperience with the federal government—into an advantage. He boasted that he had "never even been to Washington." None of the horrors of the previous decade could be attributed to him. The public was ready for an "outsider," and he provided the image.

Carter based his campaign not on ideology but on image. "My name is Jimmy Carter, and I won't lie to you" became "the speech."

Carter was aided in his image creation by a cooperative media. To the extent that he had any values or priorities, they were generally liberal, just as Reagan's were generally conservative. But neither relied much on ideology. Carter's image was that of the moral, intensely religious, small-town farmer. In Georgia he had declared himself an "ignorant and bigoted redneck" in order to defeat a liberal opponent, but after his election he charmed blacks by placing a portrait of the Reverend Dr. Martin Luther King, Jr., in the state capitol. He was a political climber, not an ideologue, and in his 1976 campaign he avoided anything more than the most vague and simple statements. The media could have ignored him, or they could have exploited his earlier racist statements. Instead, they chose to promote him. They, too, were persuaded that Americans needed a return to traditional values—humble beginnings; deep roots in the soil, hard work; success in business, the family, and the community; and Christian morals and principles.

Just as Reagan had his corporate angels, so did Carter. Early in his career Carter was befriended by J. Paul Austin, chairman of the board of the Coca-Cola Company. Carter, unlike Reagan, was a good manager of his personal finances. Through these contacts with Austin, he was nominated to the prestigious Trilateral Commission. Established in 1972 by David Rockefeller, the commission is composed of top corporate officials of multinational corporations and high government officials of the industrial democracies. It meets periodically to discuss economic relations. Through his membership in the commission, Carter was introduced to the president of the Bendix Corporation, W. Michael Blumenthal, who became his secretary of the treasury; the influential Wall Street lawyer Cyrus Vance, who became his secretary of state; the president of the California Institute of Technology, Harold Brown, who became his secretary of defense; a professor at Columbia University, Zbigniew Brzezinski, who became his national security advisor; and a U. S. senator, Walter Mondale, who became his vice-president.

Jimmy Carter thanks his supporters at the 1976 Democratic convention.

Thus, the two major contestants for the presidency in 1980 had quite similar backgrounds. Both were political amateurs with strong corporate connections, both were personally wealthy, and both projected an image of the "outsider," at least initially.

The major difference with Carter, however, was that he had to learn about the media while he ran. He did not have years of professional experience. In 1972, Carter's aide, Hamilton Jordan, wrote a memo to his boss setting the tone of the effort. "Stories in the *New York Times* and the *Washington Post* do not just happen but have to be carefully planned and planted," he wrote.[1] Jordan submitted a list of prominent print journalists. He believed that these journalists had a liberal bias and that they were imitated by television. Thus, Carter was urged to go for the "great mention." Once a prominent newspaper had declared Carter a serious candidate, then the imitators would fall in line, and his candidacy would be off and running. Jordan's blueprint for victory contained not one item related to policy or issues. His concern was winning, not the development of policy positions. It was suggested that Georgia establish trade missions abroad, thus giving Carter a reason for extensive foreign travel. Why? To learn about international relations or military alliances? No, to establish credibility as one experienced in foreign policy. The motive was image, not substance.

Reporters do not think about abstract policies; they think about winners and losers. As Stephen Hess explains, "When reporters talk with each other about public affairs, they primarily exchange speculations on the prospects of a bill getting through Congress, a candidate's chance of getting elected, the personality of a cabinet officer, or who has the real power in a department."[2] Carter was their kind of man. Yet there was trouble from the beginning. By repeating his theme—"I will never lie to you"—he was inviting reporters to judge him by a different standard. Not that all politicians are liars; rather, they hardly think it important to build a campaign around such a trivial theme.

Yet it was this special status that also attracted the major media to him. To heal the wounds of the previous decade, who could be better than a moral crusader? Carter was pious and humorless, but he was (he proclaimed repeatedly) *really* different. Carter built his media image in decentralized fashion. He sought state and local coverage initially rather than trying for the "great mention" from the networks or major newspapers. Then the *New York Times* reported that Carter was going to do better in the primaries than everybody had predicted. Other papers repeated the *Times* story, and more space was devoted to Carter. The *Times* story was an event in and of itself—"a story on the front page of the *New York Times* out of the blue, ordaining a new phenomenon, that was the most important single event in the relationship between the media and Jimmy Carter."[3]

Neither Carter nor Reagan was well-connected with the organizational apparatus of his political party. There was no need for them to be, because American political parties, as organizations, are powerless in the selection of candidates. In 1976 party leaders preferred Senator Hubert Humphrey; in 1980 Republican activists preferred George Bush. These preferences were of no consequence. Carter and Reagan were nominated because they worked hard and wanted to win badly enough to commit their complete personal resources to the task of winning for at least two years before the actual nomination.

POLITICAL PARTIES

Political parties in the United States appear impressive until you look beyond the organizational charts to the reality (see Figure 6-1 next page). The national components of the political parties are the **national committees** and the national conventions. The Democratic and Republican committees maintain permanent headquarters in Washington, and the national convention meets every four years to nominate a presidential candidate (in reality, to ratify the choice of voters in primary elections).

National committees consist of representatives from each state, most of whom meet only rarely, leaving the actual running of the committee to its professional staff. This staff does not have much to do, since campaigns are generally built around personal followings, and money comes from interest groups. Theoretically, the national committee is responsible for naming a national chairman. However, if the party controls the presidency, the president names the national chairman; if the party is out of power, leading candidates may propose their choices. The national chairman and his or her staff plan for the next convention, try to pay off debts for the last campaign, and try to look busy. The Republican National Committee, along with two congressional campaign committees, has raised substantially more money than its Democratic counterpart. The Republican committee has utilized computer technology in compiling and sorting its mailing list. Moreover, it has actively recruited candidates for state legislatures, governorships, and even Congress. It has commissioned opinion surveys independent of those conducted by presidential candidates; it has conducted workshops in understanding the media; and it has integrated finances and contributed a substantial amount to candidates it successfully recruited.[4]

National committee: The party coordinating organization, composed of representatives from each state and territory, that is concerned with party rules, publicity, fund raising, the selection of the national convention city, and the appointment of the national chairpersons.

The National Conventions: The Final Step

The most visible display of the national party is the national convention, a television extravaganza that certifies the winner of the primary elections as the nominee of the party. Of course, the convention

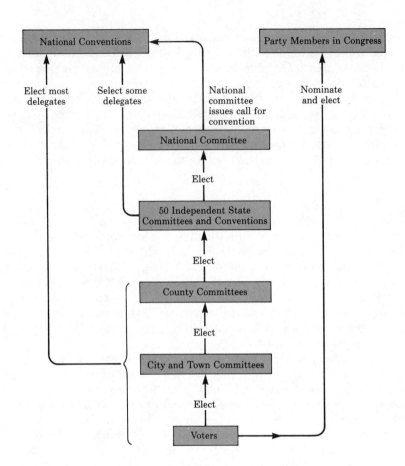

Figure 6-1. The formal organization of American political parties

Party platform: A campaign document, written by the platform committee at the convention, identifying the party's goals and its positions on the important issues of the day.

does other things, too. It fights about the **party platform,** struggles over rules for seating delegates, and the like. But the delegates are there to participate in the formality of the nomination. They themselves are allocated to each state by a variety of cumbersome and complex formulas. Most are bound to vote on the first ballot for the candidate who won the primary in their state. These delegates are selected in primary elections, although few voters know who they are.

Delegates to the national conventions are not like rank-and-file members of the party. They are more likely to be political activists, though not always party activists. In the Democratic convention, concern for minority representation has been written into the rules. In 1980 about half the delegates were women and 25 percent were black; these proportions were comparable to the distribution of women and

Senator Charles Percy, R–Ill. (third from left), discusses party politics with Republican delegates at the 1980 convention.

blacks among Democratic voters. However, convention delegates are far more likely to be ideologically "pure" than are the average voters. Republican convention delegates are more conservative than the Republican rank and file; Democratic delegates are more liberal than the Democratic rank and file. Convention delegates are less interested in supporting party regulars and more committed to ideology.[5]

> Republican convention delegates are more conservative than the Republican rank and file; Democratic delegates are more liberal than the Democratic rank and file.

Amateurs—those not active in the party and whose participation is largely limited to attending the convention—are more ideologically attached to the symbols of their party. The fact that Democratic delegates are more liberal than Democrats in the larger public can be attributed, in part, to the reforms in party organization following the defeat of Senator George McGovern for president in 1972. Goals and quotes emphasizing the participation of young people, minorities,

A convention delegate
proudly displays his
party's symbol, the
elephant.

and women open the doors of the convention to a generally more liberal group of amateurs. The Republicans have been slower to reform, mandating no requirements for the representation of women and minorities. The disparity of opinion between Democratic party delegates and Democratic voters is much greater than the disparity between Republican delegates and voters (see Table 6-1). Actually, there are not very many differences of opinion between the Democratic and Republican *voters,* but there are large differences between the conventions' *delegates.*[6]

Conventions ratify the decisions made in the primary elections. Conventions are tedious unless something unusual occurs. It is to the

Table 6-1. Convention Delegates' Opinions Compared with Voters'

	Democratic delegates	Democratic voters	Republican delegates	Republican voters
No one should live in poverty (percent agreeing)	57	22	10	13
Persons able to work should be required to work (percent agreeing)	69	28	75	79
Most important to protect rights of accused (percent agreeing)	78	36	21	28
Attitude toward military (percent favorable)	42	67	84	71

Average differences:
Democratic delegates/Democratic voters: 39%
Republican delegates/Republican voters: 7%
Republican voters/Democratic voters: 16%
Republican delegates/Democratic delegates: 42%

Source: Survey by NBC News/Associated Press, April 1982. (See *Public Opinion*, December/January, 1982, p. 36.)

advantage of the media, especially television, to change boring events into interesting ones. The media therefore exaggerate conflict during conventions. In 1980 Senator Edward Kennedy, hopelessly behind Carter in pledged delegates, launched a doomed effort for an "open convention" (that is, one in which delegates were not bound to the winner in the primary election). Although Kennedy's proposal stood absolutely no chance of being adopted by the delegates, television watchers were led to believe that the issue was in doubt and that a real fight would occur.

During the Republican convention, television was even more intrusive. Walter Cronkite, covering the convention for CBS-TV, actually became part of the decision-making process. The Republican convention, like the Democratic one, looked to be a dreary affair. Reagan had the nomination in hand well in advance. How, then, to fill three days of speeches with something that would attract viewer attention? The solution was to encourage rumors that Reagan would select former President Ford as his running mate. Ford was interviewed by Cronkite at the high point of these rumors. Although Ford and Reagan had met, it was during his interview with Cronkite that Ford set out the conditions on which he would accept the nomination. He demanded a "meaningful" role. Cronkite then defined the role more explicitly: "Something like a co-president?" Reagan had no intention of making such an unusual arrangement, but CBS was the medium through which Ford and Reagan communicated, and the definition of Ford's role was actually given by Cronkite.[7]

The Active Amateurs

The Democratic party's rules governing racial and sexual representation at national conventions have been successful. As required, women made up about 50 percent of the delegates in 1980, and blacks and youth have also gained. (See Table A.)

Table A. Changing Makeup of Democratic Convention Delegates

	Women	Blacks	Youth
1968	13%	6%	4%
1972	38	15	21
1976	34	9	15
1980	50	15	27

However, there is substantial underrepresentation of veteran politicians. The most severe decline in the proportion of U. S. senators and representatives occurred after 1968, when the changes were introduced. Governors, on the other hand, are still active (Table B).

Table B. Politicians' Participation at Democratic National Convention

	U. S. senators	U. S. representatives	Governors
1968	68%	39%	83%
1972	36	15	80
1976	18	15	47
1980	14	15	76

Party activists are more ideologically committed than most Americans. Democratic delegates are more liberal than the general population; Republican delegates are more conservative. The general public drifts toward the center, and the party activists occupy the extremes (Table C).

Table C. Ideology of 1980 Democratic and Republican Delegates

	Democratic delegates	Republican delegates	Overall U. S.
Liberal	46%	2%	19%
Moderate	42	36	43
Conservative	6	58	30

Source: CBS News delegate survey. (See *Public Opinion*, October/November 1980, p. 41.)

Former political foes, Ford, Reagan, and Bush (left to right) display the required unity once the nomination has been announced.

State and Local Parties

Since the United States is a federal (as opposed to a unitary) system of government, there are fifty state party organizations and numerous county or local organizations. These vary substantially in strength. Some, such as the party organization in Connecticut, have been genuine nominating institutions, since they use state conventions or caucuses rather than primaries to select candidates. Most state party organizations do not, and thus they are not much stronger than the national party organization. Examples of strong state and local parties are becoming rare. In Chicago, the death of Mayor Richard Daley brought about the demise of the last big-city party "machine." Nonetheless, sixteen states nominate gubernatorial candidates by convention rather than by a primary election, although some of these states allow for primary elections to contest convention choices.

There is very little connection between the various state parties and the national party organization. State party leaders do serve on the national committee. The only link that binds the state and national parties together is their mutual desire to serve up a winner in the presidential elections, on the (often mistaken) theory that presidential coattails will help state and local candidates.

THE DEVELOPMENT OF THE TWO-PARTY SYSTEM

Despite wavering and shifting party loyalties, the United States has always operated under the two-party system. George Washington in his farewell address warned of the evils of parties and said he dreaded the appearance of "two great parties, each under its leader." Yet even as Washington was speaking, the two-party system was emerging in the new nation. Figure 6-2 shows the development of these parties.

The proponents of the Constitution, known as the Federalists, were led by Alexander Hamilton, Washington's secretary of the treasury. Even though Washington believed that political parties were dangerous threats to democracy, more astute or pragmatic Federalists recognized the need to organize in the face of strong opposition from Thomas Jefferson and his Democratic-Republicans. The fear that Washington expressed about political parties was largely directed at Jefferson. The Federalists attracted the same social groups that had supported ratification of the Constitution—that is, banking and financial interests who favored a strong central government. Jefferson attracted support from agrarian interests—planters, slave owners, and farmers.

Jefferson organized with more determination than did the Federalists, actually luring James Madison into his camp. The rewards of such efforts were reaped in 1800, when Jefferson defeated the Federalists and became president. Although Jefferson proclaimed that "we are all Republicans, we are all Federalists," the Federalists were genuinely afraid. They feared that Jefferson would change the course of government as established by the Constitution. He did not. But the Federalist party became so ineffective that Democratic-Republican candidates, including Madison, won consistently, and by 1820 there was no Federalist party. Historians refer to the struggle between the Republicans under Jefferson and the Federalists under Hamilton, culminating in the disappearance of the Federalists, as the "first-party system."[8] As Jefferson's party strengthened its hold on the presidency, some of the original class distinctions between the parties became blurred. The Democratic-Republicans, originally the party of the farmers, began to attract support from some commercial and banking interests.

Andrew Jackson, hero of the War of 1812, was a vigorous proponent of the view that a new party was needed to take up the cause of Western and frontier interests. Jackson's aspirations to represent the common man coincided with an expansion of the electorate. Laws expanding the eligible electorate and the selection of presidential

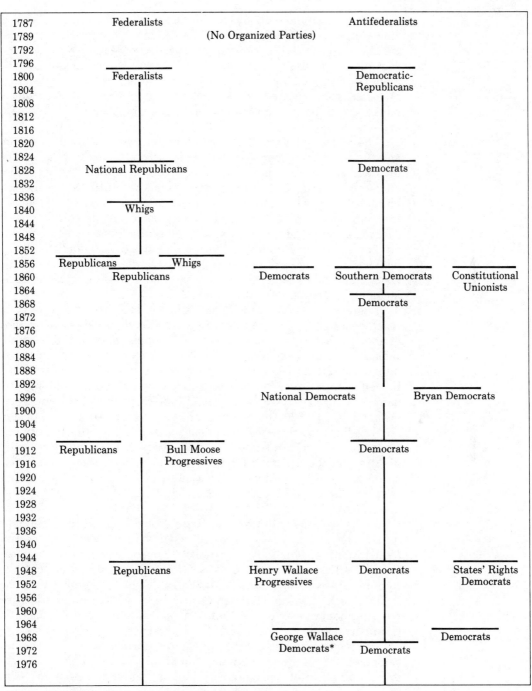

Figure 6-2. Cleavages and continuity in the two-party system

*American Independent party

electors by popular vote helped Jackson in his campaign rhetoric. However, his symbolic appeals to the common man repelled some of the more conservative members of the party. Jackson's faction became known as the Democrats, and the opposing faction adopted the name Whigs. Led by Henry Clay and Daniel Webster, the Whigs attracted the same coalition that had supported the Federalists: bankers, merchants, and large landowners, who shared a distaste for mass democracy.

The Whigs adopted the practice of the nominating convention, and the Democrats soon followed. This "second-party system" can be understood as the precursor to today's party system. The Whigs were moderately successful, winning twice from 1840 until 1854. However, both parties began to strain under the burden of slavery. Both sought to compromise an issue that ultimately could not be compromised. Jackson's Democratic party found itself divided between the Northern and Southern factions (a division that still exists), and the Whigs fell victim to a series of mediocre candidates who were crushed by the Democrats. The demoralization was complete with a Democratic landslide in 1852 for Franklin Pierce.

The deterioration of the Whigs and the inability of the party to reach consensus on the slavery issue led directly to the development of another faction, the Republicans. The appearance of the Republicans marked the beginning of the "third-party system." The new Republicans were not similar in any way to the original Republicans led by Jefferson. Former Whigs and antislavery Democrats adopted the name and promptly replaced the Whigs as the competitors to the Democrats. In 1860 the Republicans nominated Abraham Lincoln. His candidacy had very little appeal in the South; the Republican party was a Northern party. The Democrats, however, were so badly divided that the Southern Democrats and Northern Democrats nominated their own candidates. This split, plus the entry of another candidate, secured Lincoln's election with only 40 percent of the popular vote.

Following the Civil War, the Republicans became the dominant party. The Democrats were so thoroughly identified with the defeated South that it took them until 1876 to offer serious competition. The Democrats then elected Grover Cleveland twice, but the Republicans were still dominant. It was during this period that the "solid South" became the Democratic base in the competition for the presidency. Almost all Southern states supported Democratic candidates, and the North and West supported Republicans.

The neglect by both parties of the "common man" led to the development of the Progressive movement and to the Democratic party's nomination of the populist William Jennings Bryan in 1896. Speaking for the small farmers in the South and hoping to attract industrial workers in the North, Bryan saw himself as the keeper of the Jeffersonian tradition. But the nation was in the midst of an industrial revolution and expansion. It was the era of the expansion of railroads, banks, and steel; it was also an era of massive European immigration into the North. Bryan sought to move his party in the direction of protection for the masses of people against the excesses of the "robber barons." However, his massive defeat in 1896 plunged the Democratic party even more into the role of Southern representative. The victorious Republicans were supported not only by Northern and Eastern businesses but also by urban workers and Midwestern farmers. The Republican party's fiscal conservatism struck a popular chord, and the futility of protests saddled the Democrats with ineffective candidates.

Once again, however, the dominant party found itself in the grip of serious factional dispute. Theodore Roosevelt believed that the pro-business conservatism of the Republican party, although generally a good idea, needed to be tempered with protection for the victims of runaway capitalism. Roosevelt ran as a Progressive Republican ("Bull Moose") in 1912, splitting the Republican vote and allowing the Democrats to elect Woodrow Wilson. Wilson's two terms were the exception to Republican dominance. After World War I, the Republicans returned to the presidency.

It was not until the Great Depression that the Democrats regained power with the victory of Franklin Roosevelt in 1932. With the economy in complete disarray, Roosevelt succeeded where Bryan had failed. He put together the "Roosevelt coalition," adding support from urban workers in the North, immigrants, and Northern blacks to the Democrats' "solid South."

With the economy in complete disarray, Roosevelt succeeded where Bryan had failed. He put together the "Roosevelt coalition," adding support from urban workers in the North, immigrants, and northern blacks to the Democrats' "solid South."

The success of the Roosevelt coalition introduced the "fourth-party system." Democratic candidates accepted the ideas of liberal reform and held the coalition together. Republicans held to the more conservative traditions of their party. Democratic candidates attracted more support from ethnic minorities, Catholics, Jews, union members, and blacks, many of whom lived in the large metropolitan areas. Republicans attracted the support of the more-educated, Protestant, and suburban voters. Democratic candidates followed the New Deal ideology closely. Harry Truman's Fair Deal, John Kennedy's New Frontier, and Lyndon Johnson's Great Society were all based on the premise that the federal government should intervene to protect the downtrodden.

The fourth-party system endured until the solid South broke away from the coalition, largely over the civil rights issue. The Southern rebellion began in 1948 with the "Dixiecrat" party of Strom Thurmond and reached maturity with the election of 1972, when Nixon thrashed McGovern in the South. Carter regained some southern states in 1976, but he lost all but Georgia to Reagan in 1980.

The advent of a possible "fifth-party system" today reflects the increasing volatility of voters in presidential elections as well as underlying social and economic changes that may signal a realignment of the electorate. Some residual support remains for the Democratic and Republican coalitions of the fourth-party system, but these traditional coalitions are substantially less stable. In today's political

Table 6-2. Vote by Groups in Presidential Elections since 1952

	1952		1956		1960		1964	
	Stevenson	*Eisenhower*	*Stevenson*	*Eisenhower*	*Kennedy*	*Nixon*	*Johnson*	*Goldwater*
National	**44.6%**	**55.4%**	**42.2%**	**57.8%**	**50.1%**	**49.9%**	**61.3%**	**38.7%**
Sex								
Male	47	53	45	55	52	48	60	40
Female	42	58	39	61	49	51	62	38
Race								
White	43	57	41	59	49	51	59	41
Nonwhite	79	21	61	39	68	32	94	6
Education								
College	34	66	31	69	39	61	52	48
High school	45	55	42	58	52	48	62	38
Grade school	52	48	50	50	55	45	66	34
Occupation								
Prof. & business	36	64	32	68	42	58	54	46
White collar	40	60	37	63	48	52	57	43
Manual	55	45	50	50	60	40	71	29
Age								
Under 30 years	51	49	43	57	54	46	64	36
30–49 years	47	53	45	55	54	46	63	37
50 years & older	39	61	39	61	46	54	59	41
Religion								
Protestants	37	63	37	63	38	62	55	45
Catholics	56	44	51	49	78	22	76	24
Politics								
Republicans	8	92	4	96	5	95	20	80
Democrats	77	23	85	15	84	16	87	13
Independents	35	65	30	70	43	57	56	44
Region								
East	45	55	40	60	53	47	68	32
Midwest	42	58	41	59	48	52	61	39
South	51	49	49	51	51	49	52	48
West	42	58	43	57	49	51	60	40
Members of labor union families	61	39	57	43	65	35	73	27

environment, made more uncertain by "stagflation," budget deficits, and international tension, there are new signs of disaffection from the New Deal coalition.

In recent years, there has been some shift of neo-conservative intellectuals, professional managers, and both white-collar and blue-collar families from the Democratic to the Republican side (see Table 6-2). Moreover, Ronald Reagan has shown that an attractive Republican candidate can win in the Democratic South. Only in state and local elections is the "solid South" still predominantly Democratic. Spurred on by their capture of the Senate in the 1980 election, the Republicans, led by Reagan, will try to create a strategy to become the majority coalition of the future.

Table 6-2.   (*continued*)

| | 1968 | | | 1972 | | | 1976 | | | 1980 | |
Humphrey	Nixon	Wallace	McGovern	Nixon	Carter	Ford	McCarthy	Carter	Reagan	Anderson
43%	43.4%	13.6%	38%	62%	50%	48%	1%	41%	51%	7%
41	43	16	37	63	53	45	1	38	53	7
45	43	12	38	62	48	51	*	44	49	6
38	47	15	32	68	46	52	1	36	56	7
85	12	3	87	13	85	15	*	86	10	2
37	54	9	37	63	42	55	2	35	53	10
42	43	15	34	66	54	46	*	43	51	5
52	33	15	49	51	58	41	1	54	42	3
34	56	10	31	69	42	56	1	33	55	10
41	47	12	36	64	50	48	2	40	51	9
50	35	15	43	57	58	41	1	48	46	5
47	38	15	48	52	53	45	1	47	41	11
44	41	15	33	67	48	49	2	38	52	8
41	47	12	36	64	52	48	*	41	54	4
35	49	16	30	70	46	53	*	39	54	6
59	33	8	48	52	57	42	1	46	47	6
9	86	5	5	95	9	91	*	8	86	5
74	12	14	67	33	82	18	*	69	26	4
31	44	25	31	69	38	57	4	29	55	14
50	43	7	42	58	51	47	1	43	47	9
44	47	9	40	60	48	50	1	41	51	7
31	36	33	29	71	54	45	*	44	52	3
44	49	7	41	59	46	51	1	35	54	9
56	29	15	46	54	63	36	1	50	43	5

*Less than 1 percent.
Note: 1976 and 1980 results do not include vote for minor-party candidates.
Source: Gallup Poll Indexes, 1952–1980.

THE MINOR PARTIES

There has never been a really successful third-party challenge.* Occasionally, third parties have contributed to the defeat of one of the two major parties, and major parties have modified their official ideology in order to accommodate them, but the country still has a two-party system.

The persistence of two parties can be attributed to three factors. First, the party system began with *two* opposing factions: those favoring a strong central government and hence the Constitution (the Federalists) and those opposing them (Republicans). Second, Americans are culturally middle-of-the-road. They dislike extremes, and parties that become the captive of extreme elements disintegrate. Finally, the electoral system is a winner-take-all one. In congressional elections there is only one representative for a district. Whoever gets the most votes wins. Other systems (such as proportional representation) allow for seats to be allocated according to some formula reflecting percentage of votes for each party. The winner-take-all system is best illustrated by the electoral college. The candidate gaining the most votes in a state is awarded all of the state's electoral votes. Hence, Reagan won 51 percent of the popular vote but 91 percent of the electoral vote. It is difficult for minor parties to succeed under such a system, and voters are reluctant to "waste" their votes on third parties when they believe a major-party candidate will win.

> Third parties are usually formed because the members are ideologically committed to a course of action that maintains their intellectual "purity."

Third parties are usually formed because the members are ideologically committed to a course of action that maintains their intellectual "purity." They do not expect to win, but they expect that history will vindicate them. The Socialist, Socialist Labor, Socialist Workers, and Communist parties generally put forth candidates but get no more than a trace of the vote. The highest point for the parties of the ideological Left was 1912, when the Socialists won 6 percent of the vote (see Table 6-3). The Libertarian party, which advocates an absolute minimum of government interference in the economy or social life of the country, began running candidates in 1972 but never has gained more than one percent of the vote.

A different type of third party is the short-lived factional, or protest, movement, which begins within a major party. In 1912, Theodore Roosevelt's Progressive Republican (Bull Moose) party earned 27 percent of the vote and enabled Wilson to become president. How-

---

*Technically, the Republican party in 1860 was a third party, but it became a major party.

ever, such "successes" are rare. The States' Rights Democrats (Dixie-crats) of 1948, opposing the election of the Democrat Truman, did not deny him the election. Wallace's American Independent party (a more recent variant of the Dixiecrat tradition) did comparatively well in 1968, winning 13 percent of the vote. However, analysis of the election has led to the conclusion that Nixon would have won even without the Wallace candidacy. (Wallace voters hurt Nixon more than they did Humphrey.)[9]

Table 6-3.   Minor Parties in U. S. History

Year	Party	Popular votes (percent)	Electoral votes
1824	Democratic–Republican (Henry Clay)	12.99	37
	Democratic–Republican (William Crawford)	11.17	41
1832	Independent Democrat	0	11
	Anti-Masonic	7.78	7
1836	Independent Democrat	0	11
	Whig (Hugh White)	9.72	26
	Whig (Daniel Webster)	2.74	14
1840	Liberty	0.28	0
1844	Liberty	2.30	0
1848	Free Soil	10.12	0
1852	Free Soil	4.91	6
1856	Whig–American	21.53	8
1860	Southern Democrat	18.09	72
	Constitutional Union	12.61	39
1872	Straight Out Democrat	0.29	0
1876	Greenback	0.9	0
1880	Greenback	3.32	0
1884	Greenback	1.74	0
	Prohibition	1.47	0
1888	Prohibition	2.19	0
	Union Labor	1.29	0
1892	Populist	8.50	22
	Prohibition	2.25	0
1896	National Democrats	0.96	0
	Prohibition	0.90	0
1900	Prohibition	1.50	0
	Socialist	0.62	0
1904	Socialist	2.98	0
	Prohibition	1.91	0
1908	Socialist	2.82	0
	Prohibition	1.70	0
1912	Progressive	27.39	88
	Socialist	5.99	0
1916	Socialist	3.18	0
	Prohibition	1.19	0
1920	Socialist	3.42	0
	Farmer–Labor	0.99	0
1924	Progressive	16.56	13
	Prohibition	0.19	0

(Table continues)

Table 6-3. *(continued)*

Year	Party	Popular votes (percent)	Electoral votes
1928	Socialist	0.72	0
	Communist	0.13	0
1932	Socialist	2.22	0
	Communist	0.26	0
1936	Union	1.96	0
	Socialist	0.41	0
1940	Socialist	0.23	0
	Prohibition	0.12	0
1944	Socialist	0.16	0
	Prohibition	0.16	0
1948	States' Rights Democrat	2.40	39
	Progressive	2.38	0
1952	Progressive	0.23	0
	Prohibition	0.12	0
1956	Constitution	0.17	0
	Socialist–Labor	0.07	0
1960	Socialist–Labor	0.07	1 (Harry F. Byrd)
			15
1964	Socialist–Labor	0.06	0
	Socialist Workers	0.05	0
1968	American Independent	13.53	46
	Socialist–Labor	0.07	0
1972	Libertarian	0	1
	American	1.40	0
	People's	0.10	0
1976	Eugene McCarthy, independent candidate	1.00	0
1980	John Anderson, independent candidate	6.58	0
	Libertarian	1.04	0

Source: *Guide to U. S. Elections,* Congressional Quarterly, 1975.

These factional parties disappear when the leader gives up, unlike the ideological third parties, which persist regardless of the issues or the times. John Anderson, who ran as an independent, is the most recent example of the factional candidate. In 1980 Anderson, in winning about 7 percent of the vote, did no damage to an already doomed Carter. The Libertarian candidate, Ed Clark, and the Citizens Party candidate, Barry Commoner, also did not affect the outcome.

Anderson's candidacy illustrates the frustrations of third-party candidates. Failing to gain much support in the Republican primaries, Anderson launched his independent candidacy without a formal party organization. He did organize a "National Unity Coalition" with a former governor of Wisconsin, Patrick Lucey, as his running mate. Carter believed that Anderson would hurt his candidacy. Hence, he refused to appear in national debates if Anderson were to be included. Carter scornfully referred to Anderson as "the media candidate," by which he meant that the National Unity Coalition had not actually nominated Anderson. Anderson, like most minor candidates, attracted only a small core of supporters (from among the young, liberal, well-educated, and affluent) and made no inroads into either candidate's coalition. His was not a passionate candidacy. Indeed, he appeared to base his hopes on the fact that neither major-party candidate was very attractive. Although Carter argued the "wasted-vote" theory ("a vote for Anderson is a vote for Reagan"), analysis of voter preference revealed that this was an incorrect premise. Anderson gained much of his support from those who identified with neither party. As the time for the voters' decision drew near, Anderson's support declined. Initially, he was the choice of about 20 percent of the voters, but fewer than 7 percent remained loyal to him. His candidacy thus is a good illustration of the durability of the two-party system. Few voters want to protest, and when the final choice is to be made, the reality is that the president will either be a Democrat or a Republican.

John Anderson, the most recent challenger to the two-party system.

THE END OF PARTY POLITICS?

Americans have been losing their affection for the major parties for more than a decade, making media control of elections all the more likely. Before the era of the mass media, party affiliation was a reliable indicator of how a person would vote. However, with the advent of mass communication, party affiliation is far less important than candidate image. Two trends stand out: the percentage of people identifying themselves as "independent" is increasing, and the percentage of voters splitting their vote is increasing. The decline of party should come as no surprise if we examine voter perception of the parties. The majority of voters believes that there is no difference between the two parties. This may or may not be true, depending on which candidate survives the primaries; but people believe it to be true. Since the early 1960s the largest proportion of voters maintains that there is no difference between the parties with regard to ability to solve a particular problem.[10]

The Independent Electorate

The electorate, especially in presidential elections, is far less partisan than it once was. The proportion of people identifying themselves as independents has been increasing. The proportion identifying themselves as Democrats or Republicans has been declining. Today more people regard themselves as independents than Republicans or Democrats, making independents the largest category in the electorate. Even among those who still claim allegiance, more are likely to be "weak" identifiers than "strong" identifiers (Tables 6-4 and 6-5).

Independent voters tend to be younger than partisans. Younger voters are the products of the media age and its emphasis on personalities; to them, the appeal to partisan loyalties has a hollow ring.

Table 6-4. The Growth of Independents and the Decline of Strong Party Identifiers

	1952	1954	1956	1958	1960	1962
Strong Democrat	22%	22%	21%	23%	21%	23%
Weak Democrat	25	25	23	24	25	23
Independent, leaning Democrat	10	9	7	7	8	8
Independent, middle-of-the-road	5	7	9	8	8	8
Independent, leaning Republican	7	6	8	4	7	6
Weak Republican	14	14	14	16	13	16
Strong Republican	13	13	15	13	14	12

Table 6-5. Party Identification—1980

	Rep. (26%)	Ind. lean Rep. (15%)	Ind. (10%)	Ind. lean Dem. (15%)	Dem. (34%)
Age					
18–24	24	16	8	21	31
25–34	23	20	13	16	28
35–44	19	20	11	14	36
45–64	26	11	10	15	38
65 and over	38	7	9	6	40
Ideology					
Liberals	15	11	10	19	45
Moderates	22	15	10	16	37
Conservatives	36	18	6	13	27
Region					
Northeast	24	16	8	18	34
Midwest	24	14	11	16	35
South	27	14	10	11	38
White Southerners	30	16	10	10	34
West	30	15	13	14	28
Sex					
Men	24	19	9	15	33
Women	28	11	11	13	36
Education					
Less than high school graduate	24	11	11	13	41
High school graduate	25	16	7	16	36
Some college	30	13	13	15	26
College graduate +	30	21	7	14	28
Income					
First income quartile (Under $10,000)	33	6	7	10	44
Second income quartile	23	17	11	17	32
Third income quartile	25	18	8	14	35
Fourth income quartile	27	18	9	17	29
Religion					
White Protestants	34	15	11	12	28
Catholics	20	16	11	17	36
Race					
Blacks	7	7	4	16	66
Union					
Union households	19	13	10	17	41

Source: CBS News/New York Times national surveys; 1,439 April 1981 interviews, 9,902 1980 interviews, conducted January–September 1980. The 1980 partisanship figures were calculated by Solomon Barr. From *Public Opinion,* June/July 1981, p. 45.

Table 6-4. *(continued)*

1964	1966	1968	1970	1972	1974	1976	1978	1980	1981
26%	18%	20%	20%	15%	17%	15%	15%	18%	15%
25	27	25	23	25	21	25	24	23	16
9	9	10	10	11	13	12	14	11	9
8	12	11	13	13	15	14	14	13	21
6	7	9	8	11	9	10	9	10	12
13	15	14	15	13	14	14	13	14	13
11	10	10	10	10	8	9	8	9	14

Source: *National Journal,* June 13, 1981.

> Younger voters are the products of the media age and its
> emphasis on personalities; to them, the appeal to partisan
> loyalties has a hollow ring.

The frailty of party identification is also illustrated by split-ticket
voting. In the 1960s about 15 percent of the electorate regularly split
their tickets. By the 1970s, however, the proportion of ticket splitters
had doubled. Voters who split their tickets are likely to vote for congressional candidates who belong to "their" party but to reject their
party's presidential nominee.[11] The presidential election is far more
volatile and dependent on the media. It is here that image outweighs
party. Defections are far more common today than before the advent
of the primary systems and media dominance.

The Voters' Choice

The decline of parties as organizations is matched by the growing irrelevance of parties to voters. Traditionally, political scientists
have analyzed the voting choice as consisting of three components:
(1) party identification, (2) issue preference, and (3) candidate image.
Today television has made candidate image the most important component of electoral choice.

Without the stability of party identification, voters respond to the
whims of the moment. Swings in support are sharp and prompt. A
candidate's standing will rise sharply, taper off, then rise again, depending on an event, a speech, or a crisis. Carter experienced both
the greatest increase in popularity (immediately after the capture of
the hostages in Iran) and the most precipitous decrease in popularity
ever recorded.

The conventional wisdom of political science tells us that the
function of campaigns is to get out your supporters, rather than to
change minds. However, 1980 introduced a new buzzword, *volatility.*
Not only did the normal assumption that voters make up their minds
early prove wrong, but the lead also changed four times during the
election year. More than 25 percent of the voters did not reach a

decision until the final week.[12] The outcome was judged "too close to call" a week before the election, yet the actual election results were not even close. To estimate voter opinion, various pollsters tried to conduct interviews up to the day of the election. Those who did (Carter's pollsters, for example) saw Reagan's lead increasing in the final days. Inevitably, in the absence of firm ties to parties, programs, and candidates, voters' decisions come later in the campaign and are less firmly held. In 1980 the proportion of voters who were undecided was extraordinarily high in the closing weeks of the campaign. Thus, there existed a potential for a large, last-minute shift from one nominee to another. There was good reason to expect that a climactic event—such as a major debate—might prove decisive.

In such a fluid situation, issues and policy positions are relatively unimportant. When asked which party could do the best job of solving specific policy problems, astonishing majorities said there was either no difference or they did not know. Three-fourths said neither Republicans nor Democrats could do a better job of controlling inflation, solving energy shortages, or conducting foreign relations.

Mood Swing: The Volatile Electorate

Trends in electoral preference show that voters are subject to wild swings because of short-term factors. A close election is often followed by a landslide. The close presidential election of 1960 was followed by 1964's landslide; the close election of 1968 was followed by the landslide of 1972; and the close election of 1976 was followed by the landslide of 1980. (See accompanying table.)

Popular-Vote Margin in Presidential Elections

	Democrats	Republicans	Difference
1960	50%	50%	0.2%
1964	61	39	22
1968	42	43	1
1972	38	61	23
1976	50	48	2
1980	41	51	10

Adapted from *Public Opinion*, December/January 1981, p. 21.

Electorates are also volatile within a single year. Unpredictable events can doom a candidacy, as was the case with Edward Kennedy. A brief flurry of media interest can propel a candidate upward. Once the nomination was secure, Carter and Reagan exchanged the lead in the polls only once. Before the nomination there were three lead changes.

"Dealignment" from Parties

The public is undergoing a "dealignment" from parties, and the candidates are conducting campaigns without regard to the existing party structure. As a consequence of weakening party identification and the destruction of party organizations, electorates are less stable, less predictable, more fluid. Inevitably, these factors lead to a belief that neither party (or candidate) is capable of solving serious problems. During the first months of a new administration the public goes through a brief period of euphoria, with a majority believing that the newly elected president can actually do what he said he would do; but this brief respite leads only to even greater alienation and cynicism when government once again seems unresponsive.

In campaigns without an anchor, defections from party identification cannot be avoided. Why do such defections occur? A popular explanation is that, with the demise of parties, voters are more interested in selecting candidates with whom they agree on the issues, irrespective of party. "Issue voting" is said to have become more prevalent. But this popular explanation is clearly wrong. Recent presiden-

Mood swing is more apparent in the media-dominated personality contests associated with presidential elections. In congressional elections, where the play of personality is less evident, partisan loyalties are not yet dead. Hence, there has been a sharp upsurge in split-ticket voting, with voters favoring one party's candidate for Congress and another for the presidency (see figure).

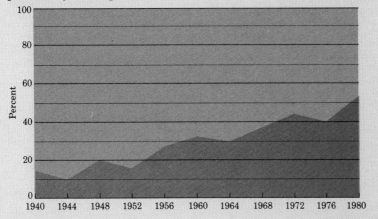

Increase in split-ticket voting for president and Congress. (Source: Richard W. Boyd, "Electoral Trends in Postwar Politics." In James D. Barber (Ed.), *Choosing the President.* © 1974 American Assembly, Columbia University. Reprinted by permission of Prentice-Hall, Inc., Englewood Cliffs, New Jersey. 1972 and 1976 data: Gallup Polls.)

tial campaigns have not been waged in terms of policy disputes between the two candidates but, instead, on the image of leadership. These "image" campaigns fit in perfectly with the media portrayal of them. Three-fourths of the coverage of campaigns by television does *not* discuss the issues. Rather, the media discuss the strategy of candidates and the size of crowds—the "horse-race" aspects of the campaign. The media deal in personalities, not issues.

To expect that voters would develop well-thought-out issue positions and link them with a candidate's policy statement is asking quite a lot. Voters do not know very much about the personnel of government, much less its policies. With television avoiding policy issues and with candidates catering to the whims of television, issues get shoved into a minor role. Even though most voters do not have

Is Anybody Listening?

Alienation of the American public from government is increasing, especially since 1977. That is, to an increasing number of people, government seems unresponsive, indifferent to their concerns, or even positively hostile. There are a variety of ways of measuring alienation; one is to determine the percentage that believes that "public officials are not really interested in the problems of the average man." (See Figure A.)

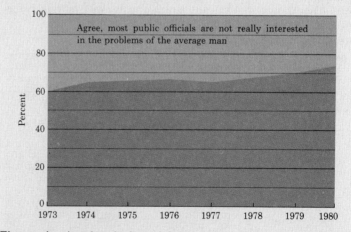

Figure A. Americans' view of how sympathetic public officials are. (Source: *Public Opinion*, October/November 1980, p. 25.)

Another manifestation of alienation is attitude toward parties and candidates. When asked to identify the "most important problem" facing the nation and then to name the party most capable of solving it, the greatest percentage an-

clear policy positions against which to measure candidates, they do tend to think in terms of "liberalism" or "conservatism." Liberal voters generally vote for Democratic candidates, and conservative voters tend to prefer Republicans, in keeping with the "image" of the two parties.[13]

The Meaning of Ideology

Many people who call themselves liberals or conservatives have no real understanding of what is meant by those terms. Many people who say they are liberals actually oppose policies traditionally associated with a liberal position.

The issue of the role of the federal government in providing jobs and a decent standard of living has been the source of an enduring

---

swers that there is no difference or offers no opinion. (See accompanying table.)

Public's View: Which Party Best Solves Problems?

	Democratic	Republican	No opinion/ No difference
October 1978	31%	21%	48%
February 1979	29	23	48
May 1979	31	21	48
October 1979	33	25	42
January 1980	34	21	45
March 1980	32	28	40
July 1980	27	30	43

Source: Surveys by the Gallup Organization, latest that of July 11–14, 1980. In *Public Opinion*, August/September 1980, p. 21.

If specific policies on which to estimate the differences between the parties are given, the same results appear.

A different problem is apathy, or lack of interest in, or caring about, government. Perhaps people are not voting because they believe that it will accomplish nothing, since public officials are believed to be indifferent. If this is so, not voting is actually a political statement, a "negative participation." This appears to be the case. Nonvoters give alienated answers more often than do voters, although even among voters there is substantial alienation. (See Figure B on the next page.) Although there are many reasons why about half of the eligible voters stay out of presidential elections, alienation is clearly a factor.

(continued)

(*continued*)

Alienation Indicators

Voters   Nonvoters

Self–described political ideology (1977 and 1978)

28%	Liberal	29%
37%	Moderate	43%
35%	Conservative	29%

"People running country don't care what happens to you" (1978)

50%	Feel	62%
50%	Don't feel	38%

"Most people with power take advantage of people like self" (1978)

51%	Feel	70%
49%	Don't feel	30%

"People in Washington out of touch with rest of country" (1978)

58%	Feel	63%
42%	Don't feel	37%

"How much confidence in Executive branch of federal government" (1977 and 1978)

21%	Great deal	21%
60%	Only some	56%
19%	Hardly any	23%

"How much confidence in Congress" (1977 and 1978)

17%	Great deal	16%
64%	Only some	63%
19%	Hardly any	21%

"Hardly fair to bring a child into the world the way things look for future" (1977)

35%	Agree	47%
65%	Disagree	53%

"Public officials not interested in problems facing the average man" (1977)

62%	Agree	72%
38%	Disagree	28%

Figure B. Comparison of the attitudes of voters and nonvoters. (Source: Surveys by National Opinion Research Center, General Social Surveys, 1977 and 1978. In *Public Opinion,* April/May 1980, p. 35.)

> Many people who call themselves liberals or conservatives have no real understanding of what is meant by those terms.

partisan debate in Congress. Liberal officeholders believe that the federal government should take an active role in the economy, whereas conservative officeholders prefer more reliance on individual initiative. Yet the ability to link abstract ideology to specific policy is lacking for most of the electorate. Many people who say they are conservative want to see the government play a large role in the economy. Reflecting on these findings, Levitin and Miller conclude that:

> . . . even an electoral victory heavily influenced by the ideological self labeling of the voters may defy interpretations in terms of a policy mandate. . . . Most voters are unable to distinguish the liberal from the conservative position on many issues. Apparently only the best educated among the most ideological of voters understand the ideological implications of their policy preferences clearly enough to link themselves ideologically to the policy preferences and to party or candidate as well as, ultimately, to the vote decision.[14]

Political Parties and the "New Class"

The growing inability of political parties to secure the stable loyalty of voters is only partially revealed by the increase in independents. As partisan identification declined, the social bases of party support also changed. The Democratic party, popularly identified as the party of working people, began to command the attention of what Ladd refers to as the **"New Class."**[15] The recent extensive growth in higher education, accompanied by the increased value placed on technical skills, has resulted in a dramatic increase in the number of people engaged in the business of the production and dissemination of knowledge—the New Class. Jeane Kirkpatrick describes this class as "symbol specialists." They are highly trained in the use of ideas and symbols and skilled in their communication.[16] The New Class found employment in higher education, of course, but also in business and government. Although its members are educated and relatively well-to-do, they do not find the Republican party very attractive. Old-style ideology has a diminished appeal for these new intellectuals who are filling positions in traditionally Republican areas. As a result, members of the New Class have contributed to a decline of support for the Republican party among what was once its natural clientele. The percentage of business executives who vote a straight Republican ticket has been steadily declining. Another clear indication is the campaign spending of business-linked political action committees (PACs). In 1978 corporate PACs gave $6.5 million to Republicans but $5 million to Democrats.

The New Class: The new governmental/academic/business elites who are skilled in the communication of political ideas and who are attracted to the Democratic Party.

> Members of the New Class have contributed to a decline of support for the Republican party among what was once its natural clientele.

This is not to suggest that the business community is no longer Republican in sympathy. The majority of chief executives of large corporations still identify themselves as Republicans. However, most have come to believe that it does not matter which party wins. Rawleigh Warner, Jr., Chairman of the Mobil Corporation, asserts "Business has fared equally well, if not better, under Democratic administrations as under Republican administrations.[17]

The values of the New Class tend to be more liberal than those of the less advantaged. Its members are more supportive of environmental legislation, efforts to solve urban problems, and efforts to improve education. They are less supportive of increased funds for the military. Socially, they are far more tolerant than are the majority.

The New Class rejected Goldwater, as did the working class; it voted for Nixon, as did the working class, and it was somewhat more enthusiastic about Reagan. As a consequence, differences between the classes are narrowing. Reagan's candidacy did not set class against class.

The diminishing differences among traditional groups of voters are apparent in the 1980 election results. The Democrat, Jimmy Carter, did win a majority of support from blacks, self-identified liberals, those earning less than $10,000 annually, the unemployed, those with less than a high school education, and those living in cities over 250,000. He also won the support of self-identified Democrats.[18] This looks like the old New Deal coalition that propelled Franklin Roosevelt into four terms in the 1930s and 1940s and has been relied on by Democratic candidates ever since. But there are some conspicuous absences from the old coalition. Carter lost among Roman Catholics, who generally support Democrats, and he did very poorly among the working classes. Labor unions, which supply a major portion of the funds for Democratic candidates, could not deliver their usual substantial majority for the president. Many of the groups that abandoned Carter were Democratic in identification. Among professionals, for example, the party identification is Republican, 27 percent; Democratic, 39 percent; and independent, 34 percent. But professionals gave Reagan 55 percent of their vote. College graduates display a similar pattern but gave Reagan 53 percent. Catholics and Jews provide a more dramatic example of the willingness of voters to shrug off party loyalty and vote for the man. Even though a majority of Catholics identify with the Democratic Party, a slim plurality preferred Reagan.

THE PRIMARY ELECTIONS

In place of strong parties we now have the personal organizations of the presidential candidates—organizations that are loyal to the candidate rather than to the party. These personal organizations must remain intact through the long primary season; to do so they must have been created and financed well in advance. Both Reagan and Carter built their organization at least a year before the first primary election was held.

The rise of the primary system, along with the decline in party identification among voters, has revolutionized presidential elections. There are no party bosses to pick candidates in smoke-filled rooms. Their place has been taken by the media. To understand the replacing of party bosses by the media, we need to understand how and why presidential primary elections have grown.

In 1968 the Democrats nominated Vice-President Humphrey at a convention torn by violence and demonstrations. Most of the delegates at the convention had *not* been elected in primaries; they had been named by state party organizations. These organizations supported Humphrey, and the various youthful demonstrators were enraged, because Humphrey supported the war in Vietnam. Humphrey was nominated without having won a single primary election. The clash in values between the party regulars and the youthful activists was stark, and it was made even more so by television. Viewers saw the symbol of the old-style politics, Mayor Daley of Chicago, use his police force to disperse the young demonstrators. Television also showed us a convention packed with Chicago municipal employees drowning out any dissent. Television commentators were clearly more sympathetic to the protestors than to the police.

Out of this televised disaster emerged the "new politics" of McGovern in 1972. He and his supporters wanted to create a more responsive and democratic national party. As a result, Democrats added a set of rules, implemented for the 1972 convention, dealing with representation of youth, blacks and other minorities, and women. These rules were so complex and cumbersome that many state leaders chose to adopt primary elections in their stead. Although McGovern was soundly beaten by Nixon in the 1972 general election, the popularity of the primary was well established. The Republicans followed the Democratic lead in switching to primary elections, and by 1980 three-fourths of the delegates to both conventions were elected by primary elections. (See Figure 6-3 on the next page.) Thirty-six states relied on primaries.

Like all reforms, this one was inspired by a genuine belief in more democracy. The results, however, were less than encouraging. Turnout in primary elections is rarely higher than 30 percent. The lower class is underrepresented, and the educated and affluent professional

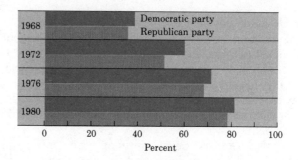

Figure 6-3. Percentage of national-convention delegates elected by presidential primary

and managerial class—the New Class—is overrepresented. Party organizations have no impact on primary election voters.

Aspiring presidential candidates move into a state with their own organization. The goal is to establish a candidate as a front-runner as early as possible. This means doing well in the New Hampshire primary, which traditionally begins the primary season.

As New Hampshire Goes ...

As we saw in Chapter 5, New Hampshire, a tiny state of little actual electoral significance, becomes the battleground in which political careers are made or broken. New Hampshire's voters account for fewer than 1 percent of all votes cast in primaries and fewer than 1 percent of the delegates to national conventions. But New Hampshire is crucial, because it has become a media event. Front-runners, or "serious candidates," are made in New Hampshire, and they are made largely by the media.

> "New Hampshire's small size, nearness to metropolitan centers of the east coast, and New England landscape and culture make it an especially attractive subject for national television. The fact that it is also the first presidential primary makes it nearly irresistible."

States hold primaries to select candidates but also because it is good for business. New Hampshire is lavishly covered by television news: "New Hampshire's small size, nearness to metropolitan centers of the east coast, and New England landscape and culture make it an especially attractive subject for national television. The fact that it is also the first presidential primary makes it nearly irresistible."[19] In 1980, network television news devoted 100 stories to New Hampshire, which held its primary on February 26. It devoted only about half as many to Massachusetts, which held its primary a week later.

The fact that Massachusetts elects nearly four times as many delegates to national conventions than does New Hampshire is of no matter. New York, with an April primary, produced only thirty stories, even though it elects nearly ten times as many delegates as does New Hampshire.

Deciding Who "Wins"

To "win," a candidate does not actually have to win, but merely to do better than the media have predicted. The strategy is clear: convince the media that you have no money or time to campaign, and then do better than they have forecast. It is probable that Carter could not have become president in 1976 without "winning" in New Hampshire. Well before the primary season, he made frequent trips to New Hampshire, achieving more familiarity with the voters there than was realized by the media. The key was establishing low expectations. Carter's manager explained:

> It had already been established in the national press that [U. S. Representative Morris] Udall was going to do well in New Hampshire, that he should win in New Hampshire. He had established that expectation. . . . We never talk about winning anywhere. We talk about doing well. And I think that the candidate and the campaign itself play a part in establishing this expectation with the media.[20]

In a crowded field Carter received 29 percent of the vote—4,300 more votes than Udall—and was declared the big winner.

Consider the fate of other candidates in other years. Senator Eugene McCarthy challenged President Johnson in New Hampshire in 1968, lost by 6 percent, but was declared the "winner." Indeed, Johnson's decision not to seek reelection was heavily influenced by McCarthy's "victory." In 1972 McGovern *lost* to Senator Edmund Muskie by 9 percent but was declared the winner by the media, thus launching his successful drive for the nomination. The enduring image of being labeled a winner or a loser in New Hampshire is remarkable.

Image Making in 1980

The 1980 campaign involved these same media strategies. Carter, now the incumbent, was challenged by Edward Kennedy. Reagan, the front-runner, was challenged by a variety of Republicans, but most seriously by Bush, the choice of the Republican establishment and the hope of the moderate wing of the party.

Kennedy's campaign was well organized, well funded, and well planned. However, the capture of American hostages by Iran and the resultant rally-'round-the-flag sentiment doomed him. Even before this lucky (for Carter) event, there were disturbing signs. Kennedy was widely regarded as an attractive personality, one whom the media could support. However, in a television interview with CBS' Roger Mudd before the primary season Kennedy appeared confused, gave vague answers to questions raised by the Chappaquiddick incident, and could not even explain why he wanted to become president. The interview, fortunately for Kennedy, was shown opposite the movie *Jaws* and did not receive as much attention as would otherwise have been expected.[21] It did tell the media something, however. The apparent nominee of the Democratic party was not good copy. Further, Kennedy could never shake the habit of shouting. He was a "hot" rather than "cool" media personality. His speeches were loud and strident, accustomed as he was to the politics of Massachusetts. As he yelled the slogans of liberalism, his media image suffered.

Kennedy's candidacy was destroyed by Iran, but its destruction was assisted by the media. Because of the hostages, the media allowed Carter to conduct an "above-politics" campaign from the White House. He was free of serious scrutiny. In the early days of the Iranian crisis Carter appeared as a calm, resolute, and clearheaded leader under stress. Comparisons with Kennedy's unfortunate behavior at Chappaquiddick were inevitable. Again we come to New Hampshire. Carter came in first, receiving about 47 percent of the vote. The media could have declared him the loser, because an incumbent president should expect a majority from his own party. However, he was the media "winner" again.

Reagan's strategy was forced on him by a poor showing in the Iowa caucuses, held before the New Hampshire primary. Bush wanted to create an image of the front-runner. He spent substantial amounts of time and money in Iowa, whereas Reagan remained aloof. The Iowa caucuses attracted an extraordinary amount of media attention, even though the voting procedure was not that of a primary election. Assembled delegates at local levels cast preference votes, but there was no way of knowing how representative they were, since self-selection, rather than party appointment, determined who would assemble. Bush narrowly edged Reagan, and the media immediately identified him as the front-runner. Whereas Bush had had trouble attracting media attention before Iowa, he now found himself surrounded by eager reporters. He added extra planes to accommodate them, a clear indication of the health of his campaign. Bush also created silly slogans to catch the eye of the media. *Momentum* was his word, gradually transformed into the "Big Mo." With the Big Mo on his side, he went into New Hampshire as the favorite.

Inadvertently, then, the media had set up Reagan to "win" in New Hampshire. By proclaiming Bush as the new leader of the pack, they gave Reagan the opportunity that he missed in 1976—to do well even if he "lost." Reagan received slightly less than half of the votes in the New Hampshire primary, with Bush coming in second. The results were interpreted as a disaster for Bush. Had he not edged Reagan in the Iowa caucuses, Bush's second-place showing might have been interpreted as a "victory."

New Hampshire thus established the nominees for both parties—Carter and Reagan. Soon thereafter, Carter's popularity began to drop as the public grew impatient over lack of progress in Iran. Carter tried to reverse the trend by a series of carefully timed announcements about Iran and the Soviet invasion of Afghanistan: presidential responses seemed obviously keyed to the electoral calendar. A boycott of the Olympic games was formally proposed the Sunday before the Iowa caucuses. The UN commission was sent to Iran a few days before the New Hampshire primary. Two days before the Illinois primary, Carter stressed his tough stand on Afghanistan by implying that he would renounce the strategic arms treaty. As the polls opened the morning of the Wisconsin primary, the president gave a televised address to announce an apparent breakthrough in negotiations with Iran. The visual symbols of these various foreign policy crises were emphasized strongly by Carter. He curtailed the traditional lighting of the national Christmas tree in Washington and referred to Iran and Afghanistan at every opportunity. Once the "outsider," Carter was now creating the image of the symbol of national unity in time of crisis.

The symbolism employed by the president was enough to get him through the primary elections against Kennedy, a candidate once regarded as unbeatable. However, as the Iranian crisis continued with no visible solution, the public became impatient. Cronkite closed each of his evening news programs on CBS-TV by recalling the number of days that the hostages had been in captivity. As the president's popularity began to wane once again, he clung doggedly to the tactics that had worked in the past; no longer the "outsider," he could nevertheless make the issue one of judgment and leadership rather than one of policy or issues. As the rally-'round-the-flag symbol began to dissipate, the challenge from Kennedy did not gain, however. The president hammered home a single theme: he did not panic under pressure. Without specifically mentioning Chappaquiddick, Carter was able to plant suspicions in the minds of many voters. Voters in the primaries were not voting for or against the president's policies; they were voting for or against a quality of leadership. Kennedy was found wanting. Voters emphasizing personal qualities disapproved of Kennedy, whereas those voters emphasizing policy or issues tended to favor him. Since most emphasized personal qualities, Carter won. After Carter's victory in Illinois, the media declared the primary season over.

If Carter won the primaries because he was judged the lesser of two evils on the dimension of leadership, just the opposite was true of Reagan. Reagan's image was of a confident, fatherly, friendly yet forceful leader. Reagan spoke simply, although occasionally without good information. The Republican establishment did not really welcome him. They believed that his support was too narrowly focused among conservative voters. Recalling the disaster of Goldwater's crushing defeat by Johnson in 1964, prominent Republicans began to search for yet another alternative. Since their man, Bush, appeared to have been damaged fatally in the eyes of the media, they turned to Ford. Ford pointed to public-opinion surveys indicating that he was preferred by Republican voters over Reagan. Before the primary-election system, Ford would have posed a serious threat. But now the only way for Ford to win was to enter the primaries. However, he had no staff, no organization, and no chance. As was the case with Kennedy, the support of state party leaders was irrelevant.

Reagan's image was of a confident, fatherly, friendly yet forceful leader.

Reagan won the Illinois primary, and the media pronounced the election over for the Republicans as well. Illinois was especially important because it was the home state of Anderson, one of the numerous moderates pursuing Reagan. His defeat by Reagan persuaded him to begin his independent candidacy. Reagan's victory was viewed by the media as decisive for one special reason. Although he did not receive an actual majority of the vote in the primary, his first-place finish was accomplished in spite of formidable obstacles. Illinois allows an "open" primary, making it possible for Democrats to vote. Reagan's victory convinced the media that he could win a general election—that Ford's assertion that he was "too conservative" was wrong. Much of Reagan's crossover vote came from Democrats, but not from liberals. Rather, Reagan drew well among working-class Democrats.

The party organization, weak as it is, had been excluded from the nominating process from the beginning. The rush to an early decision precluded much discussion of the issues. By March, choices had been made, even though not a single primary had been held west of the Mississippi. The choice went to the "media candidates." Carter and Reagan were not longtime party regulars and were opposed by the party organizations. But they had generated personal organizations, had successfully courted the media, and had "won" early. It is small wonder that, as the general-election campaign began, half the voting population indicated dissatisfaction with *both* nominees.[22]

Essentials: Securing the Right to Vote

Participation in American elections lags well behind that of other industrial democracies even though the legal impediments to voting have been disappearing almost since the beginning of the new nation. From the elimination of property requirements to court-mandated reapportionment, there has been a progressive effort to make elections more "democratic."

Property

Early in the nation's history, fear of the "common man" was so great that most states required that substantial personal income or property be acquired before the right to vote could be granted. Those without property, so the framers of the Constitution believed, might use the vote to attack property rights. So severe were these restrictions that, in the elections of the 1780s, only about 120,000 out of a population of 2 million were eligible to vote. Since the Constitution left voting requirements to the states, property qualifications remained in state laws until the early 1800s. Under the influence of Jefferson and especially Jackson, political leaders and parties competed for the support of the common man, and property qualifications were eventually dropped in all of the states.

Race

The next barrier to fall was race. Unlike property requirements, however, the struggle for the elimination of discrimination on the basis of race was long and intense. The Fifteenth Amendment, passed by Congress after the Civil War, provides that "the right of the citizens of the United States to vote shall not be denied or abridged by the United States or any state on account of race, color, or previous condition of servitude." The object was to extend the suffrage to former black slaves. The amendment gives Congress the right to enforce the rights of blacks by "appropriate" legislation. This provision proved important, as the former states of the Confederacy developed a variety of ingenious methods for preventing black voting.

One response was violence, and the Ku Klux Klan during the Reconstruction era attempted to nullify the Fifteenth Amendment by terrorizing the black population. Furthermore, states were able to prohibit blacks from voting in primary elections. Arguing that the Fifteenth Amendment ap-

(continued)

(*continued*)

plied only to general elections, the Southern legislatures declared that primary elections were a private matter. For many years in the South, winning the Democratic primary was tantamount to election. General elections were a mere formality with at best token Republican opposition. Thus, the "white primary" eliminated the effective participation of blacks. Not until 1944, in *Smith* v. *Allwright,* did the Supreme Court outlaw racial discrimination in primary elections: "When primaries become part of the machinery in choosing officials . . . as they have here, the same tests to determine the character of discrimination . . . should be applied to the primary as are applied to the general election."*

Still, despite the extension of the Fifteenth Amendment to primary elections, most blacks in the Southern states were kept from voting. Local registrars were able to turn them away by creating seemingly endless obstacles and delays. Literacy tests were a common form of discrimination. Black college graduates routinely "failed" to interpret complex legal documents that were part of the tests, whereas illiterate whites were just as routinely passed. Application forms were lengthy and complicated, and minor errors were used to disqualify blacks but not whites.

The Civil Rights Act of 1964 outlawed the unequal application of voting standards, required that literacy tests be in writing, and mandated that a sixth-grade education would be taken as a presumption of literacy. In the same year the Twenty-fourth Amendment eliminated yet another discriminatory requirement, the poll tax. By imposing such a tax, Southern states were able to depress black voting, since most blacks could not afford to pay a tax to vote.

In 1965 in Selma, Alabama, civil rights organizations demonstrated that local registrars had kept blacks from registering by closing their offices when blacks appeared, delaying black applications for months, and limiting the number of applications to be processed. In direct response to the Selma campaign, the Voting Rights Act of 1965 was passed. The act applied to any county where literacy tests or similar devices had been employed as of November, 1964, and where fewer than 50 percent of voting-age residents of either race were either registered or had cast ballots in the 1964 presidential election. In these areas the attorney general could replace local registrars with federal registrars and enroll voters without any conditions. The threat of direct federal control of elections caused most Southern counties to end voter discrimination.

The impact of the Voting Rights Act was dramatic. The act has effectively eliminated discrimination in the registration of blacks.

Sex

Legal discrimination against women in voting was not ended until the passage of the Nineteenth Amendment in 1919 and its ratification just before the 1920 presidential elections. Efforts to secure the right to vote for women actually began shortly after the conclusion of the Civil War. By the turn of the century, women's suffrage became a major issue, and well-organized protests by suffragists helped to secure the passage of the Nineteenth Amendment.

Age

In 1971 Congress approved and sent to the states for ratification the Twenty-sixth Amendment to the Constitution. The amendment states that "the right of citizens of the United States, who are eighteen years of age or older, to vote shall not be denied or abridged by the United States or by any state on account of age." The debate surrounding the ratification of this amendment occurred during the turbulence of the Vietnam War. Supporters of the amendment argued that those who fought should be allowed to vote (an argument first advanced by Governor Ellis Arnall of Georgia during World War II, when that state became the first to grant the vote to eighteen-year-olds). Supporters of the amendment also hoped to reduce protests on campuses and in the streets by extending the right to vote to students. Many Democratic supporters believed that younger voters would prefer that party; and many liberal candidates of both parties believed that idealistic young voters would be a source of electoral strength. However, the results of the amendment have been far less dramatic than anticipated. Younger voters have a lower rate of participation and do not consistently favor Democrats or liberal candidates.

Closed and Open Primary Elections

Another barrier to participation is partisanship. Since most states nominate candidates by primary election, participation in the primary can be as important as participation in the

(continued)

(*continued*)

general election. In addition to the presidential primaries, all but a handful of states nominate all other federal and state candidates by primaries. Thirty-nine states use the "closed" primary system: a voter must have previously registered as a member of the party in order to vote in that party's primary election. State requirements vary as to how long in advance of the primary this registration must occur. Those who register as independents are excluded from voting for party candidates but may vote on nonpartisan issues.

To overcome these impediments, eight states (Idaho, Michigan, Minnesota, Montana, North Dakota, Utah, Vermont, and Wisconsin) use an "open" primary. In open primaries, voters can choose a party ballot as they enter the polling place. Voters may choose one party's primary because it is more interesting, or they may vote in the "other" party's primary in order to help elect a weak opponent for "their" party in the general election. Some party leaders prefer closed primaries, because they fear this "crossover" vote. There is little evidence that much "raiding" occurs, however. In three states—Alaska, Louisiana, and Washington—a "blanket primary" allows voters to choose from among all the party candidates for each office.

Reapportionment: One Person, One Vote

The principle of "one person, one vote" was initially set forth by the Supreme Court in *Baker* v. *Carr* in 1962. In this decision and in a follow-up ruling in *Reynolds* v. *Sims* (1964), the Court ruled that both houses of state legislatures must apportion seats on the basis of population. In *Wesberry* v. *Sanders* (1964), the Court extended this principle to congressional districts. The Court has not established an absolute mathematical formula for the ratio between representatives and represented. Generally, the total population of the state is divided by the total number of representatives to obtain the average district population. Actual districts should not deviate from the average district in population by more than 2 to 3 percent.

The U. S. Constitution requires that House seats be apportioned to the states every ten years on the basis of a census of the population. Although the absolute number of representatives is not established, there have been 435 representatives since 1912.

Smith v. *Allwright*, 321 U. S. 649 (1944).

THE 1980 GENERAL ELECTION

Carter was able to avoid the issues in the 1976 presidential election. He alienated no one, and he recaptured about half of those Democrats who had bolted in 1972.

But could such a fuzzy approach succeed in 1980? For the first time since 1964, the Republicans nominated a candidate identified with the conservative wing of the party. However, Reagan had no intention of repeating the pure conservatism of Goldwater. He wanted to win. As Pomper and his associates explain,

> The party attempted to present itself and its candidate as pragmatic and patriotic. Some platform language was modified to assuage moderates, and special sections were included to appeal to blacks, urban residents, and blue-collar workers—the traditional Democratic base. Respectful attention was given to established figures in the moderate wing of the party. . . . The moderate and effective national chairman, Bill Brock, was kept in office.[23]

Most important, the vice-presidential nomination was awarded to Bush, the choice of the moderate Republican establishment.

Turnout in 1980 was 51 percent, continuing a trend toward lower participation. Since 1960 each presidential election has produced a lower turnout than the preceding one.

Public-opinion polls indicated that a majority of voters was dissatisfied with both candidates. The turnout in 1980 was 53 percent, continuing a trend toward lower participation. Since 1960 each presidential election has produced a lower turnout than the preceding one. The campaign was composed of trivia. Reagan gave "the speech," and Carter insisted that Reagan was likely to start a nuclear war. Carter's brother Billy embarrassed the president by engaging in some dubious financial arrangements with the Libyan government, but Carter's single-minded attack on Reagan continued. The issue was simply put: do you want war or peace? Reagan's single theme was economic: are you better off now than you were four years ago? Carter gradually expanded his theme; Reagan would not only lead the nation into war, he would also divide it by abandoning the poor. With regard to his own performance, little was said; he knew he was the most unpopular president in recent history. Yet he felt compelled to emphasize *something*. He chose to repeat the theme of experience. Whereas in 1976 he was the "outsider," now he was the calm helmsman of the ship of state. Almost every address contained some reference to "the Oval Office."

Carter launched a three-pronged media attack: Reagan would push the button on the Russians; Reagan would pull the plug on the poor; but Carter, speaking from the Oval Office, was a reasonable man. The strategy had some benefits; polls indicated that Reagan's lead was being eroded. As a consequence of these surveys, Reagan, who had earlier indicated no desire to debate Carter, changed his mind. Clearly, the media and the polls were controlling events.

The president was pursuing an unorthodox strategy. Rather than discussing his accomplishments (even though Reagan was attacking them), Carter tried to present Reagan as a worse alternative. He wanted the voters to regard Reagan as not sophisticated enough to

---

The Presidential Debate:
Carter Pleads for Loyalty,
Reagan Relies on Symbols

Carter: We have made good progress, and there is no doubt in my mind that the commitment to unemployment compensation, the minimum wage, welfare, national health insurance, those kinds of commitments that have typified the Democratic party since ancient history in this country's political life are a very important element of the future. In all those elements, Governor Reagan has repeatedly spoken out against them, which, to me, shows a very great insensitivity to giving deprived families a better chance in life. This, to me, is a very important difference between him and me in this election, and I believe the American people will judge accordingly.

Reagan: Next Tuesday is Election Day. Next Tuesday all of you will go to the polls, will stand there in the polling place and make a decision. I think when you make that decision, it might be well if you would ask yourself, are you better off than you were four years ago? Is it easier for you to go and buy things in the stores than it was four years ago? Is there more or less unemployment in the country than there was four years ago? Is America as respected throughout the world as it was? Do you feel ... that we're as strong as we were four years ago? And if you answer all of those questions yes, why then, I think your choice is very obvious as to whom you will vote for. If you don't agree ... then I could suggest another choice that you have.

Excerpts from the Reagan/Carter televised debate, October 28, 1980.

understand the problems of modern government. During the campaign, the president did not deliver one major policy speech.

Reagan needed the debate to continue the construction of his image. Carter was condemning him as a right-wing warmonger, but Reagan avoided an ideological label. Downplaying his opposition to the Equal Rights Amendment, he endorsed a statutory enactment of the same principle. His earlier endorsement of an amendment to ban abortion was replaced by silence. He ameliorated his hard-line approach to communist regimes by supporting the recognition of the People's Republic of China and nuclear arms negotiations with the Soviet Union. In short, Reagan presented himself not as an ideologue but as a moderate.

During the debate, Reagan successfully completed his image building. He spoke of peace, repeating the word almost as often as Carter mentioned the Oval Office. Reagan was relaxed. He joked. When he wanted to argue that Carter had misrepresented his position, he intoned, "There you go again." A genial man, not looking nearly as old as he was, was actually chiding the president of the United States! How could this relaxed and reassuring man be the maniac he was alleged to be? Carter, clearly in command of the facts, lectured and hectored. Reagan, in command of clichés, proved once again that the medium is the message.

Because Carter had harped so much on the issue of war and peace (called the "Tolstoy issue" by the press), he had been labeled as "Jimmy the mean." Carter insisted on portraying Reagan as "extremely dangerous and belligerent." Carter's tone was harsh, his manner severe. Reagan's humor not only made him appear as personally preferable but also gave the appearance of making fun of the president: "I know the president's supposed to reply to me, but sometimes I have a hard time in connecting what he is saying with what I have said or what my positions are."[24]

The debates, and the election, were not about issues; they were about images. Reagan's theme, "It's time for a change," rarely got beyond such simple phrases as "Are you better off now than you were four years ago? Is it easier to buy things in the stores than it was four years ago? Is America as respected throughout the world as it was? Do you feel that our security is as safe, that we're as strong as we were four years ago?" Carter, unable to find much strength from his incumbency, simply argued that things would be a lot worse if he lost.

All polls indicated that the debate was "won" by Reagan. (See Figure 6-4 on the next page.) "Winning" did not mean outpointing Carter in a debating contest, for he clearly did not do that, nor did he care. "Winning" meant convincing voters that he was not what Carter said he was—that he was a pleasant and reasonable man with a healthy sense of humor and a calm approach to serious problems.

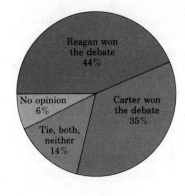

Question: Which candidate do you think did the best job—or won the debate—Carter or Reagan?

Response shown for the 83% of the sample who watched or listened to the debate.

Figure 6-4. The public judges the Carter/Reagan debate. (Source: Survey by CBS News, October 28, 1980. In *Public Opinion,* December/ January 1981, p. 34.)

ELECTIONS AS A POLICY MANDATE?

Reagan's victory was, not unexpectedly, widely interpreted by the media as a dramatic swing to the right. Of course, Reagan's administration was fond of speaking of a "mandate" from the people, as is any new administration. All politicians refer to such election mandates to do what they wish. But 1980 was especially important, because Reagan had an image as a conservative. His proposals were spoken of by television commentators as "revolutionary."

Reagan chose to interpret his election as a mandate for any number of policies. His treasury secretary remarked that for Congress to fail to approve a three-year tax reduction would be to violate the mandate of the election. David Stockman, Reagan's budget director, asserted that deep cuts in social-service agencies were also mandated. A mandate is whatever successful candidates say it is, because voters rarely have clear policies in mind. Like most recent elections, the presidential election of 1980 was an *image* election. Fewer than half of the Republicans and only one-third of the Democrats and independents who voted for Reagan favored his three-year tax cut. Most voters continued to express a long-term commitment to spending and even favored an increase in federal spending for education (Reagan proposed to abolish the Department of Education).[25]

The election was no more than a referendum on the performance of Carter. Substantial majorities did not think he could control inflation; they disapproved of his handling of the Iran crisis; and in general they regarded him as an incompetent president. They were voting against Carter. Thirty-eight percent of those who voted for Reagan gave "It's time for a change" as their reason; only eleven percent mentioned their preference for a conservative candidate.[26] The low turnout indicated little enthusiasm for either candidate, rather than a surge of support for a new conservative ideology. The coalition in support of Reagan was virtually identical to that in sup-

Suppose They Gave an Election and Nobody Came

American electoral turnout is on the decline (see figure). In the 1980 presidential election it barely exceeded the 50 percent mark. Primary elections produce substantially lower turnout than does the general election. As the accompanying table shows, turnout in the United States is the lowest of any industrial democracy.

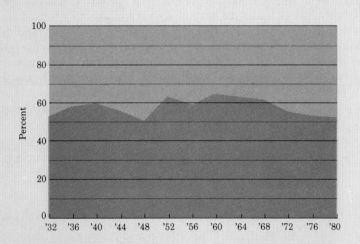

Turnout for U. S. presidential elections as a percentage of voting-age population. (Source: *Statistical Abstract of the United States,* 1973 for elections from 1932 to 1976, p. 513.) *Congressional Quarterly Weekly Report,* November 8, 1980 for 1980 election, p. 3297. In *Public Opinion,* December/January, 1981, p. 25.

Electoral Turnout in Industrial Democracies, 1977–1980

Country	Election date	Turnout
Sweden	1979	91%
West Germany	1980	89
Italy	1980	88
Netherlands	1977	88
France	1978	85
Great Britain	1979	76
Ireland	1977	74
Canada	1980	70
United States	**1980**	**51**

Source: *Public Opinion,* January, 1981, p. 25.

port of Ford in 1976. Reagan won by getting more votes from every group, rather than from a massive switching of loyalties of any particular group. The election of 1980 was *not* a "realigning" election, one in which large groups defect from an established preference, never to return. Reagan won not because of a conservative mood, but because of an unpopular incumbent.

The weak attachment of voters to parties was reinforced by the media. The media gave its attention to the candidates as individuals, and issues were largely ignored. The election was won on the basis of candidate image, an image created by expensive media campaigns.

The rise of candidate image, the decline of parties, and the continued irrelevance of issues do not mean that each party's candidate can expect to draw votes equally from all segments of the population. Certain social groups (blacks, Mexican-Americans, Jews) traditionally support Democratic candidates. Others (Protestants, suburban residents, people in business) traditionally support Republicans. How these groups react to candidates, however, is a consequence of what they learn of the candidates from the media during the campaign.

Essentials: The Electoral College

Although relatively few people are aware of it, Americans do not vote for a presidential candidate. They vote for presidential "electors." In many cases they do not know who the electors are, because their names do not appear on the ballot. These electors are pledged to vote for the candidate who wins the popular election in each state. However, there is no constitutional requirement that they do so. Indeed, it was the intention of the framers of the Constitution that electoral college votes should *not* necessarily reflect popular sentiment, but rather use their own good judgment about presidential candidates. Initially, electors were chosen by the state legislatures, but by the early 1800s most states began popular elections for slates of presidential electors who were pledged to cast their vote for one party's candidate or another. The number of electors accorded each state is equal to the sum of its U. S. representatives and senators. Three electors are allocated to the District of Columbia by the Twenty-third Amendment (1961).

The Constitution provides that, in the event that no candidate achieves a majority of the electoral vote, the House of Representatives must choose between the top three candidates, with each state delegation having one vote. The House rules provide that the vote of a state delegation is allocated to the candidate preferred by a majority of the delegation.

The electoral college has been the subject of considerable controversy. A minor complaint is that electors have occasionally failed to carry out their pledge and cast their vote for the popular winner in their state. However, only ten electors have done this since the first presidential election. A more serious objection is that the electoral college perpetuates a winner-take-all system. A candidate who receives the highest popular vote in a state will receive 100 percent of the state's electoral vote. Obviously, candidates will focus their energy on states with large populations, especially if the contest in these states is close. In the primaries, New Hampshire is the target of media and candidate attention, but in the general election this small state is ignored. In the large, urban, industrial states the competition for their votes is fierce. If a candidate can win in the big states, the election is virtually assured. For example, the combined electoral votes of California, New York, Pennsylvania, Texas, Illinois, Ohio, Michigan, New Jersey, Florida, and Massachusetts (259) are just ten short of a majority. Consequently, a president can be elected even after having lost in a majority of states and having lost in the overall popular vote. For example, candidates have occasionally won more electoral college votes while losing the popular vote (Adams in 1824, Hayes in 1876, and Harrison in 1888). The most flagrant violation of the spirit of popular elections occurred in 1824. The House elected John Quincy Adams, even though his rival, Jackson, actually had more electoral and more popular votes. (See the next page for a figure showing electoral college votes from 1952 to 1980.)

Various attempts to reform or abolish the electoral college are made from time to time, but they never seem to get very far. Proponents of direct popular election of the president believe that the electoral college creates the possibility of minor-party "spoilers." In 1968 the fear arose that Wallace would deprive either Nixon or Humphrey of a majority in the electoral college, thus creating the possibility of bargaining in the House and greater strength for the Wallace candidacy. Opponents of abolition of the electoral college wish to avoid tampering with tradition, especially the two-party tradition.

(continued)

(*continued*)

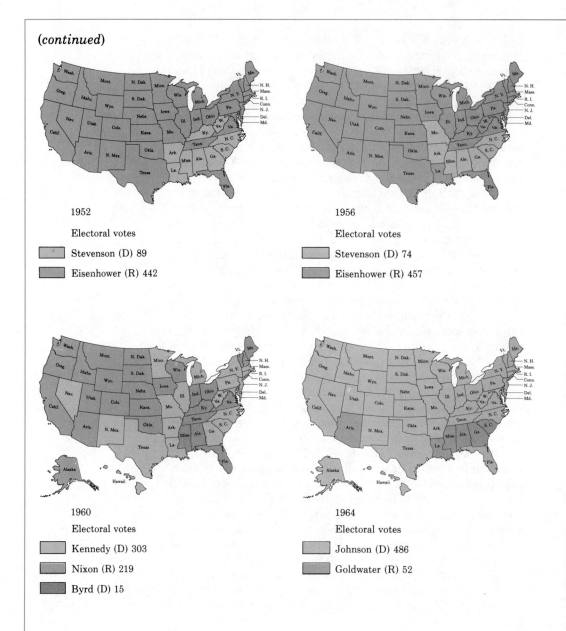

1952

Electoral votes

Stevenson (D) 89

Eisenhower (R) 442

1956

Electoral votes

Stevenson (D) 74

Eisenhower (R) 457

1960

Electoral votes

Kennedy (D) 303

Nixon (R) 219

Byrd (D) 15

1964

Electoral votes

Johnson (D) 486

Goldwater (R) 52

Electoral college votes 1952–1980.

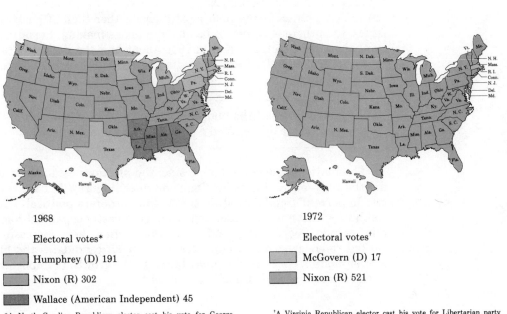

1968

Electoral votes*

Humphrey (D) 191

Nixon (R) 302

Wallace (American Independent) 45

*A North Carolina Republican elector cast his vote for George Wallace, making the official count: Nixon, 301; Humphrey, 191; Wallace, 46.

1972

Electoral votes†

McGovern (D) 17

Nixon (R) 521

†A Virginia Republican elector cast his vote for Libertarian party candidate John Hospers, making the official count: Nixon, 520; McGovern, 17; Hospers, 1.

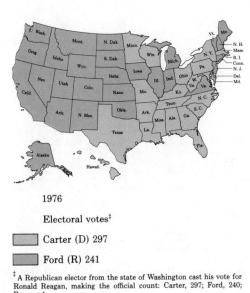

1976

Electoral votes‡

Carter (D) 297

Ford (R) 241

‡A Republican elector from the state of Washington cast his vote for Ronald Reagan, making the official count: Carter, 297; Ford, 240; Reagan, 1.

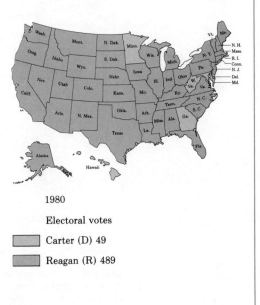

1980

Electoral votes

Carter (D) 49

Reagan (R) 489

PAYING FOR ELECTIONS

If the new politics is the politics of image rather than of party and issues, then there is money to be made in image making. Presidential campaigns are expensive, and in 1980 about half the budget of each presidential contender went to media and related expenses, particularly television.

> In 1980 about half the budget of each presidential contender went to media and related expenses, particularly television.

The limits on spending for presidential elections established under the 1974 federal campaign financing rules (Figure 6-5) have led to two important trends. First, business and corporate political action committees have proliferated and assumed a vastly expanded role in fund raising. Second, PAC and other contributions have increasingly shifted to congressional candidates. But for all candidates the high cost of modern elections has contributed to the growth in importance of the image maker and media consultant.

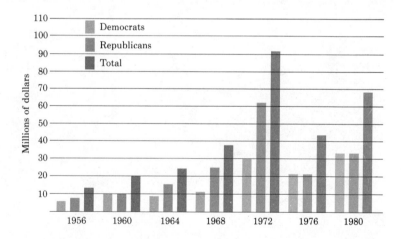

Figures are for the postconvention campaigns.

Source: Herbert E. Alexander, *Financing Politics: Money, Elections and Political Reform*, 2nd ed. (Washington, D. C.: Congressional Quarterly Press, 1980), p. 5; data for 1980 provided by Federal Election Commission; totals include the full $4.6 million maximum allotted to major-party committees.

Figure 6-5.   Presidential campaign spending. Notice that the totals for the two parties are noticeably lower—and also unlike those of previous years, equal—after the 1974 amendments to the Federal Election Campaign Act. (From *Democracy under Pressure: An Introduction to the American Political System,* 4th ed., by M. C. Cummings and D. Wise. Copyright 1981 by Harcourt Brace Jovanovich, Inc. Reprinted by permission.)

Federal Election Campaign Act (FECA)

The raising and spending of money in presidential campaigns today is governed by the Federal Election Campaign Act of 1971, as amended in 1974, 1976, and 1979. The essential components of the law are as follows.

Qualification for federal funding. To qualify for federal funding, a candidate must raise at least $100,000, consisting of at least $5,000 in twenty different states in contributions of $250 or less. *Major parties* are defined as those whose presidential candidates received more than 25 percent of the popular vote in the preceding general election, *minor parties* as those whose presidential candidates received between 5 and 25 percent. Any candidate who accepts public funding by the government is obliged to comply with the spending limits under this law. Present law does not provide federal funding for congressional candidates.

Source of federal funding. The 1974 amendments to FECA provide for a $1 checkoff by federal income-tax payers. Money raised in this way goes into a special Presidential Campaign Fund. Approximately 25 percent of U. S. taxpayers have been checking off the $1 box on their tax forms.

Presidential primaries. Federal matching funds, dollar for dollar, are available for all eligible candidates. Candidates may spend no more than a ceiling established by FECA. The ceiling is adjusted each election according to an inflation escalator based on the Consumer Price Index. In 1980, the primary spending ceiling was $17.8 million per major party candidate. Thus, a candidate raising $8.9 million would receive another $8.9 million in matching federal funds.

Nominating conventions. Eligible major party candidates could spend up to $3.9 million in 1980, all of which was federally funded.

General elections. The federal government pays for all campaign costs of major party candidates. The ceiling in 1980 was $29.5 million.

Individual contributions. In any given election, individuals may not give more than $1,000 to any candidate or the candidate's authorized committee. An individual's contributions may not exceed $20,000 per year to a national party committee or $5,000 to a political action committee, and total contributions in a year may not exceed $25,000. Some limits on individual spending were struck down by the Supreme Court in 1976 (*Buckley* v. *Valeo,* 424 U. S. 1); hence there are no limits on the amount an individual can spend on activities and advertising done independently of a candidate's campaign organization.

Political action committees. A corporation, union, or other association may establish one PAC. A PAC must register with the Federal Election Commission, have at least fifty contributors, and give to at least five candidates for federal office. PAC contributions may not exceed $5,000 to a candidate per election, $15,000 to a national party committee per year, and $5,000 to any other committee per year.

Definition of election. For purposes of individual and PAC contributions, presidential primaries, party caucuses and conventions, general elections, and run-off elections are defined as separate elections.

Disclosure of sources. Candidates and political committees must keep records of all contributions of $50 or more. All contributions of $200 or more must be reported to the Federal Election Commission, including the name, address, and occupation of the contributor. Candidates and party committees receiving or spending $5,000 or less are exempted from the requirement of filing disclosure reports. Under the 1974 amendments and the Foreign Agents Registration Act of 1938, non-citizens and illegal residents are prohibited from contributing.

Enforcement. A six-person Federal Election Commission has the authority to investigate and prosecute alleged civil violations and to refer alleged criminal violations to the Justice Department. The Commission is required to attempt settlement of alleged violations by

---

Election Eve, 1980: Carter Gets the News

When Jimmy Carter flew back to Washington on Sunday to handle the hostage crisis, he thought he was in good shape in the polls taken daily by his own expert, Pat Caddell. He had gone into the Cleveland debate one to two points ahead of Reagan by Caddell's soundings, and the trend was in his direction. "It looked good," said one of the President's aides. By Friday, however, the debate results seemed to be taking effect. Jody Powell spoke of a "pause in momentum." Carter had dropped about four points, to one or two behind. But he was still in striking distance.... He would have to campaign Monday, and so out he went.

The long day was nearly at an end when Carter's Air Force One dipped out of rainy skies into Seattle Monday night. Hamilton Jordan was on the phone from Washington with Powell. As the plane came in to land, the connection was broken. On the ground, Carter was rushed into the hangar packed with more than 1,000 cheering supporters and gave one of the best speeches of his campaign.

He was exhausted but exhilarated. It was over, and he felt a win was definitely possible. As he leaped off the stage to work the crowd, some junior staffers surprised him by putting on the public address system his 1976 campaign theme song. The tune had not been played since his last campaign. Carter started to choke with emotion when he heard it.

In the meantime, Powell was reconnected with Jordan.

conciliation before going to court. The 1976 amendments provide for penalties of up to one year in prison and $25,000.

Image Makers and Pollsters as Policy Advisors

Campaign money goes to pay for image making. Image makers do not care as much for ideology as they do for victory; if their candidate wins, they get more clients. Reagan's 1980 campaign was a marvel of image making. His media consultant, pollster, and policy advisor, Richard Wirthlin, devised a complex method of surveying public opinion, so that Reagan could modify his policy statements or appearances to correct weaknesses. Wirthlin's organization actually simulated the election several times, with different appeals, different speeches, and different outcomes. The "gaming" was comparable to that done by the Pentagon in planning defense strategy. Carter's image makers, Patrick Caddell and Gerald Rafshoon, were not in the same league.

The President's chief strategist had bad news. Caddell had just come over with his latest poll figures. Carter had dropped to ten points behind Reagan. The lead was insurmountable, Caddell had said. Jordan told Powell the election was lost. Powell was profoundly shocked. Carter was still inside shaking hands.

When the President bounded onto the plane for the long flight back to Georgia, Powell readied himself by pouring a stiff drink. He said he needed one to break that kind of news. But before he could collar the President, Carter was back in the staff cabin, talking with Domestic Affairs Adviser Stu Eizenstat and Rick Hertzberg, his chief speechwriter. They had been pleased with the day. The aides agreed that the last appearance had been great. . . .

Finally, after they were in the air more than an hour, and Carter had finished a double martini, Powell got the president alone [and] passed on Caddell's findings. Carter was devastated. He couldn't believe it. . . .

Rosalynn met her husband at the helipad when he arrived in Plains. When he told her the grim news, she was incredulous. She spent the rest of the morning fighting to maintain control . . . On the flight to Washington after voting in Plains, they were finally alone in their forward cabin. They broke down together and cried.

From "When Jimmy Knew," in *Time,* November 17, 1980. Copyright 1980 Time Inc. All rights reserved. Reprinted by permission.

> Image makers do not care as much for ideology as they do for victory.

Wirthlin and Peter Dailey (who handled the technical production) sought an image of a pragmatic and charming man, not an ideologue. Reagan achieved their expectations; he had the professional actor's ability to assume any role. If the advisors wanted warmth, he gave them warmth. If they wanted pragmatism, he gave it to them. He could speak with impressive sincerity about peace, and he could generate a teary, misty look on command (his commercials used film rather then videotape, because film creates a softer image). As Carter's campaign advisors put it, "Ronald Reagan was the best electronic media candidate in American history."[27]

Carter's image makers could obviously no longer rely on the "outsider" theme of 1976, so they chose the image of the tireless worker for the nation. Carter was seen mounting a long flight of stairs (to the Oval Office). A light appeared at night in the White House, presumably indicating how long he was working. Prominent ads also featured Carter as a peacemaker with Anwar Sadat of Egypt and Menachem Begin of Israel.

Carter's loss can be interpreted as many things—a rejection of an incompetent president, a growing fear of inflation and economic disaster, and a conviction that the nation was no longer militarily competitive with the Soviet Union. But it can also be interpreted as the victory of a well-packaged television product over a poorly packaged one.

CHAPTER SUMMARY

1. The presidential-election system encourages media-dominated campaigns, with concomitant emphasis on image and personality over issues and substance. Political amateurs with mass appeal, such as Ronald Reagan, can bypass traditional party structures and win the presidency by carefully cultivating a successful media "image."

2. The two political parties have gradually lost their hold over presidential hopefuls. Recent national conventions have been mere ratifying arrangements for the candidate who has won enough delegate support through the many primaries to secure the party's nomination.

3. Although the two-party system has seen changes in the nature of the parties and the coalitions that support them, presidential contests remain essentially two-party affairs. It is extremely difficult for a third-party challenge to succeed.

4. Party affiliation is no longer a strict predictor of the vote. The growing number of independent voters and the increase in split-ticket voting attest to the party-dealignment trend. Furthermore, an apathetic and alienated electorate is displaying a marked volatility, generated in large part by the media emphasis on dramatic events and images and the omission of issue coverage.

5. The "democratic" primary system has allowed candidates to build their own personal campaign organizations—a replacement for the party bosses and machines of the past. The primary system has also increased the power of the media in interpreting who is "winning" or "losing."

6. For many reasons, then, media strategies now dominate presidential campaigns. The emphasis on projecting a "leadership image" or portraying an opponent as a "warmonger" was evident in the 1980 preconvention and postconvention campaigns.

7. The 1980 election was hardly a mandate for the conservative policies favored by the winner, Ronald Reagan. Rather, the outcome reflected voter disenchantment with Jimmy Carter's image as a leader.

8. Campaign financing reflects the important role of the media consultants and image makers in contemporary political campaigns.

Notes

1. Jules Whitcover, *Marathon: The Pursuit of the Presidency 1972–1976* (New York: Viking Press, 1977), p. 113.
2. Stephen Hess, *The Washington Reporters* (Washington: The Brookings Institution, 1981), p. 124.
3. *Marathon,* p. 202.
4. Gerald Pomper et al., *The Election of 1980: Reports and Interpretations* (Chatham, N. J.: Chatham House, 1981), pp. 91–92.
5. Denis G. Sullivan et al., *The Politics of Representation: The Democratic Convention of 1972* (New York: St. Martin's Press, 1974), p. 124.
6. Warren J. Mitofsky and Martin Plissner, "The Making of the Delegates 1968–1980," *Public Opinion,* October/November 1980, pp. 37–43.
7. Jack Germond and Jules Whitcover, *Blue Smoke and Mirrors: How Reagan Won and Why Carter Lost the Election of 1980* (New York: Viking Press, 1981), pp. 182–183.
8. This description of the evolution of American political party systems draws from William Nisbet Chambers and Walter Dean Burnham, eds., *The American Party Systems: Stages of Political Development* (New York: Oxford University Press, 1967).
9. Philip E. Converse, Warren E. Miller, Jerrold E. Rusk, Arthur C. Wolfe, "Continuity and Change in American Politics: Parties and Issues in the 1968 Election," *American Political Science Review,* December 1969, p. 1092.
10. Thomas R. Dye and L. Harmon Zeigler, *The Irony of Democracy: An Uncommon Introduction to American Politics,* 5th ed. (Monterey, Calif.: Duxbury Press, 1981), p. 234.

11. Herbert B. Asher, *Presidential Elections and American Politics: Voters, Candidates, and Campaigns since 1952* (Homewood, Ill.: Dorsey Press, 1976), pp. 67–69.
12. Institute for Social Research survey. Reported in *Public Opinion,* December/January 1981, p. 26.
13. Pomper et al., *The Election of 1980,* pp. 86–87.
14. Teresa E. Levitin and Warren E. Miller, "Ideological Interpretations of Presidential Elections," *American Political Science Review,* September 1979, p. 769.
15. Everett Carll Ladd, Jr., "Pursuing the New Class: Social Theory and Survey Data," in B. Bruce-Briggs, ed., *The New Class?* (New York: McGraw-Hill, 1979), pp. 101–122.
16. Jeane Kirkpatrick, *The New Presidential Elite: Men and Women in National Politics* (New York: Russell Sage Foundation and Twentieth Century Fund, 1976), pp. 355ff.
17. Everett Carll Ladd, Jr., *Where Have All the Voters Gone?: The Fracturing of America's Political Parties* (New York: Norton, 1978), p. 17.
18. CBS News/*New York Times* interviews as reported in the *New York Times,* November 9, 1980, p. 28. Tabulated in Pomper et al., *The Election of 1980,* pp. 71–72.
19. Donald R. Matthews, "Winnowing: The News Media and the 1976 Presidential Nominations," in James David Barber, ed., *Race for the Presidency: The Media and the Nominating Process* (Englewood Cliffs, N. J.: Prentice-Hall, 1978), p. 65.
20. Matthews, p. 65.
21. Germond and Whitcover, *Blue Smoke and Mirrors,* p. 56.
22. *Public Opinion,* June/July 1980, p. 23.
23. Pomper et al., *The Election of 1980,* pp. 17–18.
24. *New York Times,* October 29, 1980, p. A27.
25. *Public Opinion,* December/January 1981, pp. 36–37.
26. CBS News, *New York Times* survey, November 4, 1980. Reported in *Public Opinion,* December/January 1981, p. 43.
27. "Face Off: A Conversation with the President's Pollsters Patrick Caddell and Richard Wirthlin," *Public Opinion,* December/January 1981, p. 5.

Close-Up and In-Depth Analyses

Paul Abramson, John H. Aldrich, and David W. Rohde. *Continuity and Change in the 1980 Elections.* Washington, D. C.: Congressional Quarterly Press, 1982.

Herbert E. Alexander. *Financing Politics,* 2nd ed. Washington, D. C.: Congressional Quarterly Press, 1980.

Bruce Briggs, ed. *The New Class.* New York: McGraw-Hill, 1979.

William S. Crotty and Gary C. Jacobson. *American Parties in Decline.* Boston: Little, Brown, 1980.

Thomas Ferguson and Joel Rogers. *The Hidden Election.* New York: Random House, 1981.

Everett Carll Ladd, Jr. *Where Have All the Voters Gone?,* 2nd ed. New York: Norton, 1982.

Seymour Martin Lipset, ed. *Emerging Coalitions in American Politics.* San Francisco: Institute for Contemporary Studies, 1978.

Seymour Martin Lipset, ed. *Party Coalitions in the 1980's.* San Francisco: Institute for Contemporary Studies, 1981.

Lester Milbrath. *Political Participation,* 2nd ed. Chicago: Rand McNally, 1977.

Norman H. Nie, Sidney Verba, and John R. Petrocik. *The Changing American Voter.* Cambridge, Mass.: Harvard University Press, 1976.

Dan Nimmo. *Political Communication and Public Opinion in America.* Santa Monica, Calif.: Goodyear, 1978.

Dan Nimmo and Robert L. Savage. *Candidates and Their Images.* Pacific Palisades, Calif.: Goodyear, 1976.

Thomas E. Patterson. *The Mass Media Election.* New York: Praeger, 1980.

Nelson W. Polsby and Aaron B. Wildavsky. *Presidential Elections,* 5th ed. New York: Scribner's, 1980.

Gerald Pomper et al. *The Election of 1980: Reports and Interpretations.* Chatham, N. J.: Chatham House, 1981.

Austin Ranney, ed. *The American Elections of 1980.* Washington, D. C.: American Enterprise Institute, 1981.

Ellis Sandoz and Cecil V. Crabb, Jr. *The Tide of Discontent.* Washington, D. C.: Congressional Quarterly Press, 1981.

Frank J. Sorauf. *Party Politics in America,* 4th ed. Boston: Little, Brown, 1980.

INTEREST-GROUP POLITICS

Mike Farrell has a face that most Americans recognize: he is "B. J." on the popular television comedy *M*A*S*H*. He is also a member of Common Cause, an organization dedicated to political reforms (for example, legal limits on the size of campaign contributions). Farrell has appeared on television urging viewers to join Common Cause, because if they do not, "special-interest groups" will continue to exercise undue influence in Washington. Farrell presumably believes that his organization is *not* a special-interest group. Simultaneously, his costar Alan Alda has devoted long hours to women's organizations in support of the Equal Rights Amendment. "Hawkeye" may not believe that ERA supporters are a special-interest group either.

In reality any group that tries to exert influence on government is a "special-interest group." The "special interest" represented by an organization may be relatively narrow, as is the case with occupational or single-issue groups, or it may be more expansively conceived, as is true of Common Cause. Groups that do not undertake activities on behalf of a specific occupational interest may describe themselves as "public-interest" groups, implying thereby that their interests are not really "special." This rhetorical distinction, however, does not bear up under examination.

Jeffrey Berry defines a "public-interest" group as "one that seeks a

Dr. Carl McIntire of the International Council of Christian Churches, speaks out against disarmament.

collective good, the achievement of which will not selectively and materially benefit the membership or activists of the organization."[1] This definition leaves substantial room for interpretation by the group's members. A collective good is a policy that presumably benefits all people, whether or not they are in the group. Berry gives "obvious" examples such as clean air and world peace. The problem is that, while everybody wants these things, not everybody is willing to pay the cost. Clean air may be a high priority, but so is industrial development. Manufacturers who oppose stringent air-pollution standards argue that their position is based upon a different concept of the "public interest" from that held by clean-air activists. As Berry suggests, what is a collective good to one group may be a private good to another.

All groups, no matter what they say, seek to represent a special interest.

Clearly, although we may use the term "public-interest group" to refer to certain types of organizations, this is not to say that such groups are not a kind of special-interest group. They are. In terms of political rhetoric, "special-interest groups" are those with which we disagree; they operate to the detriment of "the people." "Public-interest groups" are those with which we agree; they speak *for* "the people." Obviously, this self-serving distinction is nonsense. All groups, no matter what they say, seek to represent a special interest.

ORGANIZED GROUPS: THREATS TO DEMOCRACY?

Interest groups: Formal organizations that try to achieve their goals through influence on public policy.

A better definition of organized interest groups allows us to escape the political rhetoric. **Interest groups** are formal organizations that try to achieve their goals through influence on public policy. Generally they equate *their* goals with the public interest. Whether they are "good" or "bad" depends very much on whether you like what they advocate. But there is more to the study of interest groups, and their role in a democracy, than approval or rejection of a particular group. Are organized groups in general a desirable or a dangerous component of the political system?

The Founding Fathers believed that interest groups were evil but unavoidable. The most severe condemnation of organized groups was written by James Madison. He wrote of "factions" as "actuated by some common impulse of passion, or of interest, adverse to the rights of citizens, or to the permanent and aggregate interests of the community."[2] Thus, Madison believed that the impulse to organize such groups, bad as they were, was rooted in human nature. In order to cure the "mischiefs of faction," Madison constructed a system of checks and balances in national government as well as a federal rela-

Public Perception
of the Strength of Interest Groups

Increasingly, the public has come to believe that interest groups have grown too powerful. This belief is related to a mounting frustration with government. The accompanying figure shows the percent of survey respondents who agree that "the government is pretty much run by a few big interests looking out for themselves."*

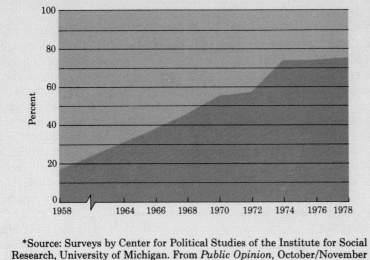

*Source: Surveys by Center for Political Studies of the Institute for Social Research, University of Michigan. From *Public Opinion,* October/November 1979, p. 29.

tionship between national and state governments. In this way it would be extremely difficult for any one faction to become dominant.

Despite the hazards pointed out by Madison, the First Amendment guaranteed the rights of citizens "to peaceably assemble and petition the government for redress of grievances." The Founding Fathers believed that groups could be dangerous but that the benefits of freedom of association overrode that danger.

Rather than a necessary evil to be controlled, organized groups are now regarded as an essential component of a healthy democracy.

Madison's view that interest groups are inevitable is now the prevailing view of political scientists. However, Madison's dislike for such groups has been reversed. Rather than a necessary evil to be controlled, organized groups are now regarded as an essential component of a healthy democracy: "Voluntary associations are the prime means by which the function of mediating between the individual and the state is performed. Through them the individual is able to relate himself effectively and meaningfully to the political system."[3] If this is so, then the media are missing out on the action, for interest groups (or *voluntary associations,* the neutral term) are rarely part of the reporter's "beat." Washington reporters know that lobbyists try hard to influence government, but few cover special-interest groups regularly.

THE BIAS OF THE GROUP SYSTEM

All groups are not equal. Some are more powerful than others. However, there is a more fundamental inequality—that is, the inequality between those who belong to groups and those who do not. The idea that groups are the primary method whereby individuals relate to government implies that this opportunity is open to everyone. Although a majority of Americans belongs to at least one organization, membership is greatest among the professional and managerial classes and among college-educated, high-income people. (See Figure 7-1.) This class bias is also expressed by the types of organization people join. Unions (which frequently are not voluntary) recruit members from among working-class Americans, whereas the U. S. Chamber of Commerce recruits members from among the business community. Many poor people and members of minority groups do not have the time, money, interest, or skills to benefit from the organized interest-group system. Sociologist Anthony Oberschall, writing

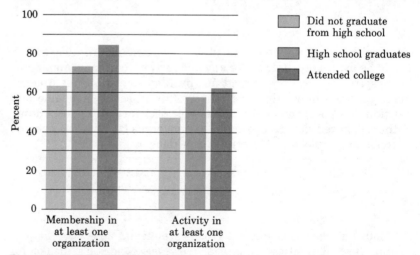

Figure 7-1. Membership and activity in organizations by Americans with different amounts of education. (Source: Samuel H. Barnes, "Some Political Consequences of Involvement in Organizations." Paper presented at the 1977 annual meeting of the American Political Science Association.)

of black organizations, reached a conclusion that applies equally well to other organizations that attempt to speak for the downtrodden:

> The main support within the black community, in terms of staff, membership, and resources . . . came from the black middle class . . . . The single most important failure of the middle class black and civil rights organization was their failure to mobilize and to organize the lower class black community . . . . The lower class segment of the black population remained by and large unorganized and unmobilized.[4]

Lobbying for the Poor

Those seeking to represent the underrepresented must find support within the overrepresented—the middle- and upper-class organizations. Consider the case of the poor. National television coverage of President Ronald Reagan's budget-reduction program gave considerable emphasis to its impact on the poor, and congressional committees heard testimony from poor people. How did these poor people get to Washington to testify and to get their message on television? If, as they said, they would be unable to live without food stamps and other income-supplement programs, how could they afford the trip? Politics is not an activity in which the poor usually participate. As a class, they rarely vote or write letters to congressmen, and they are certainly not on many legislators' "circuit" during trips to the constituency. One is not likely to encounter a food-stamp recipient at a Rotary Club luncheon; nor are welfare mothers likely to trek to Washington.

To the extent that the poor are represented at all in Washington, they are represented by "proxies"—groups that are not poor themselves but that claim to represent the poor. Many of these groups have organized and reorganized themselves under various names over the years—the National Welfare Rights Organization (dissolved in the mid-1970s), the Children's Defense Fund, the National Anti-Hunger Coalition, the Low Income Housing Coalition, and the Food Research and Action Center.

To the extent that the poor are represented at all in Washington, they are represented by "proxies"—groups that are not poor themselves but that claim to represent the poor.

Lobbyists for the poor can be divided roughly into three categories: (1) the churches, civil rights groups, and liberal organizations; (2) organized labor; and (3) administrators and lawyers for welfare programs.

Church groups (the National Conference of Catholic Bishops, the National Council of Churches, B'nai B'rith, and others) often support programs for the poor out of a sense of moral obligation. Likewise, liberal activist groups (Common Cause, Americans for Democratic Action, and others) often support social programs out of an ideological commitment. Civil rights organizations (the National Urban League, the National Association for the Advancement of Colored People, and the like) support programs for the poor as a part of their general concern for the conditions affecting minorities.

Very often the success of lobbying efforts on behalf of the poor depends on organized labor's adding its considerable political power to the coalition of churches, civil rights groups, and liberal activists. Organized labor does all of the things that the poor find difficult to do in politics—political organizing, campaign financing, letter writing, and personal lobbying. Historically, organized labor has tended to support programs for the poor, even though union pay scales have moved a great distance from the poverty line. Labor *leaders* may be more likely to support social programs than the rank and file. Of course, the first concern of organized labor is legislation dealing with labor relations, minimum wages, fair labor standards, and so on. But when labor leaders join others in support of social programs, the result is a strong political coalition.

Welfare-program administrators and lawyers have a direct financial interest in supporting social-welfare spending. These groups may take a lead in trying to organize others into coalitions in support of programs. Supporters of proposals to reduce spending for social programs complain: "Virtually all of the lobbying has come from people who are involved directly or indirectly in administering these programs."[5] The welfare bureaucracy is said to create a powerful force consisting of "people doing well by the government's doing good."[6]

Prominent among the organizations representing administrators and lawyers of social programs are the American Federation of State, County and Municipal Employees (AFSCME), the Legal Services Corporation, and the Community Services Administration. AFSCME is a labor union, affiliated with the AFL-CIO, which includes many public workers whose jobs are directly affected by cutbacks in social programs. As a union, it is funded primarily by the dues of its own members. But the Legal Services Corporation, with its 5,000 attorneys across the nation who provide legal assistance to the poor, is funded by the federal government. Its critics have charged that, to the extent that it lobbies on its own behalf, it is misusing its funds. The same charge has been leveled against the Community Services Administration, which is supposed to assist antipoverty programs throughout the country and not to lobby Congress. However, there are very few government bureaucracies—from the Defense Department to the National Aeronautics and Space Administration to the Department of Agriculture—that do not directly or indirectly lobby Congress for their own programs.

The "poverty lobby" is strongest when its separate groups— churches, civil rights organizations, liberal groups, organized labor, and social-welfare administrators—are unified and coordinated in their efforts. This is the movement that paid the expenses of the welfare mothers, food-stamp recipients, Medicaid patients, and the like to come to Washington to portray Reagan at the televised hearings as heartless. This is the "special interest" that the president warned would be working to unravel his economic package. The poverty lobby tried to wage its campaign through the media. Actual poor people make better news than does an analysis of poverty by an official or a reporter. The poverty lobby, therefore, sought to personalize poverty by bringing poor people to Washington, where reporters for the national media are concentrated.

LEADERS AND FOLLOWERS: WHY ORGANIZATIONS MISREPRESENT THEIR MEMBERS' OPINIONS

Organizations do not always represent the views of their members. People join organizations for a variety of reasons, many of which are unrelated to political goals or lobbying. Since politics is not very important to most people, many organizations find that they can attract and maintain members by providing "selective" benefits—that is, benefits that can be obtained only through membership in the organization.[7] Some doctors join the American Medical Association only to receive the *AMA Journal* and other technical publications; some veterans join the American Legion to gain access to a friendly place to drink; some retired people join the American Association of Retired Persons in order to be eligible for discount prescriptions at pharmacies; the Sierra Club organizes wilderness expeditions. People also join organizations for friendship, prestige, or "connections." The local chambers of commerce attract membership for these reasons, as do fraternal orders.

People who join an organization for selective benefits are largely unconcerned with lobbying by their organization. Lobbyists are left relatively free to pursue their goals in the name of the organization. Organized labor in Washington traditionally supports liberal causes and Democratic candidates. Unions also lobby for civil rights legislation, even though their membership does not always support such legislation. About 95 percent of the money contributed by unions to political candidates goes to the Democrats; yet in the 1980 presidential elections Reagan and Jimmy Carter split the union vote almost in half.

Douglas Fraser (front), United Auto Workers union president, joins a picket of striking PATCO union members although PATCO did not receive much support from other unions.

People who join an organization for selective benefits are largely unconcerned with lobbying by their organization.

The inability of organizations to reflect the beliefs of their members occurs most often when the group seeks to represent a large constituency such as labor, business, or the consumer. Ironically, one major resource of organized groups of substantial size—their power at the polls—is severely limited. They can use their members' money to support candidates whose position is in accord with that of the leaders of the organization, but they cannot "deliver the vote." Nor can such organizations count on public displays of solidarity. When the Professional Air Traffic Controllers Organization went on strike in 1981, other unions did not lend it much support, a bitter disappointment to PATCO. (Labor's reluctance to support the striking air controllers is partially explained by the fact that PATCO had supported Reagan in the presidential election.) When women's organizations have lobbied for the Equal Rights Amendment, their most vigorous opponent has been an organization led by a woman, Phyllis Schafly.

On the other side of the coin, freedom from membership constraint leaves organizations room to bargain, negotiate, or compromise during the passage of legislation. Since most members neither know nor care much about what their lobbyists are doing, the lobbyists strike bargains without fear of losing their jobs.

THE INTEREST-GROUP PROFESSIONALS

Membership turnover in interest groups is very high. Unless an organization can provide valuable and continuing benefits, people will drop their memberships. Many organizations are begun by professional public-relations experts. People join these groups not only because of shared attitudes (agreement about policy) but also because of newspaper appeals and mail solicitations. But once people realize that they do not need to join the organization in order to benefit from its work, membership tails off. New members must be found to replace the old ones, and most decision making is left to the professional staff.

Many organizations supplement direct mail and mass advertising by hiring professional recruiters to bolster membership. Both the National Association of Manufacturers and the U. S. Chamber of Commerce use this tactic. In both cases, fewer than 10 percent of the potential membership actually joins, and many of these members remain in the organization for only a year. The membership in such unstable organizations ebbs and flows according to the political nature of the times. Membership in Common Cause declined when President Richard Nixon resigned but bounced back with the election of Reagan. Indeed, one way to maintain membership is to identify an "enemy," someone to oppose.

Organizations as Oligarchies

Organizations are oligarchies, because only a few members will remain long enough or be active enough to influence organizational goals. Generally, the "oligarchs" are members of the professional staff and, occasionally, the board of directors. This leadership dominance is not limited to any particular kind of organization. An extreme example is the United Farm Workers Union, or *la Causa*, as the movement is called in California. It is the property of one man: Cesar Chavez. Charismatic and spectacular, he became a media figure in

Cesar Chavez (middle), the UFW leader, talking with his brother, Manuel, before announcing a contract with Coca Cola.

the 1970s. His organization is rigidly authoritarian, with Chavez himself operating without any formal restraints from his members. Work assignments are handled by the union; any worker who fails to report to a job assigned by the union is placed at the bottom of the list. Within the union, there are no bylaws and no elections. Union dues may be raised or lowered by Chavez without approval from the members. Union contracts with farmers contain clauses requiring the dismissal of any worker not in good standing with the union, but no definition of good standing exists.

> Organizations are oligarchies, because only a few members will remain long enough or be active enough to influence organizational goals.

Many "public-interest" groups are also identified with a single leader. Among the most conspicuous of these are the organizations created by Ralph Nader. Nader is passionate in his beliefs as is Chavez, but Nader's groups are more diverse and better funded. He got his start when the General Motors Corporation hired a private detective to investigate him after he published *Unsafe at Any Speed,* an attack on GM's cars. With a $400,000 settlement and with substantial royalty and speaking income, Nader has created an organizational colossus (see Figure 7-2). Each of the affiliated organizations has a staff, but many have no members. They are simply paper organizations.

Small or nonexistent membership is not limited to the conglomerate of organizations headed by Nader. Organizations are opened in Washington at the rate of about one a week. However, the total number of organizations is not increasing at that rate, because so many of them come and go. Organizations without members strengthen the hand of the professional organizers. The professionals may well have the purest of motives, but they cannot claim to "represent" anyone. Organizations that claim to speak for manufacturers, retail druggists, or trucking companies are widely regarded as special interests. Although they believe that they operate in the public interest, they cannot legitimately claim to represent anybody but a restricted clientele. These are the groups with which the public-interest groups compete.

Public-interest groups do not offer many selective benefits. However, they can often tap a resource unavailable to special-interest groups: government and foundation money. The Urban League is largely funded through federal grants; the same is true for People United to Save Humanity (PUSH), the Reverend Jesse Jackson's organization. Public-interest groups have been able to turn to private foundations, especially the Ford Foundation, for money. One-third of the public-interest groups formed in the last decade received at least half of their total income from private foundation grants. The Ford

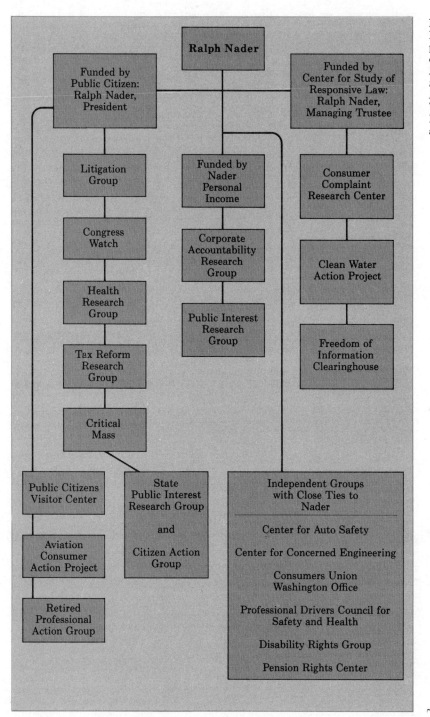

Figure 7-2. The Nader network. (Reprinted by permission of the publisher, from *American Government: Institutions and Policies,* by James Q. Wilson. Lexington, Mass.: D. C. Heath and Company, 1980.)

Foundation has made substantial grants to the Center for Law and Social Policy, to the Environmental Defense Fund and the Natural Resources Defense Council (environmental organizations), and to the Laywer's Committee for Civil Rights Under Law, Citizens Advocate Center, and Center for National Policy Review (civil rights and poverty organizations).

THE NEW SINGLE-ISSUE GROUPS

Interest groups are growing in number and financial backing. As the strength of political parties declines and candidates rely more on personal organization and media exposure, interest groups become a more important source of campaign support and financing. In Congress, party influence is diminished by reforms that create a large role for subcommittees and reduce the importance of seniority. Both the private-interest groups and the public-interest groups have become more active as a consequence. But the greatest beneficiary of the changes in political structure is another kind of group—the **single-issue interest group.**

Single-issue interest group: An interest group distinguished by zealous commitment to a single cause, such as opposition to gun control or abortion.

The traditional interest groups (for example, labor, the professions, business) have been active in politics for a long time. They were joined in the 1970s by the public-interest groups. In the 1980s the growth has been in *single-issue interest groups*. These groups are distinguished by their zealous commitment to a single cause, such as opposition to gun control or abortion. Unlike the traditional groups, which rely on selective benefits to sustain them, or the public-interest groups, which are funded by foundations, most single-issue groups are dependent solely on membership contributions. Single-issue groups must go it alone. Their major resource is passion.

When Senate hearings began on the confirmation of Sandra O'Connor, nominated by Reagan to be an associate justice of the Supreme Court, the nomination was attacked by the Life Amendment Political Action Committee and the National Right to Life Committee, prominent antiabortion single-issue groups. The issue was not whether O'Connor was competent, but whether she would support or oppose abortion. One might argue that a justice of the Supreme Court should not be judged on a single issue, but this one was "the single issue of the century, more important than slavery."[8] The antiabortion lobby is typical of single-issue groups: the single issue is the cause; no other issues matter; and no benefits other than achievement of the goal are offered to prospective members.

Single-interest groups rarely compromise.... The reason they are so rigid is that their only inducement to members is the intensity of their beliefs.

Although traditional groups can compromise, single-issue groups cannot. For example, the traditional occupational groups have always been willing to "play politics." The public-interest groups have now become part of the establishment. Environmental groups employ ex-legislators, economists, and attorneys. But single-interest groups rarely compromise. As Senator Barry Goldwater, a conservative, complained: "The uncompromising position of these groups is a divisive element that could tear apart the very spirit of our representative system, if they gain sufficient strength."[9] The reason they are so rigid is that their only inducement to members is the intensity of their beliefs.

Single-issue lobbyists are zealots. Because these groups offer only a single benefit, there is less of an opportunity for their lobbyists to ignore or misrepresent the views of their members. The National Abortion Rights Action League could not possibly take a stance even moderately at variance from absolute support for the right to abortion. Consequently, single-issue groups are *more* representative of their membership than are the more-traditional interest groups. Single-issue groups are not any more democratic in organization than are the more traditional groups. But members and leaders share a deep commitment to a single goal.

The New Right

The term "The New Right" embraces a variety of conservative organizations. The phrase itself is apparently of journalistic origin; the "New Right" isn't new. New Right groups express the "politics of resentment," concentrating on moral and social issues. Their aim is to use the political process to mandate a code of personal behavior compatible with their fundamentalist beliefs. (Neoconservatives, in contrast, are intellectuals who are more interested in economic issues than in personal morality. Their agenda has little in common with that of the New Right.)

Leaders of the New Right are skilled not at compromise but at communication. They are entrepreneurs of social conservatism in much the same way that Nader is an entrepreneur of the consumer movement. Leaders such as the Reverend Jerry Falwell of the Moral Majority and Phyllis Schafly of Stop ERA have been successful in weaving together an alliance of organizations. The network is as complex as is Nader's. It includes the National Conservative Political Action Committee; the Committee for the Survival of a Free

(continued)

(continued)

Congress; Citizens for the Republic (begun by Reagan); the Fund for the Conservative Majority; the Conservative Caucus (led by Howard Phillips, who coined the phrase *New Right*); and the American Conservative Union. In addition, the New Right umbrella organizations coordinate the activities of more-specialized groups, such as the Citizens Committee for the Right to Keep and Bear Arms.

The Rev. Jerry Falwell, leader of the Moral Majority, attains media prominence at a news conference warning about the threat of "world conquest" by the Soviet Union.

The New Right operates at various levels. Its public, media image is projected by Falwell and other political evangelists. It is Falwell who attracts media attention and creates an image of widespread support. Actually, public-opinion polls consistently indicate that political evangelism is not widely supported, even by "born-again" Christians, but it is the *image* of power that counts. Massive direct-mail campaigns, coordinated by the communications specialist of the New Right, Richard Viguerie, are said to have raised millions of dollars for sympathetic candidates ($7 million for the election of Senator Jesse Helms alone), and such campaigns can rely on contributions from a mailing list variously estimated between 2 million and 15 million contributors. The campaign efforts are organized by the National Conservative Political Action

Committee, which finances candidates, recruits them, conducts workshops in campaign strategy, and is virtually a political party in itself.

The New Right has been associated with "negative campaigns," criticizing the record of the opponents of its candidates. Prominent targets of the National Conservative Political Action Committee complained of this tactic and accused it of spreading false information. But negative campaigning did not begin with the committee. In 1970 the organization Environmental Action originated the "dirty dozen"—twelve Congressmen who had consistently opposed environmental legislation. Environmental Action produced "Wanted" posters and in general vilified the dirty dozen. Since then, negative campaigning has become standard for organizations relying on extensive publicity to further their political objectives.

Increasingly, attention is focused on the New Right because its tactics are so provocative. Furthermore, the response from liberal organizations has been to try to match the New Right in raising money and supporting candidates. They are aided by substantial contributions from prominent and wealthy liberals such as Stewart R. Mott, a leading supporter of Senator George McGovern in the 1972 presidential race. Senator Edward Kennedy has organized the Fund for a Democratic Majority; former Vice-President Walter Mondale sponsors the Committee for the Future of America; and John Anderson has created Independent Action. All these groups are affiliated with direct-mail specialists such as those used by the New Right. Their campaigns have much of the "negativism" so deplored by legislators. The National Progressive Political Action Committee, operated by the direct-mail firm of Parker, Dodd, and Associates, anticipated spending $1 million for contributors to liberal candidates, public relations services, and media attacks on conservative candidates in the 1982 Congressional elections.*

Given the publicity-conscious strategy of the single-issue groups, it is only natural that their attention came to focus on the media themselves. Supported by the umbrella organizations of the New Right, the Coalition for Better Television began a boycott of sponsors of television shows said to be too sexually explicit. Its success was substantial, and some companies agreed to remove their support from the shows targeted by the coalition.

*Maxwell Glen, "Liberal Political Action Committees Borrow a Page from the Conservatives," *National Journal*, July 4, 1981, p. 1198.

THE POLITICS OF EXPERTISE

All interest groups are using more grass-roots lobbying than they have in the past. The success of the single-issue groups has contributed to this change of tactics. But there is more to interest-group politics than conducting letter and telephone campaigns, sponsoring candidates, and soliciting funds through mass mailing. These tactics are useful during the legislative phase of policymaking, but they are of limited impact in policy administration and implementation. Once a law is on the books, *some* groups are able to continue to influence policy. The resource required for this sustained influence is *expertise*. Knowing what you are talking about in complex policy areas requires a fundamentally different strategy from that used by the ideological and single-issue groups. Even the environmental groups, initially very passionate, are learning the politics of expertise. They are shifting away from "hit lists" like the dirty dozen and are concentrating their money on acquiring people who can compete with governmental bureaucracies and legislative staffs on a technical level. Environmental groups are consciously moving away from the tactics of confrontation and adopting the politics of conciliation. When antinuclear protesters sought to delay the opening of a nuclear power plant in Diablo Canyon in California, they were given no encouragement or support from the established environmental groups. The environmental lobby includes some low-income members, but it is an increasingly slick and professional operation. The National Wildlife Federation employs 500 people in its Washington office, about the same number as the American Petroleum Institute.

Political tactics, such as this anti-nuclear demonstration in Washington, D.C. in May 1979, are being augmented by the politics of expertise.

The Oil Lobby: No Publicity, Just Power

The American Petroleum Institute (API) offers perhaps the best example of the use of expertise and information. In terms of public recognition, however, API is surely invisible. The media report on Nader, Falwell, and Chavez, but how many people know that Charles DiBona is president of the American Petroleum Institute?

API was formed in 1919 by oil executives who had coordinated petroleum supplies in World War I. It represents the interests of the major internationals, especially the "Seven Sisters"—Exxon, Mobil, Socal, Texaco, Gulf, British Petroleum, and Royal-Dutch Shell. Its membership of 356 oil and gas companies and associations plus 7,000 individual members accounts for about 85 percent of the total business volume of the industry in the non-Communist world. "Although it registers zero on public recognition polls, the giant, Washington-based API registers almost off the scale in power and influence over energy policy."[10] The institute's annual budget of $32 million puts it in a class by itself. The money is spent on lobbying, and API's lobbyists are among the best paid in Washington. But far more is spent on research.

"Although it registers zero on public recognition polls, the giant, Washington-based API registers almost off the scale in power and influence over energy policy."

API is the dominant source of information about energy in Washington. It employs economists, geologists, and engineers to develop data and has legions of consulting experts. "Its expertise on oil is placed well above that of the Department of Energy by most knowledgeable observers, including many congressmen."[11] The Department of Energy relies more on API for information than it does on its own staff. Furthermore, the interchange of personnel between the department and API is so vast as to almost erase the distinction between public agency and private organization. During the nation's recent energy shortages, Congress and the executive branch have been frustrated by their inability to obtain such basic information as the available supplies of petroleum products and reserves in the ground. Such information is the exclusive property of API. At one point, President Carter considered asking the Central Intelligence Agency to develop information about reserves.

"When outgoing Energy Secretary James Schlesinger needed vital weekly statistics on oil imports, domestic production, or refining and reserves, he consulted the latest American Petroleum Institute report. The API is the sole source of this information."[12] When reporters want information about oil, they, too, go to API. Much of this information is so technical as to be incomprehensible to the average citizen, and many of the issues that absorb the interest of the insti-

Charles DiBona, president of the relatively unknown API, and demonstrators against his organization. API does not seek public exposure.

tute are equally specialized. Narrow-based organizations such as API, with specific policy objectives, are more likely to be successful than broad-based organizations with vaguely defined, symbolic goals.

Specialized groups avoid public conflict. Unlike the single-issue groups, they do not want public exposure. They operate where expertise is highly valued and where there are no emotional issues to attract public attention. This is not always possible, so API budgets a substantial portion of its money for "institutional advertising." API is aware that public-opinion polls consistently show that people believe energy shortages are a hoax to drive up the price of gasoline. Its advertising is explicitly designed to portray its member companies as solvers of the energy shortage through exploration, rather than as causers of the shortage through corporate greed. Two advertisements by institute members show the nature of such efforts. The Mobil Corporation argues:

> We're a big company. We sell thousands of products ranging from natural gas and asphalt to gasoline and gear oil. . . . Our average profit . . . was only about two cents a gallon. That's not much when you consider how much we invest, the risks we take, and the products and services we provide.

Mobil thus portrays itself as anything but a greedy interest group.

The Gulf Oil Corporation takes a slightly different approach, addressing problems of the environment. A Gulf employee (portrayed in working clothes) declares that he is proud to work for Gulf because he knows firsthand a lot of the things Gulf does, and the precautions we take, to get the energy and preserve the environment.... Gulf and the other oil companies are making a lot of things work to get the energy we need and protect the environment. It's a tremendous challenge and I think we're handling it pretty well.

How Rich Are Oil Companies?

Oil companies spend a great deal of money on institutional advertising. In part these efforts are designed to correct what the oil companies claim are misconceptions about their financial condition. Given recurrent energy crises, there has naturally been much speculation about this issue. Jimmy Carter was quick to label the big oil companies as modern-day robber barons, and numerous polls have shown that the public believes that oil is deliberately withheld from the market in order to drive up prices.

Whether or not these allegations have much substance, public estimates of oil profits are substantially higher than the reality. Oil companies earn less than five cents' profit on each sales dollar (other manufacturers do slightly better). Further, public estimates of oil profits have been *increasing* while actual profits have been *declining*. Perhaps these common misconceptions help to explain oil companies' expenditures on institutional advertising.

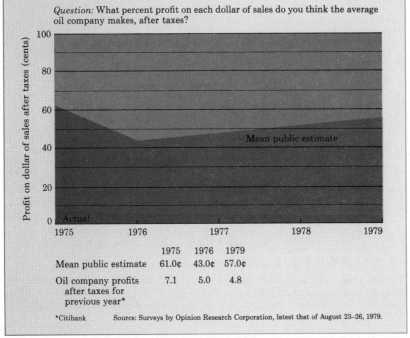

Question: What percent profit on each dollar of sales do you think the average oil company makes, after taxes?

	1975	1976	1979
Mean public estimate	61.0¢	43.0¢	57.0¢
Oil company profits after taxes for previous year*	7.1	5.0	4.8

*Citibank   Source: Surveys by Opinion Research Corporation, latest that of August 23–26, 1979.

THE GROWING INFLUENCE OF THE PACS

Organized interest groups swarm all over Capitol Hill. Many national organizations have state or local chapters (such as the major labor and business lobbies, the National Rifle Association, Common Cause), but their focus is on national policy.

As parties have declined in their ability to organize and finance campaigns, interest groups have moved rapidly to fill the gap. Interest-group spending increased especially after the passage of the Federal Election Campaign Act in 1974. This act permitted groups to form **political action committees**—PACs—to collect contributions from people, industries, and unions and make campaign contributions to candidates.

Political action committees (PACs): Organizations formed under the 1974 election law to collect campaign contributions in the name of some group or cause for disbursement to political candidates.

> As parties have declined in their ability to organize and finance campaigns, interest groups have moved rapidly to fill the gap.

PACs are growing in both numbers and influence. In 1974 there were about 600; by January 1981 there were more than 2,500 (see Figure 7-3). Some of these PACs operate almost exclusively at the mass level. They give money, instigate letter-writing campaigns, and so forth. One of the most conspicuous of these is the National Conservative Political Action Committee (NCPAC, pronounced "Nicpack"), which takes credit for the defeat in 1980 of half a dozen liberal Senate Democrats, including McGovern and Birch Bayh. Others operate as

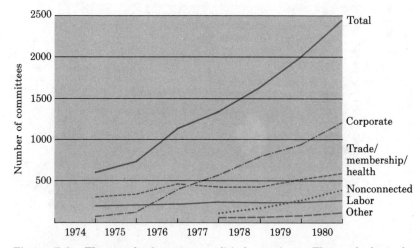

Figure 7-3. The growth of non-party political committees. The graph shows the increase in the number of political committees that are not authorized by a federal candidate or established by a political party. (Source: Federal Election Commission *Record*, March 1981, p. 2.)

the financial arm of established organizations, such as the American Medical Association.

The PACs are a major factor in congressional campaigns. Although money is given to candidates according to the degree of agreement between the group and the candidate, PACs like to invest in winners. One might suppose that corporate PACs would prefer Republican candidates and labor PACs Democrats. This supposition is only partially correct. In 1980, PACs spent in excess of $55 million on congressional candidates (see Table 7-1 on the next page). Most of the labor PAC money went to Democrats, but corporation PACs gave about 36 percent of their money to Democratic candidates. They did so with the expectation that, as the majority of Democrats would

The Military/Industrial Complex

The last speech Dwight Eisenhower gave as president warned of the growing power of the "military/industrial complex," those industries dependent on arms manufacturing and sales. Since Eisenhower's warning, the complex has grown to include not only defense contractors but also universities conducting defense research, private consulting firms, the aerospace industry, and companies that depend on subcontracts from larger firms. Like other corporations, defense contractors have jumped on the political action committee (PAC) bandwagon to further their lobbying efforts.

The Top Ten Defense Contractors

	Defense contracts, 1980 (billions)	Defense-related personnel in Washington	Defense-related professional lobbyists	PAC contributions (1979–1980)
General Dynamics Corp.	$3.5	40	0	$279,741
McDonnell Douglas Corp.	3.2	5	3	73,750
United Technologies Corp.	3.1	12–15	1	173,525
Boeing Co.	2.4	24	5	152,372
General Electric Co.	2.2	50	5	231,935
Lockheed Aircraft Corp.	2.1	15	2	129,520
Hughes Aircraft Co.	1.8	45	0	138,478
Raytheon Co.	1.7	20	0	30,750
Tenneco Inc.[a]	1.5	?	?	216,600
Grumman Corp.	1.3	7	1	282,680

[a]Would not supply information.
Sources: Defense Department Contractors Federal Election Commission.

Table 7-1. PAC Contributions to House and Senate Candidates, 1980

Type of PAC	Total contributions 1979–80 (millions)	Increase from 1977–78 cycle	Party affiliation		Candidate status		
			Democrat	Republican	Incumbent	Challenger	Open
Corporations	$19.2	+96%	36%	64%	57%	31%	12%
Trade, membership, health	16.1	+40	44	56	64	23	13
Labor	13.1	+27	93	7	71	17	12
Nonconnected	4.8	+92	32	68	32	49	19
Cooperative	1.4	+56	65	35	81	6	13
Corporations without stock	0.7	+600	56	44	73	17	10
Totals	$55.3	+58	53	47	61	26	13

Source: Federal Election Commission.

chair at least one subcommittee, it would be foolish not to establish good relations with them. Corporations and trade associations also spent most of the money on incumbents. This is another rational allocation of money, since incumbents seldom lose. More than 60 percent of all PAC contributions in 1980 were made to incumbents. Labor PACs concentrated on Democratic incumbents, but business PACs supported both Democratic and Republican incumbents.

Corporate and business PACs are becoming far more dominant than was the case a few years ago. In 1976 there was an approximately even split between contributions from labor and business PACs, but in 1980 business PACs outspent labor by over 50 percent.

What does the money buy? Money is more important for challengers than for incumbents. Challengers lack name familiarity, and, of course, they have not been able to build a record of personal service and favors. Yet most PAC money goes to incumbents. There are exceptions, the most spectacular being the well-publicized activities of NCPAC. With a computerized information and mail service operated by Viguerie, NCPAC was the object of considerable legislative interest and media attention in the 1980 campaign. Unlike most groups, this one concentrated on the defeat of unfriendly incumbents—those legislators judged to have been too "liberal" on a variety of indicators. Five Democratic senators—Birch Bayh, Frank Church, Alan Cranston, John Culver, and George McGovern—were targeted for defeat, and all but Cranston were defeated. The defeated senators blamed NCPAC, and McGovern set about the task of organizing a liberal PAC.

It is common for organizations to claim such achievements. Every group's contributions can be compared with the balance sheet of victories and losses. Not surprisingly, most groups appear very powerful; they back winners. In the case of NCPAC the claim is no more valid than is generally the case. The decline in the percentage of the vote for the five "targeted" senators was almost identical with that of non-targeted Democrats.[13]

In truth, money does not buy elections. Although a certain minimum amount is required to seriously contest a seat, large expenditures do not guarantee victory. Even in an age of media dominance, shoddy merchandise is difficult to package and sell. Money can allow a candidate to hire consultants, conduct surveys, and adjust the candidate's image accordingly, but if the image is really beyond salvation, the cause is lost. Candidates who are the targets of criminal investigations receive an extraordinary amount of (unwanted) media attention. Almost all of the representatives who were implicated in the so-called "Abscam" bribery scandal were later ousted at the polls, and there was not much they could have done about it. (There is an account of the Abscam case in the next chapter.)

The PAC Top Ten, 1980

According to the Federal Election Commission, the following were the leading political action committees in the 1980 federal election. Table A shows the leading PACs in terms of gross receipts and expenditures; Table B on the next page shows the top ten contributors to federal candidates.

Table A. Top Ten PACs in Terms of Gross Receipts and Expenditures, 1980 Election

Committee and affiliation	Category	Receipts	Expenditures
1. Congressional Club	N	$7,873,974	$7,212,754
2. National Conservative Political Action Committee	N	7,600,637	7,464,533
3. Fund for a Conservative Majority	N	3,163,528	3,150,496
4. Realtors Political Action Committee (National Association of Realtors)	T	2,753,139	2,576,077
5. Citizens for the Republic	N	2,356,751	2,384,210
6. Americans for an Effective Presidency	N	1,920,377	1,874,312
7. UAW Voluntary Community Action Program (United Auto Workers)	L	1,792,406	2,027,737
8. American Medical Political Action Committee (American Medical Association)	T	1,728,392	1,812,021
9. Committee for the Survival of a Free Congress	N	1,647,556	1,623,750
10. National Committee for an Effective Congress	N	1,570,788	1,420,238

Categories: Co–Cooperative; L–Labor; N–Nonconnected; T–Trade, membership, health. (Statistics are based on interim reports for the 1979–80 election cycle filed with the Federal Election Commission.)

(continued)

(continued)

Table B.   Top Ten PACs in Terms of Contributions to Federal Candidates, 1980 Election

Committee and affiliation	Category	Expenditures
1. Realtors Political Action Committee (National Association of Realtors)	T	$1,546,573
2. UAW Voluntary Community Action Program (United Auto Workers)	L	1,422,931
3. American Medical Political Action Committee (American Medical Association)	T	1,360,685
4. Automobile and Truck Dealers Election Action Committee (National Association of Automobile Dealers)	T	1,035,276
5. Machinists Non-Partisan Political League (International Association of Machinists and Aerospace Workers)	L	847,608
6. Committee for Thorough Agricultural Political Education (Associated Milk Producers Inc.)	Co	740,289
7. AFL-CIO COPE Political Contributions Committee (AFL-CIO)	L	715,327
8. Seafarers Political Activity Donation (Seafarers International Union of North America)	L	686,748
9. United Steelworkers Political Action Fund (United Steelworkers of America)	L	681,370
10. National Association of Life Underwriters PAC (National Association of Life Underwriters)	T	652,112

Categories: Co–Cooperative; L–Labor; N–Nonconnected; T–Trade, membership, health. (Source: *Congressional Quarterly*, Nov. 21, 1981, p. 2268. Reprinted by permission.)

THE WASHINGTON LOBBYISTS

Lobbying: Any communication by someone acting on behalf of an interest group that is directed at government decision makers with the hope of influencing decisions.

In addition to providing financial support of political campaigns through PACs, interest groups engage in direct **lobbying** to advance their causes in Washington. Lobbying is any communication by someone acting on behalf of an interest group that is directed at government decision makers with the hope of influencing decisions.

Lobbying is usually more than just an argument or emotional appeal to a lawmaker. Often it involves the collection and communication of useful technical and political information. Members of Congress are required to vote on hundreds of questions each year, and it is impossible for them to be fully informed about the wide variety of bills and issues they face. Consequently, many of them (and administrators in the executive branch as well) come to depend on skilled lobbyists to provide technical information and to inform them of the policy preferences of various groups. Congressional committee hearings usually consist of the testimony of professional lobbyists, who present not only the viewpoint of their interest group but also technical information relevant to the legislation under consideration.

Many members of Congress (and administrators in the executive branch as well) come to depend on skilled lobbyists to provide technical information and to inform them of the policy preferences of various groups.

Successful lobbyists employ a combination of "outside" and "inside" strategies. If there are members of the group in a legislator's district, the stimulation of letters and other forms of grass-roots contact are used. This tactic applies only to groups with a membership large enough, or geographically concentrated enough, to make the tactic appear legitimate. Letter-writing campaigns that have obviously been manipulated (with the identical language used, for example) are not well heeded. Perhaps more impressive is the ability of a group to stimulate letters or other more-personal communications from influential constituents and campaign contributors. This is more easily accomplished when the district or state contains a few dominant businesses or corporations that can be called on to contact their representatives or senators.

Furthermore, as we have seen, interest groups may seek to create a more favorable climate of opinion without any specific legislative goals in mind. This is done by advertising in major news magazines and newspapers. Large corporations, labor unions, and trade associations advertise on a sustained basis. The most prevalent use of institutional advertising is by corporations, since they can include ads as part of their normal marketing budget. Moreover, legislators themselves will encounter advertising, so interest groups make heavy use of the *Washington Post* for this purpose.

These outside strategies are rarely effective if they are not supplemented by direct lobbying—working the "inside." Lobbyists feel that their chances are better when there is evidence, no matter how fragmentary, that they are speaking for a "legitimate" group interest. Skillful lobbying requires a variety of political resources. Lobbyists need to have technical expertise in their field of interest, and they also need to understand the politics of the Senate and House. Reputations for technical knowledge, especially reliable and honestly presented information, are hard to come by and jealously defended. The same thing is true for political information. Therefore, the ranks of lobbyists contain a generous sprinkling of former legislators and former bureaucrats—those who know not only the subject matter but also the rules of the political game.

The media call our attention to the exchange of sexual favors and bribery in Congress, but most established lobbyists offer neither. Nonetheless, "Koreagate" revealed that legislators sometimes take bribes, and "Abscam" allowed us to watch them do it on television (see Chapter 8). Although the salaries of representatives and senators

($65,000) are not comparable to those of corporation presidents ($300,000 to $500,000 for large companies), there are substantial fringe benefits, such as travel, and most members of Congress are already fairly well off. Still, there is the occasional bribe. Perhaps the main reason that sex and bribery are not employed more often is that they invite exposure by the hungry media.

Socializing with legislators and their staffs is a routine part of lobbying. Again, however, lobbyists are in competition with others. The social life of Washington is as busy as it is varied. Members of Congress, especially chairmen of important subcommittees and committees, could spend every night of the week being entertained by lobbyists, by various research organizations, by the staffs of regulatory agencies, and the like. Experienced lobbyists use social gatherings to establish friendships; seldom do they bring up "business" on such occasions. Lawmakers are wined and dined so often that attendance at social functions is sometimes viewed as a chore.

Experienced lobbyists seldom try to threaten legislators—for example, by promising to oppose them in the next election. This is more likely to be the tactic of an amateur lobbyist or a new single-issue group. Threats often produce a defensive reaction. A threatened lawmaker may turn against the group that approaches in a hostile fashion.

Experienced lobbyists focus a great deal of attention on the members of congressional staffs. They recognize that legislators must rely heavily on committee and personal staffs for information and advice. So they try to cultivate friendships among Congressional staff people and win them over to the cause.

The only legislation on the books regulating lobbying is the Federal Registration of Lobbying Act of 1946, which is vague and ineffective. It requires the registration of names and spending reports of anyone who "solicits, collects, or receives money or any other thing of value to be used principally to aid in . . . the passage or defeat of any legislation by the Congress of the United States." Since the law does not address any activities other than direct lobbying, many organizations report only a fraction of what they spend. General advertising is not regarded as lobbying.

THE "SUPER GROUPS"

The American Petroleum Institute uses knowledge as its key to success. Less tangible but equally potent as a resource is prestige. "Super groups" rely more on the status and prestige of their members than upon other resources. They generally incorporate within their membership the largest firms or most prestigious institutions. Their power is based not upon what they know but upon who they are. Foremost among these groups are the Business Roundtable and the Council on Foreign Relations.

The Business Roundtable

Created in 1972, the Business Roundtable has only recently come to the attention of the media and the academic community. The Roundtable seeks to involve business executives, rather than lobbyists, in the formation of public policy. It comprises the chief executives of 200 of the largest corporations in the country. Each of these firms (not individuals) pays membership fees ranging as high as $50,000, depending on the size of the firm. The operating budget of the Roundtable is consequently substantial.

The image presented by Roundtable executives in their appearances before Congress and the media is one of public, rather than special, interest. Roundtable leaders contend that there is widespread misinformation about business; people need to know that business leaders do not think solely of their own narrow interests and are sensitive to broader social needs. Nevertheless, the Roundtable's lobbying debut was an effort to combat the spate of consumer-protection legislation so popular in the 1970s.

Roundtable spokespersons believe that its prestige, and hence its strength, is due in large measure to the participation by business executives rather than paid lobbyists in the policy-making process. Executive participation is organized by means of fifteen task forces on various issues of priority to the Roundtable. The issues are broadly defined rather than limited to current legislative proposals. For example, there are task forces on anti-trust policy, energy, the environment, inflation, government regulation, health, Social Security, taxation, and welfare. When the Roundtable begins to lobby, the executive responsible is backed by the considerable skills mustered by these task forces. The task forces, in turn, are financed by the substantial resources of the member companies.

Roundtable task forces send their recommendations to a forty-five-member policy committee for formal approval prior to the initiation of a lobbying campaign. Thus the executives are speaking for an apparently unified business community, as opposed to what might appear to be the narrower interests of, for example, the National Association of Manufacturers. Legislators are impressed when the chairman of the board of IBM testifies at committee hearings about taxation or when the chairman of Prudential chats informally with them about Social Security. One congressional staff member explained: "If a corporation sends its Washington representative to our office, he's probably going to be shunted over to a legislative assistant. But the chairman of the board is going to get in to see the senator."[14] Another aide echoes these sentiments: "Very few members of Congress would *not* meet with the president of a Business Roundtable corporation."[15] Additionally, Roundtable members Justin Dart and Joseph Coors have direct access to President Reagan, to whom they can personally represent the Roundtable position.

"Very few members of Congress would *not* meet with the president of a Business Roundtable corporation."

The Roundtable supported "deregulation" long before President Reagan made the phrase popular. Indeed, deregulation began, with strong Roundtable urging, under President Carter. Reagan's tax-cutting, budget-cutting, and business-incentive proposals were developed by Roundtable task forces. Under Roundtable guidance, the Reagan administration supported a proposal to require environmen-

An example of institutional advertising. Members of the Business Roundtable do not need media exposure like this since they have direct access to legislators.

"As a chemist who helps decide how industry wastes are managed, my standards are high. As a father, even higher."

Peter Briggs, Senior Advisor, Government and Industry Analysis, at a major chemical and mining company, with sons Chris and Jonathan.

"I spend most of my time on the job developing progressive company policies to protect the environment. Throughout the chemical industry, there are more than 10,000 specialists like me whose major concern is controlling pollution.

"When I was hired, I was told I was to be the conscience of my company," says Peter Briggs. "I'm concerned about the environment. I want it to be clean for my kids, as well as everybody else's.

"To dispose of chemical wastes, for instance, we use recycling, incineration and other methods, such as building secure landfills with thick, compacted clay linings. Then we check regularly to make sure liquids do not escape.

"In fact, my company has a whole internal Environmental Review Group that works constantly to monitor current operations and improve our standards. They descend on our operations for week-long investigations. Eighteen hours a day, weekends included.

"I know the whole chemical industry is concerned about the environment. We've already spent $15.3 billion controlling pollution. And our estimates show we'll spend $10 billion more over the next five years on waste disposal alone. So I know I'm not the only one with a conscience."

For a booklet that tells how we're protecting people and the environment, write: Chemical Manufacturers Association, Dept. LM-210, P.O. Box 363, Beltsville, Maryland 20705. © CMA 1982

America's Chemical Industry
The member companies of the Chemical Manufacturers Association

"We've Got the Votes"

According to a major business journal, in early 1978 the following was part of a conversation between two men, one of whom held a list of key Congressmen in his hand:

"Henry Gonzalez of San Antonio . . . should we use Sears? We have problems with Jake Pickle on this, I'm not sure we can get him . . . OK, let's ask Sears about Gonzalez . . .

"Delaney of Long Island . . . well, Delaney's a character; still, he was helpful as chairman of the Rules Committee . . . Bristol-Myers is close to Delaney, let Bill Greif handle that. . . .

"Steed of Oklahoma . . . he hasn't committed himself, maybe Phillips should call him . . . ask the Chamber of Commerce. . . .

"Gaydas of Pennsylvania . . . ask Alcoa if they'll do it, John Harper was very enthusiastic about this one . . . Hatfield of Continental could do it, but I hate to ask him. . . .

"Marks of Sharon, Pennsylvania . . . ask Ferguson of General Foods to call Kirby of Westinghouse about Marks. . . .

"Gore of Tennessee . . . Carrier Corp. and TRW . . . do we really have a chance with Gore? We really think we do? Ask Lloyd Hand of TRW. . . .

"Let's be careful . . . but if we haven't done our job by now . . . but we have, we've got the votes and we know it."*

*From Philip H. Burch, Jr., "The Business Roundtable: Its Make-up and External Ties," *Research in Political Economy,* 4, pp. 101–127.

tal regulations to be examined in terms of their economic impact. One can hardly examine the president's approach to taxing and spending without concluding that he heeded the advice of his good friend Holmes Tuttle, a Roundtable member: "The morning after the inauguration, Justin Dart and I sat down with the President and gave him our impression of the budget. We kept saying the same thing: cut, cut, and then cut some more."[16] A key ingredient of the president's program—speeding up the depreciation for tax purposes on buildings and equipment—was the work of Theodore Brophy, chairman of General Telephone and Electronics. Brophy personally directed the lobbying in Congress for faster write-offs.

While the Roundtable engages in direct lobbying on behalf of specific bills it wishes to see passed or defeated, it places even greater emphasis upon consensus building within the business community. It therefore tends to focus on issues around which such a consensus can be built. One such example is its successful opposition to the establishment of a Consumer Protection Agency in both the Ford and Carter administrations. The Roundtable does not court the media in such efforts, since it has no trouble gaining access to legislators. Its opponents, such as the various Ralph Nader organizations in the fight for the Consumer Protection Agency, rely to a far greater extent on media exposure.

The Council on Foreign Relations

Foreign policy, an issue area already confusing and remote for the mass public, provides an example of an organization just as obscure and influential as the Business Roundtable: the Council on Foreign Relations. As is true of the Business Roundtable and the American Petroleum Institute, the Council's connection with policy—in this case, foreign policy—is so pervasive as to make it a quasi-governmental organization.

The influence of the Council became apparent during the years of the Vietnam War. Initially the Council urged military intervention, a course of action followed by President Johnson. Later it suggested phased withdrawal, a course of action followed by President Nixon. Prominent Council members during this period included Johnson's Secretary of State, Dean Rusk, and his National Security Advisor, McGeorge Bundy. CIA director John McCone and Undersecretary of State George Ball were also active in Council activities.

Following the introduction of U. S. ground troops into combat in 1965, President Johnson created a "senior advisory group on Vietnam." This committee was not official, and it included more private foreign-policy specialists than it did government officials. Twelve of the fourteen members of the advisory group were Council members. This group became the arena of debate in the executive branch. George Ball, the only prominent member of the Council/government establishment who regarded military intervention as a mistake from the beginning, persuaded the Council on Foreign Relations and the advisory group to conduct a study reexamining American policy in Vietnam. This report anticipated the events of the Tet offensive in February 1968. After the Tet offensive, President Johnson held lengthy sessions with his senior advisory group. During these meetings, the Ball position began to prevail. Key Council members Douglas Dillon, Cyrus Vance, Dean Acheson, and McGeorge Bundy were persuaded to switch from the "hawk" camp to that of the "doves." The advisory group presented President Johnson with the new consensus. Five days later, Johnson announced a reduction of the American war effort and his own decision not to seek reelection.

Given the favorable response to its proposals, the senior advisory group was disbanded and reconstituted as the "Vietnam Settlement Group." Chaired by Cyrus Vance, this group devised a peace proposal requiring the immediate cessation of hostilities, the return of all prisoners, and the retention by the contesting armies of the territories then under their control. Although President Nixon's Secretary of

State, Henry Kissinger, did not attribute the terms of the ultimate settlement to the Council, the Council plan became the basis for the Paris peace agreement of January 1973.

As the focus of American foreign policy shifted away from Vietnam, the Council (now chaired by David Rockefeller of the Chase Manhattan Bank) began a long-term evaluation of American foreign policy. Key components of the Council's planning objectives were: an international campaign on behalf of "human rights," the reduction of nuclear proliferation, the reduction of international arms sales, and a reassessment of the relations between wealthy countries and underdeveloped nations. President Carter accepted each of these suggestions as fundamental elements of his foreign policy. Carter restricted international arms sales, halted development of the "fast breeder" nuclear reactor, and encouraged World Bank loans to less developed countries. Finally, and most prominently, the Carter administration based much of its foreign policy on a campaign for human rights. Foreign aid and trade with countries that did not meet the administration's rights expectations were curtailed.

Indeed, not only did Council policy become Carter policy, but Council members *were* the Carter administration. Among those prominent in the implementation of the Council's program were Council members Cyrus Vance (Secretary of State), Harold Brown (Secretary of Defense), Walter Mondale (vice-president), Zbigniew Brzezinski (National Security Advisor), Michael Blumenthal (Secretary of the Treasury), Andrew Young (U. N. Ambassador), and Paul Warnke (negotiator of the SALT II arms-limitation agreement).

The essentially liberal thrust of the Council's recommendations ran afoul of the increasing aggression of the Soviet Union and the inability of the United States to maintain a strong military presence. The Soviet invasion of Afghanistan occasioned the release of a stern Council memorandum urging that the human-rights campaign be subordinated to strategic considerations. The Council was persuaded that "détente" with the Soviet Union was possibly counterproductive and should be reexamined. The Council's new hard line, stressing that U. S./Soviet relations should be of primary concern, predated the Reagan foreign policy—a policy that (like those of Carter and Johnson) is a virtual copy of Council memoranda.

Much of the Reagan administration's reliance on Council recommendations goes unnoticed because of the more conspicuous attacks on the Council's "internationalism" by the Republican right wing. Because of these attacks and the attendant publicity, Vice-President Bush resigned from the Council. Nevertheless, as is evident from the Council's recommendations that the U. S. engage in a comprehensive military build-up and clearly state its willingness to use force to restore stability to troubled areas, the Council on Foreign Relations continues to be a dominant influence on foreign policy.

CHAPTER SUMMARY

1. Organized interest groups attempt to influence government officials and policies. Interest groups can be considered either threatening to or supportive of American democracy. James Madison and the Founding Fathers considered "factions" to be dangerous to society's stability. Today, many political scientists view interest groups as an important link between the individual citizen and the state.

2. Interest groups are mainly composed of upper- and middle-class members. The poor must be represented by "proxy" groups—churches, labor unions, and liberal/welfare organizations. This "poverty lobby" is strongest when the disparate groups are united on policy alternatives.

3. The leaders of organizations are frequently not representative of the rank-and-file membership. Where the leadership elite is mainly concerned about policy goals, regular members typically join for selective economic and social benefits. Additionally, broad-based groups suffer from internal factionalism, inhibiting the formation of an overall policy consensus. In contrast to a fluctuating mass membership, the group's professional staff is semi-permanent.

4. Single-issue interest groups are zealously devoted to one cause. They substitute passion for "selective benefits." For these groups, political compromise is virtually impossible. Both the leadership and the mass membership of single-issue groups often agree on specific policy commitments.

5. The importance of "expertise" as a group political resource is illustrated by the American Petroleum Institute. Representing major oil and gas companies, API possesses enormous influence over energy policy because of its near-monopoly of valuable information about oil production and distribution. The well-financed API also tries to sway public opinion through "institutional advertising," which attempts to place oil companies in a favorable light.

6. Political action committees (PACs) collect and disburse contributions to those candidates (mostly incumbents) deemed deserving by labor, business, or single-issue groups. The number of PACs is on the rise, and they are a major factor in congressional campaigns.

7. Interest groups use lobbyists as their "agents of influence" in Washington. Lobbyists provide valuable information to beleaguered legislators through official hearings, personal access, and socializing. Successful lobbyists usually combine "inside" and "outside" tactics to communicate their organization's policy views.

8. Prestige is another important component of organizational effectiveness, particularly with the "super groups." The Business Roundtable and the Council on Foreign Relations are two organizations that have a considerable impact on government leaders and their policies.

Notes

1. Jeffrey Berry, *Lobbying for the People* (Princeton, N. J.: Princeton University Press, 1977, p. 7.
2. Federalist 10 (Madison), in *The Federalist Papers* (New York: The New American Library, 1961), p. 78.
3. Gabriel A. Almond and Sidney Verba, *The Civic Culture: Political Attitudes and Democracy in Five Nations* (Boston: Little, Brown, 1965), p. 245.
4. Anthony Oberschall, *Social Conflict and Social Movements* (Englewood Cliffs, N. J.: Prentice-Hall, 1973), p. 213.
5. *Congressional Quarterly,* April 18, 1981, p. 660.
6. *Congressional Quarterly,* p. 662.
7. The seminal work on selective benefits is Mancur Olson, Jr., *The Logic of Collective Action* (Cambridge, Mass.: Harvard University Press, 1965). See also Terry M. Moe, *The Organization of Interests* (Chicago: University of Chicago Press, 1980), especially Chapter 2.
8. *New York Times,* July 17, 1981, p. 24.
9. *Time,* September 28, 1981, p. 27.
10. Frank Greve, *Chicago Tribune,* July 29, 1979. Reprinted in Bruce Stinebrickner (Ed.), *American Government 81/82* (Guilford, Conn.: Dushkin Press, 1981), pp. 164–165.
11. Greve, pp. 164–165.
12. Greve, pp. 164–165.
13. Seymour Martin Lipset and Earl Rabb, "The Election and the Evangelicals," *Commentary,* March 1980, p. 29.
14. *CQ Weekly Report,* June 12, 1976, p. 1512.
15. *CQ Weekly Report,* September 17, 1977, p. 1965.
16. *Time,* April 13, 1981, p. 77.

Close-Up and In-Depth Analyses

Jeffrey Berry. *Lobbying for the People.* Princeton, N. J.: Princeton University Press, 1977.

Thomas R. Dye. *Who's Running America?,* 3rd ed. Englewood Cliffs, N. J.: Prentice-Hall, 1982.

Carol S. Greenwald. *Group Power.* New York: Praeger, 1977.

Ronald J. Hrebenar and Ruth K. Scott. *Interest Group Politics in America.* Englewood Cliffs, N. J.: Prentice-Hall, 1982.

Dennis S. Ippolito and Thomas G. Walker. *Political Parties, Interest Groups, and Public Policy.* Englewood Cliffs, N. J.: Prentice-Hall, 1980.

Seymour Martin Lipset and Earl Rabb. *The Politics of Unreason.* New York: Harper & Row, 1970.

Terry R. Moe. *The Organization of Interests.* Chicago: University of Chicago Press, 1980.

Norman J. Ornstein and Shirley Elder. *Interest Groups, Lobbying, and Policymaking.* Washington, D. C.: Congressional Quarterly Press, 1978.

L. Harmon Zeigler and Wayne Peak. *Interest Groups in American Society.* Englewood Cliffs, N. J.: Prentice-Hall, 1972.

CONGRESSIONAL POLITICS

CONGRESS'S ROLE: POLICYMAKING AND REPRESENTATION

Congress is slow, unwieldy, and inefficient. It can frustrate presidents, but it cannot seize power when they stumble. This is the case because the modern Congress is largely a reactive institution. Although the balance of power between Congress and the president is constantly changing, Congress has long abandoned the idea of being the major initiator of public policy. Its policy role is to react to the proposals of the executive branch.

Presidents' success is often judged in terms of the proportion of their programs that emerge from the legislative struggle in roughly the same form in which they were presented. When Congress is in a reluctant mood, it can create the illusion of substantial independent power. But the truth of the matter is that about 80 percent of all legislation considered by Congress originates in the executive branch. Until a president decides to act, Congress is usually passive. Once presidential priorities are established, Congress reacts. As Randall Ripley explains, "The president still is, in many ways, the legislative leader. . . . A single individual with considerable formal power can inevitably declare a position and follow through on it more skillfully and rapidly than a multi-headed body like Congress."[1]

House Foreign Affairs
Committee members
vote during their work
on a resolution to
freeze nuclear
weapons.

Thus, Congress and the executive branch have reversed the roles originally assigned to them by the Founding Fathers in the Constitution. Dodd and Schott observe: "With Congress partly immobilized, and with the problems of the nation growing ever greater, the country has turned to the executive branch, both to the presidency and the bureaucracy, to fill part of the vacuum left by congressional drift. . . . [The] shifts toward leadership and budgetary control by the executive seriously threaten the ability of Congress to play a forceful role in national policymaking."[2]

About 80 percent of all legislation considered by Congress originates in the executive branch.

From a constitutional point of view, of course, the potential for power in Congress is very great. Article I empowers Congress to levy taxes, borrow and spend money, regulate interstate commerce, establish a national money supply, establish a post office, declare war, raise and support an army and navy, establish a court system, and pass all laws "necessary and proper" to implement these powers. Congress may also propose amendments to the Constitution or call a convention to do so. Congress admits new states. In the event that no candidate receives a majority of votes in the electoral college, the House of Representatives selects the president. The Senate "advises and consents" to treaties and approves presidential nominations to executive and judicial posts. The House has the power to impeach, and the Senate to try, any officer of the U. S. government, including the president. Congress may also conduct investigations, discipline its own members, and regulate its internal affairs.

Congress is better at *representation* than it is at *policymaking*. Initially, the House of Representatives was believed to be more attuned to popular preferences than was the president or the Senate. Presidents are not even popularly elected; rather, they are chosen by electors in each state. The Senate was chosen by state legislatures until 1913, when the Seventeenth Amendment provided for direct election. Only the House was originally structured so as to be directly accountable to "the people."

The Founding Fathers' distrust of public opinion, when coupled with their belief in the notion of the separation of powers, led them to create a Congress that was structured in an unwieldy fashion. The two houses have different constituencies—there are 435 House districts and 100 statewide Senate seats—and have different terms of office—two years in the House and six years in the Senate. Senators' terms are staggered so that one-third of the seats are filled every two years. Legislation, whether it is introduced in the House or the Senate, must be approved by both houses in exactly the same form. The framers of the Constitution deliberately ensured a slow response in

Congress to popular opinion. The job of policy initiation fell to
the president.

CONGRESS AND THE MEDIA

The media spend more time covering the presidency than they devote
to Congress. There is only one president, and the president can always make "news." Yet when an especially sensational story develops
in Congress—for example, the special congressional investigation of
the Watergate scandal—media attention can create celebrities out
of lawmakers. (Former U. S. Senator Sam Ervin, currently known for
never leaving home without his American Express card, owes his celebrity status to coverage of his Watergate hearings.) But even without such sensational events, the media devote a fair amount of attention to Congress. It has been estimated that, excluding stories about
elections, 15 percent of all media coverage is allocated to Congress.[3]
The Senate receives about twice as much coverage as the House.
Most of the coverage is of committees—specifically, the giving of
public testimony. When prominent cabinet officers appear before
committees, that is news. When hearings focus on controversial
topics, such as the effects of reducing federal subsidies for the poor,
interest groups try to offer compelling testimony, and that, too,
is news.

Television coverage of Congress is likely to be more negative than
its coverage of the presidency. Many network stories concern a
criticism of Congress by public figures. Attacks on Congress for

Senator Howard H.
Baker, Jr., left
(R–Tenn.) and
Senator Sam Ervin
(D–N.C.) achieved
national media
prominence during the
investigation of the
Watergate affair.

being cowardly or intransigent are most prominent. Its members are portrayed as self-seeking politicians. As Robinson and Appel explain: "Part [of the negative coverage] may [also] lie in the fact that legislatures in liberal, secular societies abound in philosophical contradictions, intense political bargaining, and what some might call the amorality of democracy. This makes for 'bad' news which is, of course, 'good' copy."[4] Certainly, Congress has a poorer image on television than the presidency or the Supreme Court.

Negativism in the media explains to some extent why Americans have such a negative view of Congress. Further, since most media coverage emphasizes committee hearings, the public's image of Congress is likely to be that of an investigative body rather than a policy-making institution.

The heavy media focus on the Senate fits well with the traditional inability of House leaders to move into positions of national prominence. House Speakers usually end their careers there, whereas Senate majority leaders are more upwardly mobile. The senators involved in the Watergate hearings reported that they received numerous proposals of marriage, comments on their appearance, and suggestions that they run for president. Only Senator Howard Baker, however, remains a media star.

Most committee hearings are no more than media events. The important compromises, bargains, and trade-offs occur outside of the glare of publicity.

Mark Twain once wrote, during his years as a reporter: "Dear Reader: Suppose you were a Congressman. Also suppose you were a thief. But I repeat myself." The media prefer stars; hence, the relatively anonymous House of Representatives is shortchanged. But by selective emphasis, much of the "real" work of Congress is neglected. Most committee hearings are no more than media events. The important compromises, bargains, and trade-offs occur outside of the glare of publicity. Many of the most influential lawmakers, admired and respected by their colleagues, are not "newsworthy." Many of the media stars in Congress are not admired or respected.

Sex and Corruption on Capitol Hill

As is the case with all public institutions, the approval rating of Congress has been plummeting. Although one can hardly argue that this decline in support has a single cause, it is nevertheless true that the media's presentation of Congress would give even the most informed voter little to cheer about. Television coverage focuses on scandal, and Congress has provided an ample opportunity for this focus. When people use the word "politics," it is common for them to apply it to inappropriate or even dishonest behavior. "That's politics" implies that politicians frequently act to promote their own welfare rather than that of "the people."

Corruption is hardly new in Congress, and Congress is not necessarily any more corrupt than other organizations. However, a series of sensational scandals has given the media an opportunity to expose the sexual and financial misdeeds of senators and representatives. The public's image of Congress as it is presented by the media is one of "politics" mixed with sex, scandal, and corruption.

Media presentation of Congress was exemplified in the "Koreagate" scandal in 1978. The *Washington Post* and *New York Times* revealed that the South Korean government, relying on the services of a businessman with good connections, Tongsun Park, had spent millions of dollars to create a "favorable legislative climate." This scandal reached to the top of the congressional hierarchy. Park asserted that he had provided thirty-one members of Congress with money, entertainment, travel, and other components of the good life in Washington. Yet only one former representative was convicted of conspiring with Park to defraud the government.

The public's image of Congress as it is presented by the media is one of "politics" mixed with sex, scandal, and corruption.

Congress tried to "clean up" its image, and it imposed strict codes of conduct on itself. Unfortunately, the 1980s began with yet another spectacular scandal, dubbed "Abscam" by the Federal Bureau of Investigation. One senator and seven representatives were accused of accepting money from an Arab (in reality, a disguised FBI agent) in exchange for legislative favors. This scandal was a ready-made media event, because the FBI had recorded the illegal transactions on videotape. Representative Michael O. Myers of Pennsylvania was shown boasting of his "inside connections" and telling the supposed Arab agent that "money talks. . . . That is the way it works in Washington." All of the Abscam legislators were convicted of bribery and conspiracy.

The media found the case of Representative John Jenrette of South Carolina especially entertaining. Jenrette not only allowed himself to be caught in the Abscam scandal but also lost control of his private life. His wife, Rita, a photogenic person, went public with allegations of sexual misconduct. Then she posed for a series of revealing photographs in *Playboy* magazine. The saga of John and Rita gave the media all they needed to fill any "slow" news days. In 1982, slow days were filled by allegations of homosexual relationships between unnamed congressmen and congressional pages.

It is hardly surprising that the public's image of Congress is negative. The public knows about the Jenrettes, but does it know much

John and Rita Jenrette became the focus of media attention because of personal impropriety.

about the organization and processes of Congress? It does not, as has been revealed by numerous surveys (see Table 8-1). Fewer than half of the American people can name both senators from their state or their representative.[5] If so many people do not even know the names of their senators or representative, it should come as no surprise that they have no idea of the policies advocated by them. Even voters who professed to know something about their senators or representative (only a minority of those interviewed) had only a vague knowledge of their policies. Usually, knowledge of a member of Congress is expressed in terms of family background, belief that he or she is "experienced," and the like.[6] Lawmakers' electoral success depends more on name familiarity and vague images of personalities, experience, and competence than it does on their voting record. (See Table 8-2.)

Table 8-1. What the American People Don't Know about Their Government

	Adults who know the right answer
How many times can an individual be elected president?	74%
Which party had the most members in the House of Representatives before the election?	64
Which party elected the most members to the House of Representatives in the election?	56
How long is the term of office for a member of the House of Representatives?	32
How long is the term of office for a United States senator?	30

Source: Data computed from the University of Michigan Center for Political Studies, 1972 National Election Study.

**Table 8-2. Percentage of Voters Who
Recognize the Names of Candidates**

	Incumbents	Challengers
House elections	93	44
Senate elections	96	86

Source: Data from the 1978 National Election Study of
the University of Michigan Center for Political Studies.

GETTING TO CAPITOL HILL

One might think that, given the negative image of Congress in the
media, members running for reelection could be defeated easily. Such
is not the case. Although the public has a low opinion of Congress as a
collective body, it has a substantially higher opinion of the individual
senator or representative serving a particular state or district. Even
though people might want to throw the rascals out, they do not punish their own rascal (presumably because he or she is not one of the
real rascals) (see Table 8-3).

**Table 8-3. Popular Support for Congress
and Reelection of Incumbents**

Year	Percent of public expressing positive rating of Congress	Percent of Senatorial incumbents reelected	Percent of House incumbents reelected
1948		65	
1950		80	
1952		74	
1954		85	95
1956		86	96
1958		65	91
1960		96	94
1962		90	96
1964		93	88
1965	64	—	—
1966	49	96	90
1967	38	—	—
1968	46	83	96
1969	34	—	—
1970	34	88	95
1971	26	—	—
1972	24	84	93
1974	29	92	90
1976	33	61	96
1978	34	68	95
1980	18	59	92

Reelecting Incumbents

In any case, getting elected to Congress is largely a matter of name familiarity and a favorable image. These are more easily attained by incumbents. Taking into account both primary and general elections, approximately 90 percent of those incumbents seeking reelection to the House have been successful, and about 80 percent of incumbents seeking to retain their seats in the Senate have been successful. *Getting elected depends most on being there in the first place.* The predicament for aspiring officeholders is not unlike that expressed on television commercials designed to attract recruits to the army: You can't get a job unless you have experience, but you can't get experience without a job. Of course, there are opportunities when incumbents retire or die. And some incumbents occasionally lose.

The Congressional Primary

Primary election: Nomination elections in which voters choose the candidates who will actually run for office in the subsequent general election.

Challengers for a seat in Congress must first win a **primary election.** Unfortunately for the ambitious candidate, incumbent success is even greater in primary elections than in general elections. Primaries, the universal mode of obtaining a political party's "nomination," are won mainly on the basis of candidate name recognition rather than ideology or issues.

Primary elections were begun by well-meaning reformers in an effort to open up the party system and eliminate the selection of candidates by bosses in smoke-filled rooms. Until the rise of the primary system in this century, candidates could become the party's choice by convincing state leaders of the merits of their case, especially if they could demonstrate long and consistent service to the party in lesser tasks. To eliminate boss rule, the primary system seemed like a good idea at the time. In fact, as the system now operates, becoming the Republican or Democratic nominee depends mostly on winning a primary election. It has less and less to do with a party's ideology or policy position or the preferences of its leadership.

The turnout in primary elections is lower than that in general elections. Therefore, the basic ingredient in success is assembling a personal campaign organization capable of turning out more supporters than the other contestants can turn out. Candidates cannot assume that their supporters will even be of the same party. Although most primary elections are "closed" rather than "open" (Chapter 6), the distinction does not mean very much. One gains the right to vote in a primary by declaring that one either has been or intends to become a "member." In most states the laws are so relaxed that changing one's party affiliation is quite simple. Furthermore, a candidate knows that the support or opposition of the active party leaders is largely irrelevant and that party hierarchies cannot control primary elections. Increasingly, *candidates find the task of turning out supporters most easily accomplished by using the media, especially television.*

Financing a Media Campaign

Both before and during the campaign, incumbent candidates can get more free time and space from the media than their challengers. They can create media events by calling press conferences to announce new legislation or a major grant for their state or district. However, both incumbents and their challengers must spend a great deal of money on media advertising.

Senate campaigns cost more than do campaigns for the House, but the costs of both have risen dramatically. The average Senate campaign costs about $1 million, and the average House campaign, about $100,000. In 1980 the most expensive Senate campaign was waged (unsuccessfully) by Indiana's Birch Bayh, who spent $2.8 million. In the House, James Corman of California spent $2 million in a successful attempt at reelection. Certainly, campaigns in excess of $1 million are no longer an exception. Most of this money does not come from party organizations; it comes from individual contributors and organized interest groups and their political action committees (Chapter 7).

> Most of the money for congressional campaigns does not come from party organizations; it comes from individual contributors and organized interest groups and their political action committees.

In 1980 interest groups gave about $45 million to various candidates, with incumbents benefitting most. Influential incumbents (such as the chairmen of major committees) benefit even more. The vast sums spent by organized groups were far greater than the amount spent by the various state and national party organizations.

Image Making

Winning elections in a media age requires that a premium be placed on image and personality, rather than issues. To win primaries, as we have seen, one need only mobilize one's most enthusiastic followers. In the general election, however, a winning coalition must be larger and more diverse. An ill-conceived issue-oriented campaign can alienate potential supporters. If a candidate wins the primary by appearing to be an extreme ideologue, you can be sure that his or her opponent in the general election will use this error to considerable advantage.

Image-oriented campaigning has two sources: first of all, the media are better at presenting images than issues; secondly, the voters themselves are attuned more to images than to issues.

THE CLASS BIAS OF CONGRESS

Technically, the requirements for becoming a senator or representative are minor. A representative must be 25 years old, a citizen for seven years, and an inhabitant of the state (but not necessarily the district) from which he or she is elected. A senator must be at least 30 years old, have been a citizen for nine years, and be an inhabitant of the state from which elected.

The "pool of eligibles," however, is considerably narrower. In reality, Congress is far from a cross section. In fact, it is a remarkably homogeneous body socially and economically. There are few blacks and few women (see Table 8-4). There are few members of the working class. Indeed, the wealth of senators and representatives is substantially higher than the national median income (about one-fourth of the members of the Senate are millionaires). Most have high-prestige occupations, such as law (see Table 8-5). Members of Congress are also older than the adult population as a whole.

Why this is the case is really quite simple. Politics is not especially interesting to most people. But it is especially attractive to those who have the time and money to indulge in the luxury of a pleasant occupation. To compete for public office, one must be wealthy enough to afford free time. Working-class Americans do not have the free time to run for high office. Members of the middle and upper classes also work, but more at their own pace. To compete for a seat in the Senate or House, one must be (at least marginally) articulate. Hence, a college education becomes an informal requirement. Although there are

Table 8-4. Blacks and Women in Congress, 1947–1982

	Senate		House	
Congress	Blacks	Women	Blacks	Women
80th (1947–1948)	0	1	2	7
81st	0	1	2	9
82nd	0	1	2	10
83rd	0	3	2	12
84th	0	1	3	16
85th	0	1	4	15
86th	0	1	4	16
87th	0	2	4	17
88th	0	2	5	11
89th	0	2	6	10
90th	1	1	5	11
91st	1	1	9	10
92nd	1	2	12	13
93rd	1	0	15	14
94th	1	0	15	19
95th	1	2	16	18
96th	0	1	16	16
97th (1981–1982)	0	2	17	19

Table 8-5. Occupations of Members of Congress (1980–1981)

Occupation	House D	House R	House Total	Senate D	Senate R	Senate Total	Congress Total
Agriculture	11	17	28	2	7	9	37
Business or banking	58	76	134	13	15	28	162
Education	39	20	59	5	5	10	69
Engineering	2	3	5	1	1	2	7
Journalism	9	12	21	4	3	7	28
Labor leaders	4	1	5	0	0	0	5
Law	114	80	194	33	26	59	253
Law enforcement	4	1	5	0	0	0	5
Medicine	2	4	6	1	0	1	7
Public service/politics	31	21	52	6	7	13	65
Clergy	2	1	3	0	1	1	4
Scientists	0	0	0	0	1	1	1

Figures add to more than the total number of senators and representatives because of multiple occupations of some members—for example, business and law.
Source: *Congressional Quarterly Weekly Report* of January 24, 1981, p. 199. Reprinted by permission.

exceptions, competitors for seats in Congress are generally following a career path from lesser to higher office. Until recently, women were largely excluded from this "apprenticeship." The skills of debate and advocacy are naturally acquired through a career in law. Hence, there are many more lawyers in the Senate and House than one would expect if a random sample of the population were drawn.

POWER IN CONGRESS
The Constitution is virtually silent on how Congress is to be organized, except to say that the vice-president will preside over the Senate and vote in case of a tie. Congress names its own officers. The Speaker of the House is elected by the House membership, and the Senate elects a president pro tempore (that is, a substitute for the occasions when the vice-president is absent).

Parties continue to organize Congress, even if they no longer organize the voters.

From the beginning political parties have provided the means whereby Congress can organize into smaller, more specialized subgroups to carry on the legislative process. Parties continue to organize Congress, even if they no longer organize the voters. The question arises why a senator or representative, who no longer owes his or her election to the party, should pay any attention to party leaders when they attempt to organize for the legislative session? The answer is to be found in the power structure of Congress.

House Speaker

The Speaker of the House, although nominally elected by the entire membership, is in fact elected by the membership of the majority party. Historically, the Speaker has been the most powerful member of the House majority party. Whether because of personal charisma or institutional authority, the Speaker is the most visible symbol of the majority. When the media attempt to capture, in a few brief moments, an important or controversial vote in the House, the behavior of the Speaker is the focus. Speakers rarely exploit this media opportunity to move up to the Senate or to compete for the presidency. Generally, it takes many years of constant service to obtain this powerful position, and there is no incentive to leave it.

The actual authority of the Speaker has gone through a number of expansions and contractions. Today, this authority is shared with other units of the majority party. Nonetheless, during debate the Speaker presides and is free to recognize any person clamoring for the floor. Given the size of the House, there are generally more representatives seeking the floor than the Speaker can accommodate. Hence, Speakers have used their authority to advance causes that they support. Deciding when to call for a vote can be equally important, since the Speaker can delay a vote until support is rounded up or until opposition dissipates.

The authority to hand out committee assignments, perhaps the Speaker's single most important source of power, has diminished somewhat over the years. Before 1910 this authority was the exclusive property of the Speaker. Since that date Speakers have been required to share their authority with other powerful party leaders but not relinquish it.

Thomas "Tip" P. O'Neill, Speaker of the House (standing), greets President Reagan prior to a meeting at the White House.

The Speaker also assigns bills to committee. This can mean that the bill may never reach the floor of the House for a vote. If the issue is one in which several competing committees have a legitimate stake, the Speaker's decision to send it to a friendly or hostile committee can be decisive.

Other House Party Leaders

Clearly, the Speaker is not the person an ambitious representative wants to antagonize. To a lesser degree, the same can be said of the second in command, the majority leader. Although without as much formal authority as the Speaker, the majority leader will probably become the Speaker on the death, retirement, or (rarely) the defeat of the Speaker. Along with minor party leaders, such as whips, the majority and minority leaders rely more on persuasion than on formal authority. They lobby for the legislation supported by the party or (more likely) the legislation supported by the executive branch if the same party controls both the House and the presidency. One answer, then, to the question of who cares what the party thinks is that the Speaker can advance or hinder a person's career in Congress.

Senate Party Leaders

The Senate, only about one-fourth the size of the House, has less need for organization. It can afford to be more deliberative. Indeed, the leisurely pace of the Senate is in stark contrast to the almost frantic rushing about that can be observed in the House. The constitutional leaders of the Senate (the vice-president and president pro tem) are nothing more than ceremonial figures. The real power in the Senate rests with the majority and minority leaders. (However, committee assignments are made by the Democratic Steering Committee and the Republican Committee on Committees, neither of which is directly accountable to these party leaders.)

Majority leader can nevertheless be a position of substantial influence, depending more on the occupant's personality than on formal authority. We can point to a consistent tradition of powerful Speakers of the House, but we can find examples of both powerful and relatively ineffective majority leaders of the Senate. Lyndon Johnson used the position of majority leader to become one of the most powerful policy leaders in the Senate. His successor, Mike Mansfield, was less driven, less compulsive, and certainly less influential. *His* successor, Robert Byrd, was more in the tradition of the negotiator and compromiser. *His* successor, Baker, used the office to become a media star. Personable, handsome, and articulate (as none of his predecessors were), Baker won more media attention than is customary. Indeed, Baker's performance may set standards for future majority leaders.

Senate majority leaders, unlike Speakers of the House, do not necessarily regard their position as the culmination of a political career. Some (Johnson, Baker) had aspirations to move on to the presidency; others (Mansfield, Byrd) did not.

Committee Chairmen

Beyond these positions, authority in both the Senate and the House resides in committees. Chairmen of important committees and, recently, chairmen of the subcomittees of such committees have as much control over the process of legislation as does the party leadership. There are 273 committees and subcommittees in Congress, each with a chairman and a staff. There are only 535 members of Congress, so the odds of everybody eventually becoming a chairman of something are good. Since such positions provide the opportunity for media exposure and, presumably, reelection, it is not surprising that efforts to reduce their number have not been successful. Indeed, the reverse is true.

> Chairmen of important committees and, recently, chairmen of the subcommittees of such committees, have as much control over the process of legislation as does the party leadership.

Seriority system:
The custom of making congressional committee and chairmanship assignments on the basis of a member's length of service.

The traditional method of selecting committee and subcommittee chairmen was the **seniority system.** Seniority helped to minimize conflict over committee assignments, but it postponed the achievement of chairman status. As a result, younger members of the Senate and House forced the adoption of a new set of rules. Committee chairmen are now elected by the party caucus. Nonetheless, seniority is still honored in most cases. There is little to be gained by violating seniority. Since most incumbents win, they can look forward to relatively quick advancement.

Quick advancement is promoted by additional changes adopted simultaneously with the removal of seniority as the sole criterion. The changes were far more dramatic in the House, but in both chambers rules spreading out committee assignments were adopted. In the House and Senate no member can chair more than one committee or (in the House) one subcommittee. In the House all committees with more than twenty members must have at least four subcommittees. Finally, committee hearings were opened to the public, and their staffs were expanded to accommodate the expansion of the subcommittee system.

Subcommittees: The Decentralization of Congress

During the 1970s Congress became more decentralized because of the rise to prominence of subcommittees. Committees found it necessary to create subcommittees with even more specialized policy concerns. Subcommittees and their staffs actually do most of the work on

Table 8-6. Standing Committees of Congress

Senate committees	*House committees*
Foreign Relations	Appropriations
Appropriations	Ways & Means
Finance	Armed Services
Budget	Banking, Finance & Urban Affairs
Agriculture, Nutrition & Forestry	Agriculture
Armed Services	Education & Labor
Judiciary	Government Operations
Commerce, Science & Transportation	Judiciary
Banking, Housing & Urban Affairs	Budget
Rules & Administration	Foreign Affairs
Governmental Affairs	Science & Technology
Veterans' Affairs	Post Office & Civil Service
Environment & Public Works	Standards of Official Conduct
Energy & Natural Resources	Small Business
Labor & Human Resources	House Administration
	Merchant Marine & Fisheries
	Veterans' Affairs
	District of Columbia
	Rules
	Interior & Insular Affairs
	Interstate & Foreign Commerce
	Public Works & Transportation

pending legislation, with meetings of the full committee serving to ratify subcommittee decisions. Ratification by full committees is the rule. There are exceptions, but given the fact that full committees rely on the expertise of subcommittees, approval is generally forthcoming.

> Subcommittees and their staffs actually do most of the work on pending legislation, with meetings of the full committee serving to ratify subcommittee decisions.

The development of subcommittee power was a product of the reforms of the 1970s. Senate subcommittees now number about 90; in the House the number of subcommittees has grown to 146. As subcommittees developed into independent bodies, they achieved more freedom from control by the chairmen of full committees. This independence was increased by the adoption of a "subcommittee bill of rights" in 1973. The majority-party members of each full committee were allowed to elect subcommittee chairmen. Normally they follow the seniority rule. Subcommittees were authorized to meet without the approval of the chairman of the full committee. They were given fixed jurisdictions, reducing the discretion of the committee chairman to reward or punish subcommittees or to help or hurt the chances of legislation by assigning bills to friendly or hostile subcommittees.

Chrysler Chairman Lee Iacocca lobbies successfully for government guaranteed loans for Chrysler Corporation.

Subcommittee budgets are under the control of the subcommittee rather than the full committee, and subcommittee staffs are selected by subcommittee chairmen and are responsible to them rather than to the full committee. Committee members who are not subcommittee chairmen have the right of appointment to at least one subcommittee of their choice, further reducing the discretion of the full committee's chairman.

The growth of subcommittees in number and power and the consequent further decentralization of Congress has had a substantial impact on the way Congress goes about its tasks. Interest groups no longer concentrate on a few powerful committee chairmen. Rather, they must work with a larger array of influential legislators. On the one hand, decentralization provides multiple access points for interest groups. On the other hand, lobbyists must spread themselves out more. Generally, interest groups have tried to establish "iron-triangle" relationships with subcommittees and bureaucrats in order to ease their task (see the section on iron triangles later in this chapter). Interest groups now open offices in Washington at the rate of one per week, suggesting that the decentralization of Congress has improved the ability of interest groups to gain access. They seek to establish policy "subgovernments," working with the subcommittee chairman, perhaps the ranking minority member, the staff, and key employees of executive bureaucracies who have an interest in the legislation that affects the interest group. As one student of Congress explains: "Every bureau and every interest group can seek out 'its' subcommittee, and if they can befriend the chairman and perhaps the ranking minority member they can help control federal policy in areas that interest them."[7]

Rule by Congressional Staff Members
The size and influence of the congressional staff has expanded rapidly in recent years. In 1960 there were about 6,500 people employed on the staffs of various congressional committees. In 1980 about 18,000 staff members were employed.

There are two separate staffs and two quite different kinds of staff personnel. On the one hand is the personal staff of the senator or representative. Although such staffs may contain quite a few policy specialists, they are actually expected to perform most of the service requests for constituents. On the other hand are the staffs of the committees and subcommittees. These staffs are employed because of their technical expertise rather than because of their loyalty to a senator or representative. As the flow of legislation increases, the role of staff experts is widened. Adding to the importance of staffs is the entry of television into the committee deliberations. Television coverage of House committee hearings had been allowed for more than ten years. The proliferation of subcommittees and their staffs has been a more recent phenomenon. However, representatives who in earlier times might have passed their legislative career in relative obscurity can now hope for the opportunity for a national forum. If the networks believe that something of dramatic importance might occur, they will be at the committee session. Representatives do not want to appear uninformed. Hence, they depend on committee and subcommittee staffs to create an image of the informed representative.

THE CONSERVATIVE COALITION
Many disloyal Democrats are Southerners. Recently these Democrats have been referred to as the "Boll Weevils." It is true, of course, that among party *followers* (that is, among the voters), party and ideology are relatively trivial in the voting decision. However, among *leaders*—candidates and officeholders—the role of party and ideology

The Reagan Budget in Congress

President Ronald Reagan, lobbying hard and effectively, won approval from Congress in 1981 for reductions in federal spending and taxation from the amounts recommended by the outgoing president, Jimmy Carter. Reagan's reduced federal budget, as well as his plan to shift spending priorities from domestic social programs to defense, had challenged the Democrats in Congress to prepare an alternative. They did, but it was not taken seriously. No more dramatic illustration of the decline of party influence can be found than the ease with which the president's program was approved by the House of Representatives, despite a Democratic majority in that body. In spite of the desperate (well-publicized) efforts of Speaker Thomas O'Neill, 62 Democrats voted with the Republicans (all 191) in support of the President's spending cuts. Later, Democrats voted with the Republicans in support of the president's tax program (Table A).

Table A. House Votes on Reagan Budget, 1981

	Budget cuts		Tax cuts		Tax increases (1982)	
	Yes	No	Yes	No	Yes	No
Republicans	191	0	189	1	103	89
Democrats	62	182	48	196	123	118
Total	253	182	237	197	192	241

These votes attracted considerable media attention. All three networks ran videotapes of O'Neill's impassioned plea to his fellow Democrats to hold the line against Reagan. The print media, but not television, contained discussions of the aftermath. These stories discussed the party leadership's consideration of possible retribution against the defectors. Little was said, however, about the fact that party discipline is *normally* very poor. The viewer and reader were given the impression that Reagan's success had been brought about by some especially remarkable or charismatic aspect of his presidency, an impression that Reagan was delighted to cultivate.

Actually, the defection of the 62 Democrats obscured the fact that the vote was a party vote—that is, that 182 Democrats agreed with Speaker O'Neill. Seventy-five percent of the Democrats opposed the president, and all the Republicans supported him. The wonder of the situation is not that 25 percent of the Democrats defected. Indeed, this percentage was lower than normal. This was virtually a classic case of party voting, a phenomenon relatively rare in congressional voting (see Table B). Yet the media gave the impression of a unique deterioration of party discipline. In fact, the 1982 vote to increase taxes showed much of the deterioration of political parties that had been alleged to have occurred earlier. The majority of both parties voted to increase taxes according to Reagan's proposal. The House Democratic leadership gave him strong support, while 46 percent of the Republicans deserted the president.

Table B.   Party Voting in Congress

	Party votes as percent of total votes	Party support— Democrats[a]	Party support— Republicans[a]
1970			
Senate	35%	58%	56%
House	27	55	60
1971			
Senate	42	64	63
House	38	61	67
1972			
Senate	36	57	64
House	27	58	61
1973			
Senate	40	69	64
House	42	68	68
1974			
Senate	44	63	59
House	29	62	63
1975			
Senate	48	68	64
House	48	69	72
1976			
Senate	37	62	61
House	36	66	67
1977			
Senate	42	63	66
House	42	68	71
1978			
Senate	45	66	59
House	33	63	69
1979			
Senate	47	68	69
House	47	69	73
1980			
Senate	46	64	65
House	38	69	71

[a]Party support: Average percentage of times a member voted with majority of party of affiliation in disagreement with the other party's majority.
Source: *Congressional Quarterly, Inc.*

is somewhat more important. Ratings by various interest groups consistently show that the majority of Democrats in Congress are liberal and the majority of Republicans are conservative. If a liberal decides to run for Congress, he or she will probably compete in Democratic party primaries. The exceptions to this generalization are Southerners.

For many years the only avenue to Congress from the South was the Democratic party. There is now some genuine competition, but it is still the case that the majority of Southern members of Congress are Democrats. Most of them are also conservative.

Thus, the decision of the Southerners to support President Reagan's budget program in 1981 was not difficult for them. The main reason that members of a party vote together is personal agreement. Since Southerners do not agree with the liberal majority of their party, they find it natural to vote with their fellow conservatives, even if these happen to be Republicans.

Conservative coalition: The voting alliance of Republicans and Southern Democrats in Congress, particularly on policy issues that tap major liberal/conservative differences.

This tendency has been institutionalized by the term **conservative coalition.** Approximately 20 percent of the votes taken in Congress involve an issue on which the conservative coalition has declared its intention to vote together. When this happens, the coalition often wins (see Table 8-7). The vote on Reagan's domestic spending and taxing programs was a classic conservative coalition victory.

Table 8-7.   Power of the Conservative Coalition

Year	Appearance[a]	Total victories[b]	Senate victories	House victories
1961	28%	55%	48%	74%
1962	14	62	71	44
1963	17	50	44	67
1964	15	51	47	67
1965	24	33	39	25
1966	25	45	51	32
1967	20	63	54	73
1968	24	73	80	63
1969	27	68	67	71
1970	22	66	64	70
1971	30	83	86	79
1972	27	69	63	79
1973	23	61	54	67
1974	24	59	54	67
1975	28	50	48	52
1976	24	58	58	59
1977	26	68	74	60
1978	21	52	46	57
1979	20	70	65	73
1980	18	72	75	67

[a]Appearance: For example, the conservative coalition appeared on 28 percent of all votes in Congress in 1961.
[b]Total victories: On 55 percent of the votes in which the coalition appeared in 1961 it was successful.

The scarcity of party-line votes should not obscure the fact that Democrats and Republicans do have different ideologies. These ideologies are, however, less the consequence of party organizational activity than they are of the self-selection process described earlier. There is not much party loyalty, but there is quite a lot of party consensus. Democrats tend to agree with other Democrats, and Republicans, with other Republicans. At one time party was the single dominant factor in explaining a vote. Since the turn of the century, however, party votes have been declining. We noted that party votes constitute a minority of all votes. In a majority of *votes,* most members of *both* parties vote the same way.

CONGRESS AND THE HOME FOLKS

Party affiliation is only one of a variety of factors in helping us to explain how senators and representatives make up their minds. Among the other factors, *constituency influence* is theoretically the most important but also the most perplexing. The source of confusion is the unclear notion of what a constituency actually is. We know the position of the president on an issue, because the executive office makes it known. But how do we know what the "folks back home" want? We know that most of them do not have the vaguest idea of the voting record of their representatives. How, then, can a constituency communicate? Clearly the whole constituency cannot. A constituency consists of many voices, some strong and articulate, others ambiguous. There are active constituents, a small minority usually relying on interest groups to represent their position, and passive constituents, whose opinions are unstable and weakly held. But even the active constituents with strong opinions do not speak with one voice. Depending on the social composition of the district or state, the active, organized constituents represent a variety of conflicting points of view.

Constituency Opinion

Members of Congress tend to listen to constituents with whom they agree. Even if lawmakers wanted to do so, on most issues it would be impossible for them to really know what a majority of their constituents wanted. Moreover, this form of representation, in which the legislator overrides personal opinion in favor of constituency opinion, is not one that enjoys much popularity in Congress. Rather, senators and representatives believe that their constituents prefer that they exercise some personal judgment. In this assessment of their appropriate role, members of Congress reject the role of **"delegate"** (that is, one whose responsibility is simply to reflect constituency opinion) in favor of the role of **"trustee"** (one whose job is to balance con-

Legislators as delegates: Role model whereby legislators' voting decisions are simply a reflection of the desires of their constituents.

Legislators as trustees: Role model whereby legislators' voting decisions are a matter of independent judgment.

stituency opinion with personal judgment and consultations with colleagues and staff).[8]

Members of Congress tend to listen to constituents with whom they agree. Even if lawmakers wanted to do so, on most issues it would be impossible for them to really know what a majority of their constituents wanted.

This is not to suggest that constituents have no influence. Instead, it is to argue that only the most active constituents come to the attention of their representative. Therefore, even legislators who believe that they are merely "delegates" necessarily receive information from an unrepresentative sample.

Legislators respond to perceived constituent opinion when that opinion is narrowly focused and deeply felt. Such issues are normally of interest to organized, economic interest groups. Although these groups usually do not pretend to represent the views of the district or state, they are rarely ignored. Senator William Proxmire of Wisconsin, who has achieved national media attention because of his crusade against useless or wasteful government spending, comes from a state in which the dairy industry is both economically essential and politically well organized. Although Proxmire frequently asserts that he is the "voice of the consumer" and has consistently supported measures to protect consumer interests, he nevertheless does what he can to

Rep. Robert H. Michel, R–Ill. (right), meets with his constituents. He is the House Minority Leader.

protect the dairy industry. Thus, Reagan's proposal to lower subsidies to dairy farmers and milk producers was opposed by Proxmire, even though the probable consequence of the Reagan program would have been to lower dairy prices to consumers.

> There is very little relationship between a legislator's vote and actual constituency opinion, but there is a strong relationship between a legislator's vote and what he or she *perceives* to be constituency opinion.

Clear and unequivocal expressions of opinion from constituents are the exception, and such expressions almost always originate from organized groups. To reach beyond the active public is a job beyond the resources of a legislator. It is reasonably safe to conclude that responding to active expressions of opinion, even though a distorted picture of constituent preference may emerge, is what legislators mean when they say that they are "representing the district." Their instructions come from citizen letters, the wishes of party leaders, expressions of opinion by the media, and the opinions of organized groups. Although many legislators cannot believe that their voting record is unknown to most of their constituents and therefore regard it as critical to their reelection, they are forced to infer constituency opinion from the active expression of various interest groups in their district. Their perception of opinions is often faulty. There is very little relationship between a legislator's vote and actual constituency opinion, but there is a strong relationship between a legislator's vote and what he or she *perceives* to be constituency opinion.[9]

Most legislators believe that they are neither instructed "delegates" nor pure "trustees." Most see their job as a blending of the two extremes. Sometimes they follow what they believe to be constituency opinion; many times they do not. Legislators frequently rationalize this approach to the job by arguing that their vote reflects what constituency opinion would be if this opinion were informed by all the information available to Congress. In other words, legislators speak for public opinion as they would like it to be.

Service to Constituents

All legislators seek to establish a good reputation for constituency service. Only a small fraction of the population (about 15 percent) ever writes to Congress.[10] When constituents do write, a good proportion of the correspondence is not about policy or voting at all. Instead, most constituents seek some kind of service. Such requests can in many cases be processed quickly and routinely. If the State Department is delaying your passport, it is probably not because of anything more than bureaucratic inertia. Is there a dispute over your Social Security check? A letter from your representative can be easily arranged and the matter resolved. Then there is the flow of mail from various civics classes, all of which need (immediately), "everything" about the Panama Canal treaty. More difficult to satisfy are those constituents looking for work or perhaps a low-interest loan from one of the many agencies with such funds available. Such requests are not so easily honored, but if the effort is made, it makes you feel good to know that somebody cares. Bureaucratic responses are likely to be impersonal. Legislative responses are not.

Casework: The vast array of personal services that members of Congress and their staffs provide for constituents.

Although some legislators gripe about "**casework**," or constituency service, they do not neglect it. This is what the personal staff of a legislator spends most of its time doing. Professional staffs attached to committees are experts in policy. The personal staff of a legislator runs errands for individual constituents. A legislator may spend about one-fourth of his or her time with casework, but his staff will devote two-thirds of its time to casework (see Table 8-8). The benefits are apparent, or so much time would not be consumed in this tedious process. Since most constituents have only a vague notion of whether they are being well served in Congress, casework is a safe way to improve an image. True, most constituents do not ask for favors, but those who do will probably talk about it. A prompt response makes them feel important. Legislators can build a strong reputation for service, and this reputation may be more important than the congruence between constituents and legislator on policy. There are some legislators (mainly senators) who have been able to stay in Washington even though their voting records appear quite out of touch with the mood of their constituency.

Table 8-8. The Congressional Workload

	Hours per week (average)	Percentage of time in each activity
Members of the House		
Legislative work	38.0	64.6
In committee	11.1	18.9
Other	26.9	45.7
Constituency service	16.3	27.6
Education/publicity	4.6	7.8
Staff		
Legislative support	30.8	14.3
Constituency service	142.1	65.5
Education/publicity	22.4	10.3
Other	21.4	9.9

Source: Data from John S. Saloma, *Congress and the New Politics* (Boston: Little, Brown, 1969), pp. 184–185. A 1977 official report using less detailed categories came up with almost the same impression of Congress' workload. Commission on Administrative Review, *Administrative Reorganization and Legislative Management*, House Doc. #95-232 (September 28, 1977), Vol. 2, especially pp. 17–19. (From *National Journal*, June 13, 1981, p. 1081. Reprinted by permission.)

"Pork Barrel"

Legislation involving special federal projects and federal spending in home districts is rarely neglected, even by the most austere legislators. Many members of Congress believe that such **"pork-barrel" projects** offer tangible evidence of their commitment to the district or the state and that these projects can help to ensure their reelection. Pork-barrel legislation is a long and honored tradition in both houses. The specific benefits vary with the times. Post offices, dams, and military contracts have always been the domain of "pork." Although they are expensive, they are also spectacular. In more recent years mass-transit systems, job-training grants to cities, and large research grants to universities have also been included in the expanding list of pork. It is an accepted courtesy to honor the needs of congressional colleagues to supply needed pork. Thus, legislators exchange support for various projects. They all fret about reelection. They worry when more than a handful of incumbents are defeated ("I could be next") and (especially in the House, with elections every two years) want to help one another out.

Like casework, pork-barrel legislation is nonthreatening, nonideological, and very helpful in creating a positive image. Of course, when all the various projects are finally added up, the price is high. When austerity budgets are in order, pork may be reduced, but it is still given a high priority. Indeed, pork may even be more impressive when it appears in a time of financial distress. It creates an image of substantial influence and argues for the return of incumbents on the ground that they can get more pork than can newcomers.

Perhaps the attention given by legislators to service work and pork-barrel legislation helps explain some otherwise puzzling aspects of the public's view of Congress. As we noted, public-opinion surveys show an erosion of confidence in Congress. However, these same surveys reveal substantially higher levels of satisfaction with the respondent's own representative. Constituents seem to make the distinction between the individual and the institution.

Pork-barrel projects: Special federal projects and spending obtained by members of Congress for their home districts.

Essentials: How a Bill Becomes a Law

The interplay of various forces—constituents, party leaders, interest groups, the president—is what the legislative process is all about. The process itself is complicated and tedious. Congress is in session for at least two-thirds of every year, and it deals with about 10,000 bills annually. Obviously, most of these bills do *not* become laws. Congress enacts about 400 laws each year.

"How a bill becomes a law," a phrase that occupies major

(continued)

(continued)

space in every civics text, is the formal process of enacting legislation. There are numerous opportunities for legislation to die, and there are insurmountable obstacles to the original legislation's remaining intact.

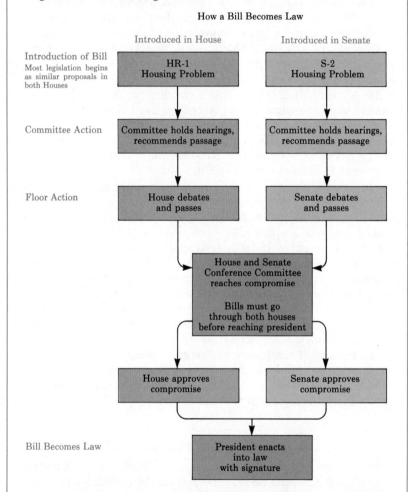

How a Bill Becomes Law

Introduction and committee work. The process begins when a bill is introduced. In the House a bill is dropped by a clerk (at the request of a representative) into the "hopper," a box on the clerk's desk. In the Senate bills are introduced by members on recognition from the presiding officer. After introduction, bills in both houses are sent to committees and, from there, to subcommittees. This is as far as most bills ever get. About 95 percent die in committee. Those that do survive begin the process with hearings at subcommittee levels. These hearings are generally bombastic, especially since both houses now provide for open meetings, with media coverage if the legislation appears to warrant it. Few minds are changed, but opinions are expressed and reputations built. After open hearings the legislation is examined in executive session, "marked up" (revised or modified), and sent to the full committee, which repeats the process. It is the full committee that votes on the bill, revises it, amends it, or defeats it (as is frequently the case). Bills normally die in committee unless they are given a favorable review. It is possible to pry bills from their respective committees by discharge petition (in the House by a majority; in the Senate by special resolution), but this procedure is rarely successful.

"JUST BETWEEN US, FORBES — HOW DOES A BILL BECOME A LAW?"

(continued)

(continued)

Rules.   From committee, the bill is placed on the calendar of the House or Senate and scheduled for debate. In the House, bills are assigned a "rule" by the Rules Committee. Given the relatively large size of the House and the pressure of the legislative calendar, the power of the Rules Committee is impressive. It can assign an "open" rule, allowing amendments from the floor, or a "closed rule." Rules can also limit debate. Clearly, a favorable rule is required for legislation to have a chance of receiving House approval. The speaker names all the majority-party members of the Rules Committee, thus making it a "traffic cop" for the party leadership. However, due to the factional nature of today's parties, the Speaker may be forced to compromise and thus lose some degree of control.

Debate.   In the Senate, in contrast to the House, debate is unlimited. Debate can be terminated only by the rule of closure, which requires a three-fifths vote and is therefore rarely successful. Thus, Senate debate can be interminable, sometimes deliberately so. In such cases a group of senators, knowing that its position is lost if a vote is taken, may try a filibuster to prevent a vote by talking the bill to death.

In both House and Senate the debate will be guided by a floor manager, generally a highly ranked member of the committee in which the bill originated. This is not an especially arduous task, as most of the conflict or controversy has been resolved during subcommittee and committee markups. Debate is therefore generally less than inspiring, although there are occasions when debates have resulted in the changing of a few crucial votes. When tourists visit the Senate or House chamber, they are often dismayed at the apparently inattentive demeanor of the legislators who happen to be present. Many do not show up until it is time for the vote; they are attending to other matters and could not possibly be in the Senate or House chamber for more than a fraction of their time.

Conference.   After a bill is passed in one chamber, it is taken up by the other chamber, where modifications and amendments may seriously violate the original intention behind the legislation. If there are basic differences in the bills passed by the two chambers, then the house that first passed the bill may request a conference. Only if the differences in the two bills are reconciled into identical language can the legislation be sent to the president. Approximately 10–15 percent of all bills go to conference.

A conference committee consists of senior members of the House and Senate committees that managed the bill. If the conference committee reaches a consensus, then a conference report is sent back to each house, where such compromise bills are routinely approved.

If the conference committee fails to reach a consensus, the bill either dies in committee or is returned to both houses for further instructions and revisions that might lead to agreement. In most cases, when the choice is between an imperfect bill and no bill at all, the choice is for the legislation. When both houses have passed the compromise bill, it is transmitted to the White House for presidential action.

Presidential signature.   Once the legislative process is complete, the president has ten days in which to either sign the bill, do nothing (in which case the bill becomes law), or veto it and return it to Congress with his objections. Congress may override the veto by a vote of two-thirds of those present in both houses. The probability of a veto suffering this fate is remote. Since the presidency of George Washington, only about 4 percent of presidential vetoes have been overriden. Even so "ineffective" a president as Carter suffered this fate only twice.

THE SENATE AND THE HOUSE: DIFFERENCES IN IDEOLOGY

The demands of the party, the constituency, the president, interest groups, colleagues, congressional staffs, and executive bureaucracies can create sufficient counterpressure to allow legislators plenty of room to express their own opinions. It is not necessarily the case that these opinions exist "out there" without regard to the various demands. An attitude or opinion is a complex notion. Taking all this into account, however, there is an immediate and long-lasting comparison to be made between the House and Senate. The Senate is more liberal. (See Table 8-9.) At the time of the drafting of the Constitution, it was assumed that the House would be more responsive to the "will of the people" and that the Senate would be more responsive to the demands of the propertied class. Given the prevailing ideologies of the time, this was a reasonable assumption. Those who spoke "for the people" generally did so from the perspective of populist ideology.

Table 8-9. Ideology of Congress

	House		Senate	
	Democrats	*Republicans*	*Democrats*	*Republicans*
Liberal	49%	8%	57%	11%
Moderate	36	26	27	29
Conservative	15	66	16	60

Based on "box scores" by liberal and conservative groups, 1975–1981.

If the Senate is more liberal and the House more conservative, which more accurately reflects the "will of the people?" It is reasonable to conclude that the more conservative House more nearly represents the views of the aggregate public, which, irrespective of how the term is defined, is more "conservative" than "liberal."[11]

Have voters in the states and congressional districts made a deliberate choice to elect liberal senators and conservative representatives? This is unlikely. A more reasonable explanation is that the senators, representing a larger constituency, do not encounter as many examples of clearly phrased opinion from various components of the active constituency. For every expression of opinion, there is another, contrary opinion. A senator's constituency is so diverse that the possibilities of balancing are unlimited. Moreover, a senator very probably has at least one large metropolitan area in the state. Such areas contain an overrepresentation of groups that benefit from liberal policies and are active in their behalf, such as labor unions and representatives of various minorities. Cities are more liberal than rural areas. Senators usually maintain residence in the largest city in the state, and much of their informal communication is in this setting.

CONGRESS AND INTEREST GROUPS

"Iron Triangles"

Iron triangle: The interest group/executive bureaucracy/congressional committee coalition that promotes a specific policy interest.

Successful lobbyists try to work closely with both the congressional staff and the executive bureaucracy. Some groups have become so skillful at this that the term **"iron triangle"** has been coined. The first side of this "triangle" is the interest group; the second side is the bureaucrats in the executive branch; and the third side is the congressional committee and its staff. Iron triangles are developed around specific policy clusters, such as insurance regulation, rivers and harbors, natural gas, environmental controls, and so forth.

Iron triangles are developed and survive because everybody wins. Lobbyists support the budget of the executive bureaucracy and contribute to the campaigns of those legislators serving on the appropriate committee. The executive bureaucracy cooperates with lobbyists in matters of implementation, possibly making regulation compatible with the goals of the interest group. Congressional staffs gain access to a useful source of information, and they can also enjoy being wined and dined by the lobbyists. Legislators are also wined and dined, and they are able to campaign successfully because of the group's PAC contributions. Admittedly, iron triangles may be expensive; budget reductions are vigorously opposed. However, the expense is borne by the least organized interest group—taxpayers.

A key ingredient in the operation of iron triangles is compromise—adjusting group goals so that a consensus is achieved. Compromise is most easily accomplished when interest groups are willing to bargain. This happens when their goals do not involve fundamental values and emotions. Economic interest groups can give a little to get a little. Their membership is rarely concerned about the details of legislation. When the membership is called on to support or oppose legislation—through the stimulation of letters, for example—this is done to set the stage for negotiation. Membership in such organizations is rarely based solely on commitment to the policy activities of the lobbyists. "Selective benefits," such as the dissemination of technical information, annual conferences, opportunities for social activities, charter flights, cheap insurance, and so on are frequently the reasons for joining a group. Thus, lobbyists can wheel and deal. It is a system well understood by legislators and one they find valuable. Media coverage of this arrangement is virtually nonexistent.

The Single-Issue Groups

There are some groups for which compromise is difficult if not impossible. These are the single-issue groups (see Chapter 7), which have accompanied the decline of parties and the emergence of emotional social issues such as gun control, abortion, and the Equal Rights Amendment. The members of these groups believe passionately in their cause. The membership of the National Rifle Association, for example, opposes *all* handgun registration or control. The Right to Life Committee opposes *all* abortions and *any* public funding for them. These groups are not part of policy clusters, and they rely almost exclusively on "outside" strategies. However, since they care only about one issue and are able to mobilize membership on that basis, they can exercise great influence. Traditional groups, such as labor organizations, can never be sure that they can deliver the vote. The NRA can be sure. No matter what else legislators do, if they favor gun control, they can be sure that the intensity of the NRA will generate opposition far in excess of what one might expect based solely on the size of the membership. Hence, many legislators dislike single-issue groups and value more traditional ones.

The intensity of the single-issue groups worries many members of Congress. There are, of course, many legislators who agree with the goals of these groups and need no prodding. Other legislators are impressed with the apparent power of these groups. Even though it is really impossible for a group to "claim victory" in an election (after all, who can really identify *the* crucial factor in any election?), conspicuous defeats, whatever the cause, create at least the impression of power. The success of the NRA is an excellent example. Public-opinion surveys reveal consistent majorities in favor of some form of gun control. With the unsuccessful attempts on the lives of President Reagan and Pope John Paul II, some opinion leaders began to speak out in favor of such legislation. Yet gun-control legislation is routinely introduced in Congress and routinely defeated. One can only suspect that the unrelenting opposition from the "gun lobby" is at least partially responsible. This outcome may be based largely on *perceptions* of influence. When a gun-control advocate loses, the "gun lobby" can claim credit, assuming that it contributed to the opposition. (In 1980 the gun lobby spent more than half a million dollars.)

Traditional groups rely on "access." They seek to establish the legitimacy of their role as representative, develop a reputation for integrity, build alliances, compromise, and socialize. Single-issue groups rely on passion.

THE PRESIDENT AND CONGRESS

Perhaps the most persistent lobbyist in Washington is the White House. Whereas most interest groups are concerned only with a relatively small portion of the policies legislated by Congress, the president and his advisors are actively involved in almost all legislation. Not only is the president the initiator of most policy; his office also lobbies extensively and with considerable impact.

Presidential Coattails

Presidential coattails: The somewhat dubious theory that a popular presidential candidate can attract additional votes for his party's congressional candidates on election day.

The president cannot rely exclusively for support on members of his own party. Loyalty to party is not that strong. And loyalty to the president does not always help at election time. The electoral theory of riding to victory on **presidential coattails** once enjoyed great popularity among scholars and politicians. But today we know that most incumbents win reelection whether they have supported the president or not. Moreover, there is a growing tendency for presidential candidates to operate with their own electoral organization, independent of the Republican or Democratic national committees. Carter and Reagan made little use of these committees. (In both cases the national committee staffs made little secret of their preference in the primaries for other candidates. The Democratic National Committee preferred Hubert Humphrey; the Republican National Committee preferred George Bush.)

Part of President Reagan's staff who help him lobby for legislation. From left: Treasury Secretary Donald Regan; Edwin Meese, presidential advisor; David Stockman, director of the Office of Management and Budget; and William Clark, national security advisor.

The party's congressional candidates run independently of the president. Even in 1980, when Republicans gained enough seats to control the Senate and make major advances in the House, Reagan's coattails did not help very much. Republican incumbents generally ran ahead of the president. (Reagan received less than 51 percent of the vote; Carter received about 42 percent; independent John Anderson got about 8 percent; and 1 percent went to minor candidates.) Even in those states in which Republicans defeated Democratic incumbents, the relationship between the Republican legislative vote and the Republican presidential vote was unclear. In half of these cases the successful Republican ran *ahead* of Reagan, and in half, *behind* him.

Presidential Lobbying

Although presidents almost always receive more legislative support from their own party, there is a great deal of presidential lobbying to be done with both parties. The president's executive office must know how to bargain, how to compromise, and even how to lose gracefully. Most importantly, the president must use the media to advantage. To say that most legislation originates in the White House is not to say that most of it emerges intact; nor is it to say that the president always gets his way. Reagan's major victory on domestic spending was followed by an equally stunning defeat of his proposal to reform Social Security. In the latter case *all* of the Republicans in the Senate

voted against the president. This defeat was comparable to the inability of Carter to persuade Congress that his energy program was
being waged in the context of the "moral equivalent of war."

> Although presidents almost always receive more legislative
> support from their own party, there is a great deal of presi-
> dential lobbying to be done with both parties.

Consider, for example, the contrasts between Carter's lobbying
and Reagan's. The differences could hardly be more dramatic. As
Carter's legislative programs were systematically mutilated, he became petulant. He placed blame first on the American people (the
famous 1979 "malaise" speech) and then on the oil companies, but
never on himself. Carter was a superb media campaigner, but he was
a terrible media lobbyist. Reagan, in stark contrast, used media lobbying to perfection. This was particularly true during his fight to cut
spending and taxing in 1981. The weekly question-and-answer television programs (*Meet the Press, Issues and Answers, Face the Nation*) were flooded with photogenic Republicans such as Senator
Robert Dole, David Stockman, and Baker. There was not an ounce of
fat among them. Reagan himself made dramatic prime-time broadcasts to ask Americans to call and write their legislators to urge support of his proposals. The Democrats, especially O'Neill, declined
television invitations. O'Neill was overweight, and Byrd, the Senate
minority leader, was no match for Baker. And, of course, none could
match Reagan's appeal on prime-time television, even though the
networks offered the Democrats "equal time" with the president.
Television pictured O'Neill pleading unsuccessfully on the floor of
the House to conservative Democrats to reject the president's proposals. The Reagan media team was displayed working to achieve a "bipartisan" victory.

The White House lobbyists.   The day-to-day lobbying for the
executive branch is handled by a congressional liaison officer. Under
Carter, Frank Moore reflected the contempt that his boss held for
Congress. Carter was not a compromiser, and his lobbyists did not
work with Congress in developing policy. Reagan enjoyed bargaining,
and his liaison officer, Max Friedersdorf, reflected his boss's pleasure.
Like all good lobbyists, the Reagan team was attentive to minor
requests and was active socially. The president's favorite jellybeans,
White House cufflinks, and other trivia were distributed to members
of Congress and their families. Furthermore, the president called
both Republican and Democratic lawmakers (particularly conservative Democrats, who are more likely to defect from the party line) for
talks in the Oval Office. Friedersdorf was particularly attentive to
telephone messages; the Carter team had a reputation for ignoring
them (even when they were from the Speaker of the House).

The result of this attention was an image of presidential deference to the traditions and preferences of Congress. The image spilled over into the media coverage of Washington news. Whereas Carter's image was one of incompetence, Reagan's was one of legislative success.

It may be humbling for a president to lobby, especially if his personality tends toward that of the "imperial president" (as was true of Nixon and Carter), but in the absence of party loyalty, effective lobbying by the president can mean the difference between an image of incompetence and one of success. As more legislators become aware of the image, it becomes more potent. In Washington the image of success is at least as important as the actual demonstration of success.

Party Affiliation of the President and Congress

Our system of elections makes it possible for the White House and Capitol Hill to be in the hands of different parties. (In European parliamentary systems, this result is not possible, since the prime minister is named by the majority party in parliament.) In recent times, Presidents Truman, Eisenhower, Nixon, Ford, and Reagan have had to deal with a Congress in which at least one house was controlled by the opposition party.

The popularity of the president is not a major factor in determining which party will control Congress. The extraordinarily popular Franklin Roosevelt had large party majorities early in his presidency and never had to face a Republican-controlled Congress; but the equally popular Eisenhower faced a Democratic-controlled Congress in the last six years of his presidency. Lyndon Johnson's landslide in 1964 was accompanied by an increase in the Democrats' congressional majorities, but with Richard Nixon's 1972 landslide Republicans gained in the House and lost ground in the Senate. With Ronald Reagan's victory in 1980 Republicans improved their party's position in both houses and gained a majority in the Senate for the first time since 1946.

Particularly troublesome for the president's party are "off-year" elections—congressional elections held in nonpresidential election years. Typically the president's party loses ground in such elections. Because the entire House of Representatives is elected every two years (whereas Senators serve staggered terms, with one-third of the Senate up for election every two years), off-year losses tend to be greater in the House. With the exception of 1934, recent presidents have consistently seen their party lose seats in the House in off-

(*continued*)

(continued)

year elections. A "normal" off-year election results in a loss of about 35 seats in the House.

Two explanations of off-year losses are (1) that voters invariably become dissatisfied as campaign promises are not kept and take out their frustration on the president's party in Congress and (2) that traditional party loyalties tend to reassert themselves to a greater degree in congressional elections than in the more personality-oriented presidential elections.

President and Congress, by Party, 1932–1980

Election year[a]	President and party		Congress	House D	House R	Senate D	Senate R	President's popular vote percentage
1932	Roosevelt	D	D	313	117	59	36	57.4%
1934	Roosevelt	D	D	322	103	69	25	
1936	Roosevelt	D	D	333	89	75	17	60.8
1938	Roosevelt	D	D	262	169	69	23	
1940	Roosevelt	D	D	267	162	66	28	54.7
1942	Roosevelt	D	D	222	209	57	38	
1944	Roosevelt	D	D	243	190	57	38	53.4
1946	Truman	D	R	188	246	45	51	
1948	Truman	D	D	263	171	54	42	49.6
1950	Truman	D	D	234	199	48	47	
1952	Eisenhower	R	R	213	221	47	48	55.1
1954	Eisenhower	R	D	232	203	48	47	
1956	Eisenhower	R	D	234	201	49	47	57.4
1958	Eisenhower	R	D	283	154	66	34	
1960	Kennedy	D	D	263	174	64	36	49.5
1962	Kennedy	D	D	259	176	68	32	
1964	Johnson	D	D	295	140	67	33	61.1
1966	Johnson	D	D	248	187	64	36	
1968	Nixon	R	D	243	192	58	42	43.4
1970	Nixon	R	D	255	180	54	44[b]	
1972	Nixon	R	D	243	192	56	42	60.7
1974	Ford	R	D	291	144	60	37[c]	
1976	Carter	D	D	292	143	61	38	50.0
1978	Carter	D	D	277	158	58	41	
1980	Reagan	R	D/R	243	192	46	53	50.8

[a]Presidential years appear in boldface.

[b]In 1970 Harry Byrd, Jr., of Virginia was elected as an independent and is therefore not included in this and subsequent totals. However, he received committee assignments as a Democrat. Also in 1970 James Buckley was elected as a Conservative from New York. He generally voted Republican but is not included in this table. In 1976 he was defeated.

[c]The total became Democrats 61, Republicans 37, after a disputed Senate contest in New Hampshire was won by the Democratic candidate in a new, special election in September 1975.

Source: Adapted from Congressional Quarterly, *Politics in America* (Washington, D. C.: Congressional Quarterly Service, 1979), pp. 120–21; 1980 data from *National Journal*, November 8, 1980, pp. 1875, 1879, and 1886, and the *New York Times*, January 6, 1981, p. A14.

THE SYMBOLIC FUNCTION OF CONGRESS

As we have seen, Congress does not pass many laws. And of those that are passed, many are "private bills," introduced as a remedy for a specific problem (for example, granting citizenship to someone). These private bills are not very interesting to most Americans.

But the function of Congress is not solely to pass laws. Congress provides an ideal arena for the articulation of conflict. There are so many points of access, so many opportunities for group interests to be expressed, and so many opportunities for "public opinion" to be expressed that, even when Congress "does nothing" (that is, most of the time), it performs a symbolic function.

> The function of Congress is not solely to pass laws. Congress provides an ideal arena for the articulation of conflict.

This symbolic function has become more visible since 1979. In that year the House voted to begin live television and radio coverage of debate. Complete coverage is provided through cable television in all fifty states. Not many people watch the full House debate, but network news shows can pick up particular segments. Thus, House members have the opportunity to try to create a national image. Individual legislators may achieve more "visibility" than they ever imagined by a dramatic speech that catches the attention of the media. Congressional "media personalities" can be created, especially since television responds primarily to strong personalities, to conflict, and to drama.

If Congress can focus and personalize policy conflict with the aid of the media, the result might be an offsetting of the tendency toward presidential domination. If Congress can capture increased attention from the media, it may slow the drift of power toward the presidency.

It is not true that Congress *never* initiates policy. However, Congress is slow to enact policy, and it is not highly regarded by the public. This low regard may be due to a perception of inefficiency. Whether Congress, in being slow, is being "responsive" to a public preference for careful deliberation is doubtful at best. The fact that most congressional decisions are in response to presidential initiative does not mean that they are automatically in contrast to the wishes of "the people." Indeed, exactly the opposite conclusion can be reached. Nor is it the case that prompt action is necessarily wise action.

CHAPTER SUMMARY

1. Congress is a much slower, less dynamic institution than the presidency. Its primary policy role is that of reacting to presidential initiatives.

2. Congress performs its representation role more effectively than its policymaking role. The Founding Fathers deliberately created a "slow" Congress to prevent the too-rapid translation of public opinion into law.

3. Congress receives far less attention from the media than does the president. Moreover, news coverage is highly selective, concentrating on public testimony before congressional committees, scandals, and allegations of corruption.

4. Despite public antipathy toward Congress in general, incumbents are usually reelected. Members of Congress tend to be wealthier, better educated, and older than the average adult; in addition, there are proportionately fewer women and minority-group members in Congress than in the population as a whole.

5. The power structure in Congress revolves around the Speaker of the House, the party leadership in the Senate, and the committee chairmen in both houses (normally chosen through seniority).

6. Strict party-line voting has declined in importance in Congress. The conservative coalition, an alliance of Republicans and southern Democrats, can wield considerable power.

7. Legislators' voting decisions are influenced by their perception of constituency opinion—a perception that can be strongly affected by organized groups in the district or state. Most members of Congress adopt a middle position between the extremes of being mere "delegates" for their constituents and being "trustees" who are expected to vote their own minds. Attention to casework and pork-barrel legislation is at least as significant as voting record when it comes to being reelected.

8. Lawmakers must deal with numerous lobbyists, who add to their leverage by means of "iron triangles"—alliances with executive and congressional staffs. Single-issue groups can exert a powerful—and, some think, unwholesome—influence on legislation.

9. Presidents vary in their ability to "lobby" Congress effectively. Because presidents cannot automatically command support for their proposals even from members of their own parties, media lobbying and day-to-day lobbying of senators and representatives can be crucial to the success of a president's legislative package.

10. In addition to its lawmaking function, Congress performs the symbolic function of providing an arena for the articulation of differences and policy conflicts.

Notes

1. Randall B. Ripley, *Congress: Process and Policy,* 2nd ed. (New York: Norton, 1978), pp. 294–295.
2. Lawrence C. Dodd and Richard L. Schott, *Congress and the Administrative State* (New York: Wiley, 1979), pp. 327–328.

3. Michael J. Robinson and Kevin R. Appel, "Network News Coverage of Congress," *Political Science Quarterly,* Fall 1979, pp. 409–410.
4. Robinson and Appel, p. 415.
5. Fred I. Greenstein, *The American Party System and the American People* (Englewood Cliffs, N. J.: Prentice-Hall, 1963), p. 12.
6. Subcommittee on Intergovernmental Relations of the Committee on Government Operations, United States Senate, *Confidence and Concern: Citizens View American Government. A Survey of Public Attitudes* (Washington, D. C.: U. S. Government Printing Office, 1973).
7. Carol S. Greenwald, *Group Power: Lobbying and Public Policy* (New York: Praeger, 1977), Chapter 8.
8. Roger H. Davidson, *The Role of the Congressman* (New York: Pegasus, 1969), p. 117.
9. Warren R. Miller and Donald E. Stokes, "Constituency Influence in Congress," *American Political Science Review,* March 1963, p. 56.
10. Sidney Verba and Norman H. Nie (Eds.), *Participation in America: Political Democracy and Social Equality* (New York: Harper & Row, 1972), p. 31.
11. *Public Opinion,* February/March 1981, p. 20.

Close-Up and In-Depth Analyses

Congressional Quarterly. *CQ Weekly Report.* Washington, D. C.: Congressional Quarterly Service.

Lawrence C. Dodd and Richard C. Schott. *Congress and the Administrative State.* New York: Wiley, 1979.

George C. Edwards. *Presidential Influence in Congress.* New York: Freeman, 1980.

Richard F. Fenno, Jr. *The Power of the Purse.* Boston: Little, Brown, 1966.

Richard F. Fenno, Jr. *Congressmen in Committees.* Boston: Little, Brown, 1973.

Richard F. Fenno, Jr. *Homestyle: House Members in their Districts.* Boston: Little, Brown, 1978.

Lewis A. Froman. *Congressmen and Their Constituencies.* Chicago: Rand McNally, 1963.

Barbara Hinckley. *Congressional Elections.* Washington, D. C.: Congressional Quarterly Press, 1981.

Walter J. Oleszek. *Congressional Procedure and the Policy Process.* Washington, D. C.: Congressional Quarterly Press, 1978.

Robert L. Peabody. *Leadership in Congress.* Boston: Little, Brown, 1976.

Nelson W. Polsby. *Congress and the Presidency,* 3rd ed. Englewood Cliffs, N. J.: Prentice-Hall, 1976.

Randall B. Ripley. *Congress: Process and Policy.* 2nd ed. New York: Norton, 1978.

PRESIDENTIAL POLITICS

THE PRESIDENCY: SUBSTANCE AND SYMBOLS

The formal powers of the presidency are rather modest. According to the Constitution, the president is to carry out legislation ("take care that the laws be faithfully executed") and to provide information to Congress ("give to Congress information of the State of the Union, and recommend to their consideration such measures as he shall judge necessary and expedient.") In addition, the president is the commander in chief of the armed forces. Treaties are made by the president but require the "advice and consent" of the Senate; "executive agreements" with foreign countries are made by the president but do not require Senate approval. Also, the president has appointive power for positions such as ambassadors and Supreme Court justices as well as all other United States officers whose appointments are not provided for in the Constitution or by statute ("nominate, and by and with the advice and consent of the Senate, shall appoint . . . "). The president may pardon someone (may "grant reprieves and pardons for offences against the United States"). Finally, the president is recognized as the chief of state ("The executive power shall be vested in a president"). (See Table 9-1.) To become president, the Constitution specifies, a person must be a natural-born citizen at least thirty-five years of age and a resident of the U. S. for fourteen years.

The Oval Office, a
symbol of American
presidency, and its
most recent occupant,
Ronald Reagan.

Table 9-1. Formal Presidential Powers in the Constitution

Chief Administrator
  Implement policy—"Take care that laws be faithfully executed"
    (Article II, Section 2).
  Supervise executive branch of government.
  Appoint and remove policy officials.
  Prepare executive budget.

Chief Legislator
  Initiate policy—"Give to the Congress information of the State of the Union and
    recommend to their consideration such measures as he shall judge necessary
    and expedient" (Article II, Section 3).
  Veto legislation passed by Congress.
  Convene special session of Congress "on extraordinary occasions"
    (Article II, Section 3).

Party Leader
  Control national party organization.
  Control federal patronage.
  Influence (not control) state and local parties through prestige.

Chief Diplomat
  Make treaties ("with the advice and consent of Senate") (Article II, Section 2).
  Make executive agreements.
  Power of diplomatic recognition—"to send and receive ambassadors"
    (Article II, Section 2).

Commander in Chief
  Command U. S. armed forces—"The President shall be commander in chief of the
    army and the navy" (Article II, Section 2).
  Appoint military officials.
  Initiate war.
  Broad war powers.

Crisis Manager and Chief of State
  "The executive power shall be vested in a president" (Article II, Section 1).
  Represent the nation as chief of state.

In an age of media technology, visibility and symbolic skills are essential to presidential power. To govern effectively, a president not only must have power resources but must be *perceived* as powerful. Both substance and symbol are necessary in forging winning coalitions on important policy issues.

Presidents can be strong or weak, depending more on their personality than on their formal powers. Decisive presidents can use their authority as both commander in chief and chief diplomat to justify a broad range of military and foreign-policy initiatives. They can use their authority over the execution of laws to undertake actions that they judge essential to national well-being. They can use their executive authority to make major initiatives in foreign and domestic policy.

The president commands the attention of the mass media. Through the power of policy initiation alone, the president has a considerable impact on the nation. The president sets the agenda for public policy. Presidential programs are presented to Congress in various messages and in the budget and thereby largely determine what the business of Congress will be in any session. Few major undertakings ever get off the ground without presidential initiation; the president frames the issues, determines their context, and decides their timing.

The political resources of presidents are vast. They are not a consequence of presidential leadership of the party, for presidents are elected largely on their own. Nor are they a consequence of presidential control of policy, for a reluctant Congress and an inert bureaucracy can frustrate any president. They are a consequence of the great reverence that Americans have for the office of president and the attention the president receives from the mass media.

Americans confer on their presidents a great deal of symbolic authority. They have high expectations of their presidents and punish them bitterly when they do not accomplish what is expected of them. The authors of the Constitution did not intend for the president to become the personal symbol of national government. But that is exactly what happened. Studies of the development of political attitudes in American children indicate that at an early age they identify the president as the government.[1]

> The authors of the Constitution did not intend for the president to become the personal symbol of national government. But that is exactly what happened.

Perhaps the first president to employ the media to create a "cult of personality" was Franklin Roosevelt. He used his "fireside chats" on radio to develop popular unity behind his programs for economic recovery from the Great Depression. It was Roosevelt who established the modern presidency. Unlike his immediate predecessors (Warren Harding, Calvin Coolidge, and Herbert Hoover), Roosevelt had a uniquely *personal* image of his job. Whether or not he believed

Franklin Roosevelt was considered by many to be the first media president.

it, he encouraged the view that the nation's future depended on his personal success. Primitive as it was by today's standards, the fireside chat was the precursor of today's use of the media by the president. The most popular presidents look and act "presidential." It is not what they do but how they appear that makes them popular.

There are a number of reasons for the cult of personality surrounding the presidency. Government social services have expanded; the president is supposed to be compassionate and caring. The nation is in a precarious nuclear balance with the Soviet Union, making foreign policy the art of "crisis management." The president has the responsibility of keeping the nation out of nuclear war. But the cult of personality owes its existence primarily to the emergence of the mass media as the major source of communication between the president, other governmental decision makers, and the public.

THE PRESIDENT AND THE MEDIA

The media love dramatic personalities. The presidency can be portrayed as a single personality and dramatized to the maximum. Congress is hard to personalize; the Supreme Court is aloof; the bureaucracy is boring. But the presidency provides a golden opportunity for the media to dramatize and personalize government.

The president and the media are engaged in a game of mutual influence. The media are accused by some presidents (Richard Nixon and Jimmy Carter) of trying to destroy them. But the media are only seeking sensational personalities, whether they are heroes or villains.

> Congress is hard to personalize; the Supreme Court is aloof; the bureaucracy is boring. But the presidency provides a golden opportunity for the media to dramatize and personalize government.

Television brings the president directly in contact with the masses, and their attachment to the president is unlike their attachment to any other public official or symbol of government. Fred I. Greenstein has classified the "psychological functions of the presidency."[2] The president:

1. "simplifies perception of government and politics" by serving as "the main cognitive 'handle' for providing busy citizens with some sense of what their government is doing"
2. provides "an outlet for emotional expression" through public interest in his and his family's private and public life
3. is a "symbol of unity" and of nationhood (as the national shock and grief over the death of a president clearly reveals)
4. provides the masses with a "vicarious means of taking political

action," in that the president can act decisively and effectively, whereas they cannot do so

5. is a "symbol of social stability" in providing the masses with a feeling of security and guidance.

The "Awesome Burden" of the Presidency

Is the presidency an "awesome burden," a heavy responsibility that all but crushes the occupant of the Oval Office? The presidency did not seem to awe Ronald Reagan in the first half of his term. Despite an unprecedented effort to halt the spiraling growth of the federal government and the battles with Congress and the bureaucracy that this effort entailed, Reagan remained comfortable, easy-going, unruffled. The oldest occupant of the White House in history, he showed little sign of his 70-plus years. Fully recovered from bullet wounds received in an assassination attempt on March 30, 1981, Reagan did not change his life-style because of his brush with death. "I think I get in the car a little quicker now," he joked.

Reagan exercised twenty minutes a day and took off Wednesday afternoons to ride horses in Virginia. On most weekends he went to the presidential retreat at Camp David, Maryland, where he rode in the morning and worked hard—splitting firewood, clearing brush, and building fences—in the afternoon. In the evening he watched television with his wife, Nancy; their favorite show, predictably, was "Little House on the Prairie."

Reagan was asked his reaction to a news story alleging that he worked only a few hours a day. "I was mad as hell," he said, laughing, "because there's no truth to that. Last night I was here until about 6:45."

Although Reagan restored considerable stateliness to the presidency, his life-style was not ostentatious. A media story about Nancy Reagan's purchase of china at $1,000 per place setting seemed to him a "bum rap." No new china had been purchased for the White House since Harry Truman, and to set a full table for a state dinner required mixing different pieces of old china. The Lenox Company sold the china at cost, the Reagans said, and the money was donated by friends.

In the face of press criticism, Reagan said that he developed a "tough hide" in 25 years as an actor. One of his movies, *King's Row*, was attacked by the critics, he pointed out, but it turned out to be "one of the all-time greats." As president, he said, "I try to remember that."

Reagan as Media Lobbyist

Ronald Reagan relied heavily on the media to win public support for his programs and to pressure Congress to enact his policies. Reagan used the media to help win two extraordinary victories over the House Democratic leadership on his budget- and tax-reduction programs of 1981. The television appeal was his most effective weapon, but it was clearly preceded by hard lobbying. Democrats who might be willing to support the president were lobbied hard, not only by the White House lobbyists but also by the president himself. Unlike his predecessor, Reagan was willing to personally lobby lawmakers—to invite them to the White House for discussions, to listen to their problems, and to trade pet projects for their support in the budget and tax fights. Of course, Reagan was not alone in lobbying for budget and tax reductions. Powerful business organizations and corporations were active, especially the U.S. Chamber of Commerce, with branches in most cities. Reagan worked closely with these business lobbyists.

All of this lobbying activity led up to the president's television presentations. Past presidents were not as successful in using television in conjunction with well-timed and strong lobbying efforts. (Carter's only serious attempt at television lobbying was his declaration of the energy crisis as "the moral equivalent of war"; but this failed to win support for his energy program.) In his television appeals Reagan was jovial and simple. The differences between the Democratic tax-cut bill and the president's were presented in simple graphic form, making minor differences appear major. His presentation was "cool." There were no "enemies" to the president; he simply gave his audience a good show, and above all he was sincere. Reagan explained to Tom Wicker, a columnist for the *New York Times*, that television picks up insincerity quicker than one might expect. He maintained that success as an actor requires belief in one's lines. Success as a television president required the same belief. He obviously believed that tax reductions and reduced federal budgets would reverse the downward spiral of the economy. His viewers, who could not possibly understand the complexities of supply-side economics, recognized his sincerity. It was not so much what he said but how he said it that won popular support. Democratic leaders reported a "telephone blitz" as a consequence of the president's television appearance. It was not that "the people" were persuaded and then persuaded the Democrats. Rather, the Reagan appearance gave both Republicans and Democrats an excuse for voting with the president.

Reagan as Media Cultivator

Style, as opposed to substance, is also important in press conferences. Most presidents come to distrust the media, and they regard press conferences as a contest of wills. Some presidents blame the media for their failures. President Lyndon Johnson contended that the media had contributed to a decline in support for the Vietnam War. (He believed that Walter Cronkite of CBS-TV was personally responsible, because he had constantly implied that the war could not be won.)[3] Carter believed that the public's perception of him as incompetent had been fostered by the media's lust for conflict, confusion, and scandal. Nixon blamed his resignation and disgrace almost solely on the media. Carter's and Nixon's hostility was apparent in their defensive and hostile mannerisms. But Reagan's personality and training as an actor made it unlikely that he would fall into a similar pattern. Not only did he identify with media personalities; he also understood the technology of the media and was comfortable with it.

On election night, for example, Cronkite was discussing Reagan's wide margin of victory in Illinois with Gerald Ford. Cronkite and Ford were in New York, and Reagan was in Los Angeles. Cronkite wanted to connect the former president and the newly elected president for a congratulatory chat. He instructed the CBS correspondent in Los Angeles to offer his headset to Reagan, thus creating the electronic link. The Washington writer Bill Hogan recalls in the *Washington Journalism Review* that

> with no trace of hesitation and with apparent recognition of what was about to happen, Reagan [took the headset]. He and Ford exchanged pleasantries, and Cronkite followed with a few questions. In a matter of minutes, with Ronald Reagan's smooth acquiescence, Cronkite and Bowen [the CBS correspondent] had scored a beat over their rival networks. This election night vignette illustrates Ronald Reagan's familiarity and ease with the television technology that catapulted him to political stardom.... One can not easily imagine, say, Jimmy Carter or Richard Nixon handling the incident with the same style. The scene also underscores ... Reagan's unflagging desire to accommodate the reporters who cover him [November/December, 1980].

In his press conferences Reagan did not answer substantive questions with much detail. Whenever possible, he simply recited a passage committed to memory from one of the speeches he had delivered from memory for years. He delegated almost all detailed work to his staff. Reporters asking questions probably knew more about the answer than he did. But only a few of his predecessors (possibly Franklin Roosevelt and John Kennedy) had such ease and grace before the media. And no previous president had actually identified with and understood the problems of journalists to the extent that Reagan did.

Reagan did well not only because he was technically trained but also because his personality was not compulsive. He appeared relaxed

President Reagan has long been a media star. Consequently, those in the media enjoy poking fun at him. Following are three examples of how other media stars treat one of their own.

New Script for Ronnie
by Art Buchwald

It is no secret that Ronald Reagan works best from a script. Therefore, the other day, just before he went out on the road to campaign for Republican candidates, his writers handed him a bunch of new pages to read.

"Okay, Ronnie, now here's the story line. You've been President of the United States for two years, and no matter what you've tried to solve the country's economic problems, nothing has worked. So you're ticked off because people are starting to blame you for their troubles. You're no longer going to be Mr. Nice Guy."

Ronnie studied the script. "Gosh, you really want me to say that the Democrats are responsible for the rotten mess we've been in for the last 40 years?"

"Right. But you must do it with feeling. The people have to believe that you inherited the biggest financial disaster of anybody who ever sat in the Oval Office. You've tried to do something about it but the fat Democratic spenders in Congress have stood in your way. Can you do it with feeling?"

"Gee whilikers. It's so out of character for me. What's my motivation for becoming a demagogue?"

"You're on the hot seat because the 1982 Senate and House elections are coming up, and the Democrats are laying the blame on you for a stagnant economy, high interest rates and two-digit unemployment. If you don't come out fighting you'll lose a Republican Senate and 40 or 50 seats in the House."

"I get it. By attacking Congress, I'm still a good guy because I'm trying to save the country."

"That's the way we wrote it. Now in this scene you are talking to the people who still believe in you, but occasionally there is a heckler in the audience who starts yelling for a job while you're talking. You never get flustered by him. You say, 'Look in the want ads.'"

"I like that line."

"It never fails to get the audience on their feet."

Ronnie went over the pages. "How about this one where I say, 'The fall elections offer a clear choice about the kind of nation we will be—whether we will continue our sure and steady course to put America back on track, or whether we will slide backward into another economic binge like the one which left us with today's pounding national hangover.' That's a big mouthful for me to say."

"We'll leave it in for Richmond, Virginia. If it doesn't get a laugh we can always drop it out on your next campaign stop."

Ronnie kept turning the pages. "Jumping bullfrogs, I see you have me blaming Washington for all our problems. Suppose they say I'm part of the problem now."

"Ignore what they say. We figure your best bet is to attack Jimmy Carter for the mess you inherited. The way we've written it whatever you can't blame on Carter you blame on Tip O'Neill. This is the part of the picture where you really go for the jugular. Can you do it, Ronnie?"

"I'm going to try my darnedest, if you're sure the people will still root for me."

"They'll root for you, Ronnie, because the way we've written it you're the white hat, and the Democrats are the bad guys. The more you say it, the more they'll believe it."

"Are all these facts in the script correct?"

"Don't worry about facts. If you read it with conviction people will believe you whether the facts are true or not. Okay, get on your horse and let's start the cameras and see how it plays."

"QUIET ON THE SET. TAKE ONE, 'THE GIPPER FIGHTS BACK.' ROLL 'EM."

Reprinted with permission of Art Buchwald and the L. A. Times Syndicate, 1982.

because he was. He was not obsessed or driven; he did not take defeat as a rejection of his presidency, nor did he have the inflated view of his personal importance that had hurt Johnson, Carter, and Nixon. Reagan's humor was spontaneous and genuine, whereas Carter's was forced and unfunny. When asked if he could have done anything differently during his first months as president, he replied, "I would not have gone to the Hilton" (the scene of the attempt on his life in 1981). Thus, television portrayed a man happy with his image of himself, confident with others, and not defensive in the face of potentially hostile questions.

POPULARITY AND POWER

A president who uses television recognizes the fact that the most important role of the presidency is symbolic. People look to the president for reassurance. When the president is not reassuring, the result is a decline in public-opinion ratings. Television allows the president to personalize government in a way that Congress cannot. Aided by the media, a successful president provides a symbol of unity and social stability. No matter what else presidents must do (and Americans are constantly told that the presidency is an "awesome" task), they must succeed symbolically, or they will serve only one term.

There is more to being president than reassuring the public, of course. The president is ultimately responsible for initiating domestic and foreign policy. However, American presidents have fewer formal powers than people believe them to have. The television president relies on the media in part because of the limitations on these formal powers. The president must confront a check-and-balance form of government as prescribed by the authors of the Constitution. The power of the purse is in Congress; a president who loses cannot dissolve Congress and call new elections (as a prime minister can do in a parliamentary democracy). Presidents must persuade rather than command. If they fail to persuade, their status at the polls will reflect the media judgment that they are incompetent. The American president is judged in terms of success or failure in persuasion.

> American presidents have fewer formal powers than people believe them to have. The television president relies on the media in part because of the limitations on these formal powers.

The people expect decisiveness from their president. The best way to give it to them is in foreign policy. In domestic policy the presidency is far more constrained. Congressional control of spending alone can make life difficult. But the president is less constrained as commander in chief. Foreign-policy initiatives can be announced in tough speeches; decisiveness can be displayed by military action; and crises can be thrust on a president by the unpredictability of international relations.

The Honeymoon

Presidents usually begin their term in office with a popular **"honeymoon"** period. The honeymoon includes high popularity in the national opinion polls and favorable reporting in the mass media. Popularity is frequently measured by the public's response to the question "Do you approve or disapprove of the way [Ronald Reagan] is handling his job as president?" (See Figure 9-1.) Evidence of the honeymoon can be found in the high approval ratings every modern president has enjoyed during his first months in office. Later in his term, the popularity of every president has declined.

Presidential "honeymoon": The early months of a new president's administration, when the public and Congress are generally supportive and consequently avoid harsh criticism.

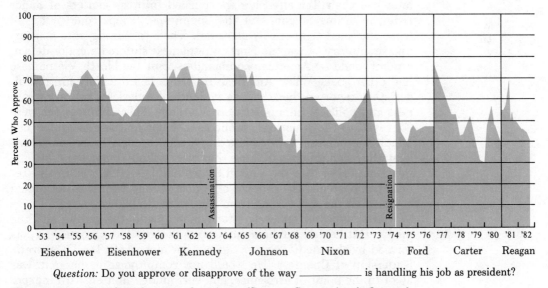

Question: Do you approve or disapprove of the way _____ is handling his job as president?

Figure 9-1. Presidential approval ratings. (Source: *Congressional Quarterly Weekly Report* of January 3, 1981, p. 38. Reprinted by permission.)

Decisive Action

Presidential popularity improves with quick and decisive action. Military victory arouses patriotism and propels presidents upward; military defeat or stalemate has the opposite result. Polls showed dramatic increases in popular support for Harry Truman at the beginning of the Korean War in 1950, for Dwight Eisenhower after the invasion of Lebanon in 1958, for Kennedy after the Cuban missile crisis in 1962, for Johnson after he committed U. S. combat troops to Vietnam in 1965, for Nixon after the Cambodian invasion of 1971, for Ford after the seizure and rescue of the *Mayaguez* in 1975, and for

Reagan after the downing of two Libyan jets over the Gulf of Sidra in
1981. But if the military situation drags on or deteriorates, public
opinion begins a decline that can be reversed only by another dramatic action. In Korea, after an initial flurry of patriotic fervor,
Truman became increasingly unpopular, especially when the United
States was forced into a massive retreat after the entry of the Chinese
into the war.

Presidential popularity improves with quick and decisive
action.

Johnson suffered an identical fate. Popular support for the war in
Vietnam was high initially, but it began a consistent decline when
military victory did not result. In 1968 the North Vietnamese
launched their Tet offensive and pushed into the centers of major
cities, including Saigon. But the Communist troops could not hold
what they had temporarily captured. Their casualties were stagger-
ing. In military terms, the North Vietnamese suffered a major defeat,
a point made by American commanders. But the North Vietnamese
had other goals. When American reporters heard enemy fire in Saigon, they reported the attack as evidence of America's military weak-
ness and political unpopularity in Vietnam. These impressions were
conveyed to the American public as a major military disaster.[4] The
North Vietnamese were conducting a war through American television; they won this war because they were willing to pay the cost. The
mistaken belief that the United States had been defeated in the Tet
offensive hastened the collapse of popular support for the war. Media
coverage of the war turned from supportive to highly critical.

Carter enjoyed an early "honeymoon" with the public and the
media. But he and public opinion soon parted. The divorce was performed by the media. Carter did not get along with the Democratic
leadership of Congress. He would not compromise or bargain, was
aloof to the point of arrogance, and surrounded himself with inexpe-
rienced aides. He failed to project an image of presidential leadership
and was portrayed by the media as weak, indecisive, and unable to
control people or events. The media cried for "leadership," whereas
during the campaign they had cried for honesty. But in response to
demands for leadership he had nothing to offer. After suffering a
major defeat in Congress on his energy program in 1979, he delivered
his infamous "national malaise" speech, blaming the American public
for his policy failures. The speech was accompanied by a shuffling of
his cabinet, again a contrived effort to create an image of the decisive
leader. It did not work, and his standing remained low, almost as low
as Nixon's immediately before his resignation. The cosmetic attempts
to project a new image failed, and Carter appeared certain to suffer
the humiliation of being denied the nomination by his own party.
The taking of the U. S. hostages in Iran and the Soviet occupation

Rallying 'Round the President

Public appraisal of presidents responds dramatically to international crises. As the following graphs show, popular support for recent presidents has risen measurably at times of trouble abroad.

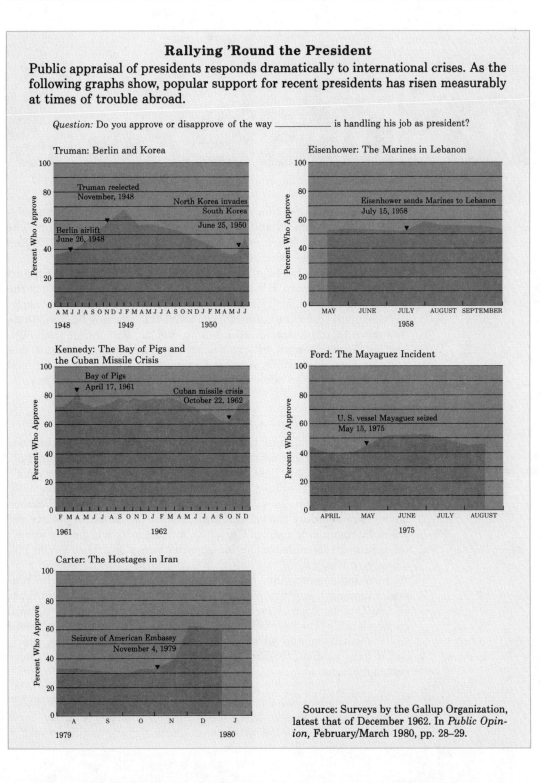

Question: Do you approve or disapprove of the way _____ is handling his job as president?

Truman: Berlin and Korea

Truman reelected
November, 1948

North Korea invades
South Korea
June 25, 1950

Berlin airlift
June 26, 1948

Eisenhower: The Marines in Lebanon

Eisenhower sends Marines to Lebanon
July 15, 1958

Kennedy: The Bay of Pigs and the Cuban Missile Crisis

Bay of Pigs
April 17, 1961

Cuban missile crisis
October 22, 1962

Ford: The Mayaguez Incident

U. S. vessel Mayaguez seized
May 15, 1975

Carter: The Hostages in Iran

Seizure of American Embassy
November 4, 1979

Source: Surveys by the Gallup Organization, latest that of December 1962. In *Public Opinion,* February/March 1980, pp. 28–29.

A horrified nation sees this assassination attempt covered on live television.

of Afghanistan saved him from humiliation. However, when no solution to either problem appeared, the public rejected him again. The Iranian crisis, which helped to give him the nomination, contributed to his defeat in the general election.

Reagan began his first term somewhat lower in popular support than his predecessors. His first dramatic act did not "play" well to the media and the public. The media did not support Reagan's attempt to "get tough" over the conflict in El Salvador. Possibly because there was more talk than action, the public was divided rather than supportive. Later, Reagan emerged from the assassination attempt as a popular hero. His public support increased dramatically. Additional popular support was achieved by the downing of the Libyan jets.

PRESIDENTS STRONG AND WEAK

Political scientist James David Barber has categorized presidential character according to whether a given president was "active" or "passive" and whether his emotional attitude was "positive" or "negative"[5] (see Table 9-2). Presidents adjudged great were generally active: only George Washington (as judged by professional historians) and Eisenhower (as judged by the general public) were perceived as passive yet great. Barber's judgment of Carter as active/positive is clearly wrong; Carter most resembled an active/negative president. How would you categorize Reagan?

Successful presidents are normally "strong" presidents. In general, nineteenth-century presidents followed the ideas of the authors of the Constitution. Reaction against strong executives, a natural consequence of the revolution, was still the dominant sentiment when the Constitution was adopted. With conspicuous exceptions, presidents were passive. William Howard Taft was typical of the passive presidency:

> The President can exercise no power which cannot be fairly and
> reasonably traced to some specific grant of power or justly
> implied and included within such express grant as proper and

Table 9-2.   Classifying Presidential Character
Emotional attitude toward the presidency

Energy level in doing the job	Positive	Negative
Active	Tends to show confidence, flexibility, a focus on producing results through rational mastery.	Tends to emphasize ambitious striving, aggressiveness, a focus on the struggle for power against a hostile environment.
	Examples: Jefferson, Franklin Roosevelt, Truman, Kennedy, Carter	Examples: John Adams, Wilson, Hoover, Johnson, Nixon
Passive	Tends to show receptiveness, compliance, other-directedness, plus a superficial hopefulness masking inner doubt.	Tends to withdraw from conflict and uncertainty and to think in terms of vague principles of duty and regular procedure.
	Examples: Madison, Taft, Harding, Ford	Examples: Washington, Coolidge, Eisenhower

From *The Presidential Character,* 2nd ed., by James David Barber. © 1977, 1972 by James David Barber. Published by Prentice-Hall, Inc.; Englewood Cliffs, N. J. 07632.

necessary to its exercise. . . . There is no undefined residuum of power which can be exercised which seems to him to be in the public interest.[6]

The exceptions to this approach were Thomas Jefferson (who had argued *before* his election in favor of the weak president model) and Abraham Lincoln. They were precursors of the twentieth-century presidency, best defined by Theodore Roosevelt:

I decline to adopt the view that what was imperatively necessary for the nation could not be done by the president unless he could find some specific authorization to do it. My belief was that it was not only his right but his duty to do anything that the needs of the nation demanded, unless such action was forbidden by the Constitution or the laws.[7]

It would be unthinkable today for a president to campaign on a platform of doing whatever Congress wanted—just sitting there until it became necessary to "take care that the laws be faithfully executed." Reagan, although he espoused a limited view of government, nonetheless came to the White House with a clear policy agenda and achieved many of his domestic policy goals in the first year in office.

Rating the Presidents

The 10 "Best"
Presidents
1. Abraham Lincoln
2. George
   Washington
3. Franklin D.
   Roosevelt
4. Theodore
   Roosevelt
5. Thomas Jefferson
6. Woodrow Wilson
7. Andrew Jackson
8. Harry S. Truman
9. Dwight D.
   Eisenhower
10. James K. Polk

The 10 "Worst"
Presidents
1. Warren G.
   Harding
2. Richard M. Nixon
3. James Buchanan
4. Franklin Pierce
5. Ulysses S. Grant
6. Millard Fillmore
7. Andrew Johnson
8. Calvin Coolidge
9. John Tyler
10. Jimmy Carter

Two of Ronald Reagan's recent predecessors rank among the 10 "worst" Presidents in a new survey of historians and political scientists.

Republican Richard M. Nixon was rated the second-worst Chief Executive, Democrat Jimmy Carter the tenth worst in a poll of 49 leading scholars.

The survey, by the *Chicago Tribune*, resembled polls done in 1948 and 1962 by historian Arthur Schlesinger, Sr., for other publications. In all three surveys, Abraham Lincoln, George Washington and Franklin D. Roosevelt led the list of "best" Presidents while Warren G. Harding was rated the very worst.

The biggest shift was the rating for Dwight Eisenhower, who rose from the tenth-worst position in 1962 to ninth best in the 1982 survey. Ike's stature among scholars is believed to have grown in part because of the troubles of his more activist successors.

Calvin Coolidge, a Chief Executive treated too harshly by historians in Reagan's judgment, was ranked as the eighth-worst President in the latest survey. He also finished in the bottom 10 in the earlier polls.

Nixon's role in the Watergate scandal and his resignation from office, it was clear, led to his next-to-lowest rating. A University of Texas historian claimed Nixon was "the most corrupt President in our history."

Carter received one vote in the 10-best category, but he got many votes for the bottom 10. A professor at the University of Illinois speculated that Carter's low rating occurred because of his "failure as a political leader and because it is so recent."

Atlanta Mayor Andrew Young, a close Carter friend, blasted the scholars for what he termed "insensitive elitism."

THE PRESIDENT AND CONGRESS

Reagan's concern with the media and with public opinion was not without justification. One of Carter's aides said: "When you go to the Hill and the latest polls show Carter isn't doing well, there isn't much reason for a member to go along with him. No president whose popularity is as low as this President has much clout on the Hill."[8]

"Clout on the Hill" is the one method of deciding whether a president is successful. Presidents are expected to set the congressional agenda, and they are expected to persuade Congress to accept the bulk of their proposals. Presidents' popularity with the public influences their ability to achieve a high "batting average" in getting bills through Congress. (For a comparison of the "clout" of recent presidents, see Figure 9-2.) Popularity is not a guarantee of success, but there is nevertheless a close relationship between it and support in Congress.[9] The correlation between presidential popularity and support in Congress is .50 for the House and .40 for the Senate. Note that these are not perfect (1.00).

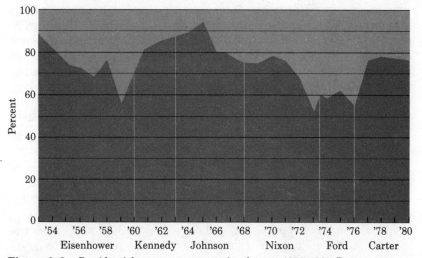

Figure 9-2. Presidential success on congressional votes, 1953–1980. Percentages are based on votes on which presidents took a position. (Source: *Congressional Quarterly Weekly Report* of January 3, 1981, p. 38. Reprinted by permission.)

Carter and Congress

The relationship between presidential popularity and congressional success may not move in the same direction. It is possible for congressional failures to reduce presidential popularity, as well as for a decline in popularity to reduce the presidential batting average. This appears to have been the case with Carter. He was inclined to define issues as moral crusades. He trusted few people, and he mistrusted the media. Perhaps because he knew media power, he feared it. Carter's failures began immediately, before there could have been any appreciable drop in public support. Rather than focusing on key points in a sequence of policies, he bombarded Congress with simultaneous demands across all policy areas. He did not consult with congressional leaders, and he disdained personal lobbying. In Carter's first year his batting average was 75 percent. But then stories of poor leadership and inadequate comprehension of the job began to surface, and he began to decline in the polls. A vicious circle began. Ultimately, Carter suffered the humiliation of having the Democratic-controlled Congress override his veto of energy legislation, the first time since 1952 that a president whose own party was in control had lost a veto. This major party revolt was encouraged by Carter's unpopularity. But the initial spiral downward was begun by media reports of congressional failures.

Reagan and Congress

Reagan's popularity, his media management, and his congressional success were very different from Carter's. During his first year he achieved two major victories over the Democratic House leadership, one on budget reductions and the other on tax reductions. In both cases his use of television was one of the keys to victory. Reagan was personally more popular than his policies. The media, as is always the case, stressed his personal attributes. One explanation for his successes frequently offered by congressional Democrats was that the president's personality made it difficult to deny him what he wanted.

> Reagan was personally more popular than his policies. The media, as is always the case, stressed his personal attributes.

The public did not really associate Reagan with his policies. This was a natural consequence of the personalization of the presidency. It did not matter whether the public understood or supported the specifics of the Reagan program. They liked the man, and Congress respects personal popularity.

Presidential Vetoes, 1789–1980

The presidential veto—or the threat of it—can be a powerful weapon in a president's dealings with Congress. It takes a two-thirds vote of both houses of Congress to override a presidential veto, and from Washington to Carter only 4 percent of vetoes have been overridden. (Of course, presidents take into account the chances of an "override" vote when they decide whether to use their veto power.) The all-time veto champion is Franklin Roosevelt, who rejected 633 pieces of legislation in his four terms as president; only 9 of his vetoes (less than 2 percent) were overridden by Congress. However, the veto power can backfire on a weak or unpopular president; Andrew Johnson saw over half of his vetoes overridden by a hostile Congress. The "modern record" is held by Gerald Ford, who lost 18 percent of his vetoes.

Much of the power of the veto is in the threat rather than in its actual use. Modern presidents do not veto very much legislation, but they frequently announce their intention to do so through the media. This kind of announcement can sometimes modify the position of congressional opponents.

Presidential Vetoes, 1789–1980

	Regular vetoes	Pocket[a] vetoes	Total vetoes	Vetoes overridden
Washington	2	—	2	—
Madison	5	2	7	—
Monroe	1	—	1	—
Jackson	5	7	12	—
Tyler	6	3	9	1
Polk	2	1	3	—
Pierce	9	—	9	5
Buchanan	4	3	7	—
Lincoln	2	4	6	—
A. Johnson	21	8	29	15
Grant	45	49	94	4
Hayes	12	1	13	1
Arthur	4	8	12	1
Cleveland	304	109	413	2
Harrison	19	25	44	1
Cleveland	43	127	170	5
McKinley	6	36	42	—
T. Roosevelt	42	40	82	1
Taft	30	9	39	1
Wilson	33	11	44	6
Harding	5	1	6	—
Coolidge	20	30	50	4
Hoover	21	16	37	3
F. Roosevelt	372	261	633	9
Truman	180	70	250	12
Eisenhower	73	108	181	2
Kennedy	12	9	21	—
L. Johnson	16	14	30	—
Nixon	24	19	43	5
Ford	44	22	66	12
Carter	13	18	31	2
Total	1375	1011	2386	92

[a]Normally, if a bill is neither signed nor vetoed by the president within ten days of its passage, it becomes law without the president's signature. However, if Congress adjourns within this ten-day period, the bill does *not* become law. At the end of a congressional session, therefore, a president can veto a bill simply by not signing it; this is called the "pocket veto."

Source: Senate Library, *Presidential Vetoes* (U. S. Government Printing Office, 1969), p. 199. Data for L. Johnson from *Congressional Quarterly Almanac, 1968* (Washington, D. C.: Congressional Quarterly Service, 1968), p. 23. Data for Nixon, Ford, and Carter from the White House Records Office.

Reagan as a "revolutionary." Well before Reagan's election, there was an emerging consensus among political and economic decision makers that a great deal of federal spending and federal regulation was counterproductive. Carter himself, while creating two new cabinet departments (Energy and Education), was able to negotiate partial deregulation of commercial airlines, and he committed himself to deregulation in the gas and oil industries. Reagan's policies were the culmination of these trends rather than their beginning. He promised to "get the government off our back" with a vigorous deregulation effort. The economy, on Reagan's election, was suffering from serious inflation. No major member of either party in Congress (with the possible exception of Senator Edward Kennedy) objected to the idea that reductions in spending and taxation were necessary. There were differences on where and how much to cut, but not on the idea of a reduction in spending.

Reagan's budget cutting was focused largely on agencies that had been created in the previous decade. American society, he contended, had experienced a virtual explosion in governmental regulation during the 1970s; between 1970 and 1979, expenditures for the major regulatory agencies had quadrupled. He added, however, that he had no intention of "dismantling" the regulatory agencies—especially those necessary to protect the environment and to ensure the public health and safety.

Hidden behind the rhetoric was the truth about the "revolution": Reagan's fiscal 1982 budget was an *increase* of 4.9 percent from Carter's 1981 budget (see Table 9-3). The "budget cutting" was in reality only a reduction in the *growth* of government spending. There were some changed priorities. Defense expenditures were increased substantially from 1981 figures (17.2 percent). Social Security and welfare ("income security") increased slightly (4.3 percent) from 1981 amounts. And Medicaid and Medicare ("health") continued their rise (11.2 percent). In short, Reagan "cut" the 1982 budget from what it *would have been* under Carter.

Reagan meets informally with George Shultz, Secretary of State; Charles Walker and Walter Wriston, economic advisors; and Rep. Jack Kemp (R–N.Y.).

Table 9-3. The Reagan Budget in Perspective

	Fiscal 1981	Fiscal 1982 (proposed)		Reagan increase over 1981
		Carter	Reagan	
National defense	$161.1	$184.4	$188.8	+ 17.2%
International affairs	11.3	12.2	11.2	− 0.1
General science, space, and technology	6.3	7.6	6.9	+ 4.7
Energy	8.7	12.0	8.7	0
Natural resources and environment	14.1	14.0	11.9	− 15.6
Agriculture	1.1	4.8	4.4	+400
Commerce and housing credit	3.5	8.1	3.1	− 11.4
Transportation	24.1	21.6	19.9	− 17.4
Community and regional development	11.1	9.1	8.1	− 27.0
Education, training, employment, and social services	31.8	34.5	25.8	− 18.8
Health	66.0	74.6	73.4	+ 11.2
Income security	231.7	255.0	241.4	+ 4.3
Veterans' benefits and services	22.6	24.5	23.6	+ 4.4
Administration of justice	4.8	4.9	4.4	− 8.3
General government	5.2	5.2	5.0	− 3.8
General-purpose fiscal assistance	6.9	6.9	6.4	− 5.8
Interest	80.4	89.9	82.5	+ 2.6
Allowances	—	1.9	1.8	—
Undistributed offsetting receipts	−27.8	−31.9	−32.0	—
Total	$662.9	$739.3	$695.3	+ 4.9%

Most of the regulatory apparatus was modified, not eliminated. Reagan sought a reduction in the regulatory roles of the Occupational Safety and Health Administration, the Equal Employment Opportunities Commission (by modifying affirmative-action guidelines), and the Environmental Protection Agency. He did not propose their abolition. He proposed to remove the Energy and Education departments from cabinet rank (both had been created by Carter). Nevertheless, the media gave great attention to Reagan's "revolution."

The President and the Party

It is true that presidents receive greater support from congressional members of their own party than from members of the opposition party. But the president is not really "the party leader." Congressional candidates run independently from the presidential campaign and independently from their own party. Presidents frequently rely on defections from the ranks of the opposition party in winning support for their programs in Congress. Reagan's successful prying away of conservative Democrats to gain victory for his budget proposals in the House was not really exceptional. His innovation was his willingness to lobby hard for virtually total support from within his own party as well as to lobby hard to gain the support of conservative Democrats.

Table 9-4 shows that Democrats in both the House and the Senate supported Carter more than Republicans in the House and Senate. Republicans in both the House and the Senate supported Ford more than Democrats in the House and Senate. Thus, *party* is an important asset to presidents in their relations with Congress.

Table 9-4. Congressional Support for Presidents' Programs by Party, 1961–1981

	House		Senate	
	Democrats	*Republicans*	*Democrats*	*Republicans*
Kennedy (Dem.)				
1961	73%	37%	65%	36%
1962	72	42	63	39
1963	72	32	63	32
Johnson (Dem.)				
1964	74	38	61	45
1965	74	41	64	48
1966	63	37	57	43
1967	69	46	61	35
1968	64	51	48	47
Nixon (Rep.)				
1969	46	58	40	64
1970	53	66	45	60
1971	47	72	40	64
1972	47	64	44	66
1973	35	62	37	61
Ford (Rep.)				
1974	41	51	39	55
1975	38	63	47	68
1976	32	63	39	62
Carter (Dem.)				
1977	63	42	70	52
1978	60	36	66	41
1979	64	34	68	47
1980	63	40	62	45

Presidential coattails, as we saw in Chapter 8, have been reduced by the individualized, personalized presidency. Reagan ran ahead of the Senate Republican victors in ten states; he trailed Republican Senate candidates in twelve states. There is no evidence to support the coattail theory. Furthermore, it is hard to be the *party* leader when you also have to be the *symbolic* leader of all the people.

The President and Foreign Policy

The president has more authority over foreign and military policy than over domestic policy. According to the Constitution, as we have seen, the president makes treaties, grants diplomatic recognition, and is commander in chief of the armed services. Clearly, the authors of the Constitution envisaged a more active role for the president in foreign policy than in domestic policy. It is in foreign policy that the greatest demand for presidential leadership has arisen, and it is in foreign policy that the swiftest expansion of presidential power has occurred. "Strong" presidents have used foreign crises to exercise extraordinary powers, and they have usually been praised for doing so.

However, presidents are not completely free to do what they wish in foreign or military policy. Congress can and does reject treaties. Carter was unable to persuade the Senate that an arms limitation treaty with the Soviet Union (SALT II) should be ratified. Carter did narrowly win ratification of the Panama Canal treaty, one of his few outstanding victories.

> It is in foreign policy that the greatest demand for presidential leadership has arisen, and it is in foreign policy that the swiftest expansion of presidential power has occurred.

Even though the president is commander in chief, Congress "declares war" and "provides for the common defense" by "raising and supporting armies." The authors of the Constitution, in defending their document in *The Federalist* papers, implied that the naming of the president as commander in chief was little more than granting the power to defend the country against invasion when Congress was not in session.[10] However, the president has exercised military power in a much more aggressive fashion. American troops have been dispatched beyond the borders of the United States on 150 occasions, but Congress has formally declared war only five times: in the War of 1812, the Mexican War, the Spanish-American War, and World Wars I and II. Congress did not declare war in either Korea or Vietnam.

> American troops have been dispatched beyond the borders of the United States on 150 occasions, but Congress has formally declared war only five times.

Supreme Court Justice William Rehnquist wrote before his appointment:

> It has been recognized from the earliest days of the Republic, by the President, by Congress, and by the Supreme Court, that the United States may lawfully engage in armed hostilities with a foreign power without Congressional declaration of war. Our history is replete with instances of 'undeclared wars' from the war with France in 1789–1800 to the Vietnamese war.[11]

The early war against the French was waged by John Adams, a president not regarded by presidential scholars as "strong." The precedent of not seeking a congressional declaration stuck. Jefferson fought pirates off the Barbary Coast; every nineteenth-century president fought Indians; Lincoln carried presidential war-making power beyond anything attempted by presidents before or since; Woodrow Wilson sent troops to Mexico and a dozen Latin American nations; Franklin Roosevelt sent U. S. destroyers to protect British convoys in the North Atlantic before Pearl Harbor; Truman committed American troops to a major war in Korea; Johnson committed troops to war in Vietnam; and Carter sent U. S. forces on the unsuccessful attempt to rescue the U. S. hostages in Iran.

Until Vietnam no congressional opposition to undeclared war was evident. The only serious dispute about the role of the president as commander in chief occurred during the Korean War, when Truman removed General Douglas MacArthur from his command for disregarding orders. As commander in chief, Truman clearly was constitutionally justified, but removing a military legend from his command undercut Truman's support at home. MacArthur came home to a hero's welcome and addressed a joint session of Congress. The dispute contributed to the premature end of Truman's career (he did not seek reelection in 1952, perhaps because he thought he would not win).

American presidents do *not* leave war to generals and admirals. From the first presidency they have been active in making strategic and tactical decisions. Washington personally led troops in the sup-

The Vietnam war was the first televised war and helped to bring about the War Powers Act.

pression of the Whiskey Rebellion in Pennsylvania. Lincoln drove his generals to rage by making detailed military decisions. Franklin Roosevelt planned strategy in World War II (allocating a large portion of resources to Europe rather than the Pacific). Truman, of course, made the decision to use nuclear weapons. Johnson personally approved bombing targets in Vietnam, as did Nixon. Carter involved himself in the attempt to rescue the American hostages in Iran.

Military failure and growing public disenchantment with presidential policies led to a successful effort by Congress to curtail the war powers of the president. In November of 1973, after evidence of presidential deception and failure in Cambodia and Vietnam, Congress passed the War Powers Act over Nixon's veto. The act was intended to restore some of the balance originally intended by the Founding Fathers, to curb the growth of an **"imperial presidency,"** and specifically to reassert congressional authority in matters involving the sending of American armed forces into combat.

> **Imperial presidency:** A term used to describe alleged abuses of power by presidents, especially in committing the nation to overseas conflict irrespective of congressional checks or consultation.

The War Powers Act is one of the first major congressional policies to define the conditions for presidential commitment of U. S. forces. Section 2(c) of the act specifies that in "situations where imminent involvement in hostilities is clearly indicated by the circumstances," the president can deploy armed forces only on condition of:

1. a declaration of war by Congress; or
2. an armed attack on the United States, an armed attack against U. S. armed forces abroad, or the imminent threat of such attacks; or
3. the need to protect and evacuate U. S. citizens whose lives are threatened in another country; or
4. specific statutory authorization by Congress

The act also requires the president to report any commitment of armed forces or initiation of hostilities to Congress within forty-eight hours. It limits the involvement of U. S. forces to sixty days unless Congress, by specific legislation, authorizes their continued use. Beyond sixty days, an additional thirty days may be authorized by Congress, but only for the purpose of withdrawing troops from a conflict. Congress can order withdrawal of troops at any time during hostilities by means of a concurrent resolution. Concurrent resolutions do not require presidential signature and thus effectively preclude a presidential veto. Finally, presidential noncompliance with the provisions of the War Powers Act may subject the president to impeachment.

Is the War Powers Act effective in checking the president's war powers? As broadly phrased as the act is, presidents have not taken it very seriously. It should first be noted that the act tacitly acknowledges the president's power as commander in chief to initiate war. Thus, presidents usually report events and actions to Congress *after* military action has begun, thereby contributing to policymaking by fait accompli. Examples include Ford and the Mayaguez incident, Carter and the aborted attempt to rescue American hostages in Iran, and Reagan and the downing of Libyan jets in the Gulf of Sidra in the Mediterranean. None of these incidents involved a significant number of troops, but the act makes no mention of a minimum number of troops. Moreover, it is well to remember that U. S. involvement in Vietnam began with only sixteen military advisors. More importantly, Congress has *never* voted to cut off appropriations in support of American armies in the field of battle.

> Presidents usually report events to Congress *after* military action has begun . . . . Congress has *never* voted to cut off appropriations in support of American armies in the field.

Congress is reluctant to meddle with presidents in time of crisis. Nobody wants to shoulder the blame if the military situation deteriorates. Presidents are assumed to have information (especially secret information) that enables them to reach a swift decision. Symbolically, the "awesome responsibility" of the president is represented by the "black box." Wherever the president goes, an aide carries the box with its coded orders for a nuclear attack. Presidents need not make overt reference to their burden but can use "national security" to blunt congressional attacks.

The Watergate Tale

Only one president ever resigned the office—Richard M. Nixon. His resignation was a direct result of two years of almost continuous nightly television news coverage of the Watergate affair. The negative news coverage of the president brought him down from his personal high in popularity in January, 1973 (following his reelection and the Vietnam peace agreement), to his low point in August, 1974 (immediately before his resignation).

The origins of Watergate are found in the climate of mass unrest in the late 1960s and early 1970s that seemed to some people to threaten the security of the nation. The White House believed that the political system was endangered by disruptive and subversive elements, that disloyal members of the administration were leaking government secrets to the press, and that extraordinary measures were required to protect the government. A Special Investigations Unit was created within the White House. The unit was known as the "Plumbers," because it was supposed to stop "leaks" of secret government information. It was placed under the supervision of a White House aide, John Ehrlichman, and his assistant, Egil Krogh. The Plumbers soon included E. Howard Hunt, Jr., a former Central Intelligence Agency agent and author of spy novels, and G. Gordon Liddy, a former agent of the Federal Bureau of Investigation. The Plumbers worked independently of the FBI and the CIA (although they received occasional assistance from the CIA) and reported directly to Ehrlichman. They undertook a variety of activities—later referred to as the "White House horrors"—including the investigation of Daniel Ellsberg and the burglary of his psychiatrist's office to learn more about his motives in releasing the Pentagon Papers. The secret papers, commissioned by Secretary of Defense Robert McNamara, were meant to provide a study of U. S. policymaking about Vietnam.

The Watergate break-in itself—the burglarizing and wiretapping of the office of the Democratic National Committee in Washington's Watergate complex—was an outgrowth of earlier undercover activities by members of the Plumbers. The work of the Plumbers had tapered off by the end of 1971, and Hunt and Liddy found new jobs with the president's campaign organization, the Committee to Re-Elect the President (CREEP), headed by former Attorney General John M. Mitchell. The "security coordinator" for CREEP was James W. McCord, Jr., who had been an FBI and CIA agent. It was easy for Hunt, McCord, and Liddy to confuse threats to national security with threats to the reelection of the incumbent president and to employ well-known "national security" tactics, including bugging and burglary, against the president's opponents. On the night of June 17, 1972, five men with burglary and wiretapping tools were arrested in the Democratic National Committee offices: McCord, Bernard L. Barker, and three Cuban exiles. Later a grand jury charged these five men, together with Hunt and Liddy, with burglary and wiretapping. At their trial in January, 1973, all seven were convicted. But U. S. District Judge John J. Sirica believed that the defendants were covering up for whoever had ordered and paid for the bugging and break-in.* The *Washington Post* reported that the defendants had been under pressure to plead guilty, that they were still being paid by an unnamed source, and that they had been promised a cash settlement and executive clemency if they went to jail and remained silent. Judge Sirica threatened the defendants with heavy

(*continued*)

(*continued*)
sentences, and soon McCord broke and told of secret payments and a cover-up.

It was not the political embarrassment of the Watergate break-in that led the White House to attempt a cover-up. (News of the burglary did not seriously affect the president's campaign, and he was re-elected overwhelmingly in November, 1972, five months *after* the break-in.) Instead, the White House seemed concerned over exposure of the whole series of repressive acts undertaken earlier. The great blunder of the Watergate operation was that some of those who were involved in the petty political burglary of the Democratic headquarters—Liddy, Hunt, and McCord—had previously served with the Plumbers.

The Senate formed a Special Select Committee on Campaign Activities—the so-called Watergate committee, headed by Senator Sam J. Ervin—to delve into Watergate and related activities. The national press, led by the prestigious *Washington Post,* which had always been hostile to Nixon, began its own investigative reporting and, along with the major television networks, launched a series of damaging stories involving Mitchell, Ehrlichman, and White House Chief of Staff H. R. Haldeman. Rumors of a White House cover-up, including secret payments of money to the Watergate burglars and promises of executive clemency, were reported.

In March, 1973, the president announced the resignation of Haldeman and Ehrlichman and at the same time dismissed the White House counsel, John Dean, who, although deeply involved in the cover-up himself, had been secretly giving information to the FBI and Senate Watergate investigators regarding the cover-up.

When the Senate Watergate committee learned that the president had regularly taped conversations in the Oval Office, it issued subpoenas for tapes that would prove or disprove charges by Dean and others of a presidential cover-up. In response, Nixon argued that the constitutional separation of powers permits the president to withhold this information from both the Congress and the courts. He relied on the doctrine of executive privilege—the assertion of the right of the president to keep information, documents, or testimony from either the Congress or the courts if in the opinion of the president it is required in the interest of national security or the proper functioning of the executive.

Eventually, the dispute over the Watergate tapes reached the Supreme Court in the important decision of *United*

States v. *Richard M. Nixon*. In an 8–0 decision, the court denied the president the power to withhold subpoenaed information from the courts under the doctrine of executive privilege when such information is essential to a criminal investigation. The Court recognized the principle of executive privilege but denied that it applies to criminal cases.

Nonetheless, the movement to impeach Nixon could not win strong support among Democrats in Congress and the influential news media as long as Spiro Agnew was vice-president. Agnew was even more offensive than Nixon to liberals and journalists. It was politically essential that Agnew be removed from the vice-presidency before any serious impeachment movement could be launched against Nixon.

Removing Agnew turned out to be a relatively easy task. Agnew had served early in his career as Baltimore County executive and later as governor of Maryland. Baltimore County politics had long been notorious for corruption. Rumors of Agnew's early involvement in corrupt local politics had circulated in Washington cocktail parties. The Justice Department, under pressure from the national news media, obtained indictments accusing Agnew of accepting money from government contractors and failing to report it on his income tax returns. In court Agnew pleaded no contest to the charge of tax fraud, resigned from office, and was given a suspended sentence. Nixon appointed Gerald Ford, Republican minority leader in the House of Representatives and a popular figure in Congress, to the vice-presidency. The removal of Agnew opened the way for a direct frontal attack on Nixon as president.

Nixon released the transcripts of the subpoenaed White House tapes in a national television broadcast in which he urged the public to read the tapes in their entirety rather than reading excerpts. Nixon contended that the tapes proved that he had had no prior knowledge of the Watergate break-in and had not participated in the cover-up. One of the key tapes involved a meeting between the president and Dean on March 21, 1973. Dean told the president that a "cancer is growing on the presidency," referring to the fact that the Watergate scandal had grown to such large proportions that the cover-up was breaking down. Dean told the president that McCord had already implicated several staff members of the Committee to Re-Elect the President. More importantly, Hunt was blackmailing the White House for immediate payment of $120,000 plus pledges of other financial payoffs and (*continued*)

(continued)

executive clemency after conviction. Dean and the president estimated that eventual payoffs to everyone to keep silent would amount to a million dollars or more. The conversations on the tape are rambling and inconclusive and are subject to varied interpretations. The most common interpretation is that Nixon approved an immediate payoff to Hunt but declined to promise him clemency. The tape's importance, however, rested not so much on its suggestion of Nixon's complicity in obstructing justice as on the tone and quality of Nixon's leadership. In many taped conversations Nixon appeared more concerned with narrow and self-serving political interests than with legal or moral questions.

The Judiciary Committee of the House of Representatives, chaired by Representative Peter Rodino of New Jersey, was convened in the spring of 1974 to consider a series of articles of impeachment against Nixon. The release of the tapes failed to persuade this committee of Nixon's innocence. Indeed, the tapes were used by the president's opponents in Congress and the news media to convince the majority on the committee of Nixon's guilt. The committee passed three articles of impeachment. Article One accused the president of obstructing justice in the Watergate investigation. Article Two accused him of misusing his executive power and disregarding his constitutional duties to take care that the laws be faithfully executed, specifically in establishing the Plumbers and approving their activities. Article Three accused him of contempt of Congress.

However, before the House of Representatives could take up these articles of impeachment, Nixon released another tape that damaged his case beyond repair. It involved a meeting between the president and Haldeman on June 23, 1972, five days after the Watergate break-in. The tape suggests that the president himself ordered the cover-up of the Watergate affair and tried to restrict the FBI's investigation by implying CIA involvement. With its release, all Republican minority members of the Judiciary Committee who had supported the president publicly announced that they had changed their minds and would vote for impeachment when the articles reached the floor of the House of Representatives. Shortly thereafter, Nixon was informed by congressional leaders of his own party that the majority of the House would vote to impeach him and that two-thirds of the Senate would vote to convict him.

THE WHITE HOUSE
WASHINGTON

August 9, 1974

Dear Mr. Secretary:

I hereby resign the Office of President of the
United States.

Sincerely,

The Honorable Henry A. Kissinger
The Secretary of State
Washington, D.C. 20520

On August 9, 1974, Nixon resigned. Ford was sworn in as president. On September 8, 1974, Ford pardoned Nixon "for all offenses against the United States which he, Richard Nixon, has committed or may have committed or taken part in" during his presidency. In accepting the pardon, Nixon expressed remorse over Watergate and acknowledged grave errors of judgment, but he did not admit personal guilt. Despite intensive questioning by the press and Congress, Ford maintained that his purpose in granting the pardon had been to end "bitter controversy and divisive national debate" and "to firmly shut and seal this book" on Watergate.

*John J. Sirica, *To Set the Record Straight* (New York: Norton, 1979), p. 91 *ff.*

THE INSTITUTIONALIZED PRESIDENCY
The executive office of the president is very institutionalized (see Figure 9-3 on the next page). Although the Constitution mentions that the president "may require the opinion, in writing, of the principal officer in each of the executive departments," there is no mention of an actual cabinet.

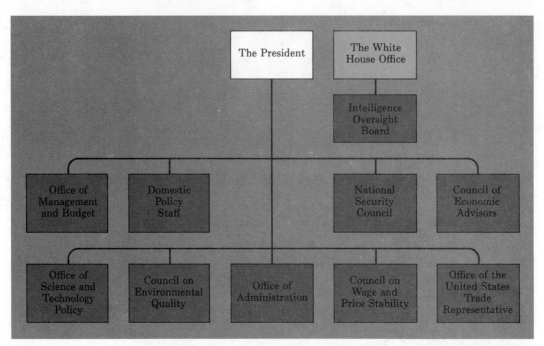

Figure 9-3. Executive office of the president. (Source: *Democracy Under Pressure: An Introduction to the American Political System,* 4th Edition, by M. C. Cummings, Jr. and D. Wise. © 1981 by Harcourt Brace Jovanovich, Inc. Reprinted by permission.)

The Cabinet

Presidents are free to use or ignore the cabinet. Usually they ignore it. The cabinet seldom acts as a body. The usual pattern is for it to serve more as a support group for policies developed by the White House staff.

Presidents always begin their first term by promising "cabinet government," but they soon lose interest. Cabinet officers (the secretaries of the thirteen executive departments) are frequently appointed on the basis of satisfying the demands of various interest groups that supported the president's election. They do not necessarily know much about their department and indeed may be virtually unknown to the president. Table 9-5 on pages 332–333 lists the current Reagan administration.

> The cabinet seldom acts as a body. The usual pattern is for it to serve more as a support group for policies developed by the White House staff.

The cabinet meets at the pleasure of the president, which may not be very often. Furthermore, members of the cabinet develop a dependence on permanent civil servants for their information. Naturally, this dependence is biased in the direction of the department and not necessarily in support of the president's overall goals. Paro-

Reagan holds his first cabinet meeting after being inaugurated. Shown from left to right are Education Secretary Terrel Bell, Health and Human Services Secretary Richard Schweiker, Interior Secretary James Watt, Secretary of State Alexander Haig, Reagan, and Secretary of Defense Caspar Weinberger.

chialism is to be expected, especially when cabinet officers have had little if any experience in the policy areas for which they are nominally responsible.

Cabinet officers have a difficult role. They must rely on their own permanent bureaucracies for information, and many eventually come to identify with "their" department. At the same time, they are expected to carry out presidential policies—even when it means cutting their own budgets or abolishing their own agencies.

The White House Staff

The White House staff is the heart of the decision-making process. Cabinet officers often find it frustrating to be denied access to the president because of staff opposition. The actual structure of the White House staff varies with each president. Presidents begin their job with the assumption that their aides and various assistants will simply help organize their time, with no assumption of decision-making authority. It seldom works this way. The temptation to rely heavily on the staff is unavoidable.

Reagan relied heavily on three members of the White House staff: Edwin Meese, counselor to the president; James Baker, chief of staff; and Michael Deaver, deputy chief of staff. Each of these officers had numerous deputies, assistants, and deputy assistants. They were named because they had proved themselves to be completely loyal to the president.

Each administration also juggles the influence of various offices in the White House. Before Reagan's administration the National Security Council was a major factor in presidential decision making, spawning such influential men as Henry Kissinger and Zbigniew

Table 9-5. The Reagan Administration

Position	Name	Age in 1980	Residence	Religion	Occupation	Previous experience	Education
President	Ronald W. Reagan	69	California	Christian Church		Sportscaster; film actor; Governor of California	B.S., Eureka College
Vice-President	George W. Bush	56	Texas	Episcopalian		Oilman; congressman; U.S. Representative to UN; Chairman, Republican National Committee; Director of CIA	B.A., Yale
Secretary of State	George P. Shultz	60	California	Episcopalian	Professor of economics	Secretary of Labor; Director, OMB; Secretary of Treasury; President, Bechtel Group, Inc.; Trilateral Commission member	B.A., Princeton; Ph.D., MIT
Secretary of the Treasury	Donald T. Regan	62	New Jersey	Roman Catholic	Chairman of brokerage firm	Stockbroker	B.A., Harvard
Secretary of Defense	Caspar W. Weinberger	63	California	Episcopalian	Columnist	State legislator; state Republican chairman; Chairman, FTC; Director, OMB; Secretary of HEW	B.A., Harvard
Attorney-General	William French Smith	63	California	Episcopalian	Attorney	Bank director; Chairman, U. of California Regents	B.A., U. of California; LL.B, Harvard
Secretary of the Interior	James G. Watt	42	Colorado	Assembly of God	Attorney	Deputy Assistant Secretary of Interior; member, Federal Power Commission	B.S., Wyoming; LL.B., Wyoming
Secretary of Agriculture	John R. Block	45	Illinois	Lutheran	Farmer	Director, Illinois Dept. of Agriculture	B.S., U.S. Military Academy
Secretary of Commerce	Malcolm Baldridge	58	Connecticut	Congregational	Business executive	State Republican finance chairman	B.A., Yale
Secretary of Health and Human Services	Richard S. Schweiker	54	Pennsylvania	Schwenkfelder	U.S. senator	Business executive	B.A., Penn State

Position	Name	Age	State	Religion	Occupation	Experience	Education
Secretary of Labor	Raymond J. Donovan	50	New Jersey	Roman Catholic	Construction company executive	Republican fundraiser; labor relations specialist	B.A., Notre Dame Seminary (New Orleans)
Secretary of Housing and Urban Development	Samuel R. Pierce	58	New York	Methodist	Attorney	Judge; General Counsel to U.S. Treasury	A.B, Cornell; LL.B, Cornell
Secretary of Transportation	Andrew (Drew) Lewis	49	Pennsylvania	Schwenkfelder	President of management consulting firm	Deputy Chairman, Republican National Committee	B.A., Haverford; M.B.A., Harvard
Secretary of Energy	James B. Edwards	53	South Carolina	Methodist	Oral surgeon	Governor of South Carolina	A.B, Coll. of Charleston; D.D.S., Louisville
Secretary of Education	Terrel H. Bell	59	Utah	Mormon	Utah Commissioner of Higher Education	U.S. Commissioner of Higher Education	B.A., Albion State (Idaho); Ed.D, Utah
Director, Office of Management and Budget	David A. Stockman	34	Michigan	Methodist	Congressman	Congressional staff member	B.A., Michigan State
United States Ambassador to UN	Jeane J. Kirkpatrick	54	Maryland	Baptist	Political scientist	Consultant, Dept. of Defense	B.A., Barnard; Ph.D., Columbia
Special Assistant to the President for National Security Affairs	Richard V. Allen	44	District of Columbia	Roman Catholic	Business consultant	Deputy National Security Adviser	A.B, Notre Dame; M.A., Notre Dame
Director of Central Intelligence	William J. Casey	67	New York	Roman Catholic	Attorney	Chairman, SEC; Under-Secretary of State; President, Export-Import Bank	B.A., Fordham; LL.B, St. John's (New York)

Brzezinski. Each powerful in his own right, they were often able to outfight the secretaries of state and defense. The NSC's original purpose was to coordinate policy from these two departments, but the personalities of national security advisors overshadowed those of the cabinet officers. Reagan pledged to reduce NSC influence.

On the other hand, Reagan elevated the Office of Management and Budget from obscurity to a major policy role. Until the appointment of David Stockman, OMB had kept a low profile of neutral competence. Stockman, in contrast, was encouraged by Reagan to become the major public spokesman for his economic policies.

All White House staff members have one thing in common: their sole responsibility to the president. They have no large governmental bureaucracy on which to depend for information. There are no alliances to be formed with organized groups.

> Presidents sometimes fall victim to "groupthink"; nobody wants to be the bearer of bad news.

Presidents sometimes fall victim to "groupthink"; nobody wants to be the bearer of bad news.[12] Groupthink is fostered when the decision-making group is bound together by a strong set of interpersonal ties, as is the case with the White House staff and personal advisors. Reagan advisors are personal friends who have known each other for many years socially and in their business activities. They are insulated from the public at large and hold a fairly uniform view of appropriate policy. The result of this process is that the president can be misinformed, and criticism can be regarded as disloyalty.

CYCLES OF LEADERSHIP

Despite these problems, the American presidency continues to be the dominant factor in policymaking. For years, strong presidents were eulogized and weak ones ridiculed. The country wanted strong leadership. But then came two successive presidents—Johnson and Nixon—who appeared to be *too* strong. The Vietnam War and the Watergate scandal led to a condemnation of the "imperial presidency" and a demand for the restoration of balance between the branches of government.[13] Carter was the direct beneficiary of this demand. He did not promise strong leadership; instead, he adopted the symbols of humility: walking to the White House for his inauguration, sending his daughter to public school, dropping the musical theme "Hail to the Chief," appearing on national television in an open collar and sweater, attending town meetings, conducting phone-ins, and so on.

There are cycles in the expansion of the presidency, but the long-term trend is clearly in the direction of even more executive leadership.

Reagan returned much of the pomp and ceremony to the White House. He and his wife enjoyed luxury and were lavish entertainers. The Reagans knew that Americans do indeed like strong presidents, if not "imperial" ones.

There are cycles in the expansion of the presidency, but the long-term trend is clearly in the direction of even more executive leadership. In a media age, we need a good performer. Congress is a multi-headed monster with no single dominant personality. The courts are aloof and the bureaucracy is boring, but the presidency is "news."

CHAPTER SUMMARY

1. The formal powers of the president have been enlarged through the media's personalizing and dramatizing of the office. The power of policy initiation is a significant one, and effective use of the media enhances that power.

2. President Reagan used the media to simplify complex legislation and to communicate a belief to the viewing public that his policies would work. Additionally, his inside knowledge of the media's operation along with his less than compulsive personality enabled him to fulfill the important presidential roles of reassurance, decisiveness, and persuasion.

3. The media image of a capable, resolute, and knowledgeable president is very important, as evidenced by the Johnson, Ford, and Carter cases. The relative popularity of presidents can be directly linked to their image.

4. The Barber active/passive and positive/negative typology relates to whether presidents feel politically confident and determined to employ (or not to employ) their power in a socially dynamic manner. Despite a professed belief in limited government, Reagan actively used the powers of his office to achieve policy goals.

5. Presidential popularity is related to success with Congress. The relationship may be circular, with congressional failures reducing presidential popularity and a decline in popularity strengthening congressional obduracy. Presidents must actively lobby to get their programs through Congress.

6. Presidential power has expanded fastest in the area of foreign policy. Presidential use (or abuse) of the war power has led to a congressional determination to restrict this power. The 1973 War Powers Act ostensibly limits presidential use of combat troops overseas to a sixty-day period, but the act has several weaknesses.

7. The cabinet and White House staff are intended to aid presidential decision making. However, the cabinet is rarely used by presidents to settle important questions. The White House staff, which is the heart of the decision-making process, sometimes tends to isolate the chief executive, induce "groupthink," and suffer factional disputes.

8. There are cycles of presidential leadership, but the trend clearly seems to be toward even more leadership from the executive branch.

Notes

1. Joseph Adelson, "The Political Imagination of the Young Adolescent," *Daedalus* 100 (1971), pp. 1013–1050. Also in Allan Elms, *Personality in Politics* (New York: Harcourt Brace Jovanovich, 1976), pp. 2–4.
2. Fred I. Greenstein, "The Psychological Functions of the Presidency for Citizens," in Elmer E. Cornwall, ed., *The American Presidency: Vital Center* (Chicago: Scott, Foresman, 1966), pp. 30–36.
3. David Halberstam, *The Powers that Be* (New York: Knopf, 1979), p. 514.
4. Peter Braestrup, *Big Story* (Garden City, N. Y.: Anchor Books, 1978). See also discussion in Doris A. Graber, *Mass Media and American Politics* (Washington, D. C.: Congressional Quarterly Press, 1980), p. 60.
5. James David Barber, *The Presidential Character: Predicting Performance in the White House* (Englewood Cliffs, N. J.: Prentice-Hall, 1977), pp. 11–13.
6. William Howard Taft, *Our Chief Magistrate and His Powers* (New York: Columbia University Press, 1938), p. 138. Reprinted in John P. Roche and L. W. Levy, eds., *The Presidency* (New York: Harcourt Brace Jovanovich, 1964), p. 23.
7. Quoted in Arthur B. Tourtellot, *Presidents on the Presidency* (Garden City, N. Y.: Doubleday, 1964), pp. 55–56.
8. George C. Edwards, III, *Presidential Influence in Congress* (San Francisco: Freeman, 1980), p. 86.
9. Edwards, p. 86.
10. Federalist 69 (Hamilton), especially pp. 417–418, in *The Federalist Papers* (New York: Mentor Books, 1961). See also Arthur M. Schlesinger, Jr., *The Imperial Presidency* (Boston: Houghton Mifflin, 1973), pp. 1–12.
11. Congressional Quarterly, *The Power of the Pentagon* (Washington, D. C.: Congressional Quarterly Press, 1972), p. 42.
12. See Irving L. Janis, *Victims of Groupthink: A Psychological Study of Foreign Policy Decisions and Fiascos* (Boston: Houghton Mifflin, 1972).
13. Schlesinger, *The Imperial Presidency,* pp. 1–12.

Close-Up and In-Depth Analyses

James David Barber. *The Presidential Character,* 2nd ed. Englewood Cliffs, N. J.: Prentice-Hall, 1977.

Thomas E. Cronin. *The State of the Presidency,* 2nd ed. Boston: Little, Brown, 1980.

Robert E. DiClerico. *The American President.* Englewood Cliffs, N. J.: Prentice-Hall, 1979.

David Halberstam. *The Best and the Brightest.* New York: Random House, 1972.

Louis W. Koenig. *The Chief Executive,* 4th ed. New York: Harcourt Brace Jovanovich, 1981.

Newton Minow. *Presidential Television.* New York: Basic Books, 1973.

Richard E. Neustadt. *Presidential Power.* New York: Wiley, 1980.

Clinton Rossiter. *The American Presidency,* 2nd ed. New York: New American Library, 1964.

Arthur Schlesinger, Jr. *The Imperial Presidency.* Boston: Houghton Mifflin, 1973.

CHAPTER 10

BUREAUCRACY AND POLITICS

THE WASHINGTON BUREAUCRACY: SOURCES OF POWER

The political struggles in the White House and Congress are generally much more visible than the struggles that take place in the labyrinths of government bureaucracies. But the "faceless bureaucrats" are just as powerful in making public policy as the president, the Congress, or the courts.

Political battles do not end with victory or defeat in Congress or the White House. The site of the battles merely shifts from the recognized political arena to an administrative arena. Organized interests do not abandon the fight and return home simply because a law has been passed and signed by the president or money appropriated by Congress. They merely shift their attention to the implementation of the law and the spending of the money by a bureaucracy. We may think that "political" questions are decided by the president and Congress and "administrative" questions by the bureaucracies. But actually political and administrative questions do not differ in content. They differ only in who decides them.

The Washington bureaucracy is a major base of power in society—largely independent of Congress, the president, the courts, or the people themselves. There are over 2 million civilian employees of the federal government.

An IRS clearing center
for income tax forms
in Albany, New York.

(There are only 2 million people in the nation's armed forces.) The *Federal Register,* which lists all of the regulations issued annually by federal bureaucracies, exceeds 60,000 pages a year. Americans are forced to submit over 2 billion forms and documents to the federal government each year. But it is not the red tape,[1] the paper shuffling, the waste and inefficiency, the impersonality and insensitivity, and the overregulation that make bureaucracy a powerful force in American life. What, then, are the sources of power of the Washington bureaucracy?

> The Washington bureaucracy is a major base of power in society—largely independent of Congress, the president, the courts, or the people themselves.

Growth of Technology

The power of bureaucracies grows with advances in technology and increases in the size and complexity of society. The influence of the "technocrats" is expanding in both the corporate and governmental sectors of society. In government it is unrealistic to believe that a president or Congress has the time, energy, or expertise to master the details of nuclear power, air quality control, communications, or aviation. So actual governance of these complex fields is turned over to specialized bureaucracies, acting under only vague and general directions from the president and Congress. The Nuclear Regulatory Commission, for example, was established to draw up specific rules to oversee the nuclear power industry. The Environmental Protection Agency was given authority to define and measure pollutants and to require industries to install controls. The Occupational Safety and Health Administration issues mountains of regulations to industries on everything from toilets to ladders. The Federal Communications Commission licenses radio and television stations and allots them specific broadcast bands and power allowances. And the Federal Aviation Administration oversees air traffic controls at commercial airports.

There are approximately 2,000 federal agencies with rule-making powers. These bureaucracies announce *twenty* rules or regulations for every *one* law of Congress.

Abdication by Congress and President

Another reason for the increased power of the Washington bureaucracy is that Congress and the president often pass and sign deliberately vague and ambiguous laws. These laws are passed for largely *symbolic* reasons—ensuring nuclear safety, protecting the environment, ensuring occupational safety, allocating broadcasting channels, guaranteeing flight safety, and so on. Bureaucracies, acting under the authority of these symbolic laws, are given the power to decide what will actually be done. Congress and the President frequently do not want to take responsibility for unpopular policies. It is much easier for political leaders to blame the bureaucrats and pretend that unpopular policies are a product of an "ungovernable" Washington bureaucracy. This delegation of authority allows the imposition of regulations for which an elected president and Congress do not wish to accept full responsibility. (Perhaps the best-known example of bureaucratic power originating from vague, symbolic phrases in legislation is the affirmative-action program of the Equal Employment Opportunity Commission.)

Policy Initiation

The Washington bureaucracy itself is now sufficiently large to have its own laws passed. Bureaucrats are the most frequent lobbyists in Congress. They recommend that their agencies expand in size, acquire greater authority, and obtain more money. The bureaucracy is self-perpetuating.

Political scientist James Q. Wilson writes: "I am impressed by the extent to which policy making is dominated by the representatives of these bureaucracies and professions having a material stake in the management and funding of the intended policy and by those political staffs who see in a new program a chance for publicity, advancement, and a good reputation for their superiors."[2]

ORGANIZATION OF THE BUREAUCRACY

All governments—federal, state, and local—collectively spend about 35 percent of the gross national product (GNP), the sum of all of the goods and services produced in the nation. The national government alone accounts for about 21 percent of the GNP, and state and local governments account for an additional 14 percent. About 16 million people work in federal, state, or local government; this is about 16 percent of the nation's total employment. In other words, about one in six employed people work for government. (See Figure 10-1.)

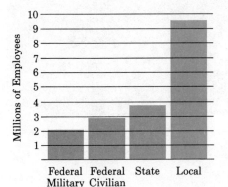

Figure 10-1. Government employment—federal, state, and local. (Source: U. S. Bureau of the Census.)

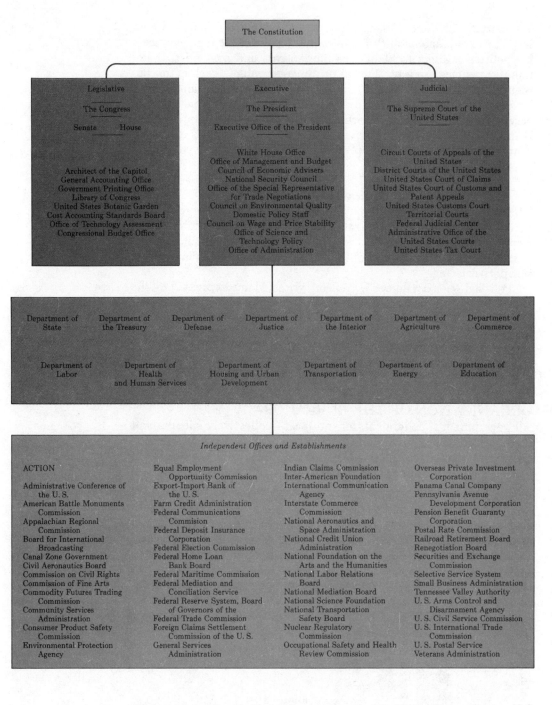

Figure 10-2. Organization of the government of the United States. (Source: *U. S. Government Manual 1981–1982.*)

The organization of the U. S. government is depicted in Figure 10-2. The executive branch employs 98 percent of the 2 million federal employees. This branch is organized into thirteen departments, fifty-six independent agencies, and a large executive office of the president.

We frequently refer to "the Washington bureaucracy," but only about 12 percent of all federal employees work in Washington. Nonetheless, Washington is the center of control of the giant apparatus that we call the federal government.

Executive Office

The **Office of Management and Budget** (OMB) is one of the most important agencies in Washington. Its function is to prepare the budget of the U. S. government for the president to submit to Congress. No money may be spent by the federal government without appropriations by Congress, and all requests for congressional appropriations must be cleared through OMB, a requirement that gives it great power over the executive branch. Since all agencies request more money than they can receive, the primary responsibility for reducing budget requests rests with OMB. It reviews, reduces, and approves estimates submitted by departments and agencies (subject, of course, to their appeal to the president), and it also continuously scrutinizes the organization and operations of executive agencies so that changes promoting efficiency and economy can be recommended. Like members of the White House staff, the top officials of OMB are responsible solely to the president, and they are supposed to reflect the president's goals and priorities in their decisions.

Office of Management and Budget: The agency whose function is to prepare the budget of the United States government for the president to submit to Congress.

The Office of Management and Budget is one of the most important agencies in Washington.

The **Council of Economic Advisers,** created by the Employment Act of 1946, is composed of three professional economists of high standing appointed by the president with the consent of the Senate. The functions of the council are to analyze trends in the economy and to recommend to the president the fiscal and monetary

Council of Economic Advisers: The agency that analyzes trends in the economy and recommends to the president fiscal and monetary policies necessary to avoid both depression and inflation.

Essentials: The Budget Process in Brief

The full budget process requires twenty months or more—from January of the year preceding the fiscal year until the following year's October 1. (Fiscal years run from October 1 to September 30, and they are named for the year in which they end; for example, the fiscal year beginning October 1, 1985, and ending September 30, 1986 is called "FY 86.")

(continued)

(continued)

The Budget Process

Approximate schedule	Actors	Tasks
January–March	President and OMB	OMB presents long-range forecasts for revenues and expenditures to the president. The president and OMB develop general guidelines for all federal agencies. Agencies are sent guidelines and forms for their budget requests.
April–July	Executive agencies	Agencies prepare and submit budget requests to OMB.
August–October	OMB and agencies	OMB reviews agency requests and holds hearings with agency officials. OMB usually tries to reduce agency requests.
November–December	OMB and president	OMB presents revised budget to president. Occasionally agencies may appeal OMB decisions directly to the president. President and OMB write budget messages for Congress.
January	President	President presents budget for the next fiscal year to Congress.
February–May	CBO and congressional committees	Standing committees review taxing and spending proposals for reports to House and Senate Budget committees. Congressional Budget Office (CBO) also reviews entire presidential budget and reports to Budget committees.
May–June	Congress; House and Senate Budget committees	House and Senate Budget committees present first concurrent resolution, which sets overall total for budget outlays in major categories. Full House and Senate vote on resolution. Committees are instructed to stay within

		Budget Committee's resolution.
July–September	Congress; House and Senate Appropriations committees and Budget committees	House and Senate Appropriations committees and sub-committees draw up detailed appropriations bills. Bills are submitted to House and Senate Budget committees for second concurrent resolution. Budget committees may force reductions through "reconciliation" provisions to limit spending. The full House and Senate vote on "reconciliations" and second (firm) concurrent resolution.
September–October	Congress and president	House and Senate pass various appropriations bills (nine to sixteen bills by major functional category, such as "defense"). Each is sent to president for signature. (If vetoed by president, the appropriations bills go back to House and Senate, which must override veto with two-thirds vote in each body or revise bills to gain president's approval.)
After October 1	Congress and president	Fiscal year for all federal agencies begins October 1. If no appropriations bill has been passed by Congress and signed by president for an agency, Congress must pass and the president sign a continuing resolution to allow the agency to spend at last year's level until a new appropriations act is passed. If no continuing resolution is passed, the agency must officially cease spending government funds and must officially shut down.

David Stockman (center), Director of OMB discusses economic reports with staff members as Howard Baker (R-Tenn.), Senate Majority Leader looks on.

policies necessary to avoid both depression and inflation. In addition, the council prepares the economic report that the Employment Act requires the president to submit to Congress each year. The economic report and the annual budget message to Congress give the president the opportunity to present broadly the administration's major policies.

National Security Council: A cabinet-like panel that advises the president on security policy and coordinates foreign, military, and domestic policies.

The **National Security Council** resembles a cabinet; it is composed of the president as chairman, the vice-president, the secretary of state, the secretary of defense, and the director of the Office of Emergency Planning (a minor unit in the executive office). The chairman of the Joint Chiefs of Staff and the director of the CIA are advisors to the Security Council. The staff of the council is headed by a special assistant to the president for national security affairs. The purposes of the council are to advise the president on security policy and to coordinate foreign, military, and domestic policies. However, presidents do not rely exclusively on the council for direction in major foreign and military decisions.

Cabinet Departments

Cabinet officers in the United States are powerful because they sit at the head of a giant administrative organization. The secretary of state, the secretary of defense, the secretary of the treasury, the attorney general, and, to a lesser extent, the other departmental secretaries are all people of power and prestige. But the cabinet, as a council, rarely makes policy. Seldom do strong presidents hold a cabinet meeting to decide important policy questions. More frequently, they know what they want and are inclined to hold cabinet meetings to help them sell their views.

The Department of Health and Human Services spends more money than any other Washington bureaucracy. Indeed, this department alone accounts for over one-third of all federal spending. Its principal operating components are the Office of Human Development Services (research, planning, and development for the aged, children, youth, families, and social service programs); the U. S. Public Health Service (medical research, health statistics, disease control, alcohol and drug abuse, mental health programs, and the activities of the Food and Drug Administration); the Health Care Financing Administration (Medicare, Medicaid); and the Social Security Administration (Social Security, Supplemental Security Income, and Aid to Families with Dependent Children, or AFDC). In addition to these operating agencies, there is a wide variety of supporting bureaucrats and minibureaucracies.

Independent Agencies

Independent agencies, functioning outside of the thirteen cabinet departments, regulate much of American society. The regulatory agencies (Table 10-1 on the next page) involve themselves in almost everything Americans do. Bank accounts are insured by the Federal Deposit Insurance Commission. Interest rates on loans are determined largely by the Federal Reserve Board. Unions are protected by the National Labor Relations Board. Safety in automobiles and buses is the responsibility of the National Transportation Safety Board. The Federal Trade Commission orders cigarette manufacturers to place a health warning on each pack. The Equal Employment Opportunity Commission investigates complaints about racial or sexual dis-

---

It is difficult to find an activity in public or private life that is *not* regulated by government.

---

crimination in jobs. The Consumer Product Safety Commission requires that toys be large enough that they cannot be swallowed. The Federal Communications Commission does not allow cigarette advertisements on television. The Environmental Protection Agency requires automobile companies to reduce exhaust emissions. The Occupational Safety and Health Administration requires construction firms to place portable toilets at work sites. The list goes on and on. Indeed, it is difficult to find an activity in public or private life that is *not* regulated by government.

Federal regulatory agencies make rules, investigate violations, adjudicate responsibility, and levy fines and penalties. They are legislature, investigator, prosecutor, judge, and jury all in one. The only appeal from their decisions is to the federal courts, and the agencies win most of the cases brought against them. Most of the independent regulatory agencies are governed by a small commission appointed by the president, with Senate confirmation, for a fixed term. During this term the commissioners cannot be fired by the president. Hence, they are considered "independent."

Table 10-1.   The Regulatory Bureaucracy

Date of legislation	Agency involved	Powers granted
1887	Interstate Commerce Commission (ICC)	Regulates water and routes of railroads, water carriers, and trucks.
1913	Federal Reserve Board (FRB)	Regulates activities of banks that are members of Federal Reserve System; sets money and credit policy.
1914	Federal Trade Commission (FTC)	Has broad powers to curb "unfair" trade practices, protect consumers, and maintain competition.
1931	Food and Drug Administration (FDA)	Originally established to regulate prescription drugs; later authorized to determine whether all prescription and nonprescription drugs are "safe."
1932	Federal Home Loan Bank Board	Regulates savings and loan associations.
1933	Federal Deposit Insurance Corporation (FDIC)	Regulates banks not in the Federal Reserve System; insures small deposits.
1934	Federal Communications Commission (FCC)	Regulates radio and television broadcasting and interstate telephone and telegraph service.
1934	Securities and Exchange Commission (SEC)	Regulates all publicly traded securities and the markets on which they are traded. Requires public disclosure and polices securities fraud.
1935	National Labor Relations Board (NLRB)	Regulates labor/management relations; defines and punishes unfair labor practices by business and labor.
1938	Food and Drug Administration (FDA)	Requires clearance of new drugs before marketing.
1938	Civil Aeronautics Board (CAB)	Regulates airline fares and routes.
1947	National Labor Relations Board (NLRB)	Powers extended to regulate union activities.
1958	Food and Drug Administration (FDA)	Clearance requirement extended to foods as well as drugs.
1962	Food and Drug Administration (FDA)	Requires proof of "effectiveness" as well as "safety" for drugs.
1962	Office of Federal Contract Compliance	Administers prohibition against discrimination by race or sex by government contractors.
1964	Equal Employment Opportunity Commission (EEOC)	Administers prohibitions against discrimination by race or sex by private employers.
1970	Environmental Protection Agency (EPA)	Regulates air and water quality, waste disposal, and toxic and hazardous materials, among other things.
1970	National Transportation Safety Board	Regulates manufacturing of autos, buses, tires, and so forth.
1971	Occupational Safety and Health Administration (OSHA)	Regulates safety and health practices in work places.
1972	Consumer Product Safety Commission (CPSC)	Establishes standards for safety, labeling, and construction of consumer products.
1973	Nuclear Regulatory Commission (NRC)	Regulates civilian nuclear safety and licenses nuclear plants.
1974	Pension Benefit Guarantee Corporation	Regulates private pension plans.
1975	Federal Trade Commission (FTC)	Powers extended to order refunds and "corrective advertising"; covers intrastate as well as interstate commerce.
1978[a]	Civil Aeronautics Board (CAB)	Control reduced over airline routes and rates.

[a]First major deregulation legislation passed.

The capture theory.   But are members of regulatory commissions really independent? Over the years many of the older commissions have worked to protect and preserve the regulated industry rather than the general public. A **"capture theory"** of regulatory agencies argues that over time the original stimulus for reform that led to the agency's creation diminishes and the agency becomes closely identified with the well-being of the industry it is supposed to regulate. Agency bureaucrats are frequently recruited from regulated industries because of their expertise. Moreover, after a few years in government, some agency bureaucrats go to work in high-paying jobs in the regulated industries. For example, many regulatory commissions attract young attorneys, fresh from prominent law schools, to their staffs. When these attorneys learn to do their job well, they are frequently offered high-paying positions by the industries they are regulating. The "best and the brightest" are siphoned off by industry to become its defenders. And, of course, these people have already learned the intricacies of government regulations, with their training having been paid for by the taxpayers.

Capture theory: The view that over time the original stimulus for reform behind the creation of an agency diminishes and that the agency becomes closely identified with the well-being of the industry it is supposed to regulate.

Federal consultants.   The Washington bureaucracy extends even beyond official agencies and employees of the federal government to include an estimated 6 million to 10 million people working indirectly for the federal government as contractors or consultants. Many of these people are working in the defense industry. However, the *Washington Post* has estimated that the federal government spends about $10 billion annually for outside consultants.[3] These consultants receive over 10,000 contracts a year, usually to do work that bureaucracies are unable or unwilling to do.

CONTROLLING THE BUREAUCRACY

The President

Presidents have constitutional authority over the executive branch of government. Their control of the bureaucracy stems primarily from their powers of (1) appointment; (2) organization and reorganization; and (3) preparing the budget for submission to Congress.

The president appoints secretaries, undersecretaries, deputy secretaries, commissioners, and most bureau directors. Of course, many of these top executive posts require Senate confirmation, but rarely is confirmation denied. Unless there is evidence of wrongdoing in an appointee's background, the Senate usually approves presidential appointments under the theory that presidents deserve to have their own "team" in office. (The president also appoints a White House staff without the need for Senate confirmation.)

> Presidential appointments often go to professional bureau-
> crats by default, because qualified political appointees can-
> not be found.

But the president only appoints about 2,500 people. About 600 of
these are in policymaking positions. Each new presidential administration goes through many months of internal squabbling, high-
powered lobbying, and difficult decision making in the process of
filling its top posts. Applicants with congressional "sponsors," friends
close to the president, or a record of effective presidential campaign
work compete for top bureaucratic jobs. Political loyalty must be
balanced against administrative competence. Yet presidential appointments often go to professional bureaucrats by default, because
qualified political appointees cannot be found.

The president tries to control the bureaucracy through the White
House staff, through the Office of Management and Budget, and
through appointed department and agency heads. But there are three
main obstacles to presidential control:

1. Some appointed political heads "go native"; that is, they yield
to the views of the permanent bureaucrats in the agency they are
supposed to head. A president's appointee sent out to control a bureaucracy ends up captured by it.
2. A majority of career bureaucrats is Democratic, so it is particularly difficult for a Republican to exercise control over the
bureaucracy.
3. Increasing the size and responsibilities of the White House
staff in order to oversee the bureaucracy creates a new bureaucracy—
the White House staff itself. Staff members, speaking "in the name of
the president," come into conflict with executive departments, dupli-
cate much of the policy research of the departments, and occasionally
make statements contradicting departmental policy pronouncements.
The president is then presented with a new problem—controlling the
White House staff.

Presidents also have the power to reorganize the federal bureaucracy, subject to congressional veto. Reorganization allows presidents
to upgrade or downgrade government activities according to their
own priorities. In the 1960s President John Kennedy created an independent National Aeronautics and Space Administration to carry out
his commitment to a space program. President Lyndon Johnson created a separate Office of Economic Opportunity in 1964 to emphasize
his War on Poverty, but in the 1970s Presidents Richard Nixon and
Gerald Ford abolished this agency and distributed its remaining
functions to regular departments. President Jimmy Carter created a
Department of Energy to symbolize national concern with energy

problems. Later, he created a Department of Education to fulfill a campaign pledge to emphasize educational matters, even though this new department was opposed by its parent bureaucracy, the Department of Health, Education, and Welfare (now the Department of Health and Human Services). In his 1980 election campaign Ronald Reagan attacked both of Carter's new departments, but once in office he apparently decided not to force a showdown with these bureaucracies. Presidents resort to reorganization only for particularly important policy priorities. Nothing arouses the fighting instincts of bureaucrats so much as the rumor of reorganization.

Finally, the president has formal control over the budget. The Office of Management and Budget works directly under the president's supervision, and its director is appointed by the president subject to Senate confirmation. The president can even withhold funds from programs and agencies, even though the money has already been appropriated by Congress. However, since the Budget and Impoundment Control Act of 1974 these presidential **"impoundments"** must be approved by Congress.

Impoundment: A president's withholding of funds appropriated by Congress to programs and agencies.

Congress

Congress can try to check the bureaucracy in several ways, including:

1. passing laws to change bureaucratic regulations or limit bureaucratic authority
2. raising or reducing a bureaucracy's budget
3. retaining specific veto powers over certain bureaucratic actions (some rules proposed by agencies must be submitted to Congress before becoming effective, and Congress may act to invalidate them)
4. conducting public investigations and hearings, with heavy media coverage, that publicize unpopular decisions, rules, or expenditures by bureaucracies
5. making direct contacts with the bureaucracy in which complaints are discussed

Yet it is difficult for Congress to use all of these powers effectively. Very few bureaucratic regulations are ever directly overturned by Congress. Members of Congress often complain publicly about bureaucratic rules and pose as defenders of the people against big government; but then these same members continue to grant authority and appropriate money to agencies to carry out the vital business of government. In this fashion Congress can have its cake and eat it too. It can avoid the difficult decisions involved in carrying out its laws and then complain about such decisions when they turn out to be unpopular.

Getting Rid of a Bureaucrat

It is very difficult to fire any of the over 2 million employees under the U. S. civil service system. These are the federal employees with a GS (General Schedule) rating, ranging from GS 1 (a messenger, for example) to GS 18 (a bureau director). The civil service system is supposed to protect government workers from partisan, political firings. But for most government workers, the system ensures that they cannot be fired except under the most unusual circumstances and only after lengthy proceedings. Only about 200 federal employees are fired for incompetence in a year—a very tiny fraction of the 2 million federal workers. To fire a federal employee requires:

1. written notice at least thirty days in advance of a hearing to determine incompetence or misconduct
2. a statement of "cause," indicating specific dates, places, and actions that are cited as incompetent or improper
3. the right to a hearing and decision by an impartial official, with the burden of proof on the agency that wishes to fire the employee
4. the employee's right to have an attorney to present witnesses in his or her favor at the hearing
5. the right to appeal any adverse action to a Merit System Protection Board
6. the right to appeal any adverse action by the Merit System Protection Board to the U. S. Court of Appeals
7. the right to remain on the job and to be paid until all appeals are exhausted

Realistically, this means that no one is fired or demoted unless his or her superior in the agency is willing to invest a great deal of time and energy in a doubtful effort.

Since, as a practical matter, bureaucrats cannot be fired, the White House and department secretaries must develop elaborate ways to encourage "voluntary" resignation:

1. They can inform incompetent employees that they are not wanted and that, if they resign, they will get a favorable letter of recommendation and a farewell luncheon. If they refuse to resign, they will be assured of no higher job in the administration and a nasty letter of recommendation if they later try to leave to get a better job elsewhere.

2. They can transfer employees to areas of the country where they do not wish to live. A transfer from Washington to the field office in Minot, North Dakota, may encourage resignation.

Joseph Wright of OMB rolls out the forms he says it takes to fire a federal employee.

3. They can reassign employees to meaningless, repetitious, boring duties, taking away their secretaries and assistants; move them into small, windowless, poorly furnished offices; or assign them distant, undesirable parking spaces.

4. They can reorganize the office to place a loyal, competent employee in charge of the disloyal or incompetent ones. Top policymaking positions are not protected by civil service.

About 2,500 *top* positions are filled by the president, sometimes with Senate confirmation. They include cabinet secretaries, undersecretaries, and assistant secretaries, most bureau chiefs, and jobs having "a confidential or policy-determining character." These jobs are listed in Washington's famous "Plum Book,"* which is eagerly read by members of incoming administrations.

*It is actually entitled *United States Policy and Supporting Positions.* It is compiled by the Committee on Post Office and Civil Service of the U. S. House of Representatives (Washington, D. C.: U. S. Government Printing Office, 1980).

Uncontrollables:
Expenditures required
by previous legislation
and considered to be
commitments.

Congressional control of bureaucratic spending is more symbolic than real. Rarely does Congress raise or lower appropriations requested in the president's budget by more than 5 percent. Many expenditures are considered "**uncontrollables**"; that is, they are required by previous legislation (Social Security, Medicare, veterans' benefits, interest on the national debt) that are considered commitments. Moreover, the practice of *incremental* budgeting focuses attention on proposed increases in agency budget requests each year. Congress rarely looks at an agency's "base"—that is, its previous year's expenditures. In short, even agencies that have seriously offended Congress can expect at most to be penalized by having their requested *increases* reduced or eliminated.

Congressional hearings can be embarrassing for high-ranking bureaucrats. They must sit quietly defending their programs while committee members make comments that they hope will capture a spot for them on the evening news. And certainly no agency likes to win Senator William Proxmire's "Golden Fleece" award, which he regularly announces to the media for what he considers to be an excessively wasteful or worthless program or project. Nonetheless, there is no conclusive evidence that these symbolic demonstrations and media events by Congress have any significant effect on bureaucratic policy.

Finally, congressional complaints passed on from constituents are handled with speed by most agencies. However, the agencies handle these complaints *within* existing rules and regulations. Bureaucrats usually do not break rules to accommodate members of Congress. The only advantage to having a member complain to an agency on one's behalf is to speed up the handling of the case.

The Courts

Decisions by executive agencies can usually be appealed to the federal courts. This is a restraint against arbitrary and unreasonable bureaucratic actions and actions that are contrary to federal laws or the Constitution itself. However, judicial control of the bureaucracy is limited by two main factors.

First, judicial oversight usually focuses on *procedural* fairness in a bureaucracy (due notice, fair hearings, opportunity to appeal, legal authority, and the like), rather than the content of the decision itself. Courts seldom overturn bureaucratic decisions simply because they are burdensome, ill-advised, pointless, or ineffective. The courts are usually concerned only with whether the bureaucracy acted within its legal authority and with due process of law.

Second, lawsuits against government bureaucracies are very expensive and time consuming. The bureaucracies have their own armies of attorneys paid for out of tax money to oppose anyone who challenges them in court. It turns out that the bureaucracies (especially the regulatory commissions) usually win in court. Rarely are their decisions overturned.[4]

REGULATION AND DEREGULATION

The regulatory commissions usually act only against the most wayward members of an industry. By attacking particular businesses that are giving an industry bad publicity, a commission may actually help improve the public image of the industry. The very existence of a regulatory commission—for example, the Securities and Exchange Commission, which regulates the stock market—provides symbolic reassurance to the public that the industry is functioning properly.

Many commission rules help to limit entry into a regulated business by small firms. Historically, federal regulations limited entry into trucking, railroading, airlines, radio, and television. Proposals to *de*regulate these areas were bitterly *opposed* by the regulated businesses. These businesses were fearful that deregulation would mean more competition and lower prices.

The New Regulators

Over the past decade, however, the civil rights movement, the environmental movement, and the consumer movement have led to the creation of new bureaucracies that pose serious challenges to industry. Unlike earlier regulatory commissions, the newer regulatory bureaucracies do not cover a single industry but instead cover all industries. Apparently, this makes them difficult, if not impossible, for industry to "capture." The Equal Employment Opportunity Commission (EEOC), the Environmental Protection Agency (EPA), and the Occupational Safety and Health Administration (OSHA) are widely resented in the business community. Rules developed by the EEOC to prevent racial or sexual discrimination in employment and promotion (affirmative-action guidelines) have been cumbersome and have been changed frequently. Many businesses do not believe that the EEOC has the insight to understand their industry or their labor market. They complain that EEOC regulations do not consider the costs of training or the availability of qualified minorities.

> The newer regulatory bureaucracies do not cover a single industry but instead cover all industries. Apparently, this makes them difficult, if not impossible, for industry to "capture."

Likewise, the EPA has been charged by industry with issuing orders that do not consider the costs, delays, or layoffs that may result from compliance. The EPA can order private industries or agencies of

An EPA check on water pollution may be followed with EPA orders to prevent more pollution.

federal, state, or local governments to halt polluting discharges or to install what the EPA defines as "the best available technology" for preventing pollution. The EPA does not need to balance the costs of following its orders with the benefits that are supposed to occur because of these orders.

The same objection has been raised by industry to the regulatory activities of OSHA. The agency has issued many thousands of safety regulations that appear costly and ridiculous to many in the affected industries. The bureaucrats who draw up the regulations have seldom had much experience in the industry.

Complaints of Overregulation

Complaints from industry concerning "overregulation" have tended to center on several main assertions.

1. Increased costs to businesses and consumers result from compliance with many separate regulations issued by many separate agencies. The costs of maintaining the regulatory bureaucracies is relatively small compared with the costs imposed on businesses and consumers in complying with their regulations. (The automobile industry asserts that safety and environmental regulations add $1,500 to the price of the average new car.) The most common estimate of

the cost of compliance is $100 billion a year, or one-seventh of the federal budget. These costs are borne by private individuals and never appear on the federal budget.

2. Regulatory agencies fail to weigh the costs of compliance with new regulations against the benefits that are presumed to flow to society. (But it is difficult to weigh costs against human life. The self-inflating automobile airbag may cost $250 to $750 per car, or $1 billion a year; but it may save 100 or 200 of the 50,000 people who die in auto accidents each year. How does one weigh an expenditure against a saving in lives?)

3. Overregulation creates a drag on innovation and productivity. The costs and delays in winning permission for a new product tend to discourage invention. (Research into new drugs is down over 75 percent from a decade ago because of the years of testing required by the FDA. Western European nations are many years ahead in life-saving drugs available; they talk of the "drug lag" in the United States. Observers charge that if aspirin were proposed for marketing today, it would not be approved by the FDA.)

4. Competition declines when regulatory bureaucracies license and limit entry into a field. The cost of complying with federal reporting requirements is itself an obstacle to small business. And larger businesses must cope with reams of reports on employee relations, taxes and Social Security, affirmative action, occupational safety and health, environmental impact, permits, licenses, fees, and so on. Only the largest corporations have high-priced legal staffs prepared to do battle with the regulators, and only the largest corporations can afford the expensive delays involved in obtaining government approval.

Deregulation

The demand for deregulation had already been heard in Washington before Reagan became president. In 1978 Carter had succeeded in getting Congress to deregulate the airline industry. Against objections by the industry itself, which *wanted* continued regulation, the Civil Aeronautics Board was stripped of its powers to allocate airline routes to various carriers and to set rates. The airline companies were "set free" to choose where to fly and what to charge. Competition on heavily traveled routes (such as from New York to Los Angeles) reduced fares dramatically, but increases in fuel prices more than wiped out the savings to the flying public. This combination of competition and higher fuel prices caused airline profits to decline.

President Carter had already committed the nation to a phased deregulation of domestic oil prices when Reagan took office. But Reagan ordered immediate decontrol of oil prices, calling these controls "a cumbersome and inefficient system of regulations that served to stifle domestic oil production, increase our dependence on foreign oil, and discourage conservation."[5] Oil prices initially increased, and domestic oil production remained the same. But after a few months the effects of conservation were felt worldwide; prices leveled off, and the industry faced a "glut" of oil.

According to President Reagan, "regulatory relief is just getting under way." He ordered all executive departments "to determine the most cost-effective approach for meeting any regulatory objective" and not to issue regulations "unless the potential benefits to society outweigh the potential costs."[6] He established a Task Force on Regulatory Relief, chaired by Vice-President George Bush. He abolished the Council on Wage and Price Stability (which had tried to halt inflation by setting wages and prices), postponed automobile airbags indefinitely, ended requirements for bilingual education in schools, and blocked new antinoise regulations. More important than these modest beginnings was Reagan's promise to make deregulation a major goal of his administration.

BUREAUCRACY AND THE MEDIA

Most media people—from reporters and writers to producers and network executives—see themselves in an "adversary relationship" with public officials. In such a relationship the media are critics of government, exposing conflict, controversy, wrongdoing, waste, and corruption. By so doing, the media hope to present exciting stories that will attract a large audience.

In contrast, public officials want to be pictured as honest, hardworking, dedicated, and successful in serving the public. Bureaucrats try to control the information released to the media so as to serve their own purposes—to project a favorable image of their agencies and programs, to suggest the need for increased appropriations and expanded authority, and to report success in accomplishing their objectives.

Bureaucrats and the media need each other, but each has its own purpose. Each tries to create the kind of "news" that furthers its own objectives. Government agencies want flattering reports to advance their own objectives. The media want sensational, attention-getting reports to advance *their* objectives—improving audience ratings, adding to their own power and status, and increasing their revenues and profits.

The media perform several important functions for the bureaucracy. First of all, they set the agenda for bureaucratic activity. When the media do a "special" on illicit drugs in Florida, they prompt the Federal Bureau of Investigation, the Drug Enforcement Administration, the Treasury Department, and state and local authorities to "crack down." When the media focus on illegal immigration into the United States, they activate the Immigration and Naturalization Service. When the media play up various ecological disasters (toxic-waste disposal, "acid rain," and the like) they encourage additional regulatory activity by the Environmental Protection Agency. Sensational media reports on "toxic shock syndrome" not only forced Proctor and Gamble to recall Rely tampons but also caused consternation in the Food and Drug Administration and the U. S. Public Health Service. The media not only direct the attention of regulatory agencies to alleged violations of existing laws; they also encourage bureaucracies to draw up new legislation and recommend new policies to the president and Congress.

The media set the agenda for bureaucratic activity.

Second, the media provide information to political leaders—in the White House, the cabinet, and Congress—that reduces their reliance on the bureaucracy itself. Most top Washington leaders read the *Washington Post* and the *New York Times* before starting their day. Both newspapers carry articles on foreign affairs well in advance of official State Department bulletins arriving in Washington. Many Washington leaders have a television set in their office, and they can respond to crisis situations as they are reported by the networks, usually well in advance of bureaucratic messages. The problem, of course, is that the media "slant" may not be the same interpretation placed on events as that of the bureaucracy itself. By the time the bureaucracy can report to Washington, the media interpretation has become accepted "truth."

Third, the media permit both political leaders and high-ranking bureaucrats to test public response to possible courses of action. The **"trial balloon"** allows information to leak to the media regarding proposed policies or programs. A trial balloon is unofficial and usually does not even carry the name of the person who is releasing it. If reaction is generally favorable, the proposal can be formalized in a legislative request or executive order. If not, it can be forgotten or even denied by official sources.

Trial balloon:
A release of information to the media regarding new policies or program proposals, designed to test popular opinion.

Political leaders and high-ranking bureaucrats can also release information to the media in off-the-record "background" briefings. A **"backgrounder"** allows an official to speak freely with the understanding that the media may not identify the source. It is an informal agreement; if it is broken, officials can deny similar information in the future to reporters who violated confidentiality. Articles or broadcasts based on background briefings usually include qualifying phrases such as "high government sources say," "it has been reliably reported that," or "a high-ranking official disclosed. . . ." Government officials like the backgrounder because it allows them to suggest policies without openly identifying themselves. In foreign affairs, officials can even warn friendly or unfriendly nations about their behavior without causing the international turmoil that an official warning

Backgrounder:
A release of information by a government official to the media with the understanding that the media may not identify the source.

would cause. The media are not very enthusiastic about background interviews and other off-the-record comments. They like having access to news that they otherwise would not get, but they dislike being forced to agree not to disclose the source.

Leak: An unauthorized release of government information.

The **"leak"** is an unauthorized release of information. Many leaks embarrass political leaders and bureaucrats by exposing unfavorable information about agencies, upsetting delicate secret negotiations, or causing political harm by disclosing the secrets of other nations. The Pentagon Papers were a series of Defense Department memos stolen from classified (officially secret) files by Daniel Ellsberg and published by the *New York Times*. Leaks of Central Intelligence Agency information have greatly reduced the confidence placed in that agency by foreign governments and foreign intelligence sources. The effectiveness of the CIA itself has been hurt by leaks, and leaks of names of foreign operatives have been associated with their deaths.

But many "leaks" are "planted" by government officials themselves.

But many "leaks" are "planted" by government officials themselves. Officials are authorized to surreptitiously release information, hiding its source and pretending that the information is *un*authorized. Occasionally these leaks are planted when various factions within the executive branch are vying for power. For example, White House advisors who are feuding with cabinet secretaries may deliberately leak information that places their opponents in a bad light.

In summary, the bureaucracy tries to use the media to serve its own purposes, just as the media try to use the bureaucracy. The result is a continuous adversary relationship between government and the media.

Parts of the Pentagon Papers published by the *New York Times*.

The Presidential Press Secretary

A small bureaucracy has grown up around the relationship between the media and the president. The presidential press secretary has become a central figure in every recent presidential administration. The press secretary is usually a close confidant of the president—someone who meets daily with the president and with top White House and cabinet officials. (Pierre Salinger served as Kennedy's press secretary; Bill Moyers served Johnson; Ron Ziegler served Nixon; Jody Powell served Carter; and James Brady, who was gravely wounded in the 1981 assassination attempt, continues to serve Reagan on a part-time basis.

The office of the press secretary is responsible for daily *press releases*—information prepared by government officials and distributed to reporters. Generally, government officials hope that the media will print a release or read it to viewers just as it is written. But the media often rewrite these releases to emphasize what they consider to be important, to add further information, or to add drama or sensationalism. The press secretary usually holds daily *news briefings*—opportunities for the media to ask direct questions. The press secretary must be careful to correctly state the president's position. Occasionally press secretaries will acknowledge that they do not know the answer and will try to find it. The press secretary is also responsible for the presidential *news conference*—an appearance before television and newspaper reporters to reply to questions. Although the news conference appears to be a wide-open question-and-answer period, a well-prepared president will have rehearsed many of the answers. The staff prepares the president to expect certain questions and suggests answers. The president decides when to call press conferences and usually begins the conference with a brief statement that sets its tone.

The press secretary maintains the White House press room. Accredited television, newspaper, wire service, magazine, and radio reporters are allowed access to the press room. Other parts of the White House are open to them only by appointment.

Media Coverage of Three Mile Island

Government is expected to protect the public interest. Government officials try to relieve anxieties and calm the masses. But the media actively exploit public fears in order to dramatize and sensationalize news stories. "Disaster" stories are favorites of the media.

Perhaps the most influential media "disaster" coverage involved the Three Mile Island accident. In 1979, the nuclear power plant at Three Mile Island near Harrisburg, Pennsyl-

(continued)

(*continued*)

vania, malfunctioned; no substantial radiation escaped the power plant itself,* although large amounts of water inside the plant were contaminated. But for several days media coverage raised the specter of an imminent nuclear explosion, implying that Harrisburg might soon look like Hiroshima. Following the story line of a movie starring Jane Fonda, "The China Syndrome," the media predicted a "meltdown" of the reactor and the danger of radiation contamination to millions of persons on the East Coast. The Nuclear Regulatory Commission (NRC) and federal, state, and local disaster officials were portrayed as incompetent. The government tried unsuccessfully to dispel fears. President Carter walked around inside the plant with live television coverage. But the media implied a government cover-up of the "real" danger. No one

Former President Carter and Mrs. Carter hold a brief news conference after touring Three Mile Island Nuclear Plant.

was injured in the accident. Yet even today the media refer to Three Mile Island as a "disaster."

Nuclear industry officials observe that no one was hurt at Three Mile Island, that radiation was contained, and that despite errors by the operators, the reactor's safety system prevented a serious accident. Indeed, no one has ever died in over thirty years of operations of commercial and military (Navy surface ships' and submarines') reactors. In contrast, over a hundred coal miners are killed each year. But it is *public perception* of danger that counts, and the media shape public perception. One nuclear power official sensed the industry's dilemma shortly after the incident: "You can look at the problem in two ways. From a technical viewpoint, Three Mile Island is no problem. It sounds bad, but there was no major accident. From a political point of view, it's a disaster. And public perception determines the political view."

Three Mile Island was indeed a "disaster" for the nuclear power industry. Media coverage of the incident forced the NRC to stop issuing licenses for any of the various stages of nuclear plant construction. The previous twelve-year delays in nuclear plant licensing and construction increased. Electric utilities were forced to cancel their orders for new nuclear plants. The costs of licensing and ever-changing safety regulations brought the nuclear power industry to a virtual halt. This was true despite the fact that Presidents Carter and Reagan, as well as the Congress, continued to support the "nuclear option." The media themselves, and the regulatory commissions so easily intimidated by them, made a major energy policy decision for the nation.**

*The Nuclear Regulatory Commission reported that the average area resident received 0.9 millirems of radiation and that the maximum cumulative dose was 80 millirems. The current standard for safety is 500 millirems per year. See Congressional Quarterly *Weekly Report*, April 7, 1979, p. 626.
**Peter Sandman and Mary Paden, "At Three Mile Island," *Columbia Journalism Review*, July/August 1979, pp. 43–58.

The FCC: Watchdog or Lapdog of the Media?

The Federal Communications Commission (FCC) was created in 1934 to regulate certain aspects of radio and television. At that time radio stations decided for themselves what wavelengths and signal strengths to use. Stations would sometimes even jam one another's signals. The FCC is an independent regulatory commission composed of seven members appointed by the president and confirmed by the Senate. It was created as a "watchdog" agency to (1) grant licenses to use the public's airways, (2) limit monopoly in broadcasting, (3) require public-service broadcasting, and (4) guarantee fair treatment on the airways. But it is widely recognized that the FCC is a "sleeping lapdog" of the media rather than a "working watchdog."

The FCC has no regulatory authority over the networks whatsoever. It has authority only over individual broadcasting stations. Even if the FCC wanted to influence network broadcasting, it could do so only by threatening the licensing of individual stations that carry network programming. (Since ABC, CBS, and NBC own five television stations apiece, the FCC could theoretically influence the networks by reviewing the licenses of these stations.)

The FCC reviews station licenses every three years. Station ownership can be very profitable, so control over licenses is a potentially significant threat. However, over the years the power of the industry itself has been so great that license renewal is almost always guaranteed. Once a license has been granted, the owners can hold it indefinitely; they can even sell it to others with little government involvement.

To limit monopoly the FCC has a variety of rules to reduce concentration of ownership. No network can own more than five television stations. (Nonetheless, by strategially placing stations in heavy market areas such as New York, Chicago, and Los Angeles, the networks can directly reach almost one-third of American households.) No one individual or corporation can own both a newspaper and a television station in the same city. (This forced the *Washington Post* to arrange a transfer of control over Washington's WTOP to the *Detroit News* in exchange for a Detroit television station.) However, when the FCC tried to enforce these rules against existing license holders in 1969, the industry turned to Congress to curtail FCC authority. Congress responded, and now these rules apply primarily to new license seekers.

The Communications Act of 1934 requires that stations "serve the public interest, convenience, and necessity." Despite demands by various interest groups over the years that it limit sexually explicit material, curtail violence, or require balanced political broadcasting, the FCC has stuck by the industry's position that the commission should keep hands off the content of broadcasting. Whatever limits exist in the broadcasting of sex, violence, or politics, these limits are imposed by the networks and stations themselves, not by the FCC. When a minor presidential candidate, Barry Commoner, broadcast a campaign advertisement in 1980 featuring a voter yelling "Bullshit" into the microphone, the FCC made no comment, despite a flood of complaints. It was *not* the FCC that established a "family hour" for early-evening television broadcasting; instead, it was the networks themselves. Likewise, public complaints convinced the networks to reduce prime-time violence; the FCC has no authority to issue orders on this topic. The networks themselves, and not the FCC, decide about explicit sex, profanity, controversial social themes, and so on.

Despite demands by various interest groups, the FCC has stuck by the industry's position that the commission should keep hands off the content of broadcasting.

The only content regulation that the FCC enforces on licensed stations is the "5-5-10 rule." This rule requires local stations to reserve 5 percent of their programming for local affairs, 5 percent for news, and 10 percent for other nonentertainment programs. Most stations exceed these required percentages.

The National Association of Broadcasters (NAB) is the powerful Washington lobby of the networks and television and radio stations. The NAB has been successful in preventing Congress or the FCC from regulating the content of broadcasts, in part by establishing its own industry code. The code prohibits specific four-letter words, frontal nudity, and explicit sex in entertainment programming, although news, educational, or documentary programming is apparently exempt. There are no penalties for code violations. The code serves primarily to blunt demands by citizen groups for government intervention to establish and enforce standards.

The **"fairness doctrine"** originates from section 315 of the Communications Act of 1934. Under it, stations that permit a candidate for political office to campaign on the air must give an equal opportunity to all other candidates for the same office. (This means that networks or stations must offer the same number of spots, at the same time, for the same price, to all competing candidates; networks or stations do *not* have to give free time to any candidate unless they have done so for the candidate's competitors.) Moreover, broadcasters who air controversial issues of public importance must provide reasonable opportunities for the presentation of conflicting views.

Fairness doctrine: The requirement that networks or stations must give equal opportunity to all candidates for a political office.

The hole in the fairness doctrine is that news programs are exempt from it.

The hole in the fairness doctrine is that news programs are exempt from it. Network newscasts can give some candidates heavy coverage while ignoring others. Newscasts can cover one side of a controversial issue and never mention any alternative approaches. Even news "specials"—half-hour, hour, or two-hour examinations of an issue—are exempt from the fairness doctrine. Presidential press conferences and special addresses to the nation are generally considered news, and they are also exempt from the doctrine. Only an explicitly political speech by a president given during a campaign would be covered by the doctrine. Generally, in order to avoid the requirements of the doctrine, the media do not broadcast political speeches or controversial films that might require air time for opposing views.

The FCC itself does little to enforce the fairness doctrine. No station has ever lost its license because of the doctrine. Indeed, the FCC generally sides with the industry in defending it from accusations of bias in broadcasting. For example, in 1969 antismoking activists sued the FCC for failing to require television stations to counter all of the prosmoking ads placed by the tobacco companies. The FCC defended the industry, but it lost the case. The federal courts ordered the FCC to require anticigarette ads.[7] But the networks knew that it would be too costly to balance all of their tobacco ads. So they urged the FCC to ban all cigarette ads and therefore eliminate the need for counterads. The FCC obliged and ordered licensed stations to stop using the public airways to advertise cigarettes, because cigarettes were a health hazard. But actually the FCC was implementing the industry's desire to avoid balancing its cigarette ads.

CHAPTER SUMMARY

1. The federal bureaucracy is a powerful force in implementing the broad, "symbolic" policies and programs of the president and Congress. The bureaucracy's power rests on its expertise, or ability to master technical aspects of policy, and its own lobbying initiatives.

2. Bureaucracies at the three levels of government—federal, state, and local—employ one out of every six Americans. (Another 6 million to 10 million people work as consultants to the federal government.) On the federal level, key executive agencies include the Office of Management and Budget, the Council of Economic Advisers, the National Security Council, and the Department of Health and Human Services.

3. Independent regulatory agencies exercise controls over a wide range of activities in American society. Although commissioners are politically independent (they cannot be fired by the president during their term of office), they are frequently "captured" by the industry that they were supposed to regulate. Thus, the agency loses its overall ability to "independently regulate." The newer regulatory agencies are more immune to capture.

4. Presidents have *some* control over the federal bureaucracy, primarily through the powers of appointment, reorganization, and budget formulation. Likewise, Congress can pass laws that override bureaucratic regulations or raise or lower an agency's budget. Congress can also conduct public hearings over an agency's performance. Finally, the courts can rule on the legal "fairness" of an agency's action, but federal judges will usually not comment on the content of bureaucratic policy.

5. Complaints about "overregulation" center on increased costs, which are passed on to producer, consumer, and the whole society, as

opposed to potential benefits. Also, critics argue that overregulation retards both product innovation and free-spirited competition among small and large businesses alike. Proponents of deregulation stress the advantages of lessened federal interference in the free market.

6. The bureaucracy and the media have mutual needs, but they face a conflict over incompatible images and objectives. The media can set the agenda for bureaucratic activity, serve as an alternative source of information to government officials, and provide both bureaucrats and political leaders the means for testing public response through the use of "trial balloons."

7. The Federal Communications Commission is supposed to regulate radio and television broadcasting. However, the FCC has been charged with being a "lapdog" of the media—that is, subservient to the media's wishes in such areas as license renewal, broadcasting content, and enforcement of the fairness doctrine.

Notes

1. *Red tape* is derived from the seventeenth-century use of reddish tape by English courts to bind legal documents. Although it is true that "everyone hates red tape," the fact that it has been around for 300 years suggests that it is not likely to go away soon. See Herbert Kaufman, *Red Tape* (Washington, D. C.: Brookings Institution, 1977).
2. James Q. Wilson, "Social Science: The Public Disenchantment," *American Scholar,* Summer 1976, p. 358.
3. *Washington Post,* June 22, 1980, p. 1.
4. Bradley Cannon and Michael Giles, "Recurring Litigants: Federal Agencies before the Supreme Court," *Western Political Quarterly,* September 1972, pp. 183–191.
5. Office of the President, *A Program for Economic Recovery* (Washington, D. C.: U. S. Government Printing Office, 1981).
6. *A Program for Economic Recovery,* pp. 18–21.
7. *Banzhaf* v. *Federal Communications Commission,* 396 U. S. 842 (1969).

Close-Up and In-Depth Analyses

Hugh Heclo. *A Government of Strangers.* Washington, D. C.: Brookings Institution, 1977.

Stephen Hess. *The Washington Reporters.* Washington, D. C.: Brookings Institution, 1981.

Herbert Kaufman. *Are Government Organizations Immortal?* Washington, D. C.: Brookings Institution, 1976.

Charles E. Lindblom. *The Intelligence of Democracy.* New York: Free Press, 1965.

Francis E. Rourke. *Bureaucracy, Politics, and Public Policy,* 2nd ed. Boston: Little, Brown, 1976.

Aaron Wildavsky. *The Politics of the Budgetary Process,* 3rd ed. Boston: Little, Brown, 1979.

Aaron Wildavsky. *Speaking Truth to Power.* Boston: Little, Brown, 1979.

James Q. Wilson. *The Politics of Regulation.* New York: Basic Books, 1980.

THE COURTS AND CIVIL LIBERTIES

In 1835 the French statesman and traveler Alexis de Tocqueville wrote: "There is hardly a political question in the United States which does not sooner or later turn into a judicial one." His comment is even more appropriate today. The Supreme Court, rather than the president, Congress, or the states, has taken the lead in:

- Eliminating racial segregation and deciding about affirmative action.
- Ensuring separation of church and state and deciding about prayer in public schools.
- Determining the personal liberties of women and deciding about abortion.
- Defining the limits of free speech and the free press and defining obscenity, censorship, and pornography.
- Ensuring equality of representation and requiring legislative districts to be equal in population.
- Defining the rights of criminal defendants, preventing unlawful searches, limiting the questioning of suspects, and preventing physical or mental intimidation.
- Deciding about life or death and permitting capital punishment.

Today the federal courts decide not only sensitive political issues but also issues that were once handled by local officials, school boards, teachers, parents, churches, and private citizens. The United States is becoming an

Part of the facade
of the Supreme
Court building in
Washington, D.C.

"adversarial" society; everyone is suing everyone else about matters large and small. For example:

• A federal court found that the Fourteenth Amendment's "equal protection of the law" gave a young female plaintiff the right to play Little League baseball.
• A federal court found that an elementary school student who was not promoted to the next grade had been denied "due process of law," because the reasons for the failure had never been adequately explained.
• A California court found that the actor Lee Marvin would have to pay his former live-in girl friend money to help her readjust to a new life, a payment quickly dubbed "palimony."

These may be trivial examples of the extension of court power into sports, schools, and personal relationships. But the trend is toward increased judicial intervention in every aspect of American life.

Essentials: Structure of the Federal Court System

The federal court system consists of three levels of courts with general jurisdiction—the Supreme Court, the Court of Appeals, and the district courts—together with various special courts (see Figure 11-1). Only the Supreme Court is established by the Constitution itself, although the number of justices—traditionally nine—is determined by Congress. Article III authorizes Congress to establish "such inferior courts" as it deems appropriate. Congress has designed a hierarchical system that includes a U. S. Court of Appeals, divided into eleven circuits, and more than ninety district courts.

District courts. U. S. district courts are the *trial courts* of the federal system. Each state has at least one district court, and larger states have more. (New York, for example, has four.) There are over 500 federal district judges, appointed for life by the president and confirmed by the Senate. The president also appoints a U. S. marshal for each district court to carry out orders of the court and maintain order in the courtroom. District courts hear criminal cases prosecuted by the U. S. Department of Justice as well as civil cases. As trial courts, the district courts make use of both grand juries (called to hear evidence and, if warranted, to indict a defendant by bringing formal criminal charges) and

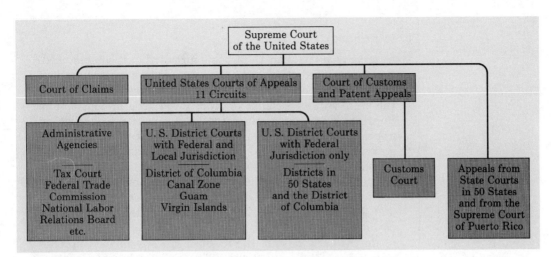

Figure 11-1. The U.S. court system. (Source: U.S. House of Representatives, Committee on the Judiciary, *The United States Courts: Their Jurisdiction and Work.* Washington, D.C.: Government Printing Office, 1969, p. 3.)

petit, or regular, juries (which determine guilt or innocence). The district courts may hear as many as 300,000 cases in a year.

Court of Appeals. The eleven circuit courts are *appellate courts.* They do not hold trials or accept new evidence but consider only the record of the trial courts and oral or written arguments (briefs) submitted by attorneys. Federal law provides that everyone has a right to appeal his or her case, so the Court of Appeals has little discretion in this regard. Appellate judges themselves estimate that over 80 percent of all appeals are "frivolous"—that is, are without any real basis.

There are more than 100 circuit judges, appointed for life by the president and confirmed by the Senate. Normally, these judges serve together on a panel to hear appeals. Over 90 percent of the cases decided by the Court of Appeals end at this level. Further appeal to the Supreme Court is not automatic; it must be approved by the Court itself. Hence, for most cases the decision of the circuit court is final.

Supreme Court. The Supreme Court of the United States is the final interpreter of all matters involving the Constitution and federal laws and treaties, whether the case began in a federal district court or in a state court. In some cases the Supreme Court has original jurisdiction (authority

(continued)

(continued)

to serve as a trial court), but this jurisdiction is seldom used. Appellate jurisdiction is the Supreme Court's major function. Appeals may come from a state court of last resort (usually the state supreme court) or from lower federal courts. The Supreme Court determines for itself whether to accept an appeal and consider a case. It may do so if there is a "substantial federal question" presented in the case or if there are "special and important reasons." Acceptance of an appeal can be granted by any four justices. However, most cases submitted to the Supreme Court, on *writs of certiorari,* are denied; and the court need not give any reason for denying appeal or certiorari.*

In the early days of the republic the size of the Supreme Court fluctuated, but since 1869 the membership has remained at nine: the chief justice and eight associate justices. The Supreme Court is in session each year from October through June, hearing oral arguments, accepting written briefs, conferring, and rendering opinions.

*The Court technically must hear writs of appeal. There are only a few matters that qualify; among them are those involving clear constitutional issues (for example, a finding that a federal law is unconstitutional, that a state law is in conflict with federal law, or that a state law is deemed a violation of the Constitution). Writs of certiorari are granted when four members agree that an issue involves a "substantial federal question."

JUDICIAL POWER AND SELF-RESTRAINT

The power of the courts stems from their authority to interpret the meaning of laws. The Constitution in Article III gives the Supreme Court (and other federal courts that Congress may establish) the "judicial power," which includes the power to interpret the meaning of laws. The Constitution itself is designated in Article VI as "the supreme law of the land." So federal courts may interpret the meaning of the Constitution itself, and the Constitution as the supreme law takes precedence over the laws of Congress or of state or local governments.

> Federal courts may interpret the meaning of the Constitution itself, and the Constitution as the supreme law takes precedence over the laws of Congress or of state or local governments.

Judicial review: The power of the federal courts to invalidate laws of Congress or of the states that the courts believe violate the Constitution.

Judicial Review

The power of **judicial review** enables federal courts to invalidate laws of Congress or of the states that the courts believe violate the

Constitution. Judicial review is not specifically mentioned in the Constitution. But it can easily be inferred from the language of that document. In *Marbury* v. *Madison* in 1803 (see Chapter 3), Chief Justice John Marshall led the Supreme Court in striking down a law of Congress as unconstitutional, arguing that:

1. The Constitution is the supreme law of the land, binding on all branches of the government—legislative, executive, and judicial.
2. The Constitution deliberately establishes a government with limited powers.
3. Consequently, "an act of the legislature, repugnant to the constitution, is void." If this were not true, then the government would be unlimited, and the Constitution would be an absurdity.
4. "It is emphatically the province and duty of the judicial department to say what the law is."
5. "So if a law be in opposition to the constitution . . . the court must determine which of these conflicting rules governs the case. This is of the very essence of judicial duty."
6. "If, then, the courts are to regard the Constitution, and the Constitution is superior to any ordinary act of the legislature, the Constitution, and not such ordinary act, must govern the case to which they both apply."
7. Hence, if a law is repugnant to the Constitution, when that law comes before a court, the judges are duty bound to declare that law void in order to uphold the supremacy of the Constitution.[1]

Since 1803 the federal courts have struck down more than eighty laws of Congress and uncounted state laws as "unconstitutional."

Judicial Activism

"The Constitution says what the Supreme Court says it says." This statement expresses the viewpoint of **judicial activism**; that is, the Supreme Court can shape the meaning of the Constitution to fit its own estimate of the needs of contemporary society. Numerous examples of judicial activism can be found:

- Federal courts have ordered state prisons to release large numbers of prisoners to reduce overcrowding, which is found to be cruel and unusual punishment.
- Federal judges have taken over the operation of city school systems to ensure that desegregation orders are carried out.
- Federal courts have told some states what kinds of care they must provide for the mentally ill.
- The U. S. Supreme Court has struck down a law requiring physi-

Judicial activism: The view that the Supreme Court can shape the meaning of the Constitution to fit its own estimate of the needs of contemporary society.

cians attending to minor children to inform the parents before performing an abortion.

- The U. S. Supreme Court has specified times during a pregnancy when a state may not interfere at all in a woman's decision to have an abortion.
- Federal courts have supervised state and local elections to ensure equality of representation.
- The U. S. Supreme Court has declared that prayer and Bible reading in the public schools as part of a daily opening ceremony violate the "no-establishment-of-religion" clause of the First Amendment.
- The U. S. Supreme Court has declared that criminal defendants must go free, regardless of evidence of guilt, if they were not fully informed of their rights to remain silent, to have an attorney, and to have free legal counsel if they cannot afford it themselves.

Judicial activism usually comes into play when courts give new interpretations to constitutional phrases, particularly general phrases such as "due process of law" (Fifth and Fourteenth Amendments), "equal protection of the laws" (Fourteenth Amendment), "establishment of religion" (First Amendment), and "cruel and unusual punishment" (Eighth Amendment).

Proponents of judicial activism argue as follows: The meaning of the Constitution must change over time if the Constitution is to remain relevant to society. The courts must recognize changes in society and reinterpret the Constitution to fit these changes. Society's changing views of what is "basically fair" must be recognized when interpreting general phrases such as "due process of law." If the courts did not shape constitutional meaning to fit society's changing needs, dozens of new constitutional amendments would be needed each generation. The strength of the Constitution lies in its flexibility.

Proponents of judicial activism argue that the strength of the Constitution lies in its flexibility.

Perhaps the best-known example of judicial activism is the famous case of *Brown* v. *Board of Education of Topeka* (1954). For many decades the U. S. Supreme Court had interpreted the phrase "equal protection of the laws" in the Fourteenth Amendment to allow state-enforced segregation of the races. In 1896 the Court ruled in *Plessy* v. *Ferguson* that separate railway accommodations for blacks and whites were "separate but equal." In the 1950s the National Association for the Advancement of Colored People (NAACP), led by its executive director, Roy Wilkins, and chief counsel, Thurgood Marshall, argued that "separate but equal" did not reflect the real conditions of segregation. They argued that laws *separating* the races created inequalities and that these laws violated the equal-protection-of-the-laws clause of the Fourteenth Amendment.

On May 17, 1954, the Supreme Court rendered its decision in *Brown*:

> Segregation of white and colored children in public schools has a detrimental effect upon the colored children. The impact is greater when it has the sanction of law, for the policy of separating the races is usually interpreted as denoting the inferiority of the Negro group. A form of inferiority affects the motivation of a child to learn. Segregation with the sanction of the law, therefore, has a tendency to retard the educational and mental development of Negro children and to deprive them of some of the benefits they would receive in a racially integrated school system....
> Whatever may have been the extent of psychological knowledge of the time of *Plessy* v. *Ferguson,* this finding is amply supported by modern authority. Any language in *Plessy* v. *Ferguson* contrary to this source is rejected.[2]

Thus, the Supreme Court recognized that the nineteenth-century doctrine of "separate but equal" did not apply in the second half of the twentieth century. The Court reinterpreted the meaning of the equal-protection clause of the Fourteenth Amendment. Although it would be many years before any significant number of black children would attend formerly segregated white schools, this decision by the nation's highest court contributed directly to the emergence of a strong civil rights movement.

Judicial Restraint

"The courts should interpret the laws, not make them.... I do not believe it is a function of the court to step in because times have changed or social mores have changed."[3] Justice Sandra O'Connor expressed these views during her Senate confirmation hearing. Her statement reflects the viewpoint of **judicial restraint**; that is, the Supreme Court should not read its own philosophies into the Constitution, and should avoid direct confrontations with Congress, the president, or the states whenever possible.

In defense of judicial self-restraint, it is argued that federal judges are not elected by the people and therefore should not substitute their own views for the views of elected representatives. Congress and the president also swear to uphold the Constitution, and federal courts should assume that these other branches of government are acting constitutionally unless the evidence is overwhelming that they

Judicial restraint: The view that the Supreme Court should not read its own philosophies into the Constitution and should avoid direct confrontations with Congress, the president, or the states whenever possible.

Justice Felix
Frankfurter.

are not. As Supreme Court Justice Felix Frankfurter once wrote: "The only check upon our own exercise of power is our own exercise of self-restraint. For the removal of unwise laws from the statute books, appeal lies not to the courts but to the ballot and to the processes of democratic government."[4] Excessive judicial activism encourages people to believe that federal courts, rather than Congress, the president, or state governments, should decide all important matters.

> In defense of judicial self-restraint, it is argued that federal judges are not elected by the people and therefore should not substitute their own views for the views of elected representatives.

Judicial activism sometimes leads to the belief that foolish laws and wrongheaded policies must be unconstitutional. This is not necessarily true. Congress or state legislatures may pass unwise laws that are nonetheless constitutional. We cannot depend on courts to reverse the errors of legislatures. Conversely, judicial restraint sometimes leads to the belief that, if a law is constitutional, it must be good. We should not confuse constitutionality with wisdom.

How does the Supreme Court exercise self-restraint?

1. The Court will not pass on the constitutionality of a law until it is presented in an actual case. The Court does not advise the president or Congress on the constitutionality of pending proposals.
2. The Court does not anticipate a question on constitutional law in advance of the necessity of deciding it. The Court does not decide hypothetical cases.
3. The Court does not decide a constitutional question if the case can be decided on some other ground.
4. The Court will not pass on the constitutionality of a law unless the complaining party shows that it has been injured by the law.
5. All possible remedies in state courts and federal courts must be exhausted before the Court accepts review.
6. If a law is held unconstitutional, the Court will confine this holding to the particular section of the law involved; the rest of the statute is unaffected by the holding.

Stare decisis: The policy of abiding by principles established in an earlier case.

Courts are also limited by the principle of **stare decisis,** which means that the issue has already been decided in an earlier case. This reliance on precedent is a fundamental notion in law. The underlying common law of England and the United States is composed simply of past cases. This foundation gives stability to the law. If every decision rested on new notions of fairness, then no one would know from day to day what the courts would decide; that is to say, no one would know what "the law" really was.

Supreme Court Justice Oliver Wendell Holmes once lectured a younger justice about the law: "Young man, about 75 years ago I learned that I was not God. And so, when the people . . . want to do something I can't find anything in the Constitution expressly forbidding them to do, I say, whether I like it or not, 'Goddamn it, let 'em do it.'"[5]

Essentials: Jurisdiction of the Federal Court System

In the American federal system, each of the fifty states maintains its own court. The federal courts are not necessarily superior to the state courts; state and federal courts operate independently. But since the U. S. Supreme Court has appellate jurisdiction over state supreme courts as well as lower federal courts, the Supreme Court oversees the nation's entire judicial system.

State courts have general jurisdiction in all criminal and civil cases. According to Article III of the Constitution, federal court jurisdiction extends to:

1. cases arising under the Constitution, federal laws, or treaties
2. cases involving ambassadors, public ministers or consuls, or maritime and admiralty laws
3. cases in which the U. S. government is a party
4. cases between two or more states
5. cases between a state and a citizen of another state
6. cases between citizens of different states
7. cases between a state or citizen and a foreign government or citizen of another nation

Obviously, it is not difficult "to make a federal case out of it," regardless of what "it" might be. There are many vaguely worded guarantees in the Constitution—"due process of law," "equal protection of the laws," "cruel and unusual punishment," "unreasonable searches and seizures," and so forth. These guarantees allow nearly every party to any case to con-

(continued)

(continued)

tend that a federal question is involved and that the case
should be heard in federal court.

The great bulk of cases begins and ends in the state court
systems, however. The federal courts do not interfere once a
case has been started in a state court, except in very rare
circumstances. And Congress has stipulated that legal disputes between citizens of different states must involve
$10,000 or more in order to be heard in federal court. More-
over, parties to cases in state courts must "exhaust their remedies"—that is, appeal their case all the way through the
state courts—before an appeal to the federal courts will be
heard. Appeals from state supreme courts go directly to the
U. S. Supreme Court and not to a federal district or circuit
court. Such appeals are usually made on the ground that a
federal question is involved in the case; that is, a question has
arisen regarding the application of the U. S. Constitution or
federal law. The U. S. Supreme Court reviews only a very
small fraction of all of the appeals from state court decisions.

Of the 10 million civil and criminal cases that are begun in
all of the nation's courts each year, only about 2 percent are
in the federal courts. About 5,000 will be appealed to the
U. S. Supreme Court each year, but the Court will only hear
about 200 of them. So the great bulk of legal cases is heard in
the state and local courts. The U. S. Constitution "reserves"
general police powers to the states. This means that crimes
and civil disputes are generally matters of state and local
concern. Murder, robbery, assault, and rape are normally
state offenses rather than federal crimes. Federal crimes generally center on offenses (1) that are against the U. S. government or its property; (2) that are against U. S. officials or
employees while they are on duty; (3) that involve crossing
state lines (such as nationally organized crime, unlawful escape across state lines, or taking kidnapping victims across
state lines); (4) that interfere with interstate commerce; and
(5) that occur in federal territories or on the seas.

Majority opinions of the Supreme Court are usually written by a single justice who summarizes majority sentiment.
Concurring opinions are written by justices who vote with the
majority but who feel that the majority opinion does not fully
explain their own reasons. A dissenting opinion is written by
a justice who is in the minority; such opinions have no impact
on the outcome of the case. Written opinions are printed,
distributed to the press, and published in *U. S. Reports* and
other legal reporting services.

THE MAKING OF FEDERAL JUDGES

Nomination

All federal judges, including Supreme Court justices, must be appointed by the president and confirmed by a majority of the Senate. The recruitment process that brings the name of potential appointees to the president's desk is highly political. Indeed, about 80 percent of federal judges have held political office.[6] Presidents almost always appoint members of their own party to the federal courts. Fewer than one-third of the nation's Supreme Court justices have had prior experience as judges. Very few of them have been promoted from lower federal courts. Political contacts and the support of the president are more important than judicial experience in securing a federal court appointment. The attorney general's office assists the president in screening candidates for all federal judgeships. This screening considers the candidates' record of political support for the president, their support of the senators from their own state, their experience in public service, the absence of scandal from their past, and their political philosophy.

> Political contacts and the support of the president are more important than judicial experience in securing a federal court appointment.

Confirmation

The Senate Judiciary Committee holds public hearings on all nominations by the president and then makes its recommendation to the full Senate before the final confirmation vote. Unless the committee discovers scandal in the nominee's background, the president's nomination will usually be approved, even by a Senate dominated by the opposition party. Over the years the prevailing view in the Senate has been that presidents deserve to appoint their own judges; that the opposition party will get its own opportunity to appoint judges when it wins the presidency; and that partisan bickering over judicial appointments should be avoided. But occasionally presidential/congressional cooperation breaks down. President Lyndon Johnson tried to appoint his confidant, the prominent Washington lawyer Abe Fortas, to be Chief Justice of the United States. Fortas was already an associate justice through an earlier Johnson appointment. But a coalition of liberal anti-Johnson Democrats and of Republicans complained of cronyism and blocked the nomination. Later when President Richard Nixon nominated two southern federal judges to the Supreme Court—Clement F. Haynsworth and G. Harold Carswell—Democratic majorities in the Senate blocked these appointments. Nixon complained that the Senate's refusal infringed on his constitutional authority to appoint judges; he had campaigned on the pledge to curb a liberal court. Later the Senate approved Nixon's nominations of Warren Burger, Harry Blackmun, Lewis Powell, and William Rehnquist.

Political Philosophy

Presidents try to nominate judges who share their political philosophy. But appointments are made for life. There is no way for a president to remove a judge, and judges can be impeached by Congress only for "high crimes and misdemeanors," not their decisions. So judges frequently become independent once they are appointed.

Presidents who have tried to appoint "liberals" or "conservatives" to the Supreme Court have sometimes been surprised by the decisions of their appointees. For example, Chief Justice Earl Warren, perhaps the most liberal and activist chief justice in the Court's history, was appointed by President Dwight Eisenhower, a Republican. Warren had no judicial experience, but as governor of California he had swung that state's delegation to Eisenhower in the Republican national convention. The grateful president rewarded him with the chief justiceship with no idea that Warren would lead the court into its most active era. Eisenhower complained later that the Warren appointment was "the biggest damn mistake I ever made."[7]

> Presidents who have tried to appoint "liberals" or "conservatives" to the Supreme Court have sometimes been surprised by the decisions of their appointees.

Social Background

Thurgood Marshall, the first black justice.

Most federal judges are recruited from well-educated, socially prominent, politically influential, financially secure, upper-class families. Over two-thirds of the justices who have served on the Supreme Court attended Ivy League or other prestigious law schools. No black had served on the Supreme Court until the appointment of Thurgood Marshall by Johnson in 1967. No woman had served on the Court until the appointment of O'Connor by Ronald Reagan in 1981. However, Jimmy Carter appointed more blacks and women to federal district and appellate courts than any other president. Nonetheless, we can still describe the typical federal judge as "white, generally Protestant . . . ; fifty to fifty-five years of age at the time of his appointment; Anglo-Saxon ethnic stock . . . ; high social status; reared in an urban environment; member of a civic-minded, politically active, economically comfortable family; legal training; some type of public office; generally well-educated."[8]

A Woman for the Supreme Court

For almost 200 years the U. S. Supreme Court had been the nation's most exclusive male club. After 101 male justices, Sandra O'Connor was named to the Supreme Court by President Reagan in 1981. She was confirmed by a unanimous Senate. Conservatives were pleased with her generally conservative views and her belief in judicial restraint, and liberals were pleased that a woman had been named to the high court.

Sandra Day O'Connor, the first woman justice and Chief Justice Warren Burger.

O'Connor had no previous experience as a federal court judge. But she had the active support of Barry Goldwater, her state's senior U. S. senator and a former Republican presidential candidate. More importantly, she was a "she." Reagan had pledged in his campaign to appoint a woman to the Supreme Court, and he was anxious to deflect criticism because of his opposition to the Equal Rights Amendment and his failure to pick very many women for his own administration. As one Reagan aide put it, "She is worth twenty-five assistant secretaries, maybe more!"

O'Connor grew up on her family's large Arizona ranch, graduated from Stanford University with honors, and then went on to Stanford Law School. She graduated near the top
(*continued*)

(continued)

of her class, together with another justice-to-be, William Rehnquist (who was first in that class). She entered Arizona Republican politics and was appointed to fill an unexpired term in the state senate. She went on to be elected twice to the senate and to become its majority leader. She left the senate in 1975 to become a Phoenix trial judge. In 1979 she was appointed to the Arizona Court of Appeals. Work on this intermediate court does not involve major constitutional questions.

Until her appointment to the U. S. Supreme Court, O'Connor was an obscure state court judge. Her service as Republican leader in the Arizona Senate qualified her as a moderately conservative party loyalist. It appears that her political and professional friendships had more to do with bringing her to the attention of Reagan than her record as a judge. She had known Rehnquist since her law school days, and she had known Chief Justice Warren Burger for many years. Moreover, Goldwater was her friend and mentor in Arizona politics. Thus, her name was passed up to Attorney General William French Smith and appeared on a very short list of conservative Republican women with some experience in public office and in the judiciary. Reagan himself interviewed her and later reassured conservatives in the Senate that O'Connor met his philosophical requirements. The appointment was widely acclaimed in the media and unanimously confirmed in the Senate.

WHEN IS A RIGHT A RIGHT?

As the federal government has expanded its role in economic and social life, Americans have come to expect "rights" that, whatever their moral justification, are not found anywhere in the U. S. Constitution. Majorities believe that they have the "right" to be protected from serious crime, to obtain effective teaching in school, to have consumer products certified as safe, to enjoy a steadily improving standard of living, to have an adequate retirement income adjusted annually for inflation, to be guaranteed a job, to have access to higher education, and to be guaranteed medical care (see Figure 11-2 on pages 384 and 385). None of these is a constitutional "right," even though the government tries to provide for them in laws. Over time legal privileges may become "rights" by implication. Is free public education a right? Most people would say it is, yet there is no mention of this "right" in the U. S. Constitution.

We need to understand the distinction between civil liberties, civil rights, and legal entitlements. *Civil liberties* are constitutional guarantees *against* governmental action. Civil liberties guarantee that we will not be subjected to arbitrary and capricious government action (see Table 11-1 for a listing of constitutional liberties). To enforce civil liberties, all that is required is that the government *not* do something. Since civil liberties are guaranteed in the Constitution, they may be claimed by individuals and minorities even against majority wishes. From a constitutional viewpoint, majorities cannot tamper with civil liberties.

Table 11-1. Liberties Guaranteed in the U. S. Constitution

Article I, Sections 8 and 10: Guarantee of habeas corpus; freedom from bills of attainder and ex post facto laws; no titles of nobility, and no laws (passed by states) impairing the obligation of contracts.

Article III, Sections 2 and 3: Right to trial by jury in federal criminal cases; restricted definition of treason.

Article IV, Section 2: Guarantee of interstate privileges and immunities for citizens of each state.

Article VI, Section 3: No religious test for public office.

First Amendment: Freedom of religion; no establishment of religion; freedom of speech and press; freedom of assembly and petition.

Second Amendment: Right to bear arms.

Third Amendment: No quartering of soldiers in private homes.

Fourth Amendment: No unreasonable searches and seizures.

Fifth Amendment: Right to federal grand jury in capital cases; freedom from self-incrimination; right to due process of law; freedom from seizure of property for public use without compensation.

Sixth Amendment: Right to fair trial procedures in federal courts.

Seventh Amendment: Right to trial by jury in federal courts.

Eighth Amendment: Prohibition of excessive bail or cruel or unusual punishment.

Ninth and Tenth Amendments: Definition of the principle of delegated powers and states' rights.

Thirteenth Amendment: Prohibition of slavery.

Fourteenth Amendment: States forbidden to abridge privileges or immunities of citizens, to deprive a person of life, liberty, or property without due process of law, or to deny any person the equal protection of the laws.

Fifteenth Amendment: Prohibition of denial of vote because of race, color, or previous condition of servitude.

Nineteenth Amendment: Prohibition of denial of vote because of sex.

Twenty-fourth Amendment: Prohibition of poll or other taxes in federal elections.

Twenty-sixth Amendment: Prohibition of denial to vote on the basis of age to persons at least eighteen years old.

Civil liberties are constitutional guarantees *against* governmental action. *Civil rights* require a more active government.

Civil rights require a more active government. They require that government prevent citizens, businesses, employers, schools, or other organizations in society from acting in an arbitrary or discriminatory manner. For example, the Civil Rights Act of 1964 prohibits private

Question: Most Americans believe that there are a number of economic, social, and political rights to which they as citizens are or should be legally or morally entitled. Differences in opinion arise in identifying just what these specific rights are (hand respondent shuffled pack of yellow cards). Here is a deck of cards which identify some of the specific things which have been debated as economic, social and political rights. Please sort them on this sorting board according to how entitled to these rights are people like yourself and your expectation of having them realized. You can put as many or as few cards in any box—there are not right or wrong answers, just your opinion that counts.

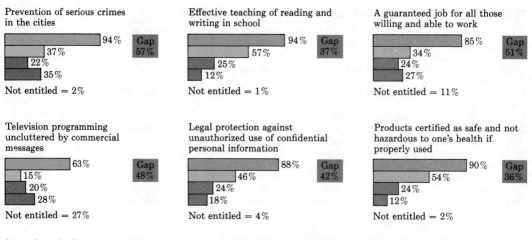

Entitled to have (Total of next three categories)
Have it now
Entitled to/expect to have in next 10 years
Entitled to/do not expect to have it in next 10 years

Prevention of serious crimes in the cities
94%
37%
22%
35%
Gap 57%
Not entitled = 2%

Effective teaching of reading and writing in school
94%
57%
25%
12%
Gap 37%
Not entitled = 1%

A guaranteed job for all those willing and able to work
85%
34%
24%
27%
Gap 51%
Not entitled = 11%

Television programming uncluttered by commercial messages
63%
15%
20%
28%
Gap 48%
Not entitled = 27%

Legal protection against unauthorized use of confidential personal information
88%
46%
24%
18%
Gap 42%
Not entitled = 4%

Products certified as safe and not hazardous to one's health if properly used
90%
54%
24%
12%
Gap 36%
Not entitled = 2%

Source: Survey by Opinion Research Corporation, General Public Caravan, for the Public Society of America, July 1979.

Figure 11-2. The philosophy of entitlement and the gap between what people feel a right to and what they feel they have. (From *Public Opinion,* April/May 1981.)

businesses that offer to serve the public from discriminating on the basis of race, and it prohibits employers from discriminating in hiring and promotion on the basis of race or sex. Majority support is usually required to get Congress and the president to pass civil rights laws, which extend the protections of individuals and minorities.

Legal entitlements are simply laws that provide government benefits to all those who meet certain requirements. Social Security is an "entitlement" program, because people who retire at age 62 are legally entitled to its benefits. Those who meet the eligibility requirements for welfare, Medicaid, or food stamps are also "entitled" to receive them. Sometimes it is argued that entitlement programs should not be changed, because there is an implied contract between the government and the people regarding their benefits. But Congress and the president frequently alter entitlement programs anyhow. There is no *constitutional* right to Social Security, welfare, or food stamps. These are merely benefits that Congress extends by law.

Legal entitlements: Laws that provide benefits to all those who meet certain requirements.

Adequate housing within each person's means

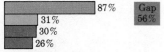

89%
36%
28%
25%

Gap
53%

Not entitled = 6%

Steadily improving standard of living

88%
39%
30%
19%

Gap
49%

Not entitled = 6%

Gradual reduction of work week to four days

52%
8%
26%
18%

Gap
44%

Not entitled = 36%

Adequate retirement income adjusted annually for inflation

87%
31%
30%
26%

Gap
56%

Not entitled = 6%

Honest and reliable reporting by the news media

90%
51%
19%
20%

Gap
39%

Not entitled = 2%

Being able to buy as much gas as one wants

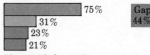

75%
31%
23%
21%

Gap
44%

Not entitled = 17%

Graduate or professional schooling free to all who qualify

59%
18%
19%
22%

Gap
41%

Not entitled = 33%

Free doctor and hospital care for everyone

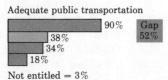

55%
16%
20%
19%

Gap
39%

Not entitled = 40%

Use of professional services, such as lawyers in public clinics

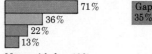

71%
36%
22%
13%

Gap
35%

Not entitled = 18%

Free dental care for everyone

53%
13%
19%
21%

Gap
40%

Not entitled = 40%

Adequate public transportation

90%
38%
34%
18%

Gap
52%

Not entitled = 3%

Right to use drugs for pleasure

15%
3%
6%
6%

Gap
12%

Not entitled = 75%

The listing in Table 11-1 of the constitutional provisions dealing with civil liberties indicates that the *constitutional* guarantees of individual rights are almost exclusively guarantees against encroachment by governments or public officials.

FREEDOM OF SPEECH

The First Amendment of the Constitution states that "Congress shall make no law . . . abridging the freedom of speech." This clause seems clear and unequivocal. According to the "absolutist" interpretation (championed by the late Justice William Douglas), "no law" means *no law.* The potential threat of public disorder or personal damage, according to this view, is less serious than the necessity of preserving this most fundamental freedom. Accordingly, those who agree with this absolutist position (as, for example, the American Civil Liberties

Union), believe that anyone can say anything anywhere. However, this interpretation is not widely shared.

Congress and the courts have imposed substantial restrictions on freedom of speech. Public-opinion polls reveal that most people do *not* want freedom of speech to mean absolute freedom. Most people are likely to favor restricting certain kinds of speech, based largely on their opposition to the ideas expressed.

Virtually nobody objects to the principle of freedom of speech, but quite a few object to its application in specific circumstances.

Most people are unable to make the connection between the abstract notion of freedom of speech and the application of the principle to a specific case. Virtually nobody objects to the principle of freedom of speech, but quite a few object to its application in specific circumstances. Suppose a person wished to express unpopular ideas about communism, racism, homosexuality, or atheism. Roughly one-third of the public would not allow such ideas to be expressed in their community. (See the box "Tolerance Does Not Extend to Teaching.") Clear majorities would not allow communists, racists, or atheists to hold teaching positions. Tolerance of unpopular ideas is directly related to education. The majority of college graduates would let people who hold controversial beliefs teach, petition, demonstrate, or speak.

Speech does not only mean talking. Some of the most controversial judicial decisions deal with demonstrations. Demonstrations actually involve both freedom of speech and freedom of assembly—the First Amendment right of the people "peaceably to assemble and to petition the government for a redress of grievances." Although demonstrations may be harmless, the negative connotations are clear. Public opinion is more tolerant of the right of the people with strange or unpopular ideas to speak than of their right to engage in demonstrations. For example, a majority would tolerate a petition circulated in favor of legalizing marijuana, but only about 40 percent would support the right of marijuana advocates to demonstrate.

Clear and Present Danger

Courts are frequently required to rule on freedom-of-speech cases, whether the speech be literal or, as it has come to be known, "symbolic." The Supreme Court tries to balance the gains in freedom to the community of unlimited speech against the costs. The Court has generally adhered to the idea of limiting speech when a "clear and present danger" can be established. Justice Holmes, who formulated the principle, explained that the key to judgement about freedom of speech is the *circumstances* of the speech. Holmes believed that

Tolerance Does Not Extend to Teaching

How far are Americans prepared to go in tolerating speeches or writings by "people whose ideas are considered bad or dangerous"? Over the years, public-opinion polls have shown an increase in the percentage of Americans who are prepared to allow atheists, communists, racists, and homosexuals to speak and write. However, most Americans are not willing to allow these people "to teach in a college or ministry."

The figures below show the attitudes of the American public toward (1) atheists, (2) communists, (3) racists, and (4) homosexuals in terms of willingness to allow them to "make a speech in your community," to allow their books in "your public library," and to permit them "to teach in a college or university."

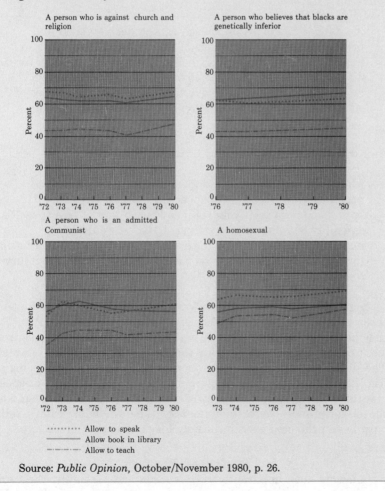

Source: *Public Opinion,* October/November 1980, p. 26.

speech can be curtailed when words are "used in such circumstances and are of such a nature as to create a clear and present danger that they will bring about the substantive evils that Congress has a right to prevent." But what is a "clear and present danger?" What is "clear," what is "present," and how "dangerous" must it be? Holmes provided only one example: "The most stringent protection of free speech would not protect a man in falsely shouting fire in a theater and causing panic."[9]

Although Holmes first used the phrase "clear and present danger," it was Justice Louis D. Brandeis who developed the doctrine in the 1930s into a valuable constitutional principle that the Supreme Court came to adopt. Brandeis explained that the doctrine involves two elements: the clearness or seriousness of the expression and the immediacy of the danger flowing from the speech. With regard to immediacy he wrote:

> No danger flowing from speech can be deemed clear and present, unless the incidence of the evil apprehended is so imminent that it may befall before there is opportunity for full discussion. If there be time to expose through discussion the falsehood and fallacies, to avert the evil by the processes of education, the remedy to be applied is more speech, not enforced silence.

And with regard to seriousness he wrote:

> Moreover, even imminent danger cannot justify resort to prohibition [of freedom of speech] . . . unless the evil apprehended is relatively serious. Prohibition of free speech and assembly is a measure so stringent that it would be inappropriate as a means for averting a relatively trivial harm to society. . . . There must be the probability of serious injury to the State.[10]

Symbolic speech also has its limits. The courts have ruled against those who burned their draft cards to protest the Vietnam War,[11] but they have ruled in favor of those who protested by discourteous treatment of the flag (such as wearing the flag on the seat of their pants).[12] The distinction between destruction of draft cards and defacing the flag illustrates the case-by-case disposition of freedom-of-speech questions. In some cases the courts have allowed speech even when the circumstances were inflammatory. The Ku Klux Klan's rallies have been protected even in heavily black or Jewish areas.

Preferred Position

By allowing such apparently risky speech and assembly, the courts are placing First Amendment freedoms in a preferred position.[13] Un-

Confrontation between the American Nazi Party and an anti-racism group tests the First Amendment of the Constitution.

less some equivalent of shouting fire in a crowded theater can be demonstrated, the only way to know if a speech or demonstration will lead to danger is to see if it does. If so, those who commit illegal acts, including those who incited them, can be prosecuted under criminal statutes. In freedom-of-speech cases, the burden of proof is on the government officials who wish to halt speech.

Liberty—for Popular People

Most Americans agree with the general principles of freedom of speech, freedom of press, freedom of religion, and the right to assemble and petition the government. But what if we asked Americans to apply these principles to specific groups— groups that they dislike?

The National Opinion Research Center at the University of Chicago asked members of a representative sample of the American public first to identify the group they liked the least from those in the following list:

Socialists
Communists
Fascists
Ku Klux Klan
John Birch Society
Black Panthers
Symbionese Liberation Army
Atheists
Proabortionists
Antiabortionists

It turned out that Communists and the Ku Klux Klan were the two least-liked groups. Everyone was then asked several

(continued)

(continued)

questions about the liberties or restrictions they would allow or impose for their *own* least-liked group; the accompanying table shows the results.

Liberties for Least-Liked Group

	Percent tolerant toward least-liked members of society
The _____ should be banned from being president of the U. S.	16%
Members of the _____ should be allowed to teach in public schools.	19%
The _____ should be outlawed.	29%
Members of the _____ should be allowed to make a speech in this city.	50%
Members of the _____ should not have their phones tapped by our government.	59%
The _____ should be allowed to hold public rallies in our city.	34%

Note that very few Americans would allow members of their least-liked group to become president. And very few would allow members of the disliked group to teach in school. Only about one-third would permit them to hold rallies in their city, and 29 percent would like to "outlaw" them. However, about half of all Americans would permit them to speak, and 59 percent would not want the government to tap their phones.

The lesson is that many Americans say they believe in the general principles of the First Amendment, but they are willing to deny these liberties to groups they dislike.

Source: John L. Sullivan, James Pierson, and Gregory E. Marcus, "An Alternative Conceptualization of Political Tolerance," *American Political Science Review*, September 1979, pp. 781–794. Used by permission.

FREEDOM OF THE PRESS

Freedom of the press, included in the same phrase of the Constitution that establishes freedom of speech, is just as controversial. The drafters of the Bill of Rights agreed with Thomas Jefferson that an open and critical press is essential to the proper functioning of a democracy: In the "marketplace of ideas," the media should be as free to write what they wish as individuals are to say what they wish. Who is to judge the merits of an idea unless the idea can be subject to free and open discussion? Although presidents may bristle when confronted with a hostile press, no one has seriously suggested that criticism of the government can be restricted.

No Prior Restraint

The courts are reluctant to impose **prior restraint** on speech and the press. Prior restraint refers to government actions to halt a speech or publication before it is uttered or published.

Prior restraint: Government actions to halt a speech or publication before it is uttered or published.

Opposition to prior restraint motivated the Supreme Court to rule against the federal government and in favor of the *New York Times* in the famous case of the Pentagon Papers.[14] The *New York Times* and the *Washington Post* had sought to publish a history of U.S. policymaking on Vietnam, based on secret information stolen from the files of the State Department and Defense Department. No one disputed the fact that stealing the secret material was illegal. What was at issue was the ability of the government to prevent publication. The documents revealed a history of lies and deception; and the war was still in progress. But what harm would occur if the papers were published? The government might be embarrassed, but would prior restraint be justifiable on the ground of national security? In seeking to block publication, the government offered national security as a legitimate reason, even though it conceded that no apparent disruption of its prosecution of the war would result. The Court was not impressed, and it allowed publication.

An even more sensational example was the effort by the *Progressive* magazine to publish detailed instructions on the manufacturing of nuclear weapons.[15] In this case the *Progressive* had no illegal access to classified documents. Indeed, one of the points of the article was that anyone could make a nuclear bomb from readily available public sources. This time the government's case was not based on the probability that publication would damage a war effort. Rather, it argued that easy access to such information would lead to such destruction that the First Amendment's freedoms would be eliminated—in other words, "You can't speak freely if you're dead." Lower courts responded sympathetically to the government's case and ruled that the information could not be published. However, the *Progressive* published the forbidden information in the form of a letter to the editor, and the government dropped its case on the grounds that it was too late. Ultimately, the original article appeared.

Television and Freedom of the Press

All media are not equal. Newspapers, magazines, and books enjoy substantially more protection from government interference than do television and radio. The authors of the Bill of Rights obviously were thinking of the printed word, and the courts have followed this tradition.

Newspapers, magazines, and books enjoy substantially more protection from government interference than do television and radio.

Radio and television are licensed by an agency of the federal government, the Federal Communications Commission. Why is there no comparable agency to license newspapers and magazines? The most frequently argued reason is that, without regulation, air-space (which, unlike newspaper space, is limited) would be overcrowded. This argument is not really accurate, especially with the development of cable systems and satellites. Nevertheless, regulation of broadcasting does exist, and this means that television and radio are supposed to conform to standards of "fairness." A newspaper can be as biased as it wishes. It can publish only conservative or only liberal views on its editorial page, and it can see that its reporters write articles with the ideological bias of the paper as their guide. But in 1969 the Supreme Court rejected the argument that similar freedoms ought to apply to radio and television.[16] Thus, local television and radio stations frequently offer free air time to those who dissent from their editorial positions. Generally, such positions are far less forthright than those of newspapers. Major networks rarely editorialize. The *New York Times* may endorse presidential candidates, but CBS does not.

Obscenity

The Supreme Court has ruled that no one has a constitutional right to speak or print obscenities under the First Amendment, but it is difficult to decide what is "obscene."

The courts apply a more severe obscenity standard to radio and television than to printed matter. Courts have argued that television is so pervasive that there is less freedom for the individual to reject it.[17] Moreover, television intrudes into the privacy of one's home. With much the same logic, laws against obscene telephone calls have also been upheld.

The question of obscenity, whatever the medium of expression, is troublesome to local and state policymakers and to the courts. Obscenity is not a freedom protected by the Bill of Rights.[18] However, the Supreme Court has floundered badly on the definition of obscenity. Justice Potter Stewart once admitted that he could not define "hard-core" pornography, "but I know it when I see it."[19] Many states ban the publication, sale, or possession of "obscene" materials, and Congress bans their shipment in the mails. But neither state nor federal law really defines obscenity, except in such terms as lewd, lascivious, filthy, indecent, and disgusting—all as vague as *obscene*. Since obscene material is not "speech," it can be banned without even an attempt to prove that it would result in a clear and present danger

An adult bookstore in Los Angeles (left) and an anti-censorship demonstration in New York City.

to society, the test that is used to adjudge the legitimacy of speech. In order to ban obscene utterances, one needs only to prove that the utterances are "obscene."

The Supreme Court has made several attempts to define obscenity.[20] It ruled, first of all, that obscenity must be determined in relation to "the average person, applying contemporary community standards" rather than in relation to particulary susceptible people. It added that the material must be considered "as a whole"; a whole book cannot be judged obscene if only a few passages are obscene. Moreover, the Court stated that it was willing to balance obscenity in material with a consideration of the material's social or literary merit. The Court defined obscenity itself as "appealing to a prurient interest—that is, a shameful or morbid interest in sex." The Court made it clear that "sex and obscenity are not synonymous.... The portrayal of sex ... in art, literature, and scientific works is not itself sufficient reason to deny material the constitutional protection of freedom of speech and press."[21] Finally, in overturning a ban on the novel *Fanny Hill,* the Court ruled that a publication cannot be proscribed unless it is "utterly without redeeming social value."[22]

> Obscenity is not a freedom protected by the Bill of Rights. However, the Supreme Court has floundered badly on the definition of obscenity.

Yet the question remains: what is obscene? Using the Court's definition, can you locate an "average" person? Can you tell what "contemporary community standards" are? Assuming that you can do both, would you trust such a person and such standards to judge whether there is any "social or literary merit" to the material? Even more difficult is discovering what people's "prurient interests" are. A related question involves what is wrong with appealing to prurient interests. Pornography may be a harmless outlet for inadequate sexual performance. If a married couple are "turned on" by watching a pornographic movie and improve their sex life, thus avoiding a divorce, is this not in the public interest?

There is, on the other hand, some wisdom in the point the Court was reaching for. In attempting to decentralize the issue, the Court was acknowledging that communities do differ substantially. There is no reason for residents of sophisticated urban communities to abide by the morality of the Bible Belt.

It should be noted that, even if communities attempt to apply the standards as set forth by the Supreme Court, there is no assumption that they will succeed. Albany, Georgia, could not prevent the showing of the film *Carnal Knowledge*,[23] nor could Chattanooga, Tennessee, ban *Hair*.[24] It is still true, however, that communities may be able to ban hard-core pornography if they can abide by the standards of the Court.

Obviously, the issue is a difficult one. We should not assume that censorship efforts are always initiated by prudes and preachers. The feminist movement has campaigned against pornography on the grounds that it degrades women and encourages rape. It argues that pornography is, in effect, a "clear and present danger" to women. (Similarly, black organizations have sought to prevent speeches by those who argue that blacks are genetically inferior to whites; they argue that acceptance of such views would lead to unequal treatment, or a denial of "equal protection of the laws.") Liberties and rights may be in conflict, and the solutions are rarely clear cut.

Libel and Slander

Libel and slander: Communications that wrongly subject a person to public ridicule or damage his or her reputation.

A more generally understood limitation of freedom of speech is the prohibition of **libel** (written) or **slander** (oral). These terms define a communication that wrongly subjects a person to public ridicule or damages his or her reputation. Generally, the injured party must demonstrate actual damage. It is a good rule of thumb that, if you knowingly lie about a person in public, you can be sued successfully. If you allege that your professor has plagiarized a book for his lectures, you can be sued. Of course, truth is a defense in any libel or slander suit. If your professor *has* plagiarized and you can prove it, then no civil or criminal penalties will apply to you. But if he has not, then freedom of speech and press cannot protect you from a lawsuit.

Libel against public officials is difficult to prove. If all newspapers, magazines, television stations, and radio stations could comment on behavior of public officials only if they were completely accurate in their remarks, there would be very little debate. The media are notoriously inaccurate, sometimes by design but mostly by carelessness. Journalists strive desperately for big stories; the print and television media live by sensationalism.

> The media can print or say anything they wish about public figures, whether it is true or not, so long as the media can claim an "absence of malice."

The Supreme Court in a landmark case, *New York Times* v. *Sullivan*,[25] set forth clear limits to libel actions by public officials. In this case the *New York Times* had run an advertisement critical of the behavior of public officials in Montgomery, Alabama, toward blacks. The advertisement contained demonstrable inaccuracies. The public officials sued the *New York Times* in Alabama, and the commissioner of police was awarded $500,000. The award was set aside on appeal. The Supreme Court ruled that inaccurate statements had to be made with "malicious intent" and with "reckless disregard of the truth." In other words, to win a libel suit a public official must prove that the journalist *knew* the information to be false but published it anyway with the intention of damaging the reputation of the official. The media can print or say anything they wish about public figures, whether it is true or not, so long as the media can claim an "absence of malice."

Truth versus Freedom of the Press

In the new media age these decisions regarding libel are very important. We are accustomed to sensational publications such as the *National Enquirer* playing fast and loose with the truth. The entertainer Carol Burnett's libel action against the *Enquirer* revealed that its reporters were far more concerned with the creation of an arresting story than with an accurate portrayal of reality. However, more-respected newspapers differ from the *Enquirer* only in degree. The "new journalism" creates "scenes" thematically. Some reporters personalize events by a variety of methods. Quotations may be created and attributed to sources as if they were real, when in fact they were never said. The composite behavior of many individuals may be assigned to a single person. (The *Washington Post*'s description of "Jimmy," a black, eight-year-old heroin addict, lead the reader to conclude that Jimmy was real, when in fact there was no such person. The *Washington Post* was embarrassed by the exposure of the false story and returned the Pulitzer Prize that the article had won.)

Television documentaries and news shows practice the art of the "new journalism" regularly. Television coverage of the hostage crisis in Iran showed violent demonstrations. The demonstrations started when the cameras began to roll and stopped when the cameras stopped.[26] The demonstrators were performers. A television portrayal of malnutrition among southern black children showed videotapes of children who were not, in fact, undernourished. Reporters were accused of urging urban rioters to throw stones for the benefit of television crews.

Restaging of events is not uncommon, and "spontaneous" interviews are frequently rehearsed off camera. Editors shorten, rearrange, and edit quotations. The order of quotations is altered to place the most dramatic questions and answers at the beginning of the story rather than in the order in which they occurred. Obviously, the "new journalism" is vulnerable to libel suits, because it seeks to tell a story in a convincing and appealing fashion rather than to describe events objectively.

Protecting News Sources

The new "investigative journalism" flourishes when sources of news are concealed. However, protection of sources makes it impossible to check the accuracy of the stories. Reporters argue that freedom of the press implies that the relationships between reporters and their sources should be confidential. Information provided by sources on the basis of confidentiality is presumed to be vital to the construction of a story; if the source were revealed, perhaps the information would be withheld from the public. However, the courts have not viewed confidential relationships between reporters and their sources as protected by the Constitution.[27] Courts have required reporters to reveal their sources or face jail sentences for obstructing justice. However, many states have enacted "shield laws" to preserve confidential relationships.

Media coverage of criminal trials is expanding, although this coverage sometimes conflicts with the Sixth Amendment guarantee of a fair jury trial. The federal Freedom of Information Act and subsequent amendments have reduced the ability of federal agencies to conceal unflattering information. Yet, as is the case with freedom of speech, freedom of the press is not absolute; it must be balanced against competing demands.

FREEDOM OF RELIGION

Perhaps the least understood provisions in the First Amendment involve freedom of religion: "Congress shall make no law respecting an establishment of religion, or prohibiting the free exercise thereof." These words are the first guarantees of the Bill of Rights, which is hardly surprising in view of the fact that early immigrants to the country were fleeing religious persecution.

Two provisions in the First Amendment deal with religion; that is, two separate prohibitions are placed on Congress (and, through the Fourteenth Amendment, on the states) regarding religion. The first is that there shall be "no law respecting an establishment of religion," and the second is that there shall be no law "prohibiting the free exercise" of religion.

The **"free-exercise" clause,** which prohibits government from interfering with or restricting religious practices, has caused comparatively little controversy or conflict. Although the wording of the First Amendment is absolute, religious freedom has never been so absolute that government could not restrict antisocial conduct carried on in the name of religion. For example, religious practices that involve human sacrifices, ritual murders, or other criminal behavior can be restricted, as can religious practices that violate public health, safety, or morals.[28]

Free-exercise clause: The Constitutional prohibition of government interference with, or restriction of, religious practices.

The **"establishment" clause,** on the other hand, has been the center of political conflict for many years. A "wall-of-separation" doctrine holds that the Constitution forbids governments to aid, encourage, support, or recognize any or all religious activities. A less stringent "no-preference" doctrine holds that government can recognize, aid, and encourage religious activities, provided that no preference is shown to any particular creed.

Establishment clause: The Constitutional prohibition of a state-established religion.

Years ago, Justice Hugo Black, speaking for the Court majority, gave the following version of the wall-of-separation doctrine:

> Neither a state nor the Federal Government can set up a church. Neither can pass laws that aid one religion, aid all religions, or prefer one religion over another.... No tax in any amount, large or small, can be levied to support any religious activities or institutions, whatever they may be called, or whatever form they may adopt to teach or practice religion. In the words of Jefferson, the clause against establishment of religion by law was intended to erect "a wall of separation between Church and State."[29]

But later, Justice Douglas countered this view:

> The First Amendment ... does not say that in every and all respects there shall be a separation of Church and State.... We

are a religious people whose institutions presuppose a Supreme Being.... When the state encourages religious instruction or cooperates with religious authorities by adjusting the schedule of public events to sectarian needs, it follows the best of our traditions.[30]

In recent years the Supreme Court has tended to support the wall-of-separation doctrine with regard to strictly religious practices. In its celebrated school-prayer decisions, the court ruled that the establishment of a religious ceremony at the beginning of each day in public schools violates the establishment clause. In the words of the Court:

> The respondent Board of Education of Union Free School District No. 9, New Hyde Park, New York, acting in its official capacity under state law, directed the School District's principal to cause the following prayer to be said aloud by each class in the presence of a teacher at the beginning of each school day: "Almighty God, we acknowledge our dependence upon Thee, and we beg Thy blessings upon us, our parents, our teachers and our country."
> ... there can, of course, be no doubt that New York's program of daily classroom invocation of God's blessings as prescribed in the Regent's prayer is a religious activity. Neither the fact that the prayer may be denominationally neutral, nor the fact that its observance on the part of the students is voluntary can serve to free it from the limitations of the Establishment Clause, as it might from the Free Exercise Clause, of the First Amendment, both of which are operative against the States by virtue of the Fourteenth Amendment.... The Establishment Clause, unlike the Free Exercise Clause, does not depend upon any showing of direct governmental compulsion and is violated by the enactment of laws which establish an official religion whether those laws operate directly to coerce non-observing individuals or not."[31]

The nation's response to the Court's decision was interesting and instructive. Even though several major religious groups supported the Court's ruling, many outraged citizens castigated the justices for "taking God out of the schools." Some advocated a constitutional amendment repealing the establishment clause, but the most common response was one of open and successful defiance of Court policy. Throughout the nation many governors and state and local school administrators declared that they would continue some type of daily religious exercise in the schools; and it seems certain that many public school systems have indeed continued this practice. Others have conformed merely to the "letter" of the ruling by substituting moments of silence for the classroom prayer. Since it is extremely unlikely that the president will send federal agents or soldiers into the nation's classrooms (the judiciary must always depend on other arms of government for enforcement of its decisions) the Court's opinion may be ignored in many communities.

The Supreme court did not "throw the Bible out of the schools"; it expressly stated that the Bible could be studied in the same fashion as other literature. But the Court objected to Bible reading as part of a devotional ceremony.[32] There are some other conspicuous gaps in the wall of separation between church and state in America. Coins bear the inscription "In God we trust"; a chaplain convenes sessions of the Senate; the pledge of allegiance to the flag contains a reference to God; and combat units of the United States armed forces are accompanied by tax-paid chaplains.

Federal Funds for Church Schools

Although it may appear initially that *any* public financing of church schools violates the establishment clause, there is some constitutional precedent for supporting public funding of private religious education. State programs for tax credits or tuition reimbursement have been ruled unconstitutional.[33] However, other forms of *indirect* public support have not: transportation to parochial schools by public agencies does not violate the establishment clause,[34] and states may give nonreligious textbooks to church schools.[35] However, *direct* aid from states to church schools to build buildings and hire teachers has been ruled an "excessive entanglement" of church and state.[36] But if the state aid is for religiously affiliated colleges or universities (as opposed to high schools and elementary schools), the Court has even been willing to tolerate general aid to religious schools (but not to the religious portions of the curriculum).[37] The justification for allowing the wall of separation to be breached in colleges and universities, but not in high schools or elementary schools, is that the intellectual freedom of colleges is substantially greater than that of high schools.

THE RIGHT TO PRIVACY

Justice Brandeis once wrote that "the right to be left alone" is "the right most valued by civilized men."[38] The Supreme Court first expressed the right to privacy in 1965.[39] The executive director of Planned Parenthood and a physician were convicted of violating a Connecticut law prohibiting the dispensation of contraceptives or medical advice about their use. The Supreme Court held the state law unconstitutional. Writing for the Court, Justice Douglas did not refer to any specific language in the Constitution but rather to general values derived from his reading of the Bill of Rights as a whole. "Various guarantees create zones of privacy," he wrote. The contraceptive devices and information given by the physician to the patient were included under this general "right of privacy."

The most important decision involving the right to privacy was the Supreme Court's controversial decision that women have a constitutional right to abortions. In *Roe* v. *Wade* in 1973, the Court ruled that the "right to privacy" that is implied by the guarantee of "liberty" in the Fifth and Fourteenth amendments includes a woman's decision to terminate her pregnancy.[40] Since 1973 the Court has consistently withstood challenges to its original decision. However, the liberty to terminate a pregnancy does not mean the right to have an abortion at government expense. Consequently, opponents of abortion have worked on two fronts: they have lobbied unsuccessfully for a new constitutional amendment prohibiting abortion; and they have lobbied successfully for the "Hyde Amendment" to halt the use of federal funds for abortions. The Supreme Court upheld the Hyde Amendment, making a distinction between the right to abort a pregnancy and the obligation of government to use public funds to support a private decision.

> The most important decision involving the right to privacy was the Supreme Court's controversial decision that women have a constitutional right to abortions.

Opponents of abortion are also seeking to have Congress declare that a fetus is a "person"—that life begins at conception. If Congress does so, then an unborn fetus would have the "right to life"—the constitutional guarantee against the taking of life without due process of law (Fifth and Fourteenth Amendments). In *Roe* v. *Wade* the Supreme Court held that the fetus was *not* a "person" within the traditional meaning of that word. It is not clear what the court would do if Congress declared that the fetus was indeed a "person" entitled to the "right to life."

RIGHTS OF DEFENDANTS

The rights of criminal defendants are most forcefully protected by (1) the prohibition against self-incrimination (Fifth Amendment); (2) the right to legal counsel (Sixth Amendment); (3) the prohibition against "unreasonable searches and seizures" (Fourth Amendment); and (4) the prohibition against "cruel and unusual punishment" (Fifth Amendment).

Self-Incrimination and the Right to Counsel

The Supreme Court under Chief Justice Warren expanded the rights of the accused in a series of decisions in the 1960s. In the *Escobedo* case,[41] the Court ruled that a suspect is entitled to legal counsel as soon as "the process shifts from investigatory to accusatory." The Court threw out a confession of murder by Danny Escobedo, because he had asked to see a lawyer before questioning but had been refused. In the *Gideon* case,[42] the Supreme Court held that criminal defendants in felony cases must be provided with an attorney at state expense if they cannot afford one themselves. In the *Miranda* case,[43] Warren wrote: "Prior to any questioning, the person must be warned that he has a right to remain silent, that any statement he does make may be used against him, and that he has the right to an attorney, either retained or appointed." Although suspects may knowingly waive these rights, they cannot be questioned further if at any point they ask to see a lawyer or indicate "in any manner" that they do not wish to be interrogated. Miranda had confessed a rape, and the victim had picked him out of a police lineup; but the Supreme Court threw out his conviction.

Whether these decisions have handicapped the police is debatable. To comply with the *Miranda* decision (and, of course, to make the arrest "stick"), police departments printed "Miranda cards" to be carried by all arresting officers (see Figure 11-3).

In *Estelle* v. *Smith, Miranda* was strengthened by a ruling about the use of psychiatric testimony.[44] Ernest Smith, accused of murder in Texas, had been interviewed by a psychiatrist (known by the nickname "Dr. Death" because he frequently testified in support of the death penalty). Smith maintained that he had no idea that his psychiatric examination would be used in evidence; had he known, he said, he would not have submitted to the interview with "Dr. Death" without an attorney. Chief Justice Burger spoke for a unanimous court in throwing out the psychiatric evidence. This case was especially significant in that it extended *Miranda* well into the sentencing process. Smith had been found guilty; at issue was the severity of the sentence.

DEFENDANT	LOCATION

SPECIFIC WARNING REGARDING INTERROGATIONS

1. YOU HAVE THE RIGHT TO REMAIN SILENT.
2. ANYTHING YOU SAY CAN AND WILL BE USED AGAINST YOU IN A COURT OF LAW.
3. YOU HAVE THE RIGHT TO TALK TO A LAWYER AND HAVE HIM PRESENT WITH YOU WHILE YOU ARE BEING QUESTIONED.
4. IF YOU CANNOT AFFORD TO HIRE A LAWYER ONE WILL BE APPOINTED TO REPRESENT YOU BEFORE ANY QUESTIONING, IF YOU WISH ONE.

SIGNATURE OF DEFENDANT	DATE
WITNESS	TIME

☐ REFUSED SIGNATURE   SAN FRANCISCO POLICE DEPARTMENT   PR.9.1.4

Figure 11-3. The "Miranda card" used by San Francisco police to inform suspects of their rights at the time of arrest.

Frisking suspects or street arrests are a matter of police judgment, as upheld by Supreme Court decisions.

As for Miranda, he was killed in a tavern fight in 1976. Although his assailant fled, the police arrested a bystander who had allegedly provided the weapon during the fight. He was read his rights from a card bearing the name of the dead victim.

"Unreasonable" Searches and Seizures

The Fourth Amendment provides that "the right of the people to be secure in their persons, houses, papers, and effects, against unreasonable searches and seizures, shall not be violated, and no warrants shall issue but upon probable cause, supported by oath or affirmation, and particularly describing the place to be searched, and the persons or things to be seized." The implication of the amendment is that "reasonable" searches are those conducted after a warrant has been issued by a judge or other judicial officer. Moreover, such warrants cannot be issued unless the agent seeking the warrant shows the judge evidence of "probable cause" that a law has been violated and unless the agent describes specifically the place to be searched and the things to be seized. Thus, a search warrant cannot be issued to find out whether a person has committed a crime if there is no probable cause for such issuance. Similarly, the indiscriminate searching of whole neighborhoods or groups of people is unconstitutional under the requirement that the place to be searched be specifically described in the warrant. (However, airline passengers may be searched on the basis that they voluntarily consented to be searched when they purchased a ticket.) The requirement that the things to be seized must be described in the warrant is meant to prevent a "fishing expedition" into a person's home and personal effects on the possibility that some evidence of unknown illegal activity might turn up.

An exception to the requirement for a warrant is made if the search is "incident to a lawful arrest." Since a "lawful arrest" can be made by police officers if they have reasonable grounds to believe that a person has committed a felony or if a misdemeanor is committed in their presence, a search of the person and the person's property is permitted without a warrant at the time of such an arrest. Evidence of a crime may be seized in such a search, even though the officers were not aware of that particular crime when the search was initiated. Searching of automobiles without warrant, even if no arrest is made, has been upheld if the officer had "probable cause" to do so.[45] A police officer who stops a car for a traffic violation may order the occupants to get out.[46] And no search warrant is required for a search or seizure if the officer is lawfully admitted to the premises. The Supreme Court has also held that police officers may "stop and frisk" a suspect on the street without a warrant if they have a reasonable suspicion that the person is armed and dangerous.[47]

Modern technology has raised new questions about government intrusion into a person's private life. "Bugging" (electronic eavesdropping) and wiretapping (listening to telephone conversations) are occasionally used by law-enforcement agencies to gather information and evidence. The Supreme Court has ruled that bugging and wiretapping are "searches" within the meaning of the Fourth Amendment and that police officers must obtain a warrant from a judge before they can legally bug or wiretap.[48]

The Supreme Court Decides about Life and Death

Before 1972 the death penalty was sanctioned officially by thirty-five states; only fifteen states had abolished capital punishment. Federal law had also retained the death penalty. However, no one had actually been executed since 1967 because of numerous legal tangles and direct challenges to the constitutionality of capital punishment.

There are several constitutional arguments against the death penalty, aside from whatever moral, ethical, or religious objections might be raised. The first is that it is "cruel and unusual punishment," which is prohibited by the Eighth Amendment to the Constitution. The problem with this argument is that the early Jeffersonians who wrote the amendment and the other sections of the Bill of Rights themselves employed the death penalty. Indeed, the death penalty is specifically mentioned in the Fifth Amendment, indicating that it was acceptable at the time. For nearly 200 years there was general agreement that death was not "cruel" or "unusual" unless it was carried out in a particularly bizarre or painful fashion. Most executions were by hanging; the electric chair was introduced in the 1920s as a "humane" alterna-

(continued)

(continued)

tive, and the gas chamber followed in some states. Nonetheless, it can be argued that by today's standards the death penalty is "cruel and unusual," recognizing that moral standards change over time.

Another constitutional argument against the death penalty is that it is used in a discriminatory fashion in violation of the equal-protection clause of the Fourteenth Amendment. Although blacks make up only 12 percent of the population of the nation, over half of those ever executed have been black. Moreover, among both blacks and whites it has generally been the less educated and less affluent who have been executed. Finally, it is argued that the death penalty is imposed in arbitrary fashion; there are no clear, consistent criteria for deciding who should be executed and who should be spared.

The principal advocate on the Supreme Court for abolishing the death penalty has been Justice Thurgood Marshall, who has argued that it is the ultimate form of racial discrimination. When a series of cases, including *Furman* v. *Georgia,* came to the Court in 1972,* there were over 700 people throughout the nation waiting under sentence of death. But Marshall was unable to convince his colleagues on the Court that the death penalty is always "cruel and unusual." Of the other liberals on the Court, only Justice William Brennan seemed to agree with him. But Justice William Douglas, together with Justices Potter Stewart and Byron White, did believe that the death penalty was being employed in an arbitrary, random, unfair, and discriminatory fashion. Some people—usually the poor, black, and uneducated—were sentenced to die for crimes for which others—usually the affluent, white, and educated—were sentenced to only a few years in prison. Douglas wrote, "A penalty should be considered 'unusually' imposed if it is administered arbitrarily or discriminatorily." So five votes were lined up by Marshall in 1972 to strike down the death penalty *as it was then imposed.* But Marshall was not able to convince a majority of the justices that the death penalty should be abolished altogether.

The minority view in 1972, to uphold the death penalty, was led by Chief Justice Warren Burger. Burger argued that the courts of the United States had always permitted the death penalty and had never held it to be cruel and unusual. Indeed, as an indicator of contemporary standards, Burger observed that most states and the federal government itself had retained the death penalty. The federal government had recently enacted death-penalty laws for airplane hijacking in which death resulted and for assassination of the president or vice-president. "The word *cruel*," said Burger, "can mean grossly out of proportion to the severity of the crime; but certainly when the crime is murder, the death penalty is not out of proportion to the crime." Burger reminded the states that the majority had not abolished the death penalty itself but had merely struck down its arbitrary use. He invited the states to reconsider and rewrite their death penalty laws. In private conversation, however, neither Burger nor Marshall expressed the belief that the states would reenact death penalty laws. Both men maintained that "there will never be another execution in this country."**

Thus, by a five-to-four vote the Supreme Court struck down all capital punishment laws as they were written and administered in 1972. The 700 people on death row were given a permanent reprieve. But the court was badly divided. Nine separate opinions were written, totaling 5,000 words on 243 pages—the longest Supreme Court decision in history.

To the surprise of many who had hoped for the abolishment of the penalty, the *Furman* v. *Georgia* case in 1972 stimulated thirty-five states to reenact the death penalty with specific guidelines to avoid arbitrary or discriminatory use. By 1976 another 600 people were waiting on death row for the Court to examine these new state laws.

The Supreme Court finally considered the new laws in a series of cases in 1976.*** Only Marshall and Brennan believed that capital punishment always violates the "cruel-and-unusual-punishment" clause of the Eighth Amendment. Justice John Paul Stevens had replaced the aging Douglas on the Court. Stevens, Burger, Harry Blackmun, Lewis Powell, and William Rehnquist provided five votes to uphold the death penalty. And Justices White and Stewart could be persuaded to uphold it if it was shown not to have been arbitrarily imposed or discriminatory.

Georgia, Florida, and Texas, as well as several other states, had enacted very carefully designed capital punishment laws after the 1972 *Furman* v. *Georgia* decision. The objective was to ensure fairness and uniformity of application. Most of these laws provided for two trials: one to determine guilt or innocence and another to determine whether to impose the death sentence. At the second trial, evidence of "aggravating" and "mitigating" factors would be presented; if
(*continued*)

(continued)
there were aggravating factors but no mitigating factors, the death penalty would be mandatory.

Justices Stewart, Powell, and Stevens together wrote the majority opinion in all of the death-penalty cases in 1976. They ruled on behalf of the Court that "the punishment of death does *not* invariably violate the Constitution." They upheld the death penalty with the following rationale: The men who drafted the Bill of Rights accepted death as a common sanction for crime. It is true that the Eighth Amendment's prohibition against cruel and unusual punishment must be interpreted in a dynamic fashion, reflecting changing moral values. But the decisions of more than half of the nation's state legislatures to reenact the death penalty since 1972 and the decisions of juries to impose the death penalty for hundreds of reasons under these laws are evidence that "a large proportion of American society continues to regard it as an appropriate and necessary criminal sanction." Moreover, said the Court majority, the social purposes of retribution and deterrence justify the use of the death penalty. This ultimate sanction is "an expression of society's moral outrage at particularly offensive conduct."

The Court reaffirmed that *Furman* had struck down the death penalty only where it was inflicted in "an arbitrary and capricious manner." The court approved the consideration of "aggravating and mitigating circumstances." It also approved of automatic review of all death sentences by state supreme courts to ensure that they had not been imposed under the influence of passion or prejudice, that aggravating circumstances were supported by the evidence, and that the sentence was not disproportionate to the crime. However, the Court disapproved of state laws making the death penalty mandatory in all first-degree murder cases, holding that such laws were "unduly harsh and unworkably rigid."

Marshall wrote a very emotional opinion dissenting from the majority view. Brennan, too, was very upset over the changing attitude of the Court. "Justice of this kind is obviously no less shocking than the crime itself," he wrote, "and a new 'official' murder far from offering redress for the offense committed against society, adds instead a second defilement to the first." But these dissents had no effect on the outcome of the case.

Furman v. *Georgia*, 408 U. S. 238 (1972).
**Bob Woodward and Scott Armstrong, *The Brethren: Inside the Supreme Court* (New York: Simon and Schuster, 1979), p. 219.
***Gregg* v. *Georgia*, 428 U. S. 153 (1976).

CHAPTER SUMMARY

1. Increasingly over the years, the federal courts have helped to decide crucial political and social issues in our "adversarial" society. Through the power of judicial review (as originally established by the 1803 case of *Marbury* v. *Madison*), laws that run counter to the Constitution can be ruled invalid. The spirit of *judicial activism*, that is, the power to shape the Constitution to a changing society, as in *Brown* v. *Board of Education of Topeka,* is criticized by those who argue for judicial restraint.

2. The federal court system consists of more than ninety district courts, eleven circuits of the U. S. Courts of Appeals, and one Supreme Court. The Supreme Court will hear a case on appeal only if it involves a "substantial federal question" or a crucial constitutional issue. Conflicts between the states will be heard *first* in the Supreme Court. Despite the publicity given to federal court actions, the vast majority of civil and criminal cases are heard in state or local courts.

3. All federal judges are appointed by the president, subject to approval by a Senate majority. Judges are selected more for their political loyalties and compatible philosophy than for their prior judicial experience. The majority of federal judges are "WASPs" who come from an upper-socioeconomic background. There are relatively few women and blacks on the federal bench.

4. Civil liberties are synonymous with constitutional guarantees *against* government action. Civil rights and legal entitlements, in contrast, depend on active governmental intervention.

5. Most Americans support free speech as a general principle but resist specific applications of it to unpopular groups or individuals. Freedom of speech is not absolute; current judicial interpretation sees speech as limited by the test of "clear and present danger." Nevertheless, the burden of proof is on the government officials who wish to halt speech.

6. The courts have been reluctant to curb freedom of the press through "prior restraint." Television and radio have been more closely supervised than newspapers and magazines, however. The difficult issue of defining "obscenity" has largely been left to local community discretion.

7. Libel and slander—written and oral defamation of character—are exceptions to the guaranteed freedoms of speech and of the press. However, public officials must prove "deliberate malice" on the part of the media in order to win a libel action. Despite the arguments of reporters, courts have not held that the confidentiality of relationships with news sources is constitutionally protected.

8. The Constitution prohibits the government from either establishing a state religion or interfering with religious practices. The "establishment" clause has been variously interpreted, and there are gaps in the "wall of separation" between church and state.

9. The case of *Roe* v. *Wade,* establishing a woman's right to abor-

tions, is the most significant decision of the Supreme Court involving the right to privacy.

10. The Warren Court's *Escobedo, Gideon,* and *Miranda* decisions held that accused persons have the right to legal counsel, at state expense if necessary, and the right to remain silent under questioning (and to be informed of that right by police).

11. The Fourth Amendment provides security against "unreasonable searches and seizures." In general, to obtain a search warrant, law-enforcement officials must show "probable cause" that a law has been violated and must specify the place to be searched.

Notes

1. *Marbury* v. *Madison,* 1 Cranch 137 (1803).
2. *Brown* v. *Board of Education of Topeka,* 347 U. S. 483 (1954).
3. *Congressional Quarterly,* September 12, 1981, p. 1731.
4. *West Virginia State Board of Education* v. *Barnette,* 319 U. S. 624 (1943).
5. Quoted by Charles P. Curtis, *Lions under the Throne* (Boston: Houghton Mifflin, 1947), p. 281.
6. Herbert Jacob, *Justice in America* (Boston: Little, Brown, 1965), p. 95.
7. Joseph W. Bishop, Jr., "The Warren Court Is Not Likely to Be Overruled," *New York Times Magazine,* September 7, 1969, p. 31.
8. John R. Schmidhauser, *The Supreme Court* (New York: Holt, Rinehart & Winston, 1960), p. 59.
9. *Schenk* v. *United States,* 249 U. S. 47 (1919).
10. *Whitney* v. *California,* 274 U. S. 357 (1927).
11. *United States* v. *O'Brien,* 391 U. S. 367 (1968).
12. *Smith* v. *Goguen,* 415 U. S. 566 (1974).
13. *United States* v. *Carolene Products Co.,* 304 U. S. 144 (1938).
14. *New York Times Co.* v. *United States,* 403 U. S. 713 (1971).
15. Howard Morland, "The H-Bomb Secret," *Progressive,* November 1979, pp. 14–23.
16. *Red Lion Broadcasting* v. *FCC,* 395 U. S. 367 (1969).
17. *FCC* v. *Pacifica Foundation,* 438 U. S. 726 (1978).
18. *Roth* v. *United States,* 354 U. S. 476 (1957).
19. *Jacobellis* v. *Ohio,* 378 U. S. 184 (1964).
20. *Miller* v. *California,* 413 U. S. 15 (1973).
21. *Roth* v. *United States,* 354 U. S. 476 (1957).
22. *A Book, etc.* v. *Attorney General of the Commonwealth of Massachusetts,* 383 U. S. 413 (1966).
23. *Jenkins* v. *Georgia,* 418 U. S. 153 (1974).
24. *Southeastern Promotions* v. *Conrad,* 420 U. S. 546 (1975).
25. *New York Times* v. *Sullivan,* 376 U. S. 254 (1964).
26. For a discussion of the background of these statements, see Herbert J. Gans, *Deciding What's News* (New York: Vintage, 1979).
27. *United States* v. *Caldwell,* 408 U. S. 665 (1972).
28. *Reynolds* v. *United States,* 98 U. S. 145 (1878).
29. *Everson* v. *Board of Education,* 330 U. S. 1 (1947).
30. *Zorach* v. *Clauson,* 343 U. S. 306, 312, 313, 314 (1952).

31. *Engel* v. *Vitale,* 370 U. S. 421 (1962).
32. *Abington School District* v. *Schempp,* 374 U. S. 203 (1963).
33. *Sloan* v. *Lemon,* 413 U. S. 825 (1973).
34. *Everson* v. *Board of Education,* 330 U. S. 1 (1947).
35. *Lemon* v. *Kurtzman,* 403 U. S. 602 (1971).
36. *Board of Education* v. *Allen,* 392 U. S. 236 (1968).
37. *Reomer* v. *Maryland Public Works Board,* 426 U. S. 736 (1976).
38. *Olmstead* v. *United States,* 277 U. S. 438 (1928).
39. *Griswold* v. *Connecticut,* 381 U. S. 479 (1965).
40. *Roe* v. *Wade,* 410 U. S. 113 (1973).
41. *Escobedo* v. *Illinois,* 398 U. S. 478 (1964).
42. *Gideon* v. *Wainwright,* 372 U. S. 335 (1963).
43. *Miranda* v. *Arizona,* 384 U. S. 436 (1966).
44. *Estelle* v. *Smith,* 101 S. Ct. 1866 (1981).
45. *Adams* v. *Williams,* 407 U. S. 143 (1972).
46. *Terry* v. *Ohio,* 392 U. S. 1 (1968).
47. *Pennsylvania* v. *Mimms,* 434 U. S. 106 (1970).
48. *Katz* v. *United States,* 389 U. S. 347 (1967).

Close-Up and In-Depth Analyses

Henry J. Abraham. *The Judicial Process.* New York: Oxford University Press, 1980.

Henry J. Abraham and Grace Doherty. *Freedom and the Court.* New York: Oxford University Press, 1977.

Jerome Barron. *Freedom of Press for Whom?* Bloomington: Indiana University Press, 1973.

Congressional Quarterly. *The Supreme Court and Individual Rights.* Washington, D. C.: Congressional Quarterly Service, 1979.

Frank J. Donner. *The Age of Surveillance.* New York: Vintage Books, 1980.

Norman Dorsen, Paul Bender, and Burt Neuhorne. *Political and Civil Rights in the United States.* Boston: Little, Brown, 1976.

Fred W. Friendly. *The Good Guys, the Bad Guys, and the First Amendment.* New York: Random House, 1975.

Nat Hentoff. *The First Freedom: The Tumultuous History of Free Speech in America.* New York: Delacorte, 1980.

Walter F. Murphy and C. Herman Pritchett (Eds.). *Courts, Judges, and Politics.* New York: Random House, 1979.

Harrison E. Salisbury. *Without Fear or Favor.* New York: Times Books, 1980.

Benno C. Schmidt, Jr. *Freedom of the Press vs. Public Access.* New York: Praeger, 1976.

Glendon Schubert. *Judicial Policy-making.* New York: Scott Foresman, 1974.

Howard Simmons and Joseph A. Califano, Jr. (Eds.). *The Media and the Law.* New York: Praeger, 1976.

THE POLITICS OF CIVIL RIGHTS

EXPANDING NOTIONS OF CIVIL RIGHTS

The early goal of the civil rights movement in the United States was to prevent discrimination that was practiced by or supported by *government,* particularly states, municipalities, and school districts. But even while the movement was achieving important victories in its efforts to prevent governmental discrimination, it began to expand its objectives to include the elimination of discrimination in *all* segments of American life, private as well as public. This more positive notion of civil rights placed on government an obligation to act forcefully to end discrimination in business, employment, housing, and all other sectors of private life.

So long as the civil rights movement was combating governmental discrimination, it could concentrate on court action to serve its objective. The Fourteenth Amendment to the Constitution prevents governments from denying "equal protection of the laws." But the Constitution does not directly govern acts of private individuals in this area. When the civil rights movement turned to combating private discrimination, it had to carry its fight into the legislative branch of government. Only Congress could prevent discrimination practiced by private owners of restaurants and hotels, private employers, and others who are not government officials.

Martin Luther King
and his followers
march on Selma,
Alabama, 1965.

The "politics of civil rights" is not solely the property of women and blacks. The politics of civil rights is one of *expansion*. The plight of blacks has occupied national attention since the end of the Civil War. Discrimination against women has been on the national agenda at various times in American political history. Another group to enter the politics of civil rights has been the elderly. "Ageism" (discrimination on the basis of age) has taken its place with racism and sexism. We are also becoming aware of discrimination against the handicapped, for whom the daily routines of life present burdensome struggles. Finally, the nation is also confronting increased demands for protection of homosexuals against discrimination.

> Just as the politics of civil rights is expanding, so are governmental remedies becoming more assertive.

Table 12-1. Family Income of Ethnic Groups (U. S. Average = 100)

Jewish	172
Japanese	132
Polish	115
Chinese	112
Italian	112
German	107
Anglo-Saxon	107
Irish	103
Filipino	99
West Indian	94
Mexican	76
Puerto Rican	63
Black	62
Indian	60

Source: U. S. Bureau of the Census and National Jewish Population Survey, 1980.

Just as the politics of civil rights is expanding, so are governmental remedies becoming more assertive. National policy has moved from the removal of legal barriers (desegregation), to the active pursuit of equality (integration), and finally to positive efforts in favor of minorities and women.

Not all minorities suffer from economic discrimination, and not all minorities are poor. There is no easy explanation why Jews, Japanese, Polish, Chinese, or Italians have fared better than Filipinos, West Indians, Mexicans, Puerto Ricans, or blacks (see Table 12-1). There are differences in regional concentration, cultural traditions, extent of violent oppression, and time of arrival. Some argue that there are "natural," or genetic, differences, but the argument is not widely accepted. The legacy of slavery for blacks and the brutal extermination of American Indians contributed to the economic position of those groups. Patterns of migration also vary. Some groups immigrated in the hope of a better future; others were captured as slaves. In any case, we need to understand that the progress of minority groups is uneven.

RACISM AND THE AMERICAN EXPERIENCE

The Thirteenth Amendment abolished slavery in the United States. The Fifteenth Amendment guaranteed that the right to vote would not be denied or abridged on account of race, color, or "previous condition of servitude." The Fourteenth Amendment declared:

> No state shall make or enforce any law which shall abridge the privileges or immunities of citizens of the United States; nor shall any state deprive any person of life, liberty, or property, without due process of law; nor deny to any person within its jurisdiction the equal protection of the laws.

All three of these amendments were passed by Congress and ratified soon after the Civil War. Their language and historical context leave little doubt that their purpose was to secure for blacks a place in American society equal to that of whites. Yet for a full century these promises went unfulfilled. Segregation became the social instrument by which blacks were "kept in their place"—that is, denied social, economic, educational, and political equality—and the vast majority of blacks remained at the bottom of the social and economic structure of American society.

Segregation was supported by a variety of social practices and institutions. In many states "Jim Crowism" followed blacks throughout life: birth in a segregated hospital ward, education in a segregated school, residence in segregated housing, employment in a segregated job, eating in segregated restaurants, and burial in a segregated graveyard. Segregation was enforced by a variety of private sanctions, from the occasional lynching mobs to country club admission committees. But government was a principal instrument of segregation both in the southern and the border states of the nation. In the northern states government was seldom used to enforce segregation, but it was also seldom used to prevent it. The results were often quite similar.

How did it come about that a governmental system specifically pledged to achieve equality for blacks actually contributed to the maintenance of segregation? And, by contrast, how did it come about that government in recent years has become the principal instrument for attacking segregation?

The Legacy of Segregation

The constitutional argument made on behalf of segregation—that the phrase "equal protection of the laws" did not prohibit the enforced separation of races so long as the races were treated equally—became known as the **separate-but-equal doctrine.** In 1896 the Supreme Court made this doctrine the official interpretation of the equal-protection clause, thus giving segregation constitutional approval. In the words of the Court in *Plessy* v. *Ferguson*:

Separate-but-equal doctrine: The view that the Constitution permitted the enforced separation of races, so long as the races were treated equally.

The object of the [Fourteenth] amendment was undoubtedly to enforce the absolute equality of the two races before the law, but in the nature of things it could not have been intended to abolish distinctions based upon color, or to enforce social, as distinguished from political, equality, or a commingling of the two races upon terms unsatisfactory to either. . . .

Legislation is powerless to eradicate racial instincts or to abolish distinctions based upon physical differences, and the attempt to do so can only result in accentuating the difficulties of the present situation. ... If one race be inferior to the other socially, the Constitution of the United States cannot put them upon the same plane.[1]

In 1896 the Supreme Court made the separate-but-equal doctrine the official interpretation of the equal-protection clause, thus giving segregation constitutional approval.

Before 1954, segregation of the races was required in seventeen states—the eleven states of the old Confederacy, together with the border states of Delaware, Kentucky, Maryland, Missouri, Oklahoma, and West Virginia (see Figure 12-1). It was authorized by local option in four states (Arizona, New Mexico, Kansas, and Wyoming). Segregation was *prohibited* in only sixteen states; the other eleven states had no legislation on the subject. Segregation was also required (by Congress) in the schools of Washington, D. C. The armed forces were not integrated until President Harry Truman ordered it in 1947.

Figure 12-1. Segregation laws in the United States in 1954. (From Thomas R. Dye, *Politics in States and Communities*, 4th ed. Englewood Cliffs, N. J.: Prentice-Hall, 1981, p. 370.)

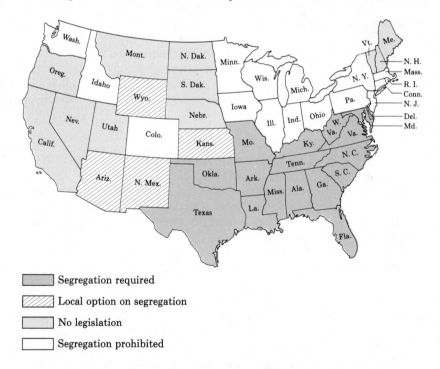

Segregation required

Local option on segregation

No legislation

Segregation prohibited

The Beginning of the Civil Rights Movement

The judicial doctrine of separate but equal was not reversed until 1954, in *Brown* v. *Board of Education of Topeka*.[2] Why Topeka? The National Association for the Advancement of Colored People

Public Attitudes toward School Integration

Expressed in the abstract, school integration meets with the approval of both black and white parents...

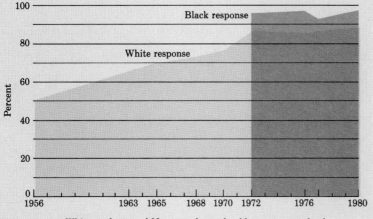

Question: Do you think white students and Negro students should go to the same school or different schools? (Question not asked for blacks until 1972. Source: Surveys by the National Opinion Research Center.)

White students and Negro students should go to same school

But many whites object to sending their children to schools in which a majority of the students are black...

Question: (asked of white parents): Would you, yourself, have any objection to sending your children to a school where a few of the children are colored? (If "no"): Where half of the children are colored? (If "no"): Where more than half of the children are colored? (In 1980, the word "black" was substituted for "colored." Source: Surveys by the Gallup Organization.)

White parents' response/would object to sending your children to school where...

More than one-half are black

One-half are black

A few children are black

(continued)

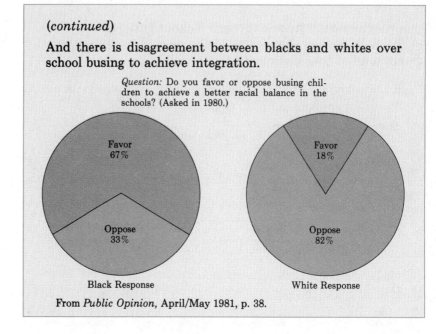

(continued)

And there is disagreement between blacks and whites over school busing to achieve integration.

Question: Do you favor or oppose busing children to achieve a better racial balance in the schools? (Asked in 1980.)

Favor
67%

Oppose
33%

Black Response

Favor
18%

Oppose
82%

White Response

From *Public Opinion,* April/May 1981, p. 38.

(NAACP), following the strategy of its chief counsel, Thurgood Marshall (who later became an associate justice of the Supreme Court) had argued successfully that, when facilities were demonstrably *un*equal, segregation was a violation of the Fourteenth Amendment. However, this strategy had to be pursued on a case-by-case basis. In Topeka, Kansas, black and white schools were equal in all measurable ways. The NAACP argument was that, even if salaries, library facilities, expenditures, and the like were equal, *segregation itself* violated the Fourteenth Amendment. If the Supreme Court accepted the case, it would have to rule on the legality of segregation itself.

> "Segregation . . . has a tendency to retard the educational and mental development of Negro children and to deprive them of some of the benefits they would receive in a racially integrated school system."

The Supreme Court could not rely on precedent in deciding the case, because the precedent was the segregationist argument of *Plessy* v. *Ferguson.* So the Court relied on the research of psychologists to support the idea that segregation damaged black children emotionally by the implication of inferiority. "Segregation . . . has a tendency to retard the educational and mental development of Negro children and to deprive them of some of the benefits they would receive in a racially integrated school system." The Court concluded that "whatever may have been the extent of psychological knowledge of the time of *Plessy* v. *Ferguson,* this finding [for integration] is amply supported by modern authority."

The Supreme Court's decision in *Brown* was symbolically very important. Although it would be many years before any significant numbers of black children would attend previously all-white schools, the decision by the nation's highest court stimulated black hopes and expectations. Indeed, *Brown* started the modern civil rights movement. The black psychologist Kenneth Clark writes: "This [civil rights] movement would probably not have existed at all were it not for the 1954 Supreme Court school desegregation decision which provided a tremendous boost to the morale of blacks by its *clear* affirmation that color is irrelevant to the rights of American citizens."[3]

The Civil Rights Act of 1964

Before 1964 Congress had been content to let other entities, including the president and the courts, struggle with the problem of civil rights. Yet Congress could not long ignore the nation's most pressing domestic issue. The civil rights movement had stepped up its protests and demonstrations and was attracting worldwide attention with organized sit-ins, freedom rides, picketing campaigns, boycotts, and mass

---

Blacks and Whites Disagree about Discrimination

Black and white Americans have markedly different perceptions of the existence of discrimination. In education, housing, skilled-employment opportunities, and job pay, many more blacks than whites perceive discrimination. The greatest numbers of both groups perceive discrimination in getting skilled jobs.

Question: In your area, would you say blacks are generally discriminated against in (read statement)?

Getting a quality education	6%	White response
	28%	Black response
Getting decent housing	17%	
	44%	
Getting skilled labor jobs	21%	
	61%	
The wages they are paid in most jobs	13%	
	57%	

Source: Survey by ABC News/*The Washington Post,* February 26–March 6, 1981. In *Public Opinion,* April/May 1981, p. 35.

marches. The mass media vividly portrayed the animosity of segregationists and helped to convince millions of Americans of the need for
national legislation. After the massive march on Washington in August, 1963, President John Kennedy asked Congress for the most
comprehensive civil rights legislation it had ever considered. After
Kennedy's assassination, President Lyndon Johnson brought heavy
pressure on Congress to pass the bill as a tribute to the late president.
Everett M. Dirksen of Illinois, the Republican leader in the Senate,
provided Johnson with the bipartisan support needed to overcome a
southern filibuster. The Civil Rights Act of 1964 finally passed both
houses of Congress by better than a two-thirds vote and with the
overwhelming support of members of both the Republican and
Democratic parties. It can be ranked with the Emancipation Proclamation, the Fourteenth Amendment, and the *Brown* case as one of
the most important steps toward full equality for blacks.

The mass media vividly portrayed the animosity of segregationists and helped to convince millions of Americans of the
need for national legislation.

The Civil Rights Act includes the following provisions:

I. It is unlawful to apply unequal standards in voter
registration procedures or to deny registration for irrelevant
errors or omissions on records or applications. Literacy tests
must be in writing, and a sixth-grade education is a
presumption of literacy.

II. It is unlawful to discriminate or segregate on the grounds
of race, color, religion, or national origin in any place of public
accommodation, including hotels, motels, restaurants, movies,
theaters, sports arenas, entertainment houses, and other places
offering to serve the public. This prohibition extends to all
establishments whose operations affect interstate commerce or
whose discriminatory practices are supported by state action.

III. The Attorney General shall undertake civil action on
behalf of any person denied equal access to a public
accommodation.

IV. The Attorney General shall undertake civil actions on
behalf of persons attempting the orderly desegregation of
public schools.

V. The U. S. Commission on Civil Rights, first established
by the Civil Rights Act of 1957, shall be empowered (1) to
investigate deprivations of the right to vote, (2) to collect and
to study information regarding discrimination in America, and
(3) to make reports to the president and Congress as necessary.

VI. Each federal department and agency shall take appropriate action to end discrimination in all programs or activities receiving federal financial assistance in any form. These actions may include the termination of assistance.

VII. It shall be unlawful for any firm or labor union employing or representing twenty-five or more persons to discriminate against any individual in any fashion because of his race, color, religion, sex, or national origin. An Equal Employment Opportunity Commission shall be established to enforce this provision by investigation, conference, conciliation, or civil action in federal court.

Martin Luther King and the Power of Protest

The civil rights movement invented new techniques through which minorities could gain power and influence in American society. Mass protest, for example, is a means of acquiring bargaining leverage for those who would otherwise be powerless. The protest may challenge established groups by threatening their reputations (where they might be harmed by unfavorable publicity), their economic position (where they might be hurt by a boycott), their peace and quiet (where noise and disruption might upset their daily activities), or their security (where violence or the threat of violence is involved).

> Mass protest is a means of acquiring bargaining leverage for those who would otherwise be powerless.

The protest technique appeals to powerless minorities who have little to bargain with except their promise not to protest. Once the protest has begun—or even *before* it has begun, if the threat of protest is made credible—the minority can promise to desist in exchange for the desired concessions. Perhaps more importantly, mass protest frequently motivates members of established elites, who have the political resources the protesters lack, to enter the political arena on behalf of the protesters.

The nation's leading exponent of nonviolent protest was the Reverend Dr. Martin Luther King, Jr. Indeed, King's contributions to the development of a philosophy of protest on behalf of blacks won him international acclaim and the Nobel Peace Prize in 1964. King first came to national prominence in 1955 when he was only twenty-five years old; he led a year-long bus boycott in Montgomery, Alabama, to protest discrimination in seating on public buses. In 1957 he formed the Southern Christian Leadership Conference (SCLC) to provide encouragement and leadership to the growing nonviolent protest movement in the South.

King explained nonviolent direct action in his famous "Letter from Birmingham Jail":

> You may well ask, "Why direct action? Why sit-ins, marches, etc? Isn't negotiation a better path?" You are exactly right in your call for negotiation. Indeed, this is the purpose of direct action. Nonviolent direct action seeks to create such a crisis and establish such creative tension that a community that has constantly refused to negotiate is forced to confront the issue. It seeks to so dramatize the issue that it can no longer be ignored. . . .
>
> You express a great deal of anxiety over our willingness to break laws. . . . One may well ask, "How can you advocate breaking some laws and obeying others?" The answer is found in the fact that there are unjust laws. I would be the first to advocate obeying just laws. One has not only a legal but a moral responsibility to obey just laws. Conversely, one has a moral responsibility to disobey unjust laws. . . .
>
> In no sense do I advocate evading or defying the law as the rabid segregationist would do. This would lead to anarchy. One who breaks an unjust law must do it openly, lovingly (not hatefully as the white mothers did in New Orleans when they were seen on television screaming "nigger, nigger, nigger") and with a willingness to accept the penalty. I submit that an individual who breaks a law that conscience tells him is unjust, and willingly accepts the penalty by staying in jail to arouse the conscience of the community over its injustice, is in reality expressing the very highest respect for law.[4]

King's technique required direct mass action against laws regarded as unjust, rather than court litigation, political campaigning, voting, or other conventional forms of democratic political activity. Mass demonstrations, sit-ins, and other nonviolent direct-action tactics usually result in violations of state and local laws. For example, those remaining at a segregated lunch counter after the owner orders them to leave are usually violating trespassing laws. Marching in the street frequently entails the obstruction of traffic and results in charges of disorderly conduct or parading without a permit. Mass demonstrations often involve disturbing the peace or refusing to obey the lawful orders of a police officer. Even though these tactics are nonviolent, they do entail disobedience to civil law.

Civil disobedience is not new to American politics. Its practitioners have played an important role in American history. They have included the patriots who participated in the Boston Tea Party, the abolitionists who hid runaway slaves, the suffragists who paraded and demonstrated for women's rights, and the labor organizers who pick-

An early 1960s sit-in in the South.

eted to form the nation's major industrial unions. Civil disobedience is a political tactic of minorities. (Since majorities can more easily change laws through conventional political activity, they seldom have to disobey them.) It is also a tactic attractive to groups wishing to change the social status quo significantly and quickly.

The political purpose of nonviolent direct action and civil disobedience is to call attention to the existence of injustices. Only laws regarded as unjust are broken, and they are broken openly without hatred or violence. Punishment is actively sought rather than avoided, since punishment will further emphasize the injustices of the law. The object of nonviolent civil disobedience is to stir the conscience of an apathetic majority and to win support for measures that will eliminate the injustices. By accepting punishment for the violation of an unjust law, persons practicing civil disobedience demonstrate their sincerity. They hope to shame the majority and to make it ask itself how far it will go to protect the status quo.

Clearly, the participation of the mass media, particularly television, contributes immeasurably to the success of nonviolent direct action. Breaking the law makes news; dissemination of the news calls the attention of the public to the existence of unjust laws or practices; the public sympathy is won when injustices are spotlighted; the willingness of the demonstrators to accept punishment provides evidence of their sincerity; and the whole drama lays the groundwork for changing unjust laws and practices. Cruelty or violence directed against the demonstrators by the police or other defenders of the status quo plays into the hands of the demonstrators by stressing the injustices they are experiencing.

The participation of the mass media, particularly television, contributes immeasurably to the success of nonviolent direct action.

The media coverage achieved by King was a key ingredient of this success. He knew that minority protest was, without powerful allies, unlikely to succeed. He wanted to find an ally with more influence to intercede with the white majority, especially in Congress. Hence, his strategy was a conscious one: he wanted to persuade the media and use the media as a "third party." To get the attention of the media he chose dramatic forms of confrontation. Civil disobedience was (and still is) an ideal technique for those denied conventional access to policymakers. King and the media developed a symbiotic relationship: King gave the media drama, and the media gave him access to policymakers.

Perhaps the most dramatic application of nonviolent direct action occurred in Birmingham, Alabama, in the spring of 1963. Under the direction of King the SCLC chose Birmingham as a major site for desegregation demonstrations during the centennial year of the Emancipation Proclamation. Birmingham was by its own description the "Heart of Dixie"; it was the most rigidly segregated large city in the United States. King believed that, if segregation could be successfully challenged in Birmingham, it might begin to crumble throughout the South. Thousands of black people, including schoolchildren, staged protest marches in Birmingham. In response, police officers and fire fighters under the direction of Police Chief "Bull" Connor attacked the demonstrators with fire hoses, cattle prods, and police dogs—all in clear view of national television cameras. Pictures of police brutality were flashed throughout the nation and the world, doubtless touching the consciences of many white Americans. The demonstrators conducted themselves in a nonviolent fashion. Thousands were dragged off to jail, including King. (It was at this time that King wrote his "Letter from Birmingham Jail" explaining and defending nonviolent direct action.)

"I have a dream that one day this nation will rise up and live out the true meaning of its creed: 'We hold these truths to be self-evident, that all men are created equal.'"

The most massive application of nonviolent direct action was the great march on Washington in August, 1963, during which more than 200,000 black and white marchers converged on the nation's capital. The march ended in a formal program at the Lincoln Memorial, where King delivered his most eloquent appeal, entitled "I Have a Dream": "I still have a dream. It is a dream deeply rooted in the American dream. I have a dream that one day this nation will rise up and live out the true meaning of its creed: 'We hold these truths to be self-evident, that all men are created equal.'"[5]

Another very significant application of nonviolent direct action occurred in Alabama in the spring of 1965—an SCLC-organized

More than 200,000 people listen as Martin Luther King delivered his famous speech, "I have a dream."

march from Selma to Montgomery to protest voting inequities. The Selma marchers convinced Congress that its earlier legislation was inadequate to the task of securely guaranteeing the right to vote for all Americans. In response to the march, Congress enacted the Voting Rights Act of 1965, which threatened federal intervention in local matters to a degree never before attempted. The act authorized the attorney general, on evidence of voter discrimination in southern states, to replace local registrars with federal examiners, who were authorized to abolish literacy tests, to waive poll taxes, and to register voters under simplified federal procedures. The impact of the Voting Rights Act of 1965 can be observed in increased black voter registration figures in the South and the election of blacks to state legislatures in every southern state and to many city and county offices as well. (See Table 12-2.)

Table 12-2. Black Registration before and after the Voting Rights Act

	Percent of blacks registered to vote	
	1960	*1976*
Alabama	13.7%	56.4%
Arkansas	38.0	56.2
Florida	39.4	61.1
Georgia	29.3	56.4
Louisiana	31.1	63.0
Mississippi	5.2	56.5
North Carolina	39.1	55.0
South Carolina	15.6	56.5
Tennessee	29.1	56.4
Texas	35.5	56.5
Virginia	23.1	56.3
Total blacks	29.4%	57.4%
Total whites	61.1%	67.9%

White racial violence in the early 1960s contributed to the success of the nonviolent direct-action movement in winning the nation's sympathy and support. Murders and bombings shocked and disgusted whites in both the North and the South. In 1963 Medgar Evers, the NAACP state chairman from Mississippi, was shot to death by a sniper as he entered his Jackson home. In that same year a bomb killed four black girls attending Sunday school in Birmingham.

On April 4, 1968, King was shot and killed by a white man in Memphis, Tennessee. The murder of the nation's leading advocate of nonviolence was a tragedy affecting all Americans. It deprived the black movement of its most charismatic leader and encouraged those who rejected the strategy of nonviolence.

Violence in Black Ghettos

Simultaneously with the establishment of civil rights in the 1964 and 1965 acts, President Johnson urged Congress to declare a War on Poverty. The Economic Opportunity Act of 1964, the central core of the "war," established the Office of Economic Opportunity and a grass-roots Community Action Program. Operation Head Start, the Legal Services Corporation, and a variety of other efforts were linked directly to the Community Action Program. It was during this period that the urban riots of the 1960s broke out. Why did violence occur then, when the federal government was obviously committing major resources to end poverty and discrimination? One reason may be that the government could not deliver what it had promised. The programs were enacted with such speed that no one had any idea if they were feasible or foolish. Turnover in personnel was very high. Communities objected to the inclusion of black activists on poverty boards. There was widespread scandal and corruption. For whatever reason, poverty was not eliminated; indeed, it was not even reduced by very much.

The promise was there; the reality was lacking. The situation was ripe for violence. The hopes and expectations of blacks had been raised by expansive rhetoric beyond the ability of the political system to respond. Hence, rising expectations and policy failures contributed to the riots. The riots in Watts (1965), Newark (1967), and Detroit (1967) were major civil disorders.

The frustration of rising expectations, a "social" cause of the riots, needs to be supplemented with the major role of television in creating a forum for public attention. The riots were well-covered by the media; the rioters gained a mass audience. Television provided legitimacy, justification, and instant access to policymakers. It also allowed whites to react in horror. The sympathy for civil rights aroused by King through television was lost by television coverage of the riots. White reaction to televised violence contributed to a strong "law-and-order" movement. By the middle of the 1970s the War on Poverty had been lost and abandoned. The civil rights era had all but ended for blacks.

The Civil Rights Act of 1968 was the last major legislative response to discrimination. The act attacked discrimination in housing, unmentioned in any previous legislation. Again relying on the inter-

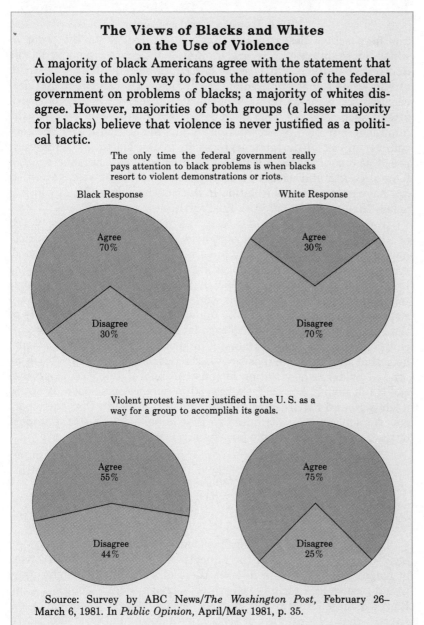

The Views of Blacks and Whites on the Use of Violence

A majority of black Americans agree with the statement that violence is the only way to focus the attention of the federal government on problems of blacks; a majority of whites disagree. However, majorities of both groups (a lesser majority for blacks) believe that violence is never justified as a political tactic.

The only time the federal government really pays attention to black problems is when blacks resort to violent demonstrations or riots.

Black Response

Agree
70%

Disagree
30%

White Response

Agree
30%

Disagree
70%

Violent protest is never justified in the U. S. as a way for a group to accomplish its goals.

Agree
55%

Disagree
44%

Agree
75%

Disagree
25%

Source: Survey by ABC News/*The Washington Post*, February 26–March 6, 1981. In *Public Opinion*, April/May 1981, p. 35.

state commerce clause, Congress prohibited discrimination in real estate exchanges of any sort. Obviously difficult to implement, the act stood little chance of passage. Then, as the act was being debated, King was assassinated. The mood of Congress changed, and its leadership passed the legislation as a tribute to King.

The Busing Controversy

Southern school desegregation has now proceeded to the point at which more black pupils are attending integrated schools in the South than in the North. Over 50 percent of black pupils in the North attend schools that are predominantly black (95 percent to 100 percent black), whereas only 19 percent of black pupils in the South attend such schools.[6] This is an important comparison between the diminishing impact of segregation *by law* in the South and the continuing impact of *de facto* segregation in the North. If the issue is posed as one of "racial isolation," it turns out that the efforts of the federal courts and executive agencies in eliminating segregation by law have reduced racial isolation in the South to the point at which it is less than racial isolation in the North.

In the important case of *Swann* v. *Charlotte Mecklenburg Board of Education*, the Supreme Court held that *southern* school districts have a special affirmative duty to eliminate all vestiges of dual school systems and that this responsibility may entail busing and the breakup of neighborhood schools.[7] Where evidence indicates that school districts once segregated students by law, these districts have a special constitutional mandate under the equal-protection clause of the Fourteenth Amendment to take whatever steps are necessary, including busing, to end all traces of dual schools. Moreover, the Court held that the racial composition of a school in such a district can be used as evidence of violation of constitutional rights. The Court was careful in saying, however, that racial imbalance in a school is not in itself a ground for ordering busing, unless it is shown that some past government action contributed to that imbalance. Thus, the impact of the *Swann* decision falls largely on southern schools.

> The Court was careful in saying, however, that racial imbalance in a school is not in itself a ground for ordering busing, unless it is shown that some past government action contributed to that imbalance.

De facto segregation: Separation of the races that is the result of housing patterns and neighborhood schools rather than direct discrimination.

In the *Brown* case the Supreme Court had stated that segregation has "a tendency to retard the educational and mental development of Negro children and to deprive them of some of the benefits they would receive in a racially integrated school system." The U. S. Civil Rights Commission reported that, even when segregation is **de facto**—that is, a product of segregated housing patterns and neighborhood schools rather than direct discrimination—the adverse effects on black students are still significant.[8] However, ending de facto segregation would require drastic changes in the prevailing concept of "neighborhood schools." Schools would no longer be a part of the neighborhood or the local community but rather part of a larger citywide or areawide school system. Inner-city students would have to be bused to the suburbs, and suburban students would have to be bused to the core city. Finally, the ending of de facto segregation would require school districts to classify students on the basis of race and to use racial categories as a basis for school placement. Although this would supposedly be a benign form of racial classification, nevertheless it would represent a return to both government-sponsored racial classification and the differential application of laws to the separate races (in contrast to the notion that the law should be "color-blind").

In *Milliken* v. *Bradley* (1974) the Supreme Court decided by a five-to-four vote that *the Fourteenth Amendment does not require busing across city/surburban school-district boundaries* to achieve integration. Where central-city schools are predominantly black and suburban schools are predominantly white, cross-district busing is not required unless it is shown that some official action brought about this segregation. The Supreme Court threw out a lower federal court order for extensive busing of students between Detroit and fifty-two suburban school districts. Although Detroit city schools were 70 percent black, none of the school districts in the area segregated students *within* their own boundaries. Chief Justice Warren Burger, writing for the majority, said:

> The constitutional right of the Negro respondents residing in Detroit is to attend a unitary school system in that district. Unless petitioners drew the district lines in a discriminatory fashion, or arranged for the white students residing in the Detroit district to attend schools in Oakland or Macomb counties, they were under no constitutional duty to make provisions for Negro students to do so.[9]

Busing is still an important political issue.

In a strong dissent, Justice Marshall wrote:

> In the short run it may seem to be the easiest course to allow
> our great metropolitan areas to be divided up each into cities—
> one white, the other black—but it is a course, I predict, our
> people will ultimately regret.

This important decision means that largely black central cities,
surrounded by largely white suburbs, will remain de facto segregated
because there are not enough white students living within the city to
achieve integration.

Note that this decision applies only to city/suburban cross-district
busing. If a federal district judge in any city, North or South, finds
that any actions by governments or school officials have contributed
to racial imbalances (for example, drawing school district attendance
lines), the judge may still order busing within the city to overcome
any racial imbalances produced by official action. In recent years an
increasing number of northern cities have come under orders from
federal district courts to improve racial balance in their schools
through busing.

Not only is busing unpopular with the white public, it is constantly being challenged by Congress. Every year, antibusing amendments are attached to various appropriation measures. But if federal
courts decide that busing is essential to meet the *constitutional* requirement of equal protection of the laws, then antibusing laws must
give way to the Constitution.

Affirmative Action

Aside from busing, perhaps the most sensitive issue affecting race
relations in the United States today is the question of how to achieve
equality in education, jobs, and income. The civil rights movement of
the 1960s opened new opportunities for black Americans. However,
equality of opportunity is not the same as equality of results. The
problem of inequality today is usually identified with continued differences in black and white family incomes (Figure 12-2), differences
in the percentages of black and white families living in poverty, and
differences in the percentages of blacks and whites in professional,
managerial, and skilled occupations.

What public policies should be pursued to achieve equality? Is
it sufficient that government eliminate discrimination, guarantee
equality of opportunity to blacks and whites, and apply "color-blind"
standards to both blacks and whites? Or should government take
affirmative action to overcome the results of past unequal treatment
of blacks—preferential or compensatory treatment that will favor
black applicants for university admission and scholarships, job hiring
and promotion, and other opportunities for advancement in life?

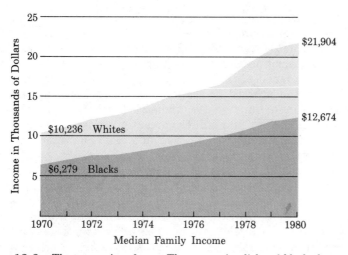

Figure 12-2. The economics of race. The economic plight of blacks has not improved in recent years. Indeed, the gap between white and black is greater than ever. In 1970, the average black family's income was about 60 percent of the average white family's; in 1980, it was about 58 percent.

Aside from busing, perhaps the most sensitive issue affecting race relations in the United States today is the question of how to achieve equality in education, jobs, and income.

Increasingly, the goal of the civil rights movement has shifted from the traditional aim of equality of opportunity through nondiscrimination alone to **affirmative action** to establish goals and timetables to achieve equality. Although usually avoiding the term *quota,* affirmative action tests the success of equal employment opportunity by observing whether blacks achieve admissions, jobs, and promotions in proportion to their numbers in the population.

The constitutional question posed by affirmative-action programs is whether they discriminate against whites in violation of the equal-protection clause of the Fourteenth Amendment. Clearly, this is a question for the Supreme Court to resolve, but unfortunately the Court has failed to develop a clear-cut answer.

In *Regents of the University of California* v. *Bakke* (1978), the Supreme Court struck down a special admissions program for minorities at a state medical school on the ground that it excluded a white applicant because of his race, violating his rights under the equal-protection clause. Allan Bakke applied to the University of California, Davis, for two consecutive years and was rejected; in both years black applicants with significantly lower grade-point averages and scores on medical aptitude tests were accepted through a special admissions program that reserved 16 minority places in a class of 100.

Affirmative action: Preferential or compensatory treatment of certain groups to overcome the results of past discrimination in education and employment.

The University of California did not deny that its admissions decisions were based on race. Instead, it argued that its racial classification was "benign"—that is, designed to assist minorities, not hinder them. The special admissions program was designed (1) to "reduce the historical deficit of traditionally disfavored minorities in medical schools and the medical profession," (2) "to counter the effects of societal discrimination," (3) to "increase the number of physicians who will practice in communities currently underserved," and (4) to "obtain the educational benefits that flow from an ethnically diverse student body."

The Court held that these objectives were legitimate and that race and ethnic background *may* be considered in reviewing applications to a state school without violating the equal-protection clause. However, the Court also held that a separate admissions program for minorities with a specified quota of openings that are unavailable to white applicants violates the equal-protection clause. "The guarantee of equal protection cannot mean one thing when applied to one individual and something else when applied to another. If both are not accorded the same protection, then it is not equal."[10] The Court ordered that Bakke be admitted to medical school and that the special

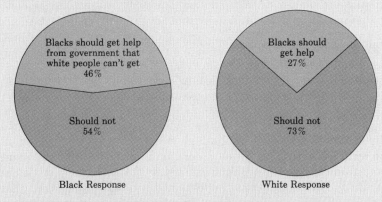

Affirmative Action: The Controversy Continues
Affirmative action is not very popular with the public, black or white. Considerably more blacks than whites favor affirmative action, but majorities of both groups are opposed to it. Respondents in the survey shown here were asked whether, because of past discrimination, blacks who need it should get help from the government that whites in similar economic circumstances do not get.

Blacks should get help from government that white people can't get
46%

Should not
54%

Blacks should get help
27%

Should not
73%

Black Response

White Response

Source: Survey by ABC News/*The Washington Post*, February 26–March 6, 1981. In *Public Opinion*, April/May 1981, p. 38.

admissions program be eliminated. It recommended that California consider an admissions program like one developed at Harvard University that considered disadvantaged racial or ethnic background a "plus" in an overall evaluation of an applicant but did not set numerical quotas or exclude anyone from competing for all positions. Since Bakke had "won" the case, most observers felt that the Court was not going to permit quota systems.

However, in *United Steelworkers of America* v. *Weber* (1979), the Supreme Court approved a plan developed by a private employer and a union to reserve 50 percent of higher-paying, skilled jobs for minorities. Kaiser Aluminum Corporation and the United Steelworkers union, under federal government pressure, had established a program to get more blacks into skilled technical jobs. Only 2 percent of the skilled jobs in the plant where Weber worked were held by blacks, whereas 39 percent of the local work force was black. When Weber was excluded from the training program and blacks with less seniority and fewer qualifications were accepted, he filed suit in federal court, contending that he had been discriminated against because of his race in violation of Title VII of the Civil Rights Act of 1964. (Weber could not contend that his rights under the Fourteenth Amendment's equal-protection clause had been violated, because this clause applied only to governmental discrimination.) Title VII prevents *all* discrimination in employment on the basis of race; it does not specify discrimination against blacks or other minorities.

The Supreme Court held that Title VII "left employers and unions in the private sector free to take such race-conscious steps to eliminate manifest racial imbalance in traditionally segregated job categories. We hold that Title VII does not prohibit such ... affirmative action plans."[11] Weber's reliance on the clear language of Title VII was held to be "misplaced." According to the court, it would be "ironic indeed" if the Civil Rights Act were used to prohibit "all voluntary private race-conscious efforts to end traditional patterns" of discrimination.

The *Weber* ruling was applauded by the U. S. Equal Employment Opportunity Commission and by various civil rights organizations, which hoped to use the decision to step up affirmative-action plans in industry and government. The decision does not directly affect women, but it may be used as a precedent to strengthen affirmative-action programs for women.

SEXUAL POLITICS

Although women constitute a slight majority of the U. S. population, they are not a *cohesive* majority. They do not stick together on political issues, even "women's issues."[12] Indeed, the reason may be that they *are* a majority. They are not segregated into ghettos or forced to ride at the back of the bus; even all-male schools are dying out. Yet the reality of economic discrimination is apparent: women earn about 59 percent of the average male income.[13] The response to discrimination against women by women reveals the extent to which they are divided. The majority of women (and men) supports the Equal Rights Amendment. Yet in 1980 women split their vote between Jimmy Carter, who supported the amendment, and Ronald Reagan, who opposed it.

> For many years discrimination against women was regarded as legitimate. All institutions of American society contributed to sex-role stereotyping.

The division among women damaged the chances of the ERA, but it should not obscure the fact that substantial legal progress toward equality between the sexes has been made. Feminist organizations led the fight for the adoption in 1920 of the Nineteenth Amendment to the Constitution, which gave women the right to vote. Black men had been accorded this right in 1870, with the Fifteenth Amendment. For many years discrimination against women was regarded as legitimate. All institutions of American society contributed to sex-role stereotyping. Even today, television commercials portray women as far more concerned about housework and family life than is actually the case. Women are shown as professionals in many entertainment series, but those who sell products through television presumably know something about their market. It is women who take the blame for "ring around the collar" or for bad-tasting coffee; and it is women whose inability to solve the problem of "waxy yellow buildup" on their floors drives them to the point of anxiety.

These forms of stereotyping are sometimes harder to attack than is the blatant discrimination against blacks. Because it is more subtle, sex discrimination does not respond so well to legislative or judicial remedies. Today, with the job market shared almost equally between the sexes (Figure 12-3), it is still "normal" for women to combine a

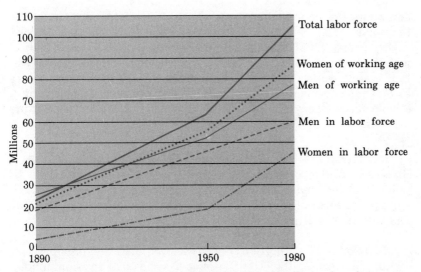

Figure 12-3. Women in the U. S. labor force, 1890–1980. Women have been entering the work force at an increasing rate. By 1980 slightly over half of all women of working age were in the labor force, representing about 43 percent of U. S. workers. (Source: U. S. Bureau of the Census and U. S. Department of Labor. In *Public Opinion*, April/May 1981, p. 22.)

career with family responsibilities. Men do not face as much job-versus-family tension; they usually do not share equally in household tasks; and they generally leave the bulk of child rearing to women.

Sexual Discrimination and the Law

There have been substantial legal gains by women in recent years. The 1964 Civil Rights Act barred discrimination on the basis of sex as well as race and created the Equal Employment Opportunities Commission with investigative authority. In 1972 Congress gave the EEOC the authority to go to court to challenge discrimination. By 1972 the phrase "women and minorities" had become standard in dealing with discrimination problems. The Equal Employment Act of 1972 declared illegal any discrimination against "women and minorities in the field of education." In the same year Title IX of the Education Amendments required schools and universities to provide equal opportunities for women in athletics. The Equal Credit Opportunity Act of 1974 prohibited sex discrimination in credit transactions. Credit cannot be denied because of sex or marital status; it can be denied, however, if the woman has no credit rating. Women who have maintained accounts in their husbands' name have found it difficult to get credit if they apply under their own name.

In spite of this legislation the economic position of women has not improved. Women are entering the professions at an accelerated rate. The number of women graduating from law school, business school, and medical school has increased nearly twelvefold since the beginning of the last decade. Yet most women still do "women's work." Eighty percent of all clerical jobs are held by women. Even in clerical jobs the pay of women lags behind that of men. Indeed, discrimination against women is most severe among clerical workers, who earn 59 percent of a male salary. Women professionals earn 64 percent of a male salary. This tells something about the opportunity structure for women.

The High Visibility Issues: Abortion and ERA

Statistical evidence of discrimination is not very interesting to the public and the media. Far more attention has been given to the conspicuous failures of feminist organizations on the issues of abortion and the Equal Rights Amendment.

Abortion. The abortion issue was initiated by organizations seeking to overturn the U. S. Supreme Court's 1973 decision upholding a woman's right to have an abortion. Since this decision about 25 percent of all pregnancies have been terminated by abortion. Moreover, until recently the federal government paid millions of dollars for abortions under Medicaid programs for the poor. The first issue to arise in Congress was whether federal funds should be used to pay for abortions. Legislative attempts to prohibit such use were undertaken in 1976, even as the presidential campaigns were under way. This further raised abortion politics to the status of a media event. Congress approved the Hyde Amendment to an appropriations bill for the Department of Health and Human Services, prohibiting federally funded abortions "except where the life of the mother would be endangered if the fetus were carried to term." Because the anti-abortion amendment was attached to the appropriation for a large, public-service bureaucracy, liberal senators and representatives were unable to muster much opposition, and the amendment became law. The law was subjected to constitutional challenges by a new proabortion (or "prochoice") organization, the National Abortion Rights Action League. However, the group was surprised and disappointed by a Supreme Court decision holding that states participating in a Medicaid program can refuse to pay for abortions.[14]

The focus of "prolife" group activity is a proposed "right-to-life" amendment to the Constitution. This amendment would declare the fetus to be entitled to the protection of law from conception onward; it would reverse the Supreme Court's 1973 abortion decision. Lobbying for and against the proposed amendment was the most "highly charged lobbying since the contentious days of the Vietnam War."[15] Many members of Congress believed that abortion was the single issue on which they had to pass the "litmus test." (Most prominent in making this argument was Senator Robert Packwood, a backer of the right to abortion whose campaign for reelection was heavily funded by various women's organizations. Similarly, right-to-life organizations donated substantial sums to Packwood's opponent. Packwood, the incumbent, was reelected.)

The prochoice groups, a loose coalition of organizations coordinated by the National Women's Political Caucus and the National Organization for Women, were severely handicapped by the necessity to pay attention to a variety of other issues. In addition to abortion, women's organizations were concerned with the implementation of Title IX of the Education Amendments of 1972, the ratification of the Equal Rights Amendment, the implementation of the Equal Credit Opportunity Act, and a variety of other matters.

Unlike these organizations, the right-to-life organizations did not deviate from their goals—an absolute ban on federally funded abortions and, ultimately, a right-to-life amendment to the Constitution. The antiabortion groups displayed "zeal, passion and organization. . . . Single-minded, angry, and persistent, the 'right to life' minority makes itself seen and heard."[16] The National Right to Life Committee, the Ad Hoc Committee in Defense of Life, and a variety of subsidiary and semiaffiliated groups were organized around this single issue. Although these groups were successful in halting most federally funded abortions, the proposed constitutional amendment generated little congressional enthusiasm.

"Single-minded, angry, and persistent, the 'right-to-life' minority makes itself seen and heard."

Single-issue interest groups are most effective at the legislative level. In this case a substantial number of members of Congress believed that their elections hung in the balance. The issue was one of emotion and great symbolic meaning, extending beyond the issue of unwanted pregnancies and touching on the delicate subject of the family and the religious doctrines of, among others, the Roman Catholic Church.

The Equal Rights Amendment.   The contours of the struggle for and against ratification of the Equal Rights Amendment were similar to those of the abortion controversy. Both involved the rights of women, and both aroused a high degree of emotion, with the accompanying manipulation of symbols.

The earliest group support for an equal rights amendment came from the National Women's Party, the more militant branch of the suffrage movement. Such an amendment was opposed by the more conservative wing of the suffrage movement, the League of Women Voters. Whereas the National Women's Party became a single-issue group, focusing its effort exclusively on the amendment, the League of Women Voters addressed itself to many issues (in alliance with upper-middle-class urban reform groups) unrelated to this amendment. The league thus adopted a posture of not identifying solely with women's equality. Not until 1937 did other women's organizations lend support to an equal rights amendment. (The backing of the National Federation of Business and Professional Women's Clubs in that year was followed by that of the General Federation of Women's Clubs in 1944.) In the late 1960s opposition to the amendment was still being expressed by the American Association of University Women, the League of Women Voters, and the National Council of Catholic Women. With the exception of the Catholic women, these groups ultimately supported the amendment.

The division among women, a division that continues today, thus delayed the congressional response. However, once opposition among established women's groups was reduced, the Equal Rights Amendment enjoyed strong national support. The ERA was approved by Congress in 1972 by a vote of 354 to 23 in the House and 84 to 8 in the Senate. It was anticipated that ratification by the states would be a mere formality. Hawaii voted unanimous ratification on the day the ERA was approved by Congress. The normal seven-year period for ratification appeared to be more than would be required. It seemed certain that thirty-eight states would ratify within a year or so. Indeed, in the first year after congressional approval twenty-two states ratified. Public-opinion polls indicated that a majority of women and men supported the amendment. However, the support was shallow; the ERA attracted the *intense* support of relatively few people. The states that had not ratified the ERA became centers of heated controversy, close media coverage, economic boycotts by women's organizations and other supporting groups, and fierce lobbying by opponents. Beneath the high level of elite attention, however, rested an astonishingly high level of public ignorance. Only 25 percent of the supporters and 40 percent of the opponents were aware that the amendment had been considered and rejected in their state.[17] According to political scientists who studied public opinion on the ERA:

What conclusions can be drawn from the above information on supporters, opponents and "don't knows" on the Equal Rights Amendment? The first conclusion we can draw is that when polls report that about 90 percent of the population has "heard of" or "read about" the ERA, it does not mean that the 90 percent has any politically useful information. In state after state the vast majority of citizens do not know the most elementary facts about the ERA in their state, namely that it has or has not been considered. For whatever reason, lack of saliency in early ratifying states, general apathy, etc., the vast army of supporters in almost all states is unable to act in behalf of their position on the issue due to ignorance.[18]

According to these scholars, once the vast majority of poorly informed, passive citizens is removed, there are only 13 percent who are informed proponents and 8 percent who are informed opponents. Thus, the distribution of opinion is ideal for the success of single-issue groups.

Action in support of the ERA was conducted by a coalition of established groups, most conspicuously the Business and Professional Women's Clubs, League of Women Voters, and National Organization for Women. Although each functioned separately, an effort toward coordination was undertaken by ERAmerica, an umbrella organization for about thirty proponent groups. Although well-financed, the pro-ERA effort suffered from divisions within their ranks over tactics and priorities.

Opposition did not really appear until 1973, after twenty-two of the required thirty-eight states had ratified. However, once the opposition began to develop, it focused largely on the single cause of stopping the ratification process. These efforts met with considerable success. In 1973 eight states ratified by an average margin of 72 percent (as opposed to 89 percent in the previous year). After that date, only five additional states ratified and they did so by a substantially reduced margin (59 percent). Additionally, five states that had previously ratified the amendment (Idaho, Kentucky, Nebraska, South Dakota, and Tennessee) later rescinded their ratification.

The process of ratification was stopped by the intense anti-ERA lobbying of a variety of traditionally active conservative organizations, but most prominently by ad hoc, single-issue groups, the most active of which was Stop ERA, led by Phyllis Schlafly. The "Phyllis Schlafly Report," begun in 1968, devoted itself largely to the alleged dangers of the ERA.

The process of ratification was stopped by the intense anti-ERA lobbying of a variety of traditionally active conservative organizations, but most prominently by ad hoc, single-issue groups.

What was the basis of opposition? What was it about the ERA that allowed Stop-ERA to stimulate the symbolic, emotional response so essential to single-issue politics? The amendment itself consists of two simple statements:

Section 1: Equality of rights under the law shall not be denied or abridged by the United States or by any state on account of sex.

Section 2: The Congress shall have the power to enforce, by appropriate legislation, the provisions of this article.

Proponents accused the anti-ERA forces of using unfair tactics, based on unfounded fears that it would initiate large-scale social changes. The arguments by Stop ERA were that the amendment would legalize homosexual marriages, place women in combat roles in the event of a draft, and destroy the traditional family. According to one observer:

> Many ad hoc local and state groups sprang up in opposition to the Amendment. Whether accurately or not, the leaders of such groups have portrayed themselves as politically inexperienced "housewives and mothers." They have been very successful in controlling the tone and content of the debate by forcing proponent groups onto the defensive. ERA supporters have been forced to reply to questions concerning coed restrooms and homosexual marriages, as well as to respond and defend their own group's stand on logically unrelated issues such as abortion and prostitution.[19]

At the state level the debate was ideological, minimizing the value of legal information as a resource. Supporters lost control of the tone of the debate:

> When it was before Congress, the Amendment was viewed as a legal issue and was discussed in abstract and technical terms by supporters and opponents. Once the ratification process began, the ERA was redefined in much broader terms by opponents in order to actively involve many subgroups of the population into conflict. The debate became more concrete, graphic, and nontechnical.... At its height, the ERA conflict has been fueled by differences in attitudes among individuals ... concerning government, society, and social change.[20]

The issue of the draft illustrates well the extent to which, according to pro-ERA forces, "the Phyllis Schlaflys of the world ... define issues which split women."[21] In states that rejected the amendment, the draft emerged as a major objection. However, legal scholars generally agree that, in the event a military draft were reinstituted, women and men would be drafted and assigned to duties (including combat) on the basis of their qualifications and the needs of the military.[22] A draft would probably provide the same exceptions for women as have been customary in the past for men. Thus, the fear that mothers would be snatched from their infants is invalid, because Congress could exempt parents.

Stalled three states short of the required number for ratification, pro-ERA groups successfully lobbied for an extension of the normal seven-year deadline to ten years—until June 30, 1982. Congress enacted the extension by simple majority vote in 1977. But no addi-

Phyllis Schlafly, the leading opponent of the ERA.

tional states ratified the amendment. Thus, fifteen states did not ratify. Nine were in the Deep South, where legislative opinions showed little sign of movement. Three were Sun Belt states, where conservative legislative opinion appeared solidified. One of the remaining three, Utah, has always had a strong Mormon legislative influence. Consequently, much attention was centered on Illinois and Missouri. In Illinois twelve attempts at ratification proved unsuccessful. In Missouri the issue became entangled in a dispute between the state and the National Organization for Women. NOW urged a nationwide boycott of Missouri, asking organizations to refuse to hold conventions in states that had not ratified the amendment. But these efforts failed to produce the necessary ratification, and time ran out.

EXPANDING CIVIL RIGHTS

Mexican-Americans

Mexican-Americans, geographically concentrated in the Southwest, have the characteristics of many of the other minority groups. They endure poverty. They have produced a charismatic leader, Cesar Chavez, and other Mexican-American leaders have spoken for those who protest against the comparative poverty of their group. Their poverty level is not as serious as that of blacks; it is bad, but not so bad as to deny hope. In the 1980 elections, Reagan gained substantially more support from Mexican-Americans than had Gerald Ford in 1976. Like blacks, the Mexican-Americans have used their geographic concentration to their advantage, winning municipal office in a number of southwestern cities. However, again like blacks, they do not have a proportion of congressional seats approaching their proportion of the population.

Officially, Mexican-Americans are the nation's second largest minority, with about 7 million people (Figure 12-4). In fact, there may be substantially more living in the United States illegally. We really do not know, then, how many there are, but estimates are in the range of 16 million. Mexican-Americans suffer far more than blacks from language barriers. Many young Mexican-Americans speak and understand only Spanish. For this reason, bilingual education was introduced by the Department of Education as a corrective. Initially developed during the Carter years, the bilingual education program required that pupils in elementary school be instructed in their native language while taking courses in English. It was reasoned that Mexican-Americans could learn math from Spanish-speaking instructors while learning English as a second language. This program was met with substantial hostility by local school administrators for fiscal and administrative reasons and by educators in general on the ground that bilingual education would delay the social integration of Spanish-speaking Americans. Reagan opposed the federal program during his campaign, and his secretary of education announced its virtual abandonment.

Possibly because of the language problem and the impoverished conditions in which Mexican-Americans live, their turnout in elections frequently lags behind that of blacks. In the 1980 presidential election blacks made up 10 percent of those who voted, compared with 2 percent for all Hispanics, including Mexican-Americans. Furthermore, although Chavez is highly regarded in the Mexican-American community, his efforts are concentrated on labor relations. No leader comparable to King has emerged in the Mexican-American community.

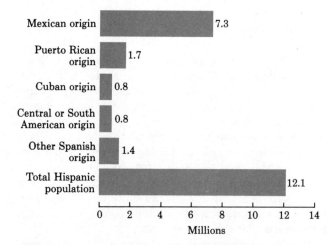

Figure 12-4. Hispanic Americans, March 1979. (Source: U. S. Bureau of the Census and the *New York Times,* February 24, 1981, pp. A1, A12.)

Mexican-Americans earn about 73 percent of the national average, substantially more than blacks or other Americans of Spanish descent.[23] Mexican-Americans have also made economic *progress*. Although black earnings and white earnings have maintained substantially the same gap for many years, Mexican-Americans have been gradually reducing the gap between their earnings and the national average. Perhaps this progress explains why 36 percent of Mexican-Americans gave Reagan their vote, a sharp increase from their Republican vote in previous years.

Homosexuals

More-complex problems exist for another group that has recently entered the politics of civil rights, homosexuals. Because of widespread social ostracism, the actual number of homosexuals is not

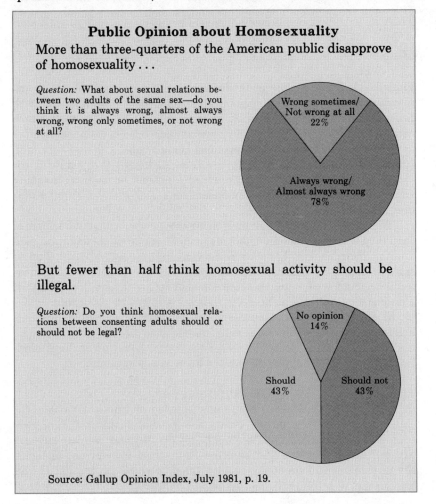

Public Opinion about Homosexuality

More than three-quarters of the American public disapprove of homosexuality . . .

Question: What about sexual relations between two adults of the same sex—do you think it is always wrong, almost always wrong, wrong only sometimes, or not wrong at all?

Wrong sometimes/
Not wrong at all
22%

Always wrong/
Almost always wrong
78%

But fewer than half think homosexual activity should be illegal.

Question: Do you think homosexual relations between consenting adults should or should not be legal?

No opinion
14%

Should
43%

Should not
43%

Source: Gallup Opinion Index, July 1981, p. 19.

Gay teachers march in San Francisco's annual Gay Freedom Day Parade.

known. Also, there is no clear definition of a homosexual. It is estimated that one-third of the population may have experimented with homosexual sex at least once. However, probably no more than 2 percent of women and 4 percent of men are exclusively homosexual.[24]

Public opinion about homosexuals is ambivalent. Some state laws still make homosexual activity a crime. Although the public is divided equally on whether homosexual relations between consenting adults should be illegal, most people favor equal job opportunities for homosexuals.

This ambivalence is not limited to the public. Until 1973, homosexuality was regarded by the American Psychiatric Association as a mental disorder. Until the Civil Service Reform Act of 1978, homosexuals could be dismissed from public employment. Intelligence-gathering and espionage agencies can still refuse to hire homosexuals. The justification is that homosexuals are subject to blackmail.

In some cities homosexuals have organized politically. In San Francisco and New York they have moved into clearly defined neighborhoods and have demonstrated substantial cohesion in local elections. In national politics they have been less successful.

The Handicapped

In 1975, with the almost unanimous passage of Public Law 94–142, called by many "the bill of rights for the handicapped," Congress responded to the demands of organizations of handicapped citizens without attracting any visible opposition. This legislation, assuring the physically and mentally handicapped of equal protection of the laws, requires public schools to educate handicapped children, whenever feasible, in the same environment with "normal" children. The intention is to give all children the same opportunity to be educated.

The problem of defining the "handicapped" is a serious one. It is not hard to identify blacks or women. Mental and physical retardation, however, allows no such easy classification. For the purpose of the federal legislation, retardation can take one of the following forms: educable mental retardation, speech retardation, physical handicaps, or learning disorders. Most teachers have no training in educating the handicapped; they have a hard enough time maintaining discipline without additional tasks. Some school districts have objected to incorporating handicapped children because of the high costs of providing special facilities and teachers. Nevertheless, another previously ignored group has taken its place in the civil rights struggle.

The Aged

The aged are different from other minority or deprived groups. Other groups are relatively stable, but the percentage of the population 65 or older is increasing rapidly (see Table 12-3). In 1900 only 4 percent of the population was 65 or over; in 1980, the figure had risen to 11 percent. This increase was due to high birth rates (slowing only in the 1970s) and substantial increases in life expectancy. The older population is not merely an older reflection of the larger population. It is disproportionately white (since blacks die younger) and female (since females live longer).

Table 12-3. Percent of the U. S. Population 65 and Over: 1900-2030

Year	Percent
1900	4.1
1910	4.3
1920	4.6
1930	5.4
1940	6.8
1950	8.1
1960	9.2
1970	9.8
1975	10.5
1980	11.0
1990 (projected)	11.7
2000	11.7
2010	11.9
2020	14.6
2030	17.0

Source: U. S. Bureau of the Census, *Current Population Reports,* Special Studies, Series P-23, No. 59, May 1976, p. 9.

It is generally assumed that the older population does not have the "shared attitudes" required for cohesive political action. It is true that people tend to become more socially conservative as they age; however, they also become more concerned about income maintenance. Many older Americans join the ranks of the poor when their retirement income makes it impossible for them to maintain the standard of living they were accustomed to when they were employed. On the average, the elderly have income levels only slightly better than half of the income levels of the under-65 population.

Social Security is the most common form of income for older Americans; indeed, it is the main source of income for most of them.[25] Although they may not have much else in common, the aged are concerned about various forms of retirement support, and their organizations lobby hard to protect Social Security. Outcries from the elderly convinced the Reagan administration that deep cuts in Social Security were unthinkable.

Discrimination on the basis of age has become a federal concern. The 1967 Age Discrimination Amendment to the 1964 Civil Rights Act added age to the list of protected categories. In 1975 the Older Americans Act provided for the withdrawal of federal funds from programs guilty of age discrimination. It also placed enforcement within the authority of the secretary of health and human services,

Rep. Claude Pepper (D-Fla.) chairman of the House Committee on Aging, greets Maria Quiroz, 100 and W. L. Dannell, M. D., 101. Pepper is 82.

with the Civil Rights Commission authorized to make investigations. Until this legislation the social mood of the country had favored early retirement, because that opens up jobs for the young. Firms sought to encourage employment by lowering the retirement age to 62. However, legislation now prohibits mandatory retirement before age 70.

RIGHTS IN CONFLICT

The politics of civil rights, as it expands, produces competing claims on the political and economic resources of society. A good example of rights in conflict can be found in efforts to solve the problem of the aged. Representative Claude Pepper—champion of the aged, the oldest member of Congress, and chairman of the House Select Committee on Aging—successfully pursued the goal of raising the mandatory retirement age. As the working population over 65 increases, however, there will be fewer jobs available for blacks, women, and other "protected categories" unless the economy expands greatly. How does one resolve this dispute? The issue is not purely academic. In 1981 the Equal Employment Opportunities Commission reported that the greatest increase in complaints had come from those alleging age discrimination.[26]

> The politics of civil rights, as it expands, produces competing claims on the political and economic resources of society.

Just as a scarce job market may result in competition between the aged and the young, so it may also result in competition between blacks and women. Women have entered the work force in ever-increasing numbers. The American economy creates about 3.5 million new jobs annually, two-thirds of which are being filled by women. White employers often concede that they prefer to hire white women rather than black men.[27] Blacks believe that this preference indicates that racism is a more durable system of discrimination than sexism. Ronald Lewis, vice-president of the National Association of Black Manufacturers, contends that "this society treats its mothers, sisters, and wives far better than its ex-slaves."[28] Women deny this assertion, stressing that the labor market still functions as a man's world, in which women are excluded from the locker rooms and luncheon clubs where many decisions are made. According to Nancy S. Barrett, an economist at the Urban Institute, "No one says that a black man does not need a job because he has a working spouse, or that he'll work for lower pay, and no one asks a black man about his baby-sitting problems."[29]

Sears, Roebuck and Company filed a lawsuit against ten federal agencies, charging that conflicting regulations made it impossible to comply with affirmative-action goals. The suit asserted that enforcement priorities had shifted from minorities to women. Sears lost the case, but the issue of rights in conflict is not subject to easy resolution.

CHAPTER SUMMARY

1. Civil rights activists have fought to eliminate both public and private discrimination against women, blacks, the aged, the handicapped, and other minorities. For black Americans in particular, the 1896 doctrine of "separate but equal" (*Plessy* v. *Ferguson*) perpetuated a segregation pattern that was not constitutionally challenged until the Supreme Court's 1954 ruling in *Brown* v. *Board of Education of Topeka*. This landmark decision noted segregation's harmful psychological effects on black children, declared the practice unconstitutional, and thus launched the modern civil rights era.

2. During the 1960s, Congress passed important civil rights legislation designed to counter *private* discrimination. (The judicial branch had already sought to counter *public,* or government-sanctioned, discrimination.) The Civil Rights Act of 1964 outlawed improper voter-registration procedures and segregation in public accommodations, and it mandated equal employment opportunities in many business firms and labor unions.

3. Nonviolent mass protest is an effort to influence the attitudes of policymakers and gain public sympathy for the protesters' cause. Media coverage of peaceful protests may strengthen their overall effectiveness (as in the Birmingham and Selma marches), but coverage of ghetto riots in the 1960s produced a "white backlash."

4. The Supreme Court's *Swann* decision on school busing accelerated integration efforts in the South while allowing a significant degree of de facto segregation to remain in the North. In 1974 (*Milliken* v. *Bradley*) the Court ruled that busing across city/suburban district lines was necessary only if school segregation had been directly caused by the actions of public officials. However, busing may still be used in many instances to overcome racial imbalances if a federal judge so orders.

5. Affirmative action seeks the achievement of equality in education and employment through preferential, compensatory programs. Do such programs result in "reverse discrimination"? The Supreme Court's *Bakke* (1978) and *Weber* (1979) decisions provide mixed answers to this question.

6. Income and employment discrimination against women continues to exist despite some congressional efforts to combat it. Two more-visible issues, abortion and the Equal Rights Amendment, have commanded public attention. The Supreme Court has ruled that women have a constitutional right to abortions—though not necessarily at government expense. ERA failed to be ratified in part because of the determined opposition of single-issue groups.

7. Mexican-Americans suffer from poverty, low educational levels, and language barriers, but unlike blacks they have been able to narrow somewhat the economic gap between themselves and whites. Homosexuals have become a politically active minority but continue to face some hostility from the public. The handicapped and the aged are two other groups that have sought equal protection under the law.

8. The competing interests of different groups can produce a situation of "rights in conflict." There is no easy resolution to the problem of competing claims advanced by different disadvantaged groups.

Notes

1. *Plessy* v. *Ferguson* 163 U. S. 537 (1896).
2. *Brown* v. *Board of Education of Topeka*, 347 U. S. 483 (1954).
3. Kenneth B. Clark, *Dark Ghetto* (New York: Harper & Row, 1965), p. 77.
4. Martin Luther King, Jr., "Letter from Birmingham Jail," April 16, 1963. Reprinted in Thomas R. Dye and Brett W. Hawkins (Eds.), *Politics in the Metropolis* (Columbus, Ohio: Charles E. Merrill, 1967), pp. 125–126.
5. *New York Times*, August 29, 1963, p. A16.
6. *Statistical Abstract of the United States*, 1980, p. 145.
7. *Swann* v. *Charlotte-Mecklenburg Board of Education*, 402 U. S. 1 (1971).
8. U. S. Commission on Civil Rights, *Racial Isolation in the Public Schools* (Washington, D. C.: Government Printing Office, 1966).
9. *Milliken* v. *Bradley*, 418 U. S. 717 (1974).
10. *Regents of University of California* v. *Bakke*, 438 U. S. 265 (1978).
11. *United Steel Workers* v. *Weber*, 443 U. S. 193 (1979).
12. Jeane Kirkpatrick, *The New Presidential Elite: Men and Women in National Politics* (New York: Russell Sage Foundation and Twentieth Century Fund, 1976), pp. 437–442.
13. U. S. Department of Commerce, Bureau of the Census, "A Statistical Portrait of Women in the United States: 1978," *Current Population Reports*, Special Studies, Series P. 23, No. 100, February 1980.
14. *Beal* v. *Doe*, 432 U. S. 438 (1977).
15. *New York Times*, June 25, 1977, Sec. IV, p. 10.
16. "The Women's Movement," *Congressional Quarterly* (1977), p. 108.
17. Debrah Bokowski and Aage Clausen, "Federalism, Representation and the Amendment Process: The Case of the Equal Rights Amendment" (paper presented to the 1979 annual meeting of the Midwest Political Science Association), p. 12.
18. Bokowski and Clausen, p. 15.
19. Janet K. Boles, *The Politics of the Equal Rights Amendment: Conflict and the Decision Process* (New York: Longman, 1979), p. 26.
20. Boles, p. 171.
21. Kristi Andersen, "Working Women and Political Participation," *American Journal of Political Science, 19* (1975), p. 453.
22. U. S. Senate, "Equal Rights for Men and Women," S. Report 92–689, 92nd Congress, 2nd session, 1972, pp. 13–14.
23. U. S. Bureau of the Census, *Current Population Reports,* Series P–20, No. 224, p. 6.

24. Elizabeth Ogg, *Changing Views of Homosexuality* (New York: Public Affairs Committee, Inc., 1978), p. 3.
25. *Congressional Quarterly Weekly Report,* November 28, 1981, p. 2333.
26. *Congressional Quarterly Weekly Report,* p. 2333.
27. Stephen V. Roberts, "Blacks and Women Clash on Access to Jobs and Aid," *New York Times,* February 20, 1979, p. A10.
28. Roberts, p. A10.
29. Roberts, p. A10.

Close-Up and In-Depth Analyses

James Baldwin. *The Fire Next Time.* New York: Dial Press, 1963.

Sandra Baxter and Marjorie Lansing. *Women in Politics.* Ann Arbor: University of Michigan Press, 1980.

Janet K. Boles. *The Politics of the Equal Rights Amendment.* New York: Longman, 1979.

Stokely Carmichael and Charles V. Hamilton. *Black Power.* New York: Random House, 1967.

Kenneth B. Clark. *Dark Ghetto.* New York: Harper & Row, 1967.

John Hope Franklin. *From Slavery to Freedom,* 5th ed. New York: Knopf, 1978.

Jo Freeman. *The Politics of the Women's Movement.* New York: McKay, 1975.

Chris F. Garcia and Rudolph O. de la Garza. *The Chicano Political Experience.* North Scituate, Mass.: Duxbury, 1977.

Jeane Kirkpatrick. *The Politics of the Women's Movement.* New York: McKay, 1975.

Anthony Oberschall. *Social Conflict and Social Movement.* Englewood Cliffs, N. J.: Prentice-Hall, 1973.

Frances Fox Piven and Richard A. Cloward. *Poor People's Movements.* New York: Pantheon, 1977.

Frances Fox Piven and Richard A. Cloward. *The New Class War.* New York: Pantheon, 1982.

Report of the National Advisory Commission on Civil Disorder. New York: Bantam, 1968.

Carol A. Whitehut. *Women in America: The Oppressed Majority.* Santa Monica, Calif.: Goodyear, 1977.

C. Vann Woodward. *The Strange Career of Jim Crow,* 3rd ed. New York: Oxford University Press, 1974.

THE CONSTITUTION
OF THE UNITED STATES
OF AMERICA*

We, the People of the United States, in order to form a more perfect
union, establish justice, insure domestic tranquility, provide for the
common defence, promote the general welfare, and secure the blessings of liberty to ourselves and our posterity, do ordain and establish
this Constitution for the United States of America.

ARTICLE I.

Section 1. All legislative powers herein granted shall be vested in
a Congress of the United States, which shall consist of a Senate and
House of Representatives.

Section 2. The House of Representatives shall be composed of
members chosen every second year by the people of the several states,
and the electors in each state shall have the qualifications requisite
for electors of the most numerous branch of the state legislature.

No person shall be a representative who shall not have attained to
the age of twenty-five years, and been seven years a citizen of the
United States, and who shall not, when elected, be an inhabitant of
that state in which he shall be chosen.

†[Representatives and direct taxes shall be apportioned among
the several states which may be included within this Union, according
to their respective numbers, which shall be determined by adding to
the whole number of free persons, including those bound to service
for a term of years, and excluding Indians not taxed, three-fifths of
all other persons.] The actual enumeration shall be made within
three years after the first meeting of the Congress of the United
States, and within every subsequent term of ten years, in such manner as they shall by law direct. The number of representatives shall
not exceed one for every thirty thousand, but each state shall have
at least one representative; and until such enumeration shall be
made, the state of New-Hampshire shall be entitled to chuse three,
Massachusetts eight, Rhode-Island and Providence Plantations one,
Connecticut five, New-York six, New-Jersey four, Pennsylvania

*The *Constitution* is reprinted in the typographic style of the final draft printed by
(John) Dunlap & Claypoole at Philadelphia for the Federal Convention of 1787 on 15
September 1787. The original text was printed in small Caslon italic and the old style
"f" has been changed to "s." This text is reprinted from U. S. Congress, House, 94th
Cong., 2d sess., H. Doc. 94-497, 1976.

†The part enclosed by brackets was changed by section 2 of Amendment XIV.

eight, Delaware one, Maryland six, Virginia ten, North-Carolina five, South-Carolina five, and Georgia three.

When vacancies happen in the representation from any state, the Executive authority thereof shall issue writs of election to fill such vacancies.

The House of Representatives shall chuse their Speaker and other officers; and shall have the sole power of impeachment.

Section 3. The Senate of the United States shall be composed of two senators from each state, *[chosen by the legislature thereof,] for six years; and each senator shall have one vote.

Immediately after they shall be assembled in consequence of the first election, they shall be divided as equally as may be into three classes. The seats of the senators of the first class shall be vacated at the expiration of the second year, of the second class at the expiration of the fourth year, and of the third class at the expiration of the sixth year, so that one-third may be chosen every second year; †[and if vacancies happen by resignation, or otherwise, during the recess of the Legislature of any state, the Executive thereof may make temporary appointments until the next meeting of the Legislature, which shall then fill such vacancies.]

No person shall be a senator who shall not have attained to the age of thirty years, and been nine years a citizen of the United States, and who shall not, when elected, be an inhabitant of that state for which he shall be chosen.

The Vice-President of the United States shall be President of the senate, but shall have no vote, unless they be equally divided.

The Senate shall chuse their other officers, and also a President pro tempore, in the absence of the Vice-President, or when he shall exercise the office of President of the United States.

The Senate shall have the sole power to try all impeachments. When sitting for that purpose, they shall be on oath or affirmation. When the President of the United States is tried, the Chief Justice shall preside: And no person shall be convicted without the concurrence of two-thirds of the members present.

Judgment in cases of impeachment shall not extend further than to removal from office, and disqualification to hold and enjoy any office of honor, trust or profit under the United States; but the party convicted shall nevertheless be liable and subject to indictment, trial, judgment and punishment, according to law.

Section 4. The times, places and manner of holding elections for senators and representatives, shall be prescribed in each state by the legislature thereof; but the Congress may at any time by law make or alter such regulations, except as to the places of chusing Senators.

The Congress shall assemble at least once in every year, and such

*The clause enclosed by brackets was changed by clause 1 of Amendment XVII.
†The part enclosed by brackets was changed by clause 2 of Amendment XVII.

meeting shall *[be on the first Monday in December,] unless they shall by law appoint a different day.

Section 5. Each house shall be the judge of the elections, returns and qualifications of its own members, and a majority of each shall constitute a quorum to do business; but a smaller number may adjourn from day to day, and may be authorized to compel the attendance of absent members, in such manner, and under such penalties as each house may provide.

Each house may determine the rules of its proceedings, punish its members for disorderly behaviour, and, with the concurrence of two-thirds, expel a member.

Each house shall keep a journal of its proceedings, and from time to time publish the same, excepting such parts as may in their judgment require secrecy; and the yeas and nays of the members of either house on any question shall, at the desire of one-fifth of those present, be entered on the journal.

Neither house, during the session of Congress, shall, without the consent of the other, adjourn for more than three days, nor to any other place than that in which the two houses shall be sitting.

Section 6. The senators and representatives shall receive a compensation for their services, to be ascertained by law, and paid out of the treasury of the United States. They shall in all cases, except treason, felony and breach of the peace, be privileged from arrest during their attendance at the session of their respective houses, and in going to and returning from the same; and for any speech or debate in either house, they shall not be questioned in any other place.

No senator or representative shall, during the time for which he was elected, be appointed to any civil office under the authority of the United States, which shall have been created, or the emoluments whereof shall have been encreased during such time; and no person holding any office under the United States, shall be a member of either house during his continuance in office.

Section 7. All bills for raising revenue shall originate in the house of representatives; but the senate may propose or concur with amendments as on other bills.

Every bill which shall have passed the house of representatives and the senate, shall, before it become a law, be presented to the president of the United States; if he approve he shall sign it, but if not he shall return it, with his objections to that house in which it shall have originated, who shall enter the objections at large on their journal, and proceed to reconsider it. If after such reconsideration two-thirds of that house shall agree to pass the bill, it shall be sent, together with the objections, to the other house, by which it shall likewise be reconsidered, and if approved by two-thirds of that house, it shall become a law. But in all such cases the votes of both houses

*The clause enclosed by brackets was changed by section 2 of Amendment XX.

shall be determined by yeas and nays, and the names of the persons voting for and against the bill shall be entered on the journal of each house respectively. If any bill shall not be returned by the President within ten days (Sundays excepted) after it shall have been presented to him, the same shall be a law, in like manner as if he had signed it, unless the Congress by their adjournment prevent its return, in which case it shall not be a law.

Every order, resolution, or vote to which the concurrence of the Senate and House of Representatives may be necessary (except on a question of adjournment) shall be presented to the President of the United States; and before the same shall take effect, shall be approved by him, or, being disapproved by him, shall be repassed by two-thirds of the Senate and House of Representatives, according to the rules and limitations prescribed in the case of a bill.

Section 8. The Congress shall have power

To lay and collect taxes, duties, imposts and excises, to pay the debts and provide for the common defence and general welfare of the United States; but all duties, imposts and excises shall be uniform throughout the United States;

To borrow money on the credit of the United States;

To regulate commerce with foreign nations, and among the several states; and with the Indian tribes;

To establish an uniform rule of naturalization, and uniform laws on the subject of bankruptcies throughout the United States;

To coin money, regulate the value thereof, and of foreign coin, and fix the standard of weights and measures;

To provide for the punishment of counterfeiting the securities and current coin of the United States;

To establish post offices and post roads;

To promote the progress of science and useful arts, by securing for limited times to authors and inventors the exclusive right to their respective writings and discoveries;

To constitute tribunals inferior to the supreme court;

To define and punish piracies and felonies committed on the high seas, and offences against the law of nations;

To declare war, grant letters of marque and reprisal, and make rules concerning captures on land and water;

To raise and support armies, but no appropriation of money to that use shall be for a longer term than two years;

To provide and maintain a navy;

To make rules for the government and regulation of the land and naval forces;

To provide for calling forth the militia to execute the laws of the union, suppress insurrections and repel invasions;

To provide for organizing, arming, and disciplining, the militia, and for governing such part of them as may be employed in the service of the United States, reserving to the States respectively, the appointment of the officers, and the authority of training the militia according to the discipline prescribed by Congress;

To exercise exclusive legislation in all cases whatsoever, over such district (not exceeding ten miles square) as may, by cession of particular States, and the acceptance of Congress, become the seat of the government of the United States, and to exercise like authority over all places purchased by the consent of the legislature of the state in which the same shall be, for the erection of forts, magazines, arsenals, dock-yards, and other needful buildings;—And

To make all laws which shall be necessary and proper for carrying into execution the foregoing powers, and all other powers vested by this constitution in the government of the United States, or in any department or officer thereof.

Section 9. The migration or importation of such persons as any of the states now existing shall think proper to admit, shall not be prohibited by the Congress prior to the year one thousand eight hundred and eight, but a tax or duty may be imposed on such importation, not exceeding ten dollars for each person.

The privilege of the writ of habeas corpus shall not be suspended, unless when in cases of rebellion or invasion the public safety may require it.

No bill of attainder or ex post facto law shall be passed.

No capitation, or other direct, tax shall be laid, unless in proportion to the census or enumeration herein before directed to be taken.*

No tax or duty shall be laid on articles exported from any state. No preference shall be given by any regulation of commerce or revenue to the ports of one state over those of another: nor shall vessels bound to, or from, one state, be obliged to enter, clear, or pay duties in another.

No money shall be drawn from the treasury, but in consequence of appropriations made by law; and a regular statement and account of the receipts and expenditures of all public money shall be published from time to time.

No title of nobility shall be granted by the United States:—And no person holding any office of profit or trust under them, shall, without the consent of the Congress, accept of any present, emolument, office, or title, of any kind whatever, from any king, prince, or foreign state.

Section 10. No state shall enter into any treaty, alliance, or confederation; grant letters of marque and reprisal; coin money; emit bills of credit; make any thing but gold and silver coin a tender in payment of debts; pass any bill of attainder, ex post facto law, or law impairing the obligation of contracts, or grant any title of nobility.

See also Amendment XVI.

No state shall, without the consent of the Congress, lay any imposts or duties on imports or exports, except what may be absolutely necessary for executing its inspection laws; and the net produce of all duties and imposts, laid by any state on imports or exports, shall be for the use of the Treasury of the United States; and all such laws shall be subject to the revision and controul of the Congress. No state shall, without the consent of Congress, lay any duty of tonnage, keep troops, or ships of war in time of peace, enter into any agreement or compact with another state, or with a foreign power, or engage in war, unless actually invaded, or in such imminent danger as will not admit of delay.

ARTICLE II.   *Section 1.* The executive power shall be vested in a president of the United States of America. He shall hold his office during the term of four years, and, together with the vice president, chosen for the same term, be elected as follows.

Each state shall appoint, in such manner as the legislature thereof may direct, a number of electors, equal to the whole number of senators and representatives to which the state may be entitled in the Congress: but no senator or representative, or person holding an office of trust or profit under the United States, shall be appointed an elector.

*[The electors shall meet in their respective states, and vote by ballot for two persons, of whom one at least shall not be an inhabitant of the same state with themselves. And they shall make a list of all the persons voted for, and of the number of votes for each; which list they shall sign and certify, and transmit sealed to the seat of the government of the United States, directed to the president of the senate. The president of the senate shall, in the presence of the senate and house of representatives, open all the certificates, and the votes shall then be counted. The person having the greatest number of votes shall be the president, if such number be a majority of the whole number of electors appointed; and if there be more than one who have such majority, and have an equal number of votes, then the house of representatives shall immediately chuse by ballot one of them for president; and if no person have a majority, then from the five highest on the list the said house shall in like manner chuse the president. But in chusing the president, the votes shall be taken by states, the representation from each state having one vote; a quorum for this purpose shall consist of a member or members from two-thirds of the states, and a majority of all the states shall be necessary to a choice. In every case, after the choice of the president, the person having the greatest number of votes of the electors shall be the vice-president. But if there should remain two or more who have equal

*This paragraph has been superseded by Amendment XII.

votes, the senate shall chuse from them by ballot the vice-president.]

The Congress may determine the time of chusing the electors, and the day on which they shall give their votes; which day shall be the same throughout the United States.

No person except a natural born citizen, or a citizen of the United States, at the time of the adoption of this constitution, shall be eligible to the office of president; neither shall any person be eligible to that office who shall not have attained to the age of thirty-five years, and been fourteen years a resident within the United States.

*In case of the removal of the president from office, or of his death, resignation, or inability to discharge the powers and duties of the said office, the same shall devolve on the vice-president, and the Congress may by law provide for the case of removal, death, resignation or inability, both of the president and vice-president, declaring what officer shall then act as president, and such officer shall act accordingly, until the disability be removed, or a president shall be elected.

The president shall, at stated times, receive for his services, a compensation, which shall neither be encreased nor diminished during the period for which he shall have been elected, and he shall not receive within that period any other emolument from the United States, or any of them.

Before he enter on the execution of his office, he shall take the following oath or affirmation:

"I do solemnly swear (or affirm) that I will faithfully execute the office of president of the United States, and will to the best of my ability, preserve, protect and defend the constitution of the United States."

Section 2. The president shall be commander in chief of the army and navy of the United States, and of the militia of the several States, when called into the actual service of the United States; he may require the opinion, in writing, of the principal officer in each of the executive departments, upon any subject relating to the duties of their respective offices, and he shall have power to grant reprieves and pardons for offences against the United States, except in cases of impeachment.

He shall have power, by and with the advice and consent of the senate, to make treaties, provided two-thirds of the senators present concur; and he shall nominate, and by and with the advice and consent of the senate, shall appoint ambassadors, other public ministers and consuls, judges of the supreme court, and all other officers of the United States, whose appointments are not herein otherwise provided for, and which shall be established by law. But the Congress may by law vest the appointment of such inferior officers, as they

*This clause has been affected by Amendment XXV.

think proper, in the president alone, in the courts of law, or in the heads of departments.

The president shall have power to fill up all vacancies that may happen during the recess of the senate, by granting commissions which shall expire at the end of their next session.

Section 3. He shall from time to time give to the Congress information of the state of the union, and recommend to their consideration such measures as he shall judge necessary and expedient; he may, on extraordinary occasions, convene both houses, or either of them, and in case of disagreement between them, with respect to the time of adjournment, he may adjourn them to such time as he shall think proper; he shall receive ambassadors and other public ministers; he shall take care that the laws be faithfully executed, and shall commission all the officers of the United States.

Section 4. The president, vice-president and all civil officers of the United States, shall be removed from office on impeachment for, and conviction of, treason, bribery, or other high crimes and misdemeanors.

ARTICLE III.   *Section 1.* The judicial power of the United States, shall be vested in one supreme court, and in such inferior courts as the Congress may from time to time ordain and establish. The judges, both of the supreme and inferior courts, shall hold their offices during good behaviour, and shall, at stated times, receive for their services, a compensation, which shall not be diminished during their continuance in office.

Section 2. The judicial power shall extend to all cases, in law and equity, arising under this constitution, the laws of the United States, and treaties made, or which shall be made, under their authority; to all cases affecting ambassadors, other public ministers and consuls; to all cases of admiralty and maritime jurisdiction; to controversies to which the United States shall be a party; to controversies between two or more States, between a state and citizens of another state,* between citizens of different States, between citizens of the same state claiming lands under grants of different States, and between a state, or the citizens thereof, and foreign States, citizens or subjects.

In all cases affecting ambassadors, other public ministers and consuls, and those in which a state shall be party, the supreme court shall have original jurisdiction. In all the other cases before mentioned, the supreme court shall have appellate jurisdiction, both as to law and fact, with such exceptions, and under such regulations as the Congress shall make.

The trial of all crimes, except in cases of impeachment, shall be by jury; and such trial shall be held in the state where the said crimes

*This clause has been affected by Amendment XI.

shall have been committed; but when not committed within any state, the trial shall be at such place or places as the Congress may by law have directed.

Section 3. Treason against the United States, shall consist only in levying war against them, or in adhering to their enemies, giving them aid and comfort. No person shall be convicted of treason unless on the testimony of two witnesses to the same overt act, or on confession in open court.

The Congress shall have power to declare the punishment of treason, but no attainder of treason shall work corruption of blood, or forfeiture except during the life of the person attainted.

ARTICLE IV.

Section 1. Full faith and credit shall be given in each state to the public acts, records, and judicial proceedings of every other state. And the Congress may by general laws prescribe the manner in which such acts, records and proceedings shall be proved, and the effect thereof.

Section 2. The citizens of each state shall be entitled to all privileges and immunities of citizens in the several states.

A person charged in any state with treason, felony, or other crime, who shall flee from justice, and be found in another state, shall, on demand of the executive authority of the state from which he fled, be delivered up, to be removed to the state having jurisdiction of the crime.

*[No person held to service or labour in one state, under the laws thereof, escaping into another, shall, in consequence of any law or regulation therein, be discharged from such service or labour, but shall be delivered up on claim of the party to whom such service or labour may be due.]

Section 3. New states may be admitted by the Congress into this union; but no new state shall be formed or erected within the jurisdiction of any other state; nor any state be formed by the junction of two or more states, or parts of states, without the consent of the legislatures of the states concerned as well as of the Congress.

The Congress shall have power to dispose of and make all needful rules and regulations respecting the territory or other property belonging to the United States; and nothing in this Constitution shall be so construed as to prejudice any claims of the United States, or of any particular state.

Section 4. The United States shall guarantee to every state in this union a Republican form of government, and shall protect each of them against invasion; and on application of the legislature, or of the executive (when the legislature cannot be convened) against domestic violence.

*This paragraph has been superseded by Amendment XIII.

ARTICLE V.   The Congress, whenever two-thirds of both houses shall deem it necessary, shall propose amendments to this constitution, or, on the application of the legislatures of two-thirds of the several states, shall call a convention for proposing amendments, which, in either case, shall be valid to all intents and purposes, as part of this constitution, when ratified by the legislatures of three-fourths of the several states, or by conventions in three-fourths thereof, as the one or the other mode of ratification may be proposed by the Congress; Provided, that no amendment which may be made prior to the year one thousand eight* hundred and eight shall in any manner affect the first and fourth clauses in the ninth section of the first article; and that no state, without its consent, shall be deprived of its equal suffrage in the senate.

ARTICLE VI.   All debts contracted and engagements entered into, before the adoption of this Constitution, shall be as valid against the United States under this Constitution, as under the confederation.

This constitution, and the laws of the United States which shall be made in pursuance thereof; and all treaties made, or which shall be made, under the authority of the United States, shall be the supreme law of the land; and the judges in every state shall be bound thereby, any thing in the constitution or laws of any state to the contrary notwithstanding.

The senators and representatives beforementioned, and the members of the several state legislatures, and all executive and judicial officers, both of the United States and of the several States, shall be bound by oath or affirmation, to support this constitution; but no religious test shall ever be required as a qualification to any office or public trust under the United States.

ARTICLE VII.   The ratification of the conventions of nine States, shall be sufficient for the establishment of this constitution between the States so ratifying the same.

[Signatures omitted]

---

*Misprinted "seven" in the original broadside of September 17, 1787, when the figures of the preceding draft were spelled out. Corrected by Dunlap & Claypoole in their Pennsylvania Packet reprint of September 19, 1787. It was the only error of text in the original print. Noted in Edmund Pendleton's copy. Correct in engrossed copy.

AMENDMENTS TO THE CONSTITUTION

Articles in addition to, and Amendment of the Constitution of the United States of America, proposed by Congress, and ratified by the Legislatures* of the several States, pursuant to the fifth Article of the original Constitution.

Congress shall make no law respecting an establishment of religion, or prohibiting the free exercise thereof; or abridging the freedom of speech, or of the press; or the right of the people peaceably to assemble, and to petition the Government for a redress of grievances.

AMENDMENT [I]†

A well regulated Militia, being necessary to the security of a free State, the right of the people to keep and bear Arms, shall not be infringed.

AMENDMENT [II]

No Soldier shall, in time of peace be quartered in any house, without the consent of the Owner, nor in time of war, but in a manner to be prescribed by law.

AMENDMENT [III]

The right of the people to be secure in their persons, houses, papers, and effects, against unreasonable searches and seizures, shall not be violated, and no Warrants shall issue, but upon probable cause, supported by Oath or affirmation, and particularly describing the place to be searched, and the persons or things to be seized.

AMENDMENT [IV]

*All the amendments except the Twenty-first Amendment were ratified by State Legislatures. The Twenty-first Amendment, by its terms, was ratified by "conventions in the several States." Only the Thirteenth, Fourteenth, Fifteenth, and Sixteenth Amendments had numbers assigned to them at the time of ratification.

†The first 10 amendments, together with 2 others that failed of ratification, were proposed to the several States by resolution of Congress on September 25, 1789. The ratifications were transmitted by the Governors from time to time. The first 10 amendments were ratified by 11 of the 14 States. Virginia completed the required three fourths by ratification on December 15, 1791, and its action was communicated to Congress by the President on December 30, 1791. The legislatures of Massachusetts, Georgia and Connecticut ratified them on March 2, 1939, March 18, 1939, and April 19, 1939, respectively.

AMENDMENT [V]

No person shall be held to answer for a capital, or otherwise infamous crime, unless on a presentment or indictment of a Grand Jury, except in cases arising in the land or naval forces, or in the Militia, when in actual service in time of War or public danger; nor shall any person be subject for the same offence to be twice put in jeopardy of life or limb; nor shall be compelled in any criminal case to be a witness against himself, nor be deprived of life, liberty, or property, without due process of law; nor shall private property be taken for public use, without just compensation.

AMENDMENT [VI]

In all criminal prosecutions, the accused shall enjoy the right to a speedy and public trial, by an impartial jury of the State and district wherein the crime shall have been committed, which district shall have been previously ascertained by law, and to be informed of the nature and cause of the accusation; to be confronted with the witnesses against him; to have compulsory process for obtaining witnesses in his favor, and to have the Assistance of Counsel for his defence.

AMENDMENT [VII]

In Suits at common law, where the value in controversy shall exceed twenty dollars, the right of trial by jury shall be preserved, and no fact tried by a jury, shall be otherwise re-examined in any Court of the United States, than according to the rules of the common law.

AMENDMENT [VIII]

Excessive bail shall not be required, nor excessive fines imposed, nor cruel and unusual punishments inflicted.

AMENDMENT [IX]

The enumeration in the Constitution, of certain rights, shall not be construed to deny or disparage others retained by the people.

AMENDMENT [X]

The powers not delegated to the United States by the Constitution, nor prohibited by it to the States, are reserved to the States respectively, or to the people.

AMENDMENT [XI]*

The Judicial power of the United States shall not be construed to extend to any suit in law or equity, commenced or prosecuted against

*The Eleventh Amendment was proposed by resolution of Congress on March 4, 1794. It was declared by the President, in a message to Congress dated January 8, 1798, to have been ratified by three fourths of the several States. Records of the National Archives show that the 11th Amendment was ratified by 13 of the 16 States. It was not ratified by New Jersey or Pennsylvania.

one of the United States by Citizens of another State, or by Citizens or Subjects of any Foreign State.

AMENDMENT [XII]*

The Electors shall meet in their respective states, and vote by ballot for President and Vice-President, one of whom, at least, shall not be an inhabitant of the same state with themselves; they shall name in their ballots the person voted for as President, and in distinct ballots the person voted for as Vice-President, and they shall make distinct lists of all persons voted for as President, and of all persons voted for as Vice-President, and of the number of votes for each, which lists they shall sign and certify, and transmit sealed to the seat of the government of the United States, directed to the President of the Senate;—The President of the Senate shall, in the presence of the Senate and House of Representatives, open all the certificates and the votes shall then be counted;—The person having the greatest number of votes for President, shall be the President, if such number be a majority of the whole number of Electors appointed; and if no person have such majority, then from the persons having the highest numbers not exceeding three on the list of those voted for as President, the House of Representatives shall choose immediately, by ballot, the President. But in choosing the President, the votes shall be taken by states, the representation from each state having one vote; a quorum for this purpose shall consist of a member or members from two-thirds of the states, and a majority of all the states shall be necessary to a choice. †[And if the House of Representatives shall not choose a President whenever the right of choice shall devolve upon them, before the fourth day of March next following, then the Vice-President shall act as President, as in the case of the death or other constitutional disability of the President.]—The person having the greatest number of votes as Vice-President, shall be the Vice-President, if such number be a majority of the whole number of Electors appointed, and if no person have a majority, then from the two highest numbers on the list, the Senate shall choose the Vice-President; a quorum for the purpose shall consist of two-thirds of the whole number of Senators, and a majority of the whole number shall be necessary to a choice. But no person constitutionally ineligible to the office of President shall be eligible to that of Vice-President of the United States.

*The Twelfth Amendment was proposed in lieu of the original third paragraph of section 1 of article II, by resolution of Congress on December 9, 1803. It was declared in a proclamation of the Secretary of State, dated September 25, 1804, to have been ratified by three fourths of the States. Records of the National Archives show that it was ratified by 14 States and rejected by Connecticut and Delaware.

†The part enclosed by brackets has been superseded by section 3 of Amendment XX.

AMENDMENT XIII*

Section 1. Neither slavery nor involuntary servitude, except as a punishment for crime whereof the party shall have been duly convicted, shall exist within the United States, or any place subject to their jurisdiction.

Section 2. Congress shall have power to enforce this article by appropriate legislation.

AMENDMENT XIV†

Section 1. All persons born or naturalized in the United States, and subject to the jurisdiction thereof, are citizens of the United States and of the State wherein they reside. No State shall make or enforce any law which shall abridge the privileges or immunities of citizens of the United States; nor shall any State deprive any person of life, liberty, or property, without due process of law; nor deny to any person within its jurisdiction the equal protection of the laws.

Section 2. Representatives shall be apportioned among the several States according to their respective numbers, counting the whole number of persons in each State, excluding Indians not taxed. But when the right to vote at any election for the choice of electors for President and Vice President of the United States, Representatives in Congress, the Executive and Judicial officers of a State, or the members of the Legislature thereof, is denied to any of the male inhabitants of such State, being twenty-one years of age, and citizens of the United States, or in any way abridged, except for participation in rebellion, or other crime, the basis of representation therein shall be reduced in the proportion which the number of such male citizens shall bear to the whole number of male citizens twenty-one years of age in such State.

Section 3. No person shall be a Senator or Representative in Congress, or elector of President and Vice President, or hold any office, civil or military, under the United States, or under any State, who, having previously taken an oath, as a member of Congress, or as an officer of the United States, or as a member of any State legislature, or as an executive or judicial officer of any State, to support the Constitution of the United States, shall have engaged in insurrection

*The Thirteenth Amendment was proposed by resolution of Congress on January 31, 1865. It was declared in a proclamation of the Secretary of State, dated December 18, 1865, to have been ratified by 27 States. Subsequent records of the National Archives show that the 13th Amendment was ratified by 7 additional States. It was rejected by Kentucky and Mississippi.

†The Fourteenth Amendment was proposed by resolution of Congress on June 13, 1866. By a concurrent resolution of Congress adopted July 21, 1868, it was declared to have been ratified by "three fourths and more of the several States of the Union," and the Secretary of State was required duly to promulgate the amendment as a part of the Constitution. He accordingly issued a proclamation, dated July 28, 1868, declaring the amendment to have been ratified by 30 States, "being more than three fourths." Records of the National Archives show that the 14th Amendment was subsequently ratified by 8 additional States. It was rejected by Kentucky.

or rebellion against the same, or given aid or comfort to the enemies thereof. But Congress may by a vote of two-thirds of each House, remove such disability.

Section 4. The validity of the public debt of the United States, authorized by law, including debts incurred for payment of pensions and bounties for services in suppressing insurrection or rebellion, shall not be questioned. But neither the United States nor any State shall assume or pay any debt or obligation incurred in aid of insurrection or rebellion against the United States, or any claim for the loss of emancipation of any slave; but all such debts, obligations and claims shall be held illegal and void.

Section 5. The Congress shall have power to enforce, by appropriate legislation, the provisions of this article.

Section 1. The right of citizens of the United States to vote shall not be denied or abridged by the United States or by any State on account of race, color, or previous condition of servitude.

Section 2. The Congress shall have power to enforce this article by appropriate legislation.

AMENDMENT XV*

The Congress shall have power to lay and collect taxes on incomes, from whatever source derived, without apportionment among the several States, and without regard to any census or enumeration.

AMENDMENT XVI†

The Senate of the United States shall be composed of two Senators from each State, elected by the people thereof, for six years; and each Senator shall have one vote. The electors in each State shall have the qualifications requisite for electors of the most numerous branch of the State legislatures.

AMENDMENT [XVII]‡

---

*The Fifteenth Amendment was proposed by resolution of Congress on February 26, 1869. It was declared in a proclamation of the Secretary of State, dated March 30, 1870, to have been ratified by 29 States, which "constitute three fourths." Records of the National Archives show that the 15th Amendment was subsequently ratified by 6 more of the States. It was rejected by Kentucky, Maryland, and Tennessee.

†The Sixteenth Amendment was proposed by resolution of Congress on July 12, 1909. It was declared in a proclamation of the Secretary of State, dated February 25, 1913, to have been ratified by 38 States, which "constitute three fourths." Subsequent records of the National Archives show that the 16th Amendment was ratified by 4 additional States. It was rejected by Connecticut, Florida, Rhode Island, and Utah.

‡The Seventeenth Amendment was proposed by resolution of Congress on May 13, 1912. It was declared in a proclamation of the Secretary of State, dated May 31, 1913, to have been ratified by 36 States, which "constitute three fourths." Records of the National Archives show that the 17th Amendment was subsequently ratified by 1 additional State. It was rejected by Utah and Delaware.

When vacancies happen in the representation of any State in the Senate, the executive authority of such State shall issue writs of election to fill such vacancies: *Provided,* That the legislature of any State may empower the executive thereof to make temporary appointments until the people fill the vacancies by election as the legislature may direct.

This amendment shall not be so construed as to affect the election or term of any Senator chosen before it becomes valid as part of the Constitution.

AMENDMENT [XVIII]*

[*Section 1.* After one year from the ratification of this article the manufacture, sale, or transportation of intoxicating liquors within, the importation thereof into, or the exportation thereof from the United States and all territory subject to the jurisdiction thereof for beverage purposes is hereby prohibited.

[*Section 2.* The Congress and the several States shall have concurrent power to enforce this article by appropriate legislation.

[*Section 3.* This article shall be inoperative unless it shall have been ratified as an amendment to the Constitution by the legislatures of the several States, as provided in the Constitution, within seven years from the date of the submission hereof to the States by the Congress.]

AMENDMENT [XIX]†

The right of citizens of the United States to vote shall not be denied or abridged by the United States or by any State on account of sex.

Congress shall have power to enforce this article by appropriate legislation.

---

*The Eighteenth Amendment was proposed by resolution of Congress on December 18, 1917. It was declared in a proclamation of the Acting Secretary of State, dated January 29, 1919, to have been ratified by 36 States, which "constitute three fourths." Subsequent records of the National Archives show that the 18th Amendment was ratified by 10 additional States. It was rejected by Rhode Island. By its own terms the 18th Amendment became effective one year after its ratification, which was consummated on January 16, 1919, and therefore went into effect on Janury 16, 1920.

Repeal of the 18th Amendment on December 5, 1933, was proclaimed by the President in his proclamation of that date, when the ratification of the 21st Amendment was certified by the Acting Secretary of State.

†The Nineteenth Amendment was proposed by resolution of Congress on June 4, 1919. It was declared in a proclamation of the Secretary of State, dated August 26, 1920, to have been ratified by 36 States, which "constitute three fourths." Subsequent records of the National Archives show that the 19th Amendment was ratified by 5 additional States. It was rejected by Georgia, South Carolina, Mississippi, Delaware, and Louisiana.

Section 1. The terms of the President and Vice President shall end at noon on the 20th day of January, and the terms of Senators and Representatives at noon on the 3d day of January, of the years in which such terms would have ended if this article had not been ratified; and the terms of their successors shall then begin.

Section 2. The Congress shall assemble at least once in every year, and such meeting shall begin at noon on the 3d day of January, unless they shall by law appoint a different day.

Section 3. If, at the time fixed for the beginning of the term of the President, the President elect shall have died, the Vice President elect shall become President. If a President shall not have been chosen before the time fixed for the beginning of his term, or if the President elect shall have failed to qualify, then the Vice President elect shall act as President until a President shall have qualified; and the Congress may by law provide for the case wherein neither a President elect nor a Vice President elect shall have qualified, declaring who shall then act as President, or the manner in which one who is to act shall be selected, and such person shall act accordingly until a President or Vice President shall have qualified.

Section 4. The Congress may by law provide for the case of the death of any of the persons from whom the House of Representatives may choose a President whenever the right of choice shall have devolved upon them, and for the case of the death of any of the persons from whom the Senate may choose a Vice President whenever the right of choice shall have devolved upon them.

Section 5. Sections 1 and 2 shall take effect on the 15th day of October following the ratification of this article.

Section 6. This article shall be inoperative unless it shall have been ratified as an amendment to the Constitution by the legislatures of three-fourths of the several States within seven years from the date of its submission.

AMENDMENT [XX]*

Section 1. The eighteenth article of amendment to the Constitution of the United States is hereby repealed.

AMENDMENT [XXI]†

*The Twentieth Amendment was proposed by resolution of Congress on March 2, 1932. It was declared in a proclamation of the Secretary of State, dated February 6, 1933, to have been ratified by 39 States, which "constitute more than the requisite three fourths." Subsequent records of the National Archives show that the 20th Amendment was ratified by all 48 States before sections 1 and 2 became effective on October 15, 1933. The other sections of the amendment became effective on January 23, 1933, when its ratification was consummated by three fourths of the States.

†The Twenty-first Amendment was proposed by resolution of Congress on February 20, 1933. It was certified in a proclamation of the Acting Secretary of State, dated December 5, 1933, to have been ratified by conventions of 36 States, which "constitute the requisite three fourths of the whole number of States." Subsequent records of the National Archives show that the 21st Amendment was ratified by 2 additional States. It was rejected by the convention of South Carolina. North Carolina voted against holding a convention.

Section 2. The transportation or importation into any State, Territory, or possession of the United States for delivery or use therein of intoxicating liquors, in violation of the laws thereof, is hereby prohibited.

Section 3. This article shall be inoperative unless it shall have been ratified as an amendment to the Constitution by conventions in the several States, as provided in the Constitution, within seven years from the date of the submission hereof to the States by the Congress.

AMENDMENT [XXII]*

Section 1. No person shall be elected to the office of the President more than twice, and no person who has held the office of President, or acted as President, for more than two years of a term to which some other person was elected President shall be elected to the office of the President more than once. But this Article shall not apply to any person holding the office of President when this Article was proposed by the Congress, and shall not prevent any person who may be holding the office of President, or acting as President, during the term within which this Article becomes operative from holding the office of President or acting as President during the remainder of such term.

Section 2. This article shall be inoperative unless it shall have been ratified as an amendment to the Constitution by the legislatures of three-fourths of the several States within seven years from the date of its submission to the States by the Congress.

AMENDMENT [XXIII]†

Section 1. The District constituting the seat of Government of the United States shall appoint in such manner as the Congress may direct:

A number of electors of President and Vice President equal to the whole number of Senators and Representatives in Congress to which the District would be entitled if it were a State, but in no event more than the least populous State; they shall be in addition to those appointed by the States, but they shall be considered, for the purposes of the election of President and Vice President, to be electors appointed by a State; and they shall meet in the District and perform

*The Twenty-second Amendment was proposed by resolution of Congress on March 24, 1947. Ratification was completed on February 27, 1951, when the thirty-sixth State (Minnesota) approved the amendment. On March 1, 1951, the Administrator of General Services certified that "the States whose Legislatures have so ratified the said proposed Amendment constitute the requisite three-fourths of the whole number of States in the United States." Records of the National Archives show that the 22nd Amendment was subsequently ratified by 5 additional States.

†The Twenty-third Amendment was proposed by resolution of Congress on June 16, 1960. The Administrator of General Services certified the ratification and adoption of the amendment by three-fourths of the States on April 3, 1961. It was rejected by Arkansas.

such duties as provided by the twelfth article of amendment.

Section 2. The Congress shall have power to enforce this article by appropriate legislation.

Section 1. The right of citizens of the United States to vote in any primary or other election for President or Vice President, for electors for President or Vice President, or for Senator or Representative in Congress, shall not be denied or abridged by the United States or any State by reason of failure to pay any poll tax or other tax.

Section 2. The Congress shall have power to enforce this article by appropriate legislation.

AMENDMENT [XXIV]*

Section 1. In case of the removal of the President from office or of his death or resignation, the Vice President shall become President.

Section 2. Whenever there is a vacancy in the office of the Vice President, the President shall nominate a Vice President who shall take office upon confirmation by a majority vote of both Houses of Congress.

Section 3. Whenever the President transmits to the President pro tempore of the Senate and the Speaker of the House of Representatives his written declaration that he is unable to discharge the powers and duties of his office, and until he transmits to them a written declaration to the contrary, such powers and duties shall be discharged by the Vice President as Acting President.

Section 4. Whenever the Vice President and a majority of either the principal officers of the executive departments or of such other body as Congress may by law provide, transmit to the President pro tempore of the Senate and the Speaker of the House of Representatives their written declaration that the President is unable to discharge the powers and duties of his office, the Vice President shall immediately assume the powers and duties of the office as Acting President.

Thereafter, when the President transmits to the President pro tempore of the Senate and the Speaker of the House of Representatives his written declaration that no inability exists, he shall resume

AMENDMENT [XXV]†

*The Twenty-fourth Amendment was proposed by resolution of Congress on August 27, 1962. It was declared in a Proclamation of the Administrator of General Services, dated February 4, 1964, to have been ratified by three-fourths of the States. It was rejected by the legislature of Mississippi on December 20, 1962.

†The Twenty-fifth Amendment to the Constitution was proposed by the Congress on July 6, 1965. It was declared in a certificate of the Administrator of General Services, dated February 23, 1967, to have been ratified by the legislatures of 39 of the 50 States. Ratification was completed on February 10, 1967.

The amendment was subsequently ratified by Connecticut, Montana, South Dakota, Ohio, Alabama, North Carolina, Illinois, and Texas.

the powers and duties of his office unless the Vice President and a majority of either the principal officers of the executive department or of such other body as Congress may by law provide, transmit within four days to the President pro tempore of the Senate and the Speaker of the House of Representatives their written declaration that the President is unable to discharge the powers and duties of his office. Thereupon Congress shall decide the issue, assembling within forty-eight hours for that purpose if not in session. If the Congress, within twenty-one days after receipt of the latter written declaration, or, if Congress is not in session, within twenty-one days after Congress is required to assemble, determines by two-thirds vote of both Houses that the President is unable to discharge the powers and duties of his office, the Vice President shall continue to discharge the same as Acting President; otherwise, the President shall resume the powers and duties of his office.

AMENDMENT [XXVI]*

Section 1. The right of citizens of the United States, who are eighteen years of age or older, to vote shall not be denied or abridged by the United States or by any State on account of age.

Section 2. The Congress shall have power to enforce this article by appropriate legislation.

*The Twenty-sixth Amendment was proposed by resolution of Congress on March 8, 1971. It was declared in a certificate of the Administrator of General Services, dated July 5, 1971, to have been ratified by the legislatures of 39 of the 50 States.
Ratification was completed on July 1, 1971.
The amendment was subsequently ratified by Virginia and Wyoming.

INDEX

Credits (Continued from copyright page)

Frontispiece photo © Peter Southwick/Stock, Boston.

CHAPTER 1: Scattered quotations, from *Mass Media and American Politics,* by Doris A. Graber. © 1980 by Congressional Quarterly Press. Reprinted by permission. Photos, pages 2–3 © Alex Webb/Magnum; page 4 © Gilles Peress/Magnum; page 6 © Bohdan Hrynewych/Stock, Boston; page 9 © Jan Lukas; page 12 © Owen Franken/Stock, Boston; page 17 © Daniel S. Brody/Stock, Boston; pages 19 and 20 courtesy of UPI; page 25 © Alex Webb/Magnum.

CHAPTER 2: Photos, pages 30–31 © Jan Lukas; page 34 © George Bellerose/Stock, Boston; page 36 © Charles Gatewood/Stock, Boston; page 47 courtesy of SOVFOTO; page 50 by Yang Baokun/New China Pictures Co.

CHAPTER 3: Photo on pages 62–63 courtesy of Wide World Photos; Colonial newspaper on page 65 courtesy of Smithsonian Institution; art on pages 76 (top), 83, and 84 courtesy of the Library of Congress; photo on page 76 courtesy of Historical Pictures Agency, Chicago; portraits on pages 82 and 84 courtesy of Culver Pictures.

CHAPTER 4: Photos, pages 88–89 © Chick Harrity/US News & World Report; page 91 © David A. Krathwohl/Stock, Boston; page 92 © Jean-Claude Lejeune/Stock, Boston; page 94 courtesy of Smithsonian Institution; portrait on page 96 courtesy of Culver Pictures; page 99 © Burt Glinn/Magnum; page 106 © J. P. Laffont/Sygma.

CHAPTER 5: Scattered quotations, from *The Washington Reporter,* by Stephen Hess. © 1981 by The Brookings Institution. Reprinted by permission. Photos, pages 120–121 © Barbara Alper/Stock, Boston; page 122 © Elizabeth Hamlin/Stock, Boston; page 129 © Roland L. Freeman/Magnum; page 131 © Marc Riboud/Magnum; page 143 © Arthur Grace/Stock, Boston; page 150 © Bob McNeely/Magnum; page 158 © James A. Parcell, The Washington Post.

CHAPTER 6: Electoral college maps, pages 214–215, from *Democracy Under Pressure: An Introduction to the American Political System,* 3rd Edition, by M. C. Cummings and D. Wise. © 1977 by Harcourt Brace Jovanovich, Inc. Reprinted by permission. Photos, pages 162–163 © Gilles Peress/Magnum; page 167 courtesy of UPI; page 169 © Elliott Erwitt/Magnum; pages 173 and 174 © Richard Kalvar/Magnum; page 177 © Alex Webb/Magnum; 187 © Michael Rothstein/Jeroboam.

CHAPTER 7: Photos, pages 224–225 © Mark Antman/Stock, Boston; pages 232, 238, and 242 (two photos) courtesy of UPI; page 233 © Hap Stewart/Jeroboam; page 240 © Anne Dorfman/Jeroboam; page 252 courtesy of Chemical Manufacturers Association, © CMA 1982.

CHAPTER 8: Photos, pages 258–259 © James K. W. Atherton/Washington Post; page 261 © Wally McNamee/Newsweek; pages 264, 270, and 291 courtesy of UPI; page 274 © James K. W. Atherton/The Washington Post; page 280 © Jeff Lowenthal/Newsweek; cartoon on page 285 © Sidney Harris.

CHAPTER 9: Photos pages 298–299 by Mary Anne Fackelman/The White House; page 301 courtesy of Wide World Photos; page 307 Ohman cartoon reprinted by permission of Tribune Company Syndicate, Inc.; page 312 (three photos) by Ron

Edmonds/Wide World Photos; pages 318, 322, and 331 courtesy of UPI; Nixon resignation letter on page 329 courtesy of National Archives and Records Service.

CHAPTER 10: Photos pages 338–339 © Joseph Schuyler/Stock, Boston; pages 346, 356, 360, and 362 courtesy of UPI; page 353 © James M. Thresher/The Washington Post.

CHAPTER 11: Scattered quotations, from "Consensus and Ideology in American Politics," by Herbert McClosky. In *American Political Science Review,* Vol. 63 (June, 1964), pp. 366–367. Reprinted by permission.
Photos, pages 358–359 © Patrick McCabe; pages 376, 380, 381, and 393 (left) courtesy of UPI; page 389 © Jean-Claude Lejeune/Stock, Boston; page 393 (right) © Jim Anderson/Stock, Boston; page 402 © Leonard Freed/Magnum.

CHAPTER 12: Photos, pages 440–441 © James Karales/Design Photographers International; page 421 © Danny Lyon/Magnum; page 423 courtesy of Wide World Photos; page 427 © Lucinda Freeson/Stock, Boston; page 439 Bruce Hoertel; page 444 courtesy of UPI.

To the owner of this book:

We hope that you have enjoyed *American Politics in the Media Age* as much as we have enjoyed writing it. We'd like to know as much about your experiences with the book as you care to offer. Only through your comments and the comments of others can we learn how to make this a better book for future readers.

School: _____ Your instructor's name: _____

1. What did you like most about *American Politics in the Media Age?*

   _____

   _____

2. What did you like least about the book? _____

   _____

3. Were all of the chapters of the book assigned for you to read? _____

   If not, which ones weren't? _____

4. If you used the glossary terms, how helpful were they as an aid in understanding political concepts

   and terms? _____

   _____

5. Were other books assigned for you to read? _____

   If so, which ones? _____

   _____

6. In the space below, or in a separate letter, please let us know what other comments about the book

   you'd like to make. (For example, were any chapters *or* concepts particularly difficult?) We'd be

   delighted to hear from you!

Optional:

Your name: _____ Date: _____

May Brooks/Cole quote you, either in promotion for *American Politics in the Media Age* or in future publishing ventures?

Yes _____ No _____

Sincerely,

Thomas R. Dye

L. Harmon Zeigler

CUT PAGE OUT AND FOLD HERE

|||| |||

NO POSTAGE
NECESSARY
IF MAILED
IN THE
UNITED STATES

BUSINESS REPLY MAIL
FIRST CLASS   PERMIT NO. 84   MONTEREY, CALIF.

POSTAGE WILL BE PAID BY ADDRESSEE

Professor Thomas R. Dye
Dr. L. Harmon Zeigler
Brooks/Cole Publishing Company
Monterey, CA 93940